Answers to the Most
Perplexing and Amusing
Mysteries of Everyday Life

IMPONDERABLES

David Feldman

Reader's
Digest

The Reader's Digest Association, Inc.
Pleasantville, New York | Montreal

Project Staff

EDITOR
Neil Wertheimer

ART DIRECTOR
Rich Kershner

COVER DESIGNER
Christopher Tobias

COPY EDITOR
Jeanette Gingold

INDEXER
Nanette Bendyna

EDITORIAL ASSISTANTS
Blossom Beason
Alison Palmer Dupree

Reader's Digest Home & Health Books

PRESIDENT, HOME &
GARDEN AND
HEALTH & WELLNESS
Alyce Alston

EDITOR IN CHIEF
Neil Wertheimer

CREATIVE DIRECTOR
Michele Laseau

EXECUTIVE MANAGING
EDITOR
Donna Ruvituso

ASSOCIATE DIRECTOR,
NORTH AMERICA PREPRESS
Douglas A. Croll

MANUFACTURING MANAGER
John L. Cassidy

MARKETING DIRECTOR
Dawn Nelson

The Reader's Digest Association, Inc.

PRESIDENT AND CHIEF
EXECUTIVE OFFICER
Mary Berner

PRESIDENT, GLOBAL
CONSUMER MARKETING
Dawn Zier

The material in this book originally appeared in the following books, all published by HarperCollins Publishers, Inc.: *Do Elephants Jump?; How Do Astronauts Scratch an Itch? How Does Aspirin Find a Headache?; Are Lobsters Ambidextrous?; Do Penguins Have Knees?; Why Do Dogs Have Wet Noses?; When Do Fish Sleep?; Who Put the Butter in Butterfly?; Why Do Clocks Run Clockwise?;* and *Why Don't Cats Like to Swim?*

This special deluxe edition was compiled and published by The Reader's Digest Association, Inc., by permission of HarperCollins Publishers Inc., New York.

Library of Congress Cataloging-in-Publication Data
Feldman, David, 1950-
 Imponderables : answers to the most perplexing and amusing mysteries of every-day life / David Feldman.
   p. cm.
 Includes index.
 ISBN 978-0-7621-0749-0 (hardcover)
 1. Questions and answers. 2. Questions and answers—Humor. 3. Curiosities and wonders. 4. Curiosities and wonders—Humor. I. Title. II. Title: Answers to the most perplexing and amusing mysteries of everyday life.
 AG195.F449 2006
 031.02—dc22
        2006014040

Address any comments about *Imponderables* to:
The Reader's Digest Association, Inc.
Editor-in-Chief
Reader's Digest Books
Reader's Digest Road
Pleasantville, NY 10570-7000

To order copies of *Imponderables,* call 1-800-846-2100.

Visit our online store at rdstore.com

Printed in the United States of America
   3 5 7 9 10 8 6 4 2
US 4918/L

Why are some potato chips green?

What's the difference between a kit and a caboodle? Or flotsam and jetsam?

What does the "Q" in Q-tips stand for?

What causes the holes in Swiss cheese?

Why are barns red?

Finally: answers to the questions of life!

Not the big questions, mind you, but so many of the little ones that nag us every day—questions so unusual, so perplexing, so honest, no other book dares to ask!

On the pages ahead, David Feldman takes you on his never-ending quest to solve the mysteries of daily life.

How do they put the hole in a syringe needle?

How do astronauts scratch an itch?

Why do power lines hum?

Why is "Rx" the symbol for a prescription?

Why do golf balls have dimples?

contents

1

People

Why do we have earlobes? Wisdom teeth? Runny noses? Goose bumps? Indentations on our upper lips? Answers to dozens of questions about ourselves.

2

Animals

Why do dogs have black lips? Do skunks think skunks stink? Why do gulls congregate in parking lots? The mysteries of the animal kingdom, revealed!

3

Food

How do they put the pockets in pita bread? Where did 7UP get its name? Why do onions make you cry? Read this, and dinner will never be the same.

4

Procedures and Traditions

Who decides the boundaries between oceans? Why do unlisted phone numbers cost extra? Solutions to the baffling questions of daily life.

(5)

Machines and Devices 247

Why do they call large trucks "semis"? Why aren't there A- or B-sized batteries? Little-known truths about the equipment of modern living.

(6)

Everyday Stuff 303

Why is Rhode Island called an island? What makes a glue "super"? Why do ceiling fans get dusty? Answers to these and other random observations.

(7)

Science and Nature 333

How does aspirin find a headache? How do you get Teflon to stick to the pan? How do you measure a food's caloric value? Science to the rescue!

(8)

Popular Culture 359

Why does Bazooka Joe wear an eye patch? What makes theater "legitimate"? No gossip—just fun answers about the stuff that entertains us.

(9)

Sports 395

Why are tennis balls fuzzy? Why nine innings in baseball? Why are there dimples on golf balls? These questions will stump the smartest sports fan.

the never-ending quest
to answer life's little questions

Have you ever wondered why dogs eat standing up but cats eat sitting down? Or why power lines hum? Or whether there ever was a real Dr. Pepper?

Some folks can enjoy a perfectly pleasant life without finding the answers to these mysteries. Unfortunately, I'm not one of those people. Since early childhood, I annoyed anyone within earshot with questions that started with the dreaded "Why?"

On a Saturday afternoon more than twenty years ago, I was in the cereal section of a local grocery store. I was on a diet and wanted to find a low-calorie cereal, but I realized I had never read the cereal boxes' nutritional panels carefully. Much to my shock, I found that virtually every cereal was exactly 110 calories per ounce. How, I wondered, could Kellogg's Corn Flakes and Kellogg's Sugar Frosted Flakes have the same number of calories per ounce?

On the way home from the grocery store, the word "Imponderables" popped into my mind to describe these little mysteries of everyday life that drive us nuts. We never find the answers because we don't know where to go to find the solution or because we become preoccupied with other annoying things, like going to school or doing our jobs. I vowed to compile these Imponderables, mysteries that weren't discussed in standard reference books, and to find the answers by consulting experts in these fields. My goal was nothing less than eradicating Imponderability.

I learned an important lesson in searching out the answer to my breakfast cereal conundrum, and that is that the answers are often simpler than you'd think, and more interesting than you'd expect. In the case of breakfast cereal, the answer proved almost embarrassingly easy. (For the record, here it is: Equal weights of all carbohydrates and proteins contain the exact same amount of calories: 4 calories per gram. It doesn't matter whether it is a simple carbohydrate, like refined sugar, or the most healthy whole grain on the planet—in terms of calories, they are equal).

When I published my first book, I ended the book with a page that asked readers to send in their own Imponderables. Ever since, I've been answering the mysteries of my readers. The folks who have bought my books tend to fall into two camps: those who cannot sleep at night until their own Imponderables are solved; and those who hope my books will keep their loved ones from harassing them with their Imponderable obsessions.

The fun part of my job is talking to experts in every conceivable field—from funeral directors to zipper manufacturers; from neurologists to the world's foremost expert on fly swatters. These experts, who are so generous with their time, are the backbone of my work.

I've long since given up on the fantasy of eliminating Imponderability. As soon as one mystery is solved, two more rear their ugly heads. But I'm resigned to fighting the good fight. Each new Imponderable is a challenge.

If you're itching to find the solution to any of the Imponderables I've posed in this introduction (all of which are answered in the volume you're reading), I think you'll discover what I have concluded: As long as you are curious, you'll never be bored.

—David Feldman

1

PEOPLE

Sometimes just being a person is confusing. Why do tiny paper cuts hurt so much? Why don't we get goose bumps on our faces? Why does our skin itch? Why does helium make your voice squeak like a chipmunk? Be prepared—the answers are often stranger than the questions.

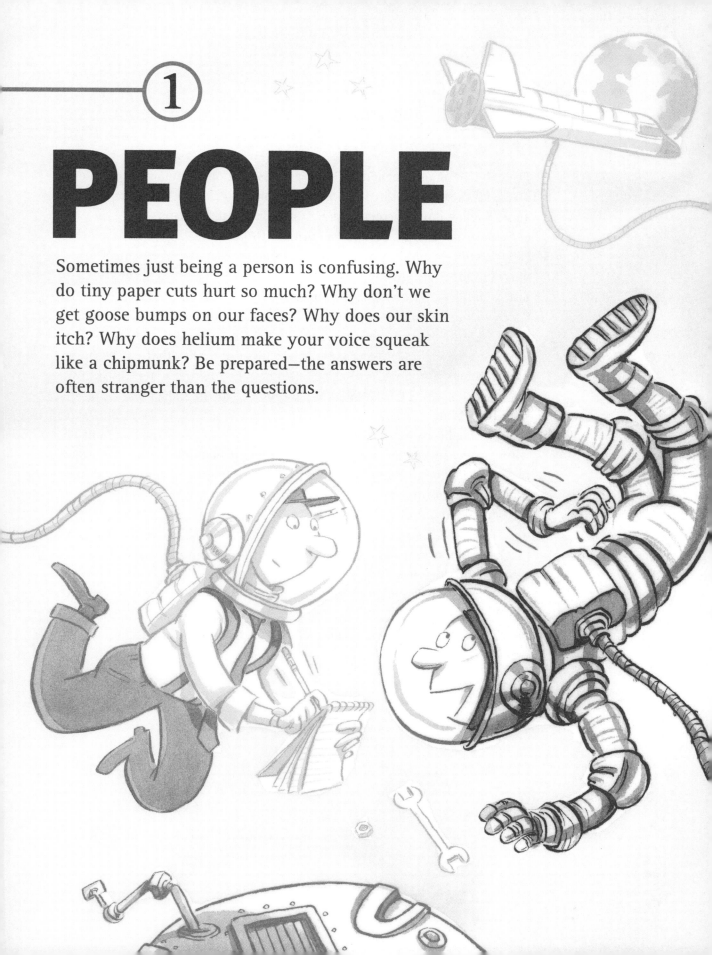

who put E on top
of the eye chart? And why?

Professor Hermann Snellen, a Dutch professor of ophthalmology, put the E on top of the eye chart in 1862. Although his very first chart was headed by an A, Snellen quickly composed another chart with E on top.

Snellen succeeded Dr. Frans Cornelis Donders as the director of the Netherlands Hospital for Eye Patients. Donders was then the world's foremost authority on geometric optics. Snellen was trying to standardize a test to diagnose visual acuity, to measure how small an image an eye can accept while still detecting the detail of that image. Dr. Donders' complicated formulas were based on three parallel lines; of all the letters of the alphabet, the capital E most closely resembled the lines that Dr. Donders had studied so intensively. Because Donders had earlier determined how the eye perceives the E, Snellen based much of his mathematical work on the fifth letter.

The three horizontal limbs of the E are separated by an equal amount of white space. In Snellen's original chart, there was a one-to-one ratio between the height and width of the letters, and the gaps and bars were all the same length (in some modern eye charts, the middle bar is shorter).

Louanne Gould of Cambridge Instruments says that the E, unlike more open letters like L or U, forces the observer to distinguish between white and black, an important constituent of good vision. Without this ability, E's begin to look like B's, F's, P's or many other letters.

Of course, Snellen couldn't make an eye chart full of only E's, or else all his patients would have 20-10 vision. But Snellen realized that it was important to use the same letters many times on the eye charts, to ensure that the

IN WHAT DIRECTION ARE OUR EYES FACING WHEN WE ARE ASLEEP?

Upward, usually. Our eye muscles relax when we are asleep, and the natural tendency, known as Bell's Phenomenon, is for the eyes to roll back above their usual position. Of course, when we experience rapid eye movements during sleep, our eyes dart back and forth.

—Submitted by Nadine Sheppard of Fairfield, California.

failure of an observer to identify a letter was based on a visual problem rather than the relative difficulty of a set of letters. Ian Bailey, professor of optometry and director of the Low Vision Clinic at the University of California at Berkeley, says that it isn't so important whether an eye chart uses the easiest or most difficult letters. Most eye charts incorporate only ten different letters, ones that have the smallest range of difficulty.

Today, many eye charts do not start with an E—and there is no technical reason why they have to—but most still do. Dr. Stephen C. Miller of the American Optometric Association suggests that the desire of optical companies to have a standardized approach to the production of eye charts probably accounts for the preponderance of E charts. And we're happy about it. It's a nice feeling to know that even if our vision is failing us miserably, we'll always get the top row right.

—Submitted by Merry Phillips of Menlo Park, California.

how do blind people discriminate between different denominations of paper money?

Sandra Abrams, supervisor of Independent Living Services for Associated Services of the Blind, points out that the government defines "legally blind" as possessing 10% or less of normal vision. Legally blind people with partial vision usually have few problems handling paper money:

> Individuals who are partially sighted may be able to see the numbers on bills, especially in certain lighting conditions. Some people with low vision must hold the money up to their noses in order to see the numbers; some people have been asked by members of the public if they are smelling their money. Other persons with low vision might use different types of magnification. Some people with partial sight have pointed out that the numbers on the top corners of bills are larger than those on the bottoms.

The U.S. government certainly doesn't make it easy for blind people to identify currency. Virtually every other nation varies the size and color of denominations. One reader asked whether a five-dollar bill *feels* different from a twenty-dollar bill. Although suggestions have been made to introduce slight differences in texture, a blind person can't now discriminate between bills by touching them.

Initially blind people must rely on bank tellers or friends to identify the denomination of each bill, and then they develop a system to keep track of which bill is which. Gwynn Luxton of the American Foundation for the Blind uses a popular system with her clients:

- One-dollar bills are kept flat in the wallet.

- Five-dollar bills are folded in half crosswise, so that they are approximately three inches long.

- Ten-dollar bills are folded in thirds crosswise, so that they are about two inches long.

- Twenty-dollar bills are folded in half lengthwise, so that they are half the height of the other bills and sit down much farther in the wallet or purse than the other bills.

Machines have been created to solve this problem as well. The relatively inexpensive Talking Wallet reads out the denomination of bills it receives. The more expensive Talking Money Identifier can be hooked up to cash registers and be used for commercial use. Many newspaper vendors are blind, and the Money Identifier can save them from being shortchanged.

Blind people have so many pressing problems imposed on them by a seeing culture that identifying paper money is a minor irritant. As Sandra Abrams puts it, "Frankly, of all the things I do daily, identifying money is one of the easiest."

—Submitted by Jon Gregerson of Marshall, Michigan.

what causes bags under the eyes?

Let us count the ways, in descending order of frequency:

1. Heredity. That's right. It wasn't that night on the town that makes you look like a raccoon in the morning. It's all your parents' and grandparents' fault. Some people are born with excess fatty tissue and liquid around the eyes.

2. Fluid retention. The eyelids are the thinnest and softest skin in the entire body, four times as thin as "average" skin. Fluid tends to pool in thin portions of the skin.

What causes the fluid retention? Among the culprits are drugs, kidney or liver problems, salt intake, and very commonly, allergies. Cosmetics drum up more business for dermatologists and allergists than just about anything else. Allergic reactions to mascara and eyeliner are the usual culprits.

3. **Aging.** The skin of the face, particularly around the eyes, loosens with age. Age is more likely to cause bags than mere sleepiness or fatigue.

4. **Too many smiles and frowns.** These expressions not only can build crow's feet but bags. We can safely disregard this answer to explain Bob Newhart's bags, however.

Another less fascinating explanation for many sightings of bags under the eyes was noted by Dr. Tom Meek of the American Academy of Dermatology in *The New York Times:* "The circles are probably caused by shadows cast from overhead lighting."

—Submitted by Stephen T. Kelly of New York, New York.

why do we have to close our eyes when we sneeze?

We thought we'd get off easy with this mystery. Sure, a true Imponderable can't be answered by a standard reference work, but would a poke in a few medical texts do our readers any harm?

We shouldn't have bothered. We understand now that a sneeze is usually a physiological response to an irritant of some sort. We learned that there is a $10 word for sneezing (the "sternutatory reflex") and that almost all animals sneeze. But what exactly happens when we sneeze? Here's a short excerpt from one textbook's explanation of a sneeze:

> When an irritant contacts the nasal mucosa, the trigeminal nerve provides the affect limb for impulses to the pons, and medullai Preganglionic efferent fibers leave these latter two structures via the intermediate nerve, through geniculate ganglion to the greater petrosal nerve, through the vividian nerve and then synapse at the sphenopalatine ganglion ...

Get this outta here! Until CliffsNotes comes out with a companion to rhinology textbooks, we'll go to humans for the answers. Our rhinologist friend, Dr. Pat Barelli, managed to read those textbooks and still writes like a human being. He explains that the sneeze reflex is a protective phenomenon:

The sneeze clears the nose and head and injects [oxygen] into the cells of the body, provoking much the same physiological effect as sniffing snuff or cocaine. When a person sneezes, all body functions cease. Tremendous stress is put on the body by the sneeze, especially the eyes.

As Dr. G. H. Drumheller of the International Rhinological Society put it, "We close our eyes when sneezing to keep the eyes from extruding." While nobody is willing to test the hypothesis, there is more than a grain of truth to the folk wisdom that closing your eyes when you sneeze keeps them from popping out, but probably not more than three or four grains.

—Submitted by Linda Rudd of Houston, Texas. Thanks also to Michelle Zielinski of Arnold, Missouri; Helen Moore of New York, New York; Jose Elizondo of Pontiac, Michigan; Amy Harding of Dixon, Kentucky; and Gail Lee of Los Angeles, California.

what causes floaters, or spots, in the eyes?

The innermost part of the eye is a large cavity filled with a jellylike fluid known as vitreous humor. Floaters are small flecks of protein, pigment, or embryonic remnants (trapped in the cavity during the formation of the eye) that suspend in the vitreous humor.

The small specks appear to be in front of the eye because the semitransparent floaters are visible only when they fall within the line of sight. Most people might have specks trapped in the vitreous humor from time to time but not notice them. Eyes have a way of adjusting to imperfections, as any eyeglass wearer with dirty lenses could tell you. Floaters are most likely to be noticed when one is looking at a plain background, such as a blackboard, a bare wall, or the sky.

What should one do about floaters? An occasional spot is usually harmless, although sometimes floaters can be precursors of retinal damage. Most often, a home remedy will keep floaters from bothering you. The American Academy of Ophthalmology suggests:

> If a floater appears directly in your line of vision, the best thing to do is to move your eye around, which will cause the inside fluid to swirl and allow the floater to move out of the way. We are most accustomed to moving our eyes back and forth, but looking up and down will cause different currents within the eye and may be more effective in getting the floaters out of the way.

Although you may be aware of their presence, it is often surprisingly difficult to isolate floaters in your line of vision. Because the floaters are actually within the eye, they move as your eyes move and seem to dart away whenever you try to focus on looking at them directly.

—Submitted by Gail Lee of Los Angeles, California.

why do your eyes hurt when you are tired?

Why do couch potatoes have such a bad reputation? While lying on the sofa perusing an Archie comic book or studying the impact of television violence on children by viewing Bugs Bunny cartoons, they are actually exercising what ophthalmologist James P. McCulley of the University of Texas Medical School calls "among the most active muscles in the body."

Actually, your eyes contain three sets of muscle groups:

- Each eye has six *extraocular muscles* attached to the outside of the eyeball, which turn the eyes in all directions. The extraocular muscles must coordinate their movements so that both eyes look in the same direction at the same time.

- The *sphincter and dilatory muscles* open or close the pupils, defining how much light is allowed into the eye.

- The *ciliary muscles* attach to the lens inside the eye. When these muscles contract or relax, they change the shape of the lens, altering its focus.

Concentrated reading or close work provides a workout for these muscle groups strenuous enough to make Richard Simmons proud. Unfortunately, as in all aerobic programs, the saying "no pain, no gain" applies, as Winnipeg, Manitoba, optometrist Steven Mintz explains:

> The human eye is designed so that, if perfectly formed, it will form a clear image on the retina (at the back of the eye) of any distant object without having to use any of the muscles. In order to see closer objects clearly, however, each set of muscles has to work. The extraocular muscles must turn each eye inward; the sphincter muscles must work to make the pupil smaller; and the ciliary muscles must contract to allow the lens to change to a shape that will produce a clearer image.
>
> This minimal muscular effort is significant in itself. However, no human eye is perfectly formed and these imperfections will increase the amount of effort required. For instance, people who are farsighted must exert more than the normal amount of effort on the part of the ciliary muscles. Many people have extraocular muscle imbalances that force them to work harder. Virtually every person, as [he or she]

approaches or passes the age of forty, suffers from a stiffening of the lens inside the eye, which forces those ciliary muscles to work even harder. Reading under poor light (either too much or too little) will cause the sphincter and dilatory muscles to work excessively.

Just like doing 100 push-ups can cause the arm muscles to become pain[ed], so can the muscular effort ... described above cause sore eyes. Add to this that after several hours of close work, all of your body's muscles are going to be more fatigued, your level of tolerance or your pain threshold for sore eyes will be less than when you are fresh.

Ophthalmologists we consulted speculated that much of the eyestrain attributed to tiredness is in reality caused by dryness. Dr. Ronald Schachar of the Association for the Advancement of Ophthalmology notes that when one is tired, the blink rate slows down and the eyes are not properly lubricated. Close work also slows down the blink rate. Eye specialists are finding that workers at computer visual display terminals experience decreased blinking. This is one reason most consultants recommend stepping away from VDTs at least once an hour. While most of us are more than happy to rest our muscles after doing a few push-ups, we expose our eyes to a marathon just about every day.

—Submitted by Martin Nearl of Monsey, New York.

what do you call that little groove in the center of our upper lips?

Sorry, we can't answer this question. It is hardly an Imponderable, since it has been answered in scores of trivia books. Heck, this question has been posed by so many stand-up comedians on bad cable television shows, we refuse to answer on principle.

—Submitted by too many readers.

what is the *purpose* of the little indentation in the center of our upper lips?

If you rephrase your Imponderable in the form of a proper question, you can weasel just about anything out of us. How can we write about the indentation without mentioning its name? OK guys ... it's called the *philtrum*. You'll be proud to know that we have a groove running down our upper lip for absolutely no good reason, as William P. Jollie, professor and chairman of anatomy at the Medical College of Virginia, explains:

> The indentation in the center of our upper lip is a groove, or raphe, that forms embryonically by merging paired right and left processes that make up our upper jaw. It has no function, just as many such midline merger marks, or raphes, have no function. We have quite a few merger-lines on our bodies: a raphe down the upper surface of our tongues; a grooved notch under the point of our chins; and a raphe in the midline of our palates. There are also several in the genital area, both male and female.
>
> Anatomically, the raphe on our upper lip is called the *philtrum,* an interesting word derived from the Greek word *philter,* which even in English means a love potion. I confess I don't see a connection, but many anatomical terms are peculiar in origin, if not downright funny.

Speaking of funny, it is our earnest hope that after the information in this chapter is disseminated, every stand-up comedian, standing before the inevitable brick wall, will stop doing routines about philtrums. Enough is enough.

—Submitted by Bruce Hyman of Short Hills, New Jersey. Thanks also to three-year-old Michael Joshua Lim of Livonia, Michigan.

what purpose do wisdom teeth serve?

They serve a powerful purpose for dentists, who are paid to extract them. Otherwise, wisdom teeth are commonly regarded as being useless to modern man. But because nature rarely provides us with useless body parts, a little investigation yields a more satisfying answer.

Primitive man ate meats so tough that they make beef jerky feel like mashed potatoes in comparison. The extra molars in the back of the mouth, now known as wisdom teeth, undoubtedly aided in our ancestors' mastication.

As humans have evolved, their brains have gotten progressively larger and the face position has moved farther downward and inward. About the time that primitive man started walking in an upright position, other changes in the facial structure occurred. The protruding jawbones of early man gradually moved backward, making the jaw itself shorter and leaving no room for the wisdom teeth (also known as third molars). Most people's jaws no longer have the capacity to accommodate these four, now super-fluous, teeth.

why do many elderly people, especially those missing teeth, display a chewing motion?

Dr. John Rutkauskas of the American Society for Geriatric Dentistry consulted with two of his geriatric dentistry colleagues, Dr. Saul Kamen and Dr. Barry Ceridan, and told *Imponderables* that this chewing motion is found almost exclusively in people who have lost teeth. On rare occasions, certain tranquilizers or antidepressants (in the phenothiazine family) may cause a side effect called tardive dyskinesia, an inability to control what are ordinarily voluntary movements. These movements are as likely to involve the nose as the mouth or jaws, though.

In most cases, Rutkauskas believes that the chewing motion is a neuromuscular response to the lack of teeth: an attempt by the oral cavity to achieve some form of equilibrium. In particular, these sufferers can't position their upper and lower jaws properly. With a full set of ivories, the teeth act as a stop to keep the jaws in place.

Of course, most people who lose teeth attempt to remedy the problem by wearing dentures. And most people adapt well. But Ike House, a Louisiana dentist and *Imponderables* reader (we're sure he is prouder of the first qualification), told us that a significant number of elderly people have lost the ability to wear dentures at all because of an excessive loss of bone:

WHY IS AN OLD PERSON SAID TO BE *LONG IN THE TOOTH*?

The first recorded use of *long in the tooth* was in J. C. Snaith's *Love Lane* (1919): "One of the youngest R.A.s [rear admirals] on record, but a bit long in the tooth for the Army."

The meaning is the same today, but the words don't seem to apply to humans. The answer is that *long in the tooth* originally referred only to horses. As horses age, their gums recede. Their teeth don't actually get longer, but they *look* longer. The older the horse, the longer its teeth look.

They can close their mouth much fuller than they would with teeth present, resulting in the "nose touching skin" appearance of many elderly folks. Since the normal "rest position" of about 2 to 3 mm between the upper and lower natural or artificial teeth is not able to be referenced, they may be constantly searching for this position.

Many elderly people who wear dentures feel that the prostheses just don't feel normal. And restlessness leads to "chewing in the air," as House amplifies:

> If you had two objects in your hands, such as two pecans or two coins, you would probably manipulate them in some way. When not using a pen or pencil, for example, but holding it passively, we usually move it in our hand. It may be that folks wearing dentures constantly manipulate them in some way just because objects being held but not used are often moved by unconscious habit.
>
> I have a great-uncle who lets his upper teeth fall down between words and pushes them back up against his palate. This is a most disconcerting habit to his family! I know some elderly patients cannot tolerate dentures in their mouths unless they are eating because they can't leave them alone.

Barnet B. Orenstein, an associate clinical professor of dentistry at New York University's College of Dentistry, told *Imponderables* that the tongue is often the culprit in creating the chewing motion:

> Elderly people often display a constant chewing motion because, having lost their lower teeth, their tongue is no longer confined to the space within the dental arch. The tongue spreads out and actually increases in size. What appears to be a chewing motion is actually a subconscious effort to find a place for the tongue.

The last time we were at the *Imponderables* staff's official dentist, Phil Klein of Brooklyn Heights, we asked him to wrestle with this mystery while he mauled our molars (and we pondered whether we could deduct the office visit from our income tax as a research as well as medical expense). Much to our relief, Dr. Klein concurred with the theories stated above but raised the possibility of a few others, including rare neurological conditions and grinding of teeth to the point where the lower and upper jaws can't mesh comfortably.

Klein also mentioned that problems with salivation, and particularly dryness, is a constant problem for numerous elderly people, and many with this problem move their mouth and jaw in response to this dryness.

And then he told us we had no cavities.

—Submitted by Dennis Kingsley of Goodrich, Michigan.
Note to IRS: We deducted our trip to Dr. Klein as a medical expense.

do we really need to put thermometers under our tongues? Couldn't we put them above our tongues if our mouths were closed?

Anyone who has ever seen a child fidgeting, desperately struggling to keep a thermometer under the tongue, has probably wondered, Why do physicians want to take our temperature in the most inconvenient places?

No, there is nothing intrinsically important about the temperature under the tongue or, for that matter, in your rectum. The goal is to determine the "core temperature," the temperature of the interior of the body.

The rectum and tongue are the most accessible areas of the body that are at core temperature. Occasionally the armpit will be used, but the armpit is more exposed to the ambient air, and tends to give colder readings. Of course, drinking a hot beverage, as many schoolchildren have learned, is effective in shooting one's temperature up. But barring tricks, the area under the tongue, full of blood vessels, is almost as accurate as the rectal area, and a lot more pleasant place to use.

So what are the advantages of putting the thermometer *under* the tongue as opposed to over it? Let us count the ways:

1. **Accuracy.** Placing the thermometer under the tongue insulates the area from outside influence, such as air and food. As Dr. E. Wilson Griffin III told *Imponderables*, "Moving air would evaporate moisture in the mouth and on the thermometer and falsely lower the temperature. It is important to have the thermometer under the tongue rather than just banging around loose inside the mouth, because a mercury thermometer responds most accurately to the temperature of liquids or solids in direct contact with it."

2. **Speed.** The soft tissues and blood vessels of the tongue are ideal resting spots for a thermometer. Dr. Frank Davidoff of the American College of Physicians points out that compared to the skin of the armpit, which is thick and nonvascular, the "soft, unprotected tissues under the tongue wrap tightly around the thermometer, improving the speed and completeness of heat transfer."

3. **Comfort.** Although you may not believe it, keeping the thermometer above the tongue would not be as comfortable. The hard thermometer, instead of being embraced by the soft tissue below the tongue, would inevitably scrape against the much harder tissues of the hard palate (the roof of your mouth). Something would have to give—and it wouldn't be the thermometer.

Why Does Your Voice Sound Higher and Funny When You Ingest Helium?

The kiddie equivalent of the drunken party-goer putting a lampshade on his head is ingesting helium and speaking like a chipmunk with a caffeine problem. When we saw *L.A. Law*'s stolid Michael Kuzak playing this prank, we were supposed to be smitten with his puckish, fun-loving, childlike side. We were not convinced.

Still, many *Imponderables* readers want to know the answer to this question, so we contacted several chemists and physicists. They replied with unanimity. Perhaps the most complete explanation came from George B. Kauffman:

> Sound is the sensation produced by stimulation of the organs of hearing by vibrations transmitted through the air or other mediums. Low-frequency sound is heard as low pitch and higher frequencies as correspondingly higher pitch. The frequency (pitch) of sound depends on the density of the medium through which the vibrations are transmitted; the less dense the medium, the greater the rate (frequency) of vibration, and hence, the higher the pitch of the sound.
>
> The densities of gases are directly proportional to their molecular weights. Because the density of helium (mol. wt. 4) is much less than that of air, a mixture of about 78 percent nitrogen (mol. wt. 28) and about 20 percent oxygen (mol. wt. 32), the vocal cords vibrate much faster (at a higher frequency) in helium than in air, and therefore the voice is perceived as having a higher pitch.
>
> The effect is more readily perceived with male voices, which have a lower pitch than female voices. The pitch of the voice [can] be lowered by inhaling a member of the noble (inert) gas family (to which helium belongs) that is heavier than air, such as xenon (mol. wt. 131.29)....

Brian Bigley, a chemist at Systech Environmental Corporation, told *Imponderables* that helium mixtures are used to treat asthma and other types of respiratory ailments. Patients with breathing problems can process a helium mixture more easily than normal air, and the muscles of the lungs don't have to work as hard as they do to inhale the same volume of oxygen.

—Submitted by Jim Albert of Cary, North Carolina. Thanks also to James Wheaton of Plattsburgh AFB, New York; Nancy Sampson of West Milford, New Jersey; Karen Riddick of Dresden, Tennessee; Loren A. Larson of Altamonte Springs, Florida; and Teresa Bankhead of Culpeper, Virginia.

Davidoff concedes that in a pinch, placing the thermometer above the tongue might not be a total disaster:

> In principle, you could get a reasonably accurate temperature reading with a thermometer above your tongue *if* you hadn't recently been mouth breathing or hadn't recently eaten or drunk anything, *if* you held the thermometer reasonably firmly between your tongue and the roof of your mouth, and *if* you kept it there long enough.

why do our noses run in cold weather?

Otolaryngologist Dr. Steven C. Marks, on behalf of the American Rhinologic Society, explains the physiology:

> The nose and sinuses are lined by a mucous membrane that contains both mucus-secreting glands and small cells called goblet cells, which also secrete a component of mucus. This mucus is produced in normal mucous membranes and in those that are infected or inflamed.

Many medical problems, such as viral or bacterial infections or allergies, can cause your nose to run. But the nose's response to cold is a little different, as Marks explains:

> The nasal and sinus mucous membranes are innervated [stimulated] by nerves which control, to some extent, the rate of mucus secretion. The response of the nose to cold air is in part a reflex mediated by these nerves. The cold air is sensed by the mucosa [mucous membrane], which then sends a signal back to the brain, which then sends a signal back to the mucosa: the result is a secretion of mucus.

WHY DO WOMEN TEND TO HAVE HIGHER VOICES THAN MEN? WHY DO SHORT PEOPLE TEND TO HAVE HIGHER VOICES THAN TALL PEOPLE?

Daniel Boone, a University of Arizona professor and expert on vocal mechanisms, provides the answer: "Fundamental frequency or voice pitch level is directly related to the length and thickness of the individual's vocal folds [or vocal cords]." The average man's vocal-fold length is approximately eighteen millimeters; the average woman's is ten millimeters.

The tall person of either gender is likely to have longer vocal cords than a shorter person of the same sex.

What good does a runny nose do anyone but Kleenex? Keith Holmes, an ear, nose, and throat specialist from Dubois, Wyoming, believes that it is "a natural physiologic phenomenon of the organ to protect the warm lining of the nose," as cold irritates the mucous membrane. Marks speculates that "the increased mucus flow may be necessary to improve the humidification and cleaning of the air in the cold environment."

—Submitted by John Miller of Lacona, New York. Thanks also to L. Gualtierie of Brampton, Ontario.

what is the purpose of that piece of skin hanging from the back of our throat?

Actually, that isn't skin hanging down. It's mucous membrane and muscle. And it has a name: the uvula.

The uvula is a sort of anatomical tollgate between the throat and the pharynx, the first part of the digestive tract. The uvula has a small but important role in controlling the inflow and outflow of food through the digestive system. Dr. William P. Jollie, chairman, Department of Anatomy, the Medical College of Virginia, explains: "The muscle of both the soft palate and the uvula elevates the roof of the mouth during swallowing so that food and liquid can pass from the mouth cavity into the pharynx."

Dr. L. J. A. DiDio of the Medical College of Ohio adds that the uvula also helps prevent us from regurgitating food during swallowing. Without the uvula, some of our food might enter the nasal cavity, with unpleasant consequences.

—Submitted by Andy Garruto of Kinnelon, New Jersey.

what causes the ringing sound you get in your ears?

Unless you are listening to a bell, a ringing sensation means you are suffering from tinnitus. Someone with tinnitus receives auditory sensations without any external auditory source. While most of us rarely experience tinnitus, it is a chronic problem for over 30 million Americans.

Tinnitus is a symptom, not a disease in itself. Virtually anything that might disturb the auditory nerve is capable of causing tinnitus. Because the function of the auditory nerve is to carry sound, when the nerve is irritated for any reason the brain interprets the impulse as noise.

Some of the most common causes for temporary tinnitus are:

1. Reaction to a loud noise.

2. Vascular distress after a physical or mental trauma.

3. Allergic reaction to medication. (Aspirin is the most common pharmaceutical cause of tinnitus. Many people who take more than twenty aspirin per day are subject to tinnitus attacks.) Luckily, the symptoms usually disappear upon discontinuance of the drug.

Causes of more chronic tinnitus conditions are myriad. Here are some of the most common: clogging of the external ear with earwax; inflammation of any part of the ear; drug overdoses; excessive use of the telephone; vertigo attacks; nutritional deficiencies (particularly a lack of trace minerals); muscle spasms in the ear; infections; allergies.

Chronic tinnitus sufferers have to live not only with annoying buzzing, but usually with accompanying hearing loss. Unfortunately, there is no simple cure for the condition. Much research is being conducted on the role of nutrition in helping treat tinnitus, but for now, the emphasis is on teaching sufferers how to live with the problem. Devices are sold to mask the ringing sound. Techniques such as hypnosis and biofeedback are used to distract the patient from the annoying ringing.

Ear problems may not be the most glamorous medical problems, but they are the most prevalent, as a booklet from the House Ear Institute, prepared by the Otological Medical Group, Inc. of Los Angeles explains: "Loss of hearing is America's largest, yet least recognized, physical ailment. More people suffer from it than heart disease, cancer, blindness, tuberculosis, multiple sclerosis, venereal disease, and kidney disease combined."

—Submitted by Bobby Dalton of Maryland Heights, Missouri.

do earlobes serve any particular or discernible function?

Our authorities answered as one: Yes, earlobes do serve a particular function. They are an ideal place to hang earrings.

Oh sure, there are theories. Ear, nose, and throat specialist Dr. Ben Jenkins of Kingsland, Georgia, remembers reading about a speculation that when our

WHY IS OUR LITTLE FINGER CALLED A *PINKIE*?
WHY IS THE DRINK CALLED A *PINK LADY*?

We have the Dutch to blame for this piece of baby talk. *Pinck* in Middle Dutch meant "small." Their word for the little finger was *pinkje*.

At least a *pink lady* is pink (although why it is called a "lady" probably has more to do with sexism—froth equals femininity—than linguistics). John Ciardi points out that the diminutive ending of *pinkie* is a redundancy, for it means, in effect, "small little finger." At least the Dutch derivation explains why one finger has been singled out for its pinkness.

—Submitted by Steve Hajewski of New Berlin, Wisconsin.

---

predecessors walked on four feet, our earlobes were larger "and that they fell in[ward] to protect the ear canal." Biologist John F. Hertner recounts another anthropological theory: that earlobes served as "an ornament of interest in sexual selection."

Doctors and biologists we confront with questions like these about seemingly unimportant anatomical features are quick to shrug their shoulders. They are quite comfortable with the notion that not every organ in our body is essential to our well-being and not every obsolete feature of our anatomy is eliminated as soon as it becomes unnecessary.

Actually, the opposite is closer to the truth. Anatomical features of earlier humankind tend to stick around unless they are an obvious detriment. As Professor Hertner puts it,

> Nature tends to conserve genetic information unless there is selection pressure against a particular feature. Our bodies serve in some respect as museums of our evolutionary heritage.

> —*Submitted by Dianne Love of Seaside Park, New Jersey.*

why are people immune to their own body odor?

How can so many otherwise sensitive people expose others to their body odors? Surely, they must not know that they (or their clothes) are foul-smelling, or they would do something about it. Right?

Right. Compared to most animals, humans don't have an acutely developed sense of smell. According to Dr. Pat Barelli, secretary of the American Rhinologic Society, "The olfactory nerve easily becomes 'fatigued' in areas where there are odors." In order not to be overloaded with information, your nervous system decides not to even try being "bothered" by your body odor unless it changes dramatically. Whether you regularly smell like a spring bouquet or like last night's table scraps, you're unlikely to notice—even if you're sensitive to the body odor of other people.

Dr. Morley Kare, director of the Monell Institute at the University of Pennsylvania, adds that this fatigue principle applies to many of the senses. Workers at automobile factories must learn to block out the sounds of machinery or risk being driven insane. Residents of Hershey, Pennsylvania, stop noticing the smell of chocolate that permeates the town.

Students often can't discriminate the taste of different dishes served in their school cafeteria. Of course, this phenomenon might be explained by the fact that all the cafeteria dishes *do* taste alike, but we would need a government grant to confirm the thesis.

—Submitted by Karole Rathouz of Mehlville, Missouri.

why did men thrust their right hand into their jacket in old photographs?

Most of the photo historians we contacted discounted what we considered to be the most likely answer: These subjects were merely imitating Napoleon and what came to be known as the Napoleonic pose. Instead, the experts reasoned that just as subjects couldn't easily maintain a sincere smile during long exposure times, trying to keep their hands still was also a challenge. Frank Calandra, secretary/treasurer of the Photographic Historical Society wrote us:

> The hand was placed in the jacket or a pocket or resting on a fixed object so that the subject wouldn't move it [or his other hand] and cause a blurred image. Try holding your hands at your sides motionless for fifteen minutes or so—it's not easy.

Grant Romer, director of education at the George Eastman House's International Museum of Photography, adds that this gesture not only solved the problem of blurring and what to do with the subject's hands while striking a pose but forced the subject to hold his body in a more elegant manner.

Still, if these technical concerns were the only problem, why not thrust both hands into the jacket? Or pose the hands in front of the subject, with fingers intertwined? John Husinak, professor of art history at Middlebury College, assured us that this particular piece of body language was part of a trend that was bigger and more wide-ranging than simply an imitation of Napoleon.

Early portrait photographers understood the significance of particular gestures to the point where they were codified in many journals and manuals about photography. Some specific examples are cited in an article by William E. Parker in *After Image,* an analysis of the work of early photographer Everett A. Scholfield. Parker cites some specific examples: Two men shaking hands or touching each other's shoulders "connoted familial relationship or particular comradeship"; if a subject's head was tilted up with the eyes open or down with eyes closed, the photographer meant "to suggest speculative or contemplative moods."

Harry Amdur of the American Photographic Historical Society told us that early photographers tried to be "painterly" because they wanted to gain respect as fine artists. Any survey of the portrait paintings of the early and mid-nineteenth century indicates that the "hand-in-jacket" pose was a common one for many prominent men besides Napoleon.

Another boon to the Napoleonic pose was the invention of the *carte de visite,* a photographic calling card. Developed in France in the 1850s, small portraits were mounted on a card about the size of today's business card. Royalty and many affluent commoners had their visages immortalized on *cartes*. In France, prominent figures actually sold their *cartes*—ordinary citizens collected what became the baseball cards of their era. *Cartes de visite* invaded the United States within years.

These photos were far from candid shots. Indeed, Roy McJunkin, curator of the California Museum of Photography at the University of California, Berkeley, told *Imponderables* that *carte de visite* studios in the United States used theatrical sets, and that subjects invariably dressed in their Sunday best. The hand-in-jacket pose was only one of many staged poses, including holding a letter or Bible, holding a gun as if the subject were shooting, or pointing to an unseen (and usually nonexistent) point or object.

Some of the pretensions of this period were downright silly—silly enough to inspire Lewis Carroll to write a parody of the whole enterprise. In Carroll's poem, actually a parody of Longfellow's *Hiawatha*, Hiawatha is transformed into a harried, frustrated portrait photographer:

From his shoulder Hiawatha
Took the camera of rosewood,
Made of sliding, folding rosewood;
Neatly put it all together,
In its case it lay compactly,
Folded into nearly nothing;
But he opened out the hinges,
Pushed and pulled the joints and hinges,
Till it looked all squares and oblongs,
Like a complicated figure
In the second book of Euclid,
   This he perched upon a tri-pod—
   Crouched beneath its dusty cover—
Stretched his hand enforcing silence—
Mystic, awful was the process,
   All the family in order
Sat before him for their pictures:

Each in turn, as he was taken,
Volunteered his own suggestions.
   First the governor, the father:
He suggested velvet curtains
Looped about a messy Pillar;
And the corner of a table.
He would hold a scroll of something
Hold it firmly in his left hand;
He would keep his right hand buried
(Like Napoleon) in his waistcoat;
He would contemplate the distance
With a look of pensive meaning,
As of ducks that die in tempests.
Grand, heroic was the notion:
Yet, the picture failed entirely:
Failed, because he moved a little,
Moved because he couldn't help it!

Who would have ever thought of Lewis Carroll summarizing the answers to an Imponderable, while simultaneously contemplating the plight of a Sears portrait photographer?

—Submitted by Donald McGurk of West Springfield, Massachusetts.
Thanks also to Wendy Gessel of Hudson, Ohio, and Geoff Rizzie of Cypress, California.

why does heat make us sleepy in the afternoon when we're trying to work but restless when we're trying to sleep at night?

Fewer experiences are more physically draining than sitting in an over-heated library in the winter (why *are* all libraries overheated in the winter?) trying to work. You can be reading the most fascinating book in the world, and yet you would kill for a spot on a vacant cot rather than remaining on your hardback chair. So you trudge home, eventually, to your overheated house and try to get a good night's sleep. Yet the very heat that sent your body into a mortal craving for lassitude now turns you into a twisting and turning repository of frustration. You can't fall asleep. Why?

There is no doubt that heat saps us of energy. Many Latin, Asian, and Mediterranean cultures routinely allow their work force to take siestas during the hottest portions of the day, aware both that productivity would slacken during the early P.M. hours without a siesta and that workers are refreshed after an hour or so of sleep.

Yet all of the sleep experts we consulted agreed with the declaration of the Better Sleep Council's Caroline Jones: "Heat is not what makes us sleepy in the afternoon. Researchers have documented a universal dip in energy levels that occurs in the P.M. regardless of the temperature." These daily fluctuations of sleepiness within our body are known as "circadian rhythms." David L. Hopper, president of the American Academy of Somnology, told *Imponderables* that late evening and early afternoon are the "two periods during the twenty-four-hour cycle when sleep is possible or likely to occur under normal conditions."

Some sleep specialists believe that circadian rhythms indicate humans have an inborn predisposition to nap. But somnologists seem to agree that the natural sleepiness most of us feel in the afternoon, when it happens to be hottest outside, has little or nothing to do with the other very real enervating effects heat has upon us.

Environmental temperatures *do* affect our sleep patterns, though. Most people sleep better in cool environments, which explains why many of us are restless when trying to sleep in hot rooms even when we are exhausted at night. And if the temperature should shift while we are asleep, it can cause us to awaken, as Hopper explains:

> Our body temperature is lowest in the early morning hours and highest in the evening. During deep NREM and REM sleep, we lose our ability to effectively regulate body temperature, so if the outside temperature is too warm or too cold, we must arouse somewhat in order to regulate our body temperature more effectively. During sleep we are not unconscious, so signals are able to get through to arouse us when needed, much as when we awaken from sleep when we need to go to the bathroom.

—Submitted by Mark Gilbey of Palo Alto, California.
Thanks also to Neal Riemer of Oakland, California.

WHY DOES *KNUCKLE UNDER* MEAN "TO SUBMIT" OR "TO GIVE IN"?

Knuckle once referred to the joint of any bone, including the knee and elbow. *Knuckling under* originally meant "to bend down on one's knee and kneel in submission." The knuckles of the knees were hitting the ground and under (and supporting) the body of the supplicant.

why are humans most comfortable at 72°F? Why not at 98.6°F?

We feel most comfortable when we maintain our body temperature, so why don't we feel most comfortable when it is 98.6°F in the ambient air? We would—if we were nudists.

But most of us cling to the habit of wearing clothes. Clothing helps us retain body heat, some of which must be dissipated in order for us to feel comfortable in warm environments. Uncovered parts of our body usually radiate enough heat to meet the ambient air temperature halfway. If we are fully clothed at 72°F, the uncovered hands, ears, and face will radiate only a small portion of our heat, but enough to make us feel comfortable. Nude at 72°F, we would feel cold, for our bodies would give off too much heat.

Humidity and wind also affect our comfort level. The more humid the air, the greater ability it has to absorb heat. Wind can also wreak havoc with our comfort level. It hastens the flow of the heat we radiate and then constantly moves the air away and allows slightly cooler air to replace it.

—Submitted by Joel Kuni of Kirkland, Washington.

why do superficial paper cuts tend to hurt more than grosser cuts?

Perhaps paper cuts hurt more because they are so emotionally maddening. How can such a trivial little cut, sometimes without a hint of blood, cause such pain?

The sensory nerve endings are located close to the skin surface, and the hands, where most paper cuts occur, contain more nerve endings than almost any other area of the body. Dr. John Cook of the Georgia Dermatology and Skin Cancer Clinic adds that a trivial laceration such as a paper cut creates the worst of both worlds: "It irritates these nerve endings but doesn't damage them very much." Damaged nerve endings can lead to more serious complications, but sometimes to less pain than paper cuts.

Dr. Cook and Dr. Elliot of the American Dermatological Association also mentioned that most patients tend not to treat paper cuts as they would

grosser ones. After any kind of cut, the skin starts drying and pulling apart, exposing nerve endings. Cuts are also exposed to foreign substances, such as soap, liquids, perspiration, and dirt. Putting a bandage over a paper cut will not make it heal faster, necessarily, but if the cut stays moist, it won't hurt as much.

why don't you feel or see a mosquito bite until after it begins to itch?

We would like to think that the reason we don't feel the mosquito biting us is that Mother Nature is merciful. If we were aware that the mosquito was in the process of sinking its mouth into our flesh, we might panic, especially because a simple mosquito bite takes a lot longer than we suspected.

A female mosquito doesn't believe in a casual "slam bam, thank you, ma'am." On the contrary, mosquitoes will usually rest on all six legs on human skin for at least a minute or so before starting to bite. Mosquitoes are so light and their biting technique so skillful that most humans cannot feel them, even though the insect may be resting on their skin for five minutes or more.

When the mosquito decides to finally make her move and press her lancets into a nice, juicy capillary, the insertion takes about a minute. She lubricates her mouthparts with her own saliva and proceeds to suck the blood for up to three minutes until her stomach is literally about to burst. She withdraws her lancets in a few seconds and flies off to deposit her eggs, assuring the world that the mosquito will not soon make the endangered species list.

A few sensitive souls feel a mosquito's bite immediately. But most of us are aware of itching (or in some cases, pain) only after the mosquito is long gone not because of the bite or the loss of blood but because of the saliva left behind. The mosquito's saliva acts not only as a lubricant in the biting process but as an anesthetic to the bitee. For most people, the saliva is a blessing, since it allows us to be oblivious to the fact that our blood is being sucked by a loathsome insect. Unfortunately, the saliva contains anticoagulant components that cause allergic reactions in many people. This allergic reaction, not the bite itself, is what causes the little lumps and itchy sensations that make us wonder why mosquitoes exist in this otherwise often wonderful world.

—Submitted by Alesia Richards of Erie, Pennsylvania.

why does the skin on the extremities wrinkle after a bath? And why only the extremities?

Despite its appearance, your skin isn't shriveling after your bath. Actually, it is expanding.

The skin on the fingers, palms, toes, and soles wrinkles only after it is saturated with water (a prolonged stay underwater in the swimming pool will create the same effect). The stratum corneum—the thick, dead layer of the skin that protects us from the environment and that makes the skin on our hands and feet tougher and thicker than that on our stomachs or faces—expands when it soaks up water. This expansion causes the wrinkling effect.

So why doesn't the skin on other parts of the body also wrinkle when saturated? Actually, it does, but there is more room for the moisture to be absorbed in these less densely packed areas before it will show. One doctor we contacted said that soldiers whose feet are submerged in soggy boots for a long period will exhibit wrinkling all over the covered area.

—Submitted by Michelle L. Zielinski of Arnold, Missouri.

how do astronauts scratch an itch when they have space suits on?

Most of the time, an itch presents no problem for an astronaut in space. If an itch is pesky, the astronaut reaches to the offending nerve endings and scratches. If the itch is in an "unfortunate" place, perhaps the astronaut will look around the cabin, make sure no one else is looking, and then scratch. Still, no problem.

That's because most of the time when an astronaut is in space, he, and increasingly, she, is in street clothes—typically comfortable trousers or shorts and a polo shirt. There are only three times when the space suit conspires to foil an itch: upon launch, during reentry, and during "extravehicular activity" in space, such as a space walk.

During launch and reentry, astronauts wear an "LES" (launch-and-entry suit), the bright orange garb we see the astronauts wear when boarding the

shuttle. These are "partial pressure" suits, designed to pressurize in case the cabin has a sudden loss of pressure during launch or entry and are not unlike the suits worn by jet fighter pilots. Of course, a helmet is an essential component of the LES.

The "EVA" (extravehicular activity) suit is far bulkier and designed to withstand the rigors of outer space. This is the "big white uniform" that we associate with astronauts and with space walks, and that dominated the imagery in the movie *Apollo 13*. But even back in the Apollo days, astronauts rid themselves of the bulky suits once they were in orbit. Today, space shuttle astronauts wear EVAs while doing repair work on satellites or the Hubble telescope.

While EVAs are more flexible than the old Apollo suits, they are hardly a model of comfort. An astronaut first dons a bodysuit, akin to long johns, made of thin fabric. Over this go many layers of insulation and life-support equipment, including many tubes carrying liquid and gas. Then the "HUT" (hard upper torso), a stiff upper suit, is placed over all these other layers. The suit proper ends at the neck, with a hard metal locking ring, which clamps the helmet. Once the suit is pressurized, it puffs up, making it difficult to move freely within the EVA.

The helmet is locked rigidly at the neck clamp. If an astronaut swivels her head to the left, the helmet doesn't turn with her. So if she wants to see something at "three o'clock," she had better move her whole body in that direction.

In the Apollo days, suits were individually constructed for each astronaut. Now, they come "off the rack." No, there is no Gap for Astronauts, but they are sized "small, medium, and large," with allowances for long and short limbs.

By all accounts, the LES suits are more comfortable than the EVA suits. Astronauts are ordinarily in these suits, before takeoff, for at least one and one-half hours before launch. With delays, they can be stuck, unable to move freely, for up to four or five hours: plenty of time to contemplate itchiness, and what they are going to do about it. But once the launch takes place, the shuttle is in orbit within eight and one-half minutes; at that point, they can put on street clothes and scratch to their heart's (or other body part's) content.

So, is itchiness a burning issue among astronauts? Have they come up with solutions to this intractable problem? To find out, we assembled a group of five experts:

1. Wendy Lawrence, a former naval aviator and current astronaut, who flew on shuttle flight STS-67, an historic sixteen-day mission, which was the second flight of the ASTRO observatory.

2. G. David Low, who retired in 1996 after a ten-year career as an astronaut. Dave has flown on three shuttle missions and performed a six-hour space walk. He currently works at Orbital Sciences Corporation.

3. Mike Lounge, a former astronaut who trained for space walks but never did one. He currently works for Space Habitat.

4. James Hartsfield, NASA public affairs director.

5. Glen Lutz, a NASA "subsystem manager," whose specialty is the design of space suits.

We asked the three astronauts if itching bothered them, particularly when wearing the stiff EVA suits. They all agreed that the biggest problem was with facial itches, particularly on the nose. Luckily for them, that is one of the few parts of the anatomy that the space suit is equipped to help—but not because NASA was concerned about itching!

Built into the side of an EVA helmet is a V-shaped object called a "Valsalva device," which is designed to relieve earaches created by pressure changes in the cabin. To execute the "Valsalva maneuver," you hold your nose shut and blow through your nose to equalize pressure in the middle ear and clear the Eustachian tubes. Obviously, an astronaut can't "hold his nose" (there's that nasty little problem of the helmet being in the

WHY CAN'T HAIR GROW ON A VACCINATION MARK?

A vaccination mark is nothing more than scar tissue. A vaccination causes an inflammation intense enough to destroy the hair follicles in its vicinity. Any deep injury to the skin will destroy hair follicles and cause hair loss, a condition known to dermatologists as "scarring alopecia." One can easily transplant hair onto a vaccination mark, if desired, but one can never bring a dead hair follicle back to life.

—Submitted by David Wilsterman of Belmont, California.

way), so instead the astronauts rest their heads on the "V" of the Valsalva device and blow. The Valsalva device is built into the side of the helmet, so astronauts can simply turn their heads and place their proboscises right on it.

Ingenious astronauts discovered that they seldom needed the device for ear problems; they more frequently could use it for itch problems! In his funny and informative book, *How Do You Go to the Bathroom in Space?*, ex-astronaut William R. Pogue addresses this issue directly:

> Not only did my nose itch occasionally, but also my ears. Because a scratch is almost an involuntary reaction, I frequently reached up to scratch my nose and hit my helmet—which can make you feel really dumb. I scratched my nose by rubbing it on a little nose pincher device we used to clear our ears [the Valsalva device].
>
> If our ears itched, we just had to tolerate it, I usually tried rubbing the side of my head against the inside of the helmet, but it didn't help much. The best thing to do was to think of something else.

Some of our astronauts had their own workarounds:

> **LAWRENCE:** On an EVA you don't have direct access to your face. Hopefully you can wiggle your nose to satisfy it. You just try to move your nose around, maybe see if you can get your nose down to the base of the mounting ring on the inside—you see if that'll work.

> **LOUNGE:** The Valsalva device can help you with your nose. If you get an itch [elsewhere] on your face, you kind of move your head around and find something inside the helmet to rub against it.

Astronaut David Low had a hate relationship with the Valsalva device that turned into love:

> I had hundreds of hours in EVA training. I'd probably used that Valsalva device only a few times on a couple of different training runs. It always got in my way. In fact, a lot of times when just moving my head around, I'd bump into it and it became somewhat of a pain to me. I found I could always clear my ears by just moving my jaw around.
>
> In training, I never used it for what it was intended for. I was considering asking them to remove it from my helmet for the mission. But for some reason, about two weeks before flight, I was sitting in my office one day and I thought, What if I have to use the Valsalva device on my real space walk? I called our support guy and asked if they could make sure that there was a Valsalva device on my helmet.
>
> It turns out that I had the worst ear block I've ever had in my life when I was coming back in from my space walk and repressurizing. If you've ever had one of those, they're very uncomfortable and you can have a lot of pain. Nothing you can do about it. You can't get your hands in there to blow your nose. I was so happy that I had that Valsalva device.

Included on every EVA helmet is a straw, leading to a water pouch, and a food bar. Dehydration is a problem during space walks, so astronauts are encouraged to drink. Although it is possible to try to satisfy itches with these two devices, James Hartsfield indicates it isn't wise:

> The water straw is within reach of your mouth. You can get a drink by just bending your head down to get your lips onto the straw. There's also a food bar. But you don't want to use them to scratch facial itches. If you jiggle them around, they might come loose.

> LUTZ: On an EVA, it's possible to scratch a facial itch with the water straw and/or the food bar. But because both those things are going to be ingested, you probably want to avoid as much body contact with them as you can. Most of the guys eat that food bar before they get outside or quickly because the EVA is usually pretty task-intensive and they don't want to be messing around eating things.

The prognosis for nasty facial itches in the LES suit is much more favorable, because the visor is flexible:

> LOW: You can raise the visor on the helmet of an LES suit. For most of the ride uphill and downhill, we leave the visor open. We close them for the first two minutes of each launch, until solid rocket booster separation occurs. After that, we raise the visor. So when the visor is open, you can easily scratch a face itch. But if the orbiter lost pressurization, you'd have to leave the visor down.

What about body itches? In some cases, the space suit is as unforgiving as the helmet. It's difficult to work in an EVA suit; David Low compared it to being inside the Pillsbury Doughboy:

> It's hard to move in the things. They are pressurized and they balloon up. It wants to stay in the same, blown-up state. Anytime you bend it, it pops back to that original state.

Our other experts had slight disagreements about how easy it was to scratch an itch in the EVA suits:

> LOUNGE: The EVA suits are pressurized enough that you can't feel sensation if you try to scratch from the outside. It's not like a soft garment; it's like a hard shell. The tips of the gloves are rubber. You can move your fingers, but you don't have a good tactile sense.

> LUTZ: When the suit's not fully pressurized, that is, before you go out the door as you're getting ready for the space walk, if you get an itch on the soft part of the suit, like your arms, for instance, you can sort of compress it a little bit. You do that by squeezing with your arms from the outside of the suit.

However, once it's pressurized and you're on the space walk, the suit makes a pretty rigid balloon. It's feasible to rub your body against the inside of the suit. We're trying to make the suits as close as we can to a snug fit, but there is enough free volume that you can move around some. You can often get enough friction to scratch a bit.

LOW: It depends where the itch is. You can feel certain skin parts from the inside. The space suit is fairly tight. It looks bulky, but there are enough layers on the inside that you're almost touching something everywhere. You can just bend your leg or elbow [if you had an itch there]. You also typically have a little bit of room inside the chest cavity. If your shoulder itched, you could just contort yourself around there and scratch it the best you can.

If you get a muscle cramp or charley horse, you're out of luck. You can't rub muscles from the outside at all. You can try to bend joints and flex them. You can try to rub from the inside, but basically you just have to grin and bear it.

HARTSFIELD: I've asked the suit technicians about this. The best you can do is try to rub against some part of the suit that might be close by. If you can't do that, you're out of luck. You just grin and bear it. [Where did we hear that line before?]

If your leg itched, you couldn't scratch it. That is, you wouldn't feel it through the suit at all if you reached there with your hand. Externally, you can't scratch through the outside of the suit. The pressure in the suit is such that, for instance, if you work with your hands and you have to make a grip, it's like trying to squeeze a balloon. If you push your leg, the pressure would go somewhere else. There are just too many layers to go through. In fact, once you're in the suit, you wouldn't even try—it's obvious that it isn't going to work.

If you were lucky enough to have an itch somewhere close by some part of the suit you could feel on the skin, you could try to scratch it up and down but that would still be hard to do because you're wearing a liquid cooling vent garment, like a pair of long underwear. You'd have to try to scratch through that by rubbing your leg against some part of the suit.

LES space suits, much to the relief of the astronauts, are much more forgiving. Barring an emergency, they are not inflated, so they are not as stiff as EVA suits:

LUTZ: It is a soft suit, so you can kind of press in and get to whatever [itch] you have.

LAWRENCE: For the most part, the suits are comfortable. What makes it uncomfortable is if there's a launch delay—you're lying on your back maybe four hours, strapped to a seat. That's the uncomfortable part. But if you had an itch, you could scratch it through the outside of the suit.

This is a substantial improvement from the earlier Apollo days. In his book *Liftoff,* astronaut Michael Collins talks about the exigencies of itches and other physical discomforts during the Gemini era:

> Inside the suit were other odds and ends, such as biomedical sensors taped to the chest with wires running to electronic amplifiers placed in pockets in the underwear. Finally, there was a "motorman's friend," a triangular urine bag with a condomlike device into which the astronaut inserted his penis before donning the suit. Once you're locked inside the suit, none of this gear could be adjusted, nor could an eye be rubbed, a nose blown, or an itch scratched. Some of the most fundamental amenities that we take for granted on Earth are difficult or impossible for an extravehicular astronaut.

To be honest, we were surprised that itching wasn't more of a complaint or concern. But look at it this way: When the astronauts are performing a space walk or about to launch, they might actually have *other things* on their minds. Hartsfield, who has worked with so many astronauts, comments:

> Most astronauts, when they do a space walk, are so enthralled by the experience that their mind doesn't wander to small things like this. But perhaps we will confront this when we get into the construction of the station and we do space walks regularly—essentially construction work in orbit.
>
> It might get to the point where an itch here or there would be something the astronauts actually talk about. Today, I think it doesn't even enter their minds with the six hours they've got on a typical space walk.
>
> Also, they've trained in these suits for hundreds of hours. They are very comfortable with the suits already. If they're comfortable on the ground, they're going to be really comfortable out in the weightlessness of space.

And it's not as if astronauts lean toward the wimpy or whiny. Many astronauts have a military background, and even those that don't tend to share the stiff-upper-lip demeanor depicted in *The Right Stuff* and *Apollo 13.* Perhaps astronaut Wendy Lawrence put it best:

> You just deal with it. My background is that of a Navy pilot. If you get an itch when you are in military formation and standing in ranks, you just can't scratch it. You do what you can to alleviate the discomfort, but at the same time you realize that you have to stay at attention. You come up with ways to work around the problem and try to alleviate it, but you can't get out of your main responsibility.
>
> But let me tell you. When the engines are on, and you're on solid rocket boosters, it's a nit! I was so wrapped in what was going on with the launch, and all my responsibilities with the launch, I didn't even notice any of that stuff.

—Submitted by Dallas Brozik of Huntington, West Virginia.

why don't people get goose bumps on their faces?

Be proud of the fact that you don't get goose bumps on your face. It's one of the few things that separate you from chimpanzees.

We get goose bumps only on parts of our bodies that have hair. The purpose of body hair is to protect us from the cold. But when our hair doesn't provide enough insulation, the small muscles at the bottom of each hair tighten, so that the hair stands up.

In animals covered with fur, the risen strands form a protective nest of hairs. Cold air is trapped in the hair instead of bouncing against delicate skin. The hair thus insulates the animals against the cold.

Although humans have lost most of their body hair, the same muscular contractions occur to defend against the cold. Instead of a mat of hair, all we have to face the elements are a few wispy tufts and a multitude of

WHY ARE TATTOOS USUALLY BLUE (WITH AN OCCASIONAL TOUCH OF RED)?

Most tattoos are not blue. The pigment, made from carbon, is actually jet black. Since the pigment is lodged *underneath* the skin, tattoos appear blue because of the juxtaposition of black against the yellowish to brown skin of most Caucasians. Although red is the second most popular color, many other shades are readily available; in fact, most tattoo artists buy many different colorings, premade, from DuPont.

We spoke to Spider Webb, perhaps the most famous tattooist in the United States and leader of the Tattoo Club of America, about the prevalence of black pigment in tattoos. Webb felt that most clients, once they decide to take the plunge, want to show off their tattoos: Black is by far the strongest and most visible color. Webb added that in the case of one client, albino guitarist Johnny Winter, a black tattoo does appear to be black and not blue.

—Submitted by Venia Stanley of Albuquerque, New Mexico.

mounds of skin, which used to support an erect hair and now must go it alone. When a male lion gets goose bumps, his erect hair makes him ferocious; our goose bumps only make us look vulnerable.

—Submitted by Pam Cicero of Madison, Ohio.

why do older women dye their hair blue?

In the 1960s, it was fashionable to tint or bleach hair in pastel shades. Some older women, perhaps, are choosing to stick with a trend that has come and gone.

The majority, however, use a blue rinse (not a dye or tint) to combat the yellow shadings that discolor their gray or white hair. Blue helps mask yellow.

Advancing age is not the sole reason for yellow hair. Some chemicals used in other hair preparations can cause yellowing. But the biggest culprit of all is smoke. Cosmetician Richard Levac told *Imponderables* that as we get older, the hair becomes more porous. Smoke coats the hair and embeds itself in the hair shaft, causing yellowing.

Levac adds that very few women are intentionally trying to emerge from a salon with blue hair. Blue rinses are much lighter than they were twenty years ago. If you can notice the blue, the hairdresser has done a poor job.

—Submitted by Daniel A. Placko, Jr., of Chicago, Illinois.

why do your feet swell up so much in airplanes?

We talked to two specialists in aviation medicine who assured us that there is no reason why atmospheric changes in airplanes would cause feet to swell. Both assured us that the reason your feet swell up on a plane is the same reason they swell up on the ground—inactivity.

Your heart is not the only organ in the body that acts as a pump; so do the muscles of the legs. Walking or flexing a leg muscle assists the pumping effect. On a plane, you are not only confined in movement but sitting with the legs perpendicular to the floor. If you sit for prolonged periods without muscular activity, blood and other fluids collect in the foot with the assistance of gravity.

It doesn't really matter whether you leave your shoes on or off during periods of inactivity. If left on, they will provide external support, but they will inhibit circulation, feel tight—and will not prevent feet from swelling, in any case. If you take your shoes off, you will feel more comfortable, but you'll have a tough time putting your shoes back on, and most of us don't take our shoehorns along on planes.

The pooling of fluids in the feet can happen just as easily in a bus, a train, or an office. Most people's feet swell during the day, which is why the American Podiatric Association recommends buying shoes during the middle of the afternoon. Many people require a shoe a half size to a full size larger in the afternoon than when they wake up.

If your feet swelling becomes a problem, consider airplane aerobics. A few laps around a wide-body plane will do wonders for your feet and will build up your appetite for that wholesome and delicious airplane meal that awaits you.

—Submitted by Christal Henner of New York, New York.

WHY IS ROYALTY REFERRED TO AS "BLUE-BLOODED"?

In the eighth century, a group of Islamic warriors, the Moors, invaded and occupied Spain. And they ruled over the country for five centuries.

This didn't sit too well with the aristocrats of Castile, who began referring to themselves as *sangre azul* ("blue blood") to differentiate themselves from the Moors. No, the Castilians' blood was no different in color than the Moors', but their skin complexion was lighter than that of their conquerors.

The Castilian pride in their "blue blood" was a thinly veiled proclamation of pride in their light complexions, and a subtle way of indicating that they were not, as the *Oxford English Dictionary* puts it, "contaminated by Moorish, Jewish, or other foreign admixture." For the paler the complexion of the skin, the more blue the veins appear.

—Submitted by Daniel A. Placko of Chicago, Illinois.

why is pubic hair curly?

If you want to know the anatomical reason why pubic hair is curly, we can help you. Dr. Joseph P. Bark, diplomate of the American Board of Dermatology, explains:

> Pubic hair is curly because it is genetically made in a flat shape rather than in a round shape. Perfectly round hair, such as the hair seen on the scalps of Native Americans, is straight and has no tendency to curl. However, ribbonlike hair on the scalps of African Americans is seen to curl because it is oval in construction. The same is true with pubic hair.

But answering what function curly pubic hair serves is a much trickier proposition. Some, such as Samuel T. Selden, a Chesapeake, Virginia, dermatologist, speculate that pubic hair might be curly because if it grew out straight and stiff, it might rub against adjacent areas and cause discomfort. (Dermatologist Jerome Z. Litt of Pepper Pike, Ohio, who has been confronted with the question of why pubic and axillary hair doesn't grow as fast as scalp hair, facetiously suggests that "not only wouldn't it look sporty in the shower room, but we'd all be tripping over it.")

Before we get carried away with our theories, though, we might keep in mind a salient fact—not all pubic hair is curly. Early in puberty, it is soft and straight. And Selden points out that if this book were published in Japan or China, this Imponderable likely would never have been posed. The pubic hair of Orientals tends to be sparser and much straighter than that of whites or blacks.

—Submitted by Suzanne Saldi of West Berlin, New Jersey.

why are some parts of our bodies more ticklish than others?

The experts who tackled this Imponderable focused on serious benefits that ticklishness might bestow on us mortals, all agreeing that what we now consider a benign tingling sensation at one time in our evolution might have warned us against serious trauma.

San Francisco biophysicist Joe Doyle notes that some parts of our body are more richly endowed with nerves than others—including such tickling meccas as the bottom of the feet, the underarms, and the hands and fingers.

Evolutionists, notes Neil Harvey of the International Academy for Child Brain Development, "would say that the reason for the heavier concentration may be whatever survival benefits we derive from being more sensitive in those places."

How could, say, the armpit possibly be necessary to survival? "The axilla warns of a touch that might progress to a wound of the brachial plexus, which could paralyze an arm," answers University of Chicago neurosurgeon Sean F. Mullan. Other sensitive sites such as the nostrils, ear canals, and eye sockets are all subject to invasion by foreign objects or creeping or flying insects.

What about the underside of the foot, then? Mullan is slightly more tentative:

> The role of the foot is more perplexing. Is it a warning against the snake that crawled up the tree when we lived in its branches? Is it a hypersensitivity resulting from the removal of the thicker skin of our soles, which was normal before we began to wear shoes? I prefer the former explanation.
>
> —*Submitted by a caller on the Mike Rosen Show, KOA-AM, Denver, Colorado.*

during a hernia exam, why does the physician say, "Turn your head and cough"? Why is the cough necessary? Is the head turn necessary?

Although a doctor may ask you to cough when listening to your lungs, the dreaded "Turn your head and cough" is heard when the physician is checking for hernias, weaknesses or gaps in the structure of what should be a firm body wall.

According to Dr. Frank Davidoff of the American College of Physicians, these gaps are most frequently found in the inguinal area in men, "the area where the tube (duct) that connects each testicle to the structures inside the body passes through the body wall." Some men are born with fairly large gaps to begin with. The danger, Davidoff says, is that

> repeated increases in the pressure inside the abdomen, as from repeated and chronic coughing, lifting heavy weights, etc., can push abdominal contents into the gap, stretching a slightly enlarged opening into an even bigger one, and leading ultimately to a permanent bulge in contents out through the hernia opening.
>
> Inguinal hernias are obvious and can be disfiguring when they are large and contain a sizable amount of abdominal contents, such as pads of fat or loops of intestine. However, hernias are actually more

dangerous when they are small, because a loop of bowel is likely to get pinched, hence obstructed, if caught in a small hernia opening, while a large hernia opening tends to allow a loop of bowel to slide freely in and out of the hernia "sac" without getting caught or twisted.

Doctors are therefore particularly concerned about detecting inguinal hernias when they are small, exactly the situation in which they have not been obvious to the patient. A small inguinal hernia may not bulge at all when the pressure inside the abdomen is normal. Most small hernias would go undetected unless the patient increased the pressure inside the abdomen, thus causing the hernia sac to bulge outward, where it can be felt by the doctor's examining finger pushed up into the scrotum.

And the fastest, simplest way for the patient to increase the intra-abdominal pressure is to cough, since coughing pushes up the diaphragm, squeezes the lungs, and forces air out past the vocal cords. By forcing all the abdominal muscles to contract together, coughing creates the necessary increase in pressure.

If the physician can't feel a bulge beneath the examining finger during the cough, he or she assumes the patient is hernia-free.

And why do you have to turn your head when coughing? Dr. E. Wilson Griffin III, a family physician at the Jonesville Family Medical Center, in Jonesville, North Carolina, provided the most concise answer: "So that the patient doesn't cough his yucky germs all over the doctor."

−Submitted by Jeffrey Chavez of Torrance, California.
Thanks also to J. S. Hubar of Pittsburgh, Pennsylvania.

why do pregnant women get strange food cravings? And why do they suddenly start hating foods they used to love?

Is there something specific about being in the family way that produces a sudden passion for a pickle sundae? A pork-and-banana sandwich? Or Twinkies with a dollop of mustard?

A few social scientists subscribe to the notion that cravings are "all in pregnant women's heads," but the nutritionists and medical experts we consulted dissent. Food cravings are prevalent all over the world: We found scores of studies that found at least some food cravings in one-half to more than 90 percent of pregnant women, with most falling in the 65 to 75 percent range.

Cravings are likely a result of hormonal changes that alter taste perception. One strong argument for hormones as the culprit is that women tend also to undergo strong food cravings (and aversions) during menopause,

another period when hormones are raging and changing. Janet Pope, an associate professor of nutrition and dietetics at Louisiana Tech University, told *Imponderables* that pregnant women evaluate flavor differently, so they may try different foods or combinations of foods to find foods that will now satisfy them.

And then there is the indisputable fact that the little fetus is draining some nutrition from the mother. "You are now eating for two," so the cliché goes. But most nutritionists believe the average female need consume only 300 extra calories a day of a well-balanced diet to compensate for the other life she is carrying. It would seem logical to assume that the fetus is taking in nutrients unevenly, and that is the reason for weird cravings and aversions. Ethiopian women believe that their sudden aversion to usual staples can be explained by their babies' distaste for that particular food. But biologists and nutritionists still can't explain the unpredictability in food preferences during pregnancy.

Some cravings are relatively easy to explain on a strictly nutritional basis. For example, a woman who craves olives or pickles might be low in sodium. A newfound peanut-butter fanatic might need additional protein, fat, or B vitamins. But sodium can be obtained from Triscuits or pretzels, too. Protein, fat, and B vitamins are contained in fish or meat, as well. Cross-cultural studies indicate that most mothers crave nutritious items that are *not* part of their regular diet. In the West, many expectant mothers swear off meat; where meat is prized but scarce, it is among the most common cravings. Unusual food cravings may also be, in part, an attempt to find new food combinations to stave off some of the unpleasant symptoms of pregnancy, such as morning sickness.

Almost as many women experience food aversions as strong cravings, often from foods and drinks that they enjoyed before pregnancy. One theory is that aversions are nature's way of assuring the fetus obtains good nutrition by diversifying the diet of the mother. This might explain why in Third World countries, poor women often experience aversions to staple grains—many mothers' normal diets contain too much cereal and starch, and not enough protein and fat.

Others contend that food aversions are a way of safeguarding the fetus by making dangerous substances unpalatable to the mother. Some chain-smoking, coffee-sipping, booze-guzzling females find it remarkably easy to shed their vices when pregnant. They might maintain that their sudden upgrading of habits is done out of altruism, but studies indicate that these were among the most common aversions even before their potential damage to the fetus was known. Likewise, many women find themselves nauseated at even the thought of consuming raw meat, sushi, or soft cheeses, substances that are usually safe to consume but do offer increased health risks if prepared inadequately.

But some cravings have no conceivable nutritional advantage. Perhaps the most popular craving of pregnant women is ice: *ice*, not water, a Popsicle, or a soda. Ella Lacey, a nutritionist at Southern Illinois University's medical school, says that nobody understands why women often crave foods that offer few, if any nutrients, let alone the particular nutrients she might lack. She theorizes that it may be some form of addictive behavior, where there is a drive to gain satisfaction, even if the outcome doesn't fulfill the deficiency.

The most aberrant addictive craving is pica, a condition most prevalent in the South of the United States and Central America, in which folks crave and eat non-food substances, often dirt, clay, chalk, dishwasher detergent, and, least scary, ice chips. Pregnant women comprise the largest, but by no means

WHAT'S THE PURPOSE OF THE WHITE HALF-MOONS ON THE BASES OF OUR FINGERNAILS AND TOENAILS? WHY DON'T THEY GROW OUT WITH THE NAILS?

Those white moons are called lunulae. The lunula is the only visible portion of the nail matrix, which produces the nail itself. The matrix (and the lunulae) never moves, but new nails continually push forward, away from the matrix.

Why does a lunula appear white? Dermatologist Harry Arnold explains:

The nail beds distal to the lunulae look pink because capillaries with blood in them immediately underlie the nail plate. The lunulae look white because the thin, modified epidermis of the nail bed is three or four times thicker there, being the busy factory where nail plate is manufactured. The lunula is avascular [without blood vessels], so it looks white.

—Submitted by Joanna Parker of Miami, Florida.
Thanks also to Jo Hadley of Claremont, California.

only, group of pica practitioners, but in most, the desire goes away once the baby is born.

Pica is more prevalent among poor folks, many of whom have nutritional deficiencies, leading some nutritionists to believe that pica, and especially geophagy (eating of dirt and clay), is a response to an iron or calcium deficiency. The more affluent woman is likely to detect such a deficiency by consulting a doctor or nutritionist, and once diagnosed, more likely to turn to spinach and liver than the backyard for a remedy.

All of a sudden, that pickle sundae is starting to sound awfully tempting.

—Submitted by Angela Burgess of Los Angeles, California.
Thanks also to Jerry De Duca of Montreal West, Quebec;
and Steffany Aye of Lawrence, Kansas.

why don't women faint
as much as they used to?

The most common cause of fainting is a lack of sufficient blood flow to the brain because of a sudden drop in blood pressure. Serious heart problems, including arrhythmia and ventricular tachycardia, can also be the culprit and less frequently, neurological irregularities. Some phobics truly do faint at the sight of blood or a coiling snake, but this is the result of a sudden loss of blood pressure.

None of these medical conditions has been eradicated, so it's always a shock to pick up a Victorian novel and find damsels fainting when they are frightened, fainting when they are ecstatic, fainting when their heart is heavy, and most of all, fainting when it is convenient to their purposes. What ever happened to swooning?

The most often cited faint-inducer in the past was a torture device known as the corset, an undergarment so tight that according to Lynda Stretton's essay "A Mini-History of the Corset":

> By the time they were teenagers, the girls were unable to sit or stand for any length of time without the aid of a heavy canvas corset reinforced with whalebone or steel. The corset deformed the internal organs, making it impossible to draw a deep breath, in or out of a corset. Because of this, Victorian women were always fainting and getting the vapours.

What was the purpose of this torture? The mark of a beautiful woman was thought to be the thinnest possible waist. Stretton reports that although the

literature refers to corseted waists as small as twelve to eighteen inches in adult women, most of these figures were probably fantasies:

> Measurements of corsets in museum collections indicate that most corsets of the period 1860 to 1910 measured from twenty to twenty-two inches. Furthermore, those sizes do not indicate how tightly the corsets were laced. They could easily have been laced out by several inches, and probably were, because it was prestigious to buy small corsets.

Even so, trying to cinch in a waist six or eight inches tighter than nature intended could do damage to the circulatory system.

Corsets, with certain Madonna-like exceptions, are no longer a fashion rage. Has fainting stopped? Nope. As Louis E. Rentz, executive director of the American College of Neuropsychiatrists, wrote us:

> [Fainting] is one of the most common complaints that present to a physician's office and certainly one of the most common things neurologists and cardiologists see. It is common at all ages.

Two U.S. studies of more than 5,000 healthy people indicate that somewhere between 3 to 6 percent of the population report at least one fainting episode over an extended period of time (ten years in one study, twenty-six in another).

One statistic popped out on all of the research about fainting we consulted: Men fainted almost as much as women. Could all the reports of female swooning in the nineteenth century be inaccurate? Exaggerated?

Upper-crust society in England, the subject of most of the Victorian novels we read in English 101, were living in times when women were considered to be delicate creatures. Corsets were thought not only to make women look more attractive, but to help them medically (children as little as three or four wore corsets, in the mistaken belief that such support would help strengthen their posture and musculature).

Even more bizarre were the beliefs about the "delicate sensibilities" of ladies. The Society for the Reformation of Manners, founded in London in 1690, first started fighting against prostitution and drunkenness, but by the nineteenth century became preoccupied with "cleaning up" the language. *Bloody* became a taboo word, and no host would serve a woman a rare cut of beef for fear that the sight of blood would send a delicate lady to the fainting couch for a swoon. In her review of etiquette books of the period, *The Best Behavior,* Esther B. Aresty notes that not only sticks and stones but words were believed to be able to hurt Victorian females:

> Well-bred English people never spoke of going to bed; they retired. Even a bureau could not have "drawers." To refer to a female as a "woman" was insulting and a foreigner might cause a fainting spell if

he said "woman" to a lady's face.... Delicacy was, in fact, being carried to such extremes that Lady Gough's *Etiquette* ruled that even *books* by male and female authors should "be properly separated on bookshelves. Their proximity unless they happen to be married should not be tolerated."

Women in the nineteenth century lived in a culture in which fainting was seen as a badge of femininity. When Alexis de Tocqueville came to the United States as a young man in the 1830s, he observed that European women were:

seductive and imperfect beings ... [who] almost consider it a privilege that they are entitled to show themselves futile, feeble, and timid.... The women of America claim no such privileges.

In this environment, who could blame a woman for timing a swoon so that it coincided with the approach of her intended? If you wanted to avoid a nasty confrontation, why not faint instead?

Our theory is that fainting was largely a cultural phenomenon, a benign form of mass hysteria. No doubt, tight corsets constricted blood flow and caused fainting, especially in women with low blood pressure. But Victorian society rewarded fainting—it was considered feminine and attractive behavior. The faint became an all-purpose excuse for ducking difficult obligations, the nineteenth-century equivalent of "the dog ate my homework," with the added benefit of garnering sympathy.

We bet that the actual incidence of fainting hasn't changed that much over centuries. Indeed, we recently encountered a reality show that proved that not only Victorian damsels feign fainting. On Fox TV's reality show, *Boot Camp*, a drill instructor found macho Meyer dawdling on a hot day. Meyer decided to evade doing his required push-ups by "fainting." He didn't fool his comrades, just as we suspect most swooning damsels didn't. But maybe Meyer's fate explains why you don't see folks bragging about fainting anymore: he was unanimously booted off the show.

—Submitted by Nathan Trask of Herrin, Illinois.

How come we never see left-handed string players in orchestras?

We posed this Imponderable to reader-cellist Craig Kirkland, who responded:

> I know two lefty violinists and both were taught as youngsters to play the same way righties do, so it's never been an issue for them. "Backwards" instruments may exist, like those lefty electric bassist Paul McCartney uses, but I've never seen a string equivalent.

Precisely, Craig. Although there were isolated lefty sightings (Jeannine Abel, secretary of the American Musical Instrument Society, spotted a left-handed violinist in the St. Luke's orchestra), they are few and far between, and for a perfectly logical reason. Imagine two violinists bowing furiously during the crescendo of a symphony: The bows would be moving in opposite directions. The applied pressure on the strings would be different, and the bows would look as if they were engaged in a duel rather than a musical enterprise. Furthermore, left-handed bowing would ruin the visual symmetry that is part of the concertgoing experience.

We spoke to William Monical, a violin restorer and dealer in New York City, who emphasized the difficulty in retrofitting high-quality violins for left-handers. Although the violin might be symmetrical on the outside, the inside is not. For example, there is a bass bar (a long, vertical piece of wood) glued to the inside top of the violin that runs along the G-string. A sound post lies behind the bridge near the D-string (in layman's terms, this is a dowel held in place by the pressure of the D-string). These pieces must be moved with great delicacy to accommodate left-handers. Likewise, the strings cannot simply be reversed for left-handers; the fingerboard would also have to be changed as well.

And how would a left-hander know if it was worth making the change? Monical suggests it would cost several thousand dollars to make the adjustments. Some of the valuable seventeenth- and eighteenth-century violins were made slightly asymmetrically to accommodate the sound post, adding even more difficulties (and costs) to the process.

Monical has a half dozen or so clients who are left-handed, and two of them have asked for left-handed modifications. But others fear harming the sound of their instrument and have decided to make the best of the fate that the right-handed world has bestowed upon them: accommodation to the dominant right-handed style of playing.

—Submitted by Solomon Marmor of Portland, Oregon.
Thanks also to Phyllis Diamond of Cherry Valley, California;
and Sean Campbell-Brennan of Middleton, Idaho.

do identical twins have identical fingerprints? Identical DNA?

Let's put it this way: If identical twins had identical fingerprints, do you really think David Kelley wouldn't have fashioned a murder plot about it on *The Practice?* Or Dick Wolf on one of the seventy-four *Law & Order* spinoffs?

Scientists corroborate our TV-based evidence. Identical twins result when a fertilized egg splits and the mother carries two separate embryos to term. The key to the creation of identical twins is that the split occurs *after* fertilization. The twins come from the same sperm and egg—and thus have the same DNA, the identical genetic makeup.

Because their DNA is an exact match, identical twins will always be the same sex, have the same eye color, and share the same blood type. "Fraternal twins," on the other hand, are born when two separate eggs are fertilized by *two different* sperms. Their DNA will be similar, but no more of a match than any other pair of siblings from the same parents. Not only do fraternal twins not necessarily look that much alike (think, for example, of the Bee Gees brothers, Maurice and Robin Gibb), but can be of the opposite sex and may possess different blood types.

Even though identical twins share the same DNA, however, they aren't carbon copies. Parents and close friends can usually tell one identical twin from the other without much difficulty. Their personalities may differ radically. And their fingerprints differ. If genetics doesn't account for these differences, what does? Why aren't the fingerprints of identical twins, er, identical?

The environment of the developing embryo in the womb has a hand in determining a fingerprint. That's why geneticists make the distinction between "genotypes" (the set of genes that a person inherits, the DNA) and "phenotypes" (the characteristics that make up a person after the DNA is exposed to the environment). Identical twins will always have the same genotype, but their phenotypes will differ because their experience in the womb will diverge.

Edward Richards, the director of the program in law, science, and public health at Louisiana State University, writes:

> In the case of fingerprints, the genes determine the general characteristics of the patterns that are used for fingerprint classification. As the skin on the fingertip differentiates, it expresses these general characteristics. However, as a surface tissue, it is also in contact with other

parts of the fetus and the uterus, and their position in relation to uterus and the fetal body changes as the fetus moves on its own and in response to positional changes of the mother. Thus the microenvironment of the growing cells on the fingertip is in flux, and is always slightly different from hand to hand and finger to finger. It is this microenvironment that determines the fine detail of the fingerprint structure. While the differences in the microenvironment between fingers are small and subtle, their effect is amplified by the differentiating cells and produces the macroscopic differences that enable the fingerprints of twins to be differentiated.

Influences as disparate as the nutrition of the mother, position in the womb, and individual blood pressure can all contribute to different fingerprints of identical twins.

Richards notes that the physical differences between twins widen as they age: "In middle and old age [identical twins] will look more like non-identical twins."

About 2 percent of all births are twins, and only one third of those are identical twins. But twins' fingerprints are like snowflakes—they may look alike at first blush, but get them under a microscope, and the differences emerge.

—Submitted by Mary Quint, via the Internet. Thanks also to Rachel P. Wincel, via the Internet; and Stephanie Pencek of Reston, Virginia.

why are children taught how to print before they learn cursive handwriting?

While most of us were taught how to print in kindergarten and learned how to write in late second or third grade, this wasn't always the case. Until the early 1920s, children were taught only cursive handwriting in school. Margaret Wise imported the idea of starting kids with manuscript writing (or printing) from England in 1921, and her method has become nearly universal in North America ever since.

Wise used two arguments to promote the radical change: With limited motor skills, it was easier for small children to make print legible; and print, looking more like typeset letters than cursive writing, would enable children to learn to read faster and more easily. Subsequent experimental research has confirmed that Wise's suppositions were correct.

In the seventy years since Wise revolutionized kindergarten penmanship, other reasons for teaching children printing have been advanced: Print is easier for teachers and students to read; students learn print more quickly and easily than cursive writing; and despite protestations from some, children can print as fast as they can write. While adults tend to write faster than they can print, experiments have indicated that this is only true because most adults rarely print; those who print as a matter of course are just as fast as cursive writers.

We have pored over many academic discussions about children's writing and haven't found anyone strenuously objecting to teaching children how to print first. What surprised us, though, is the lack of reasoned justification for weaning children from printing and, just after they have mastered the technique, teaching them cursive writing. After reviewing the literature on the subject, Walter Koenke, in an article in *The Reading Teacher,* boiled the rationales down to two—tradition and parental pressure:

> Since printing can be produced as speedily as cursive handwriting while being as legible and since it is obvious that the adult world generally accepts printing, it seems that the tradition rather than research calls for the transition from some form of printing to cursive handwriting.

A litany of justifications for cursive writing has been advanced, but none of them holds up. If print is easier to read and write, why do we need to learn cursive script? Why do we need to teach children duplicate letter forms when there is hard evidence that the transitionary period temporarily retards students' reading and compositional ability? (One study indicated that for each semester's delay in introducing cursive handwriting, students' compositional skill improved.)

In a wonderful article, "Curse You, Cursive Writing," the University of Northern Iowa's Professor Sharon Arthur Moore argues passionately that there is no need to teach children cursive writing and rebuts most of the arguments that its proponents claim. It is not true, as conventional wisdom might have it, that cursive writing is harder to forge than manuscript print, nor is it true that only cursive writing can be a valid signature on legal documents (X can still mark the spot).

Moore feels that parental pressure and a belief that cursive is somehow more "grown up" or prestigious than print permeates our society and leads to an unnecessary emphasis on cursive style:

> From the time they enter school, children want to learn to "write"; near the end of second or the beginning of third grade, the wish comes true. The writing done to that point must not be very highly valued, or why would there be such a rush to learn to do "the real thing"? Perceptions

are so much more powerful than reality at times that it may not even occur to people to question the value of cursive writing.

Why, she argues persuasively, do business and legal forms ask us to "please print carefully"? The answer, of course, is that even adults print more legibly than they write cursively. If cursive is superior, why aren't cursive typefaces for typewriters and computer printers more popular? Why aren't books published in cursive?

Moore, like us, can't understand the justification for teaching kids how to write, and then changing that method in two years for no pedagogical purpose. She endorses the notion of teaching cursive writing as an elective in eighth or ninth grade.

Several handwriting styles have been advanced to try to bridge the gap between manuscript and cursive styles—most prominently, the "D'Nealian Manuscript," which teaches children to slant letters from the very beginning and involves much less lifting of the pencil than standard printing. Proponents of the D'Nealian method claim that their style requires fewer jerky movements that may prove difficult and time-consuming for five- and six-year-olds and eases the transition from manuscript to cursive by teaching kids how to "slant" right away. And the D'Nealian method also cuts down the reversal of letters that typifies children's printing. It is far less likely that a child, using D'Nealian, will misspell "dad" as "bab," because the "b" and "d" look considerably different. In standard manuscript, the child is taught to create a "b" by making a straight vertical line and then drawing a circle next to it. But in D'Nealian, the

---

WHY DO WE SAY THAT SOMEONE IN A STATE OF ANXIETY OR SUSPENSE IS *ON TENTERHOOKS?*

After fabric was woven and milled, the material used to be stretched on a frame, called a *tenter,* to dry the cloth evenly. The cloth was kept snugly in place by hooks (or bent nails), which were known as, appropriately enough, *tenterhooks.*

Tenter probably derives from the Latin *tendere* ("to stretch"). *On tenterhooks,* then, always has been a metaphor for being "on the rack." Novelist Tobias Smollett so used *tenterhooks* as early as 1748: "I left him upon the tenterhooks of impatient uncertainty."

pencil is never picked up: the straight but slanted vertical line is drawn, but the "circle" starts at the bottom of the line, and the pencil is brought around and up to form what they call the "tummy" of the "b."

We'll leave it to the theorists to debate whether the D'Nealian, or more obscure methods, are superior to the standard "circle stick" style of manuscript. But we wish we could have found a clearer reason why it's necessary to change from that style into cursive writing—ever. We couldn't argue the cause more eloquently than Janice-Carol Yasgur, an urban elementary schoolteacher:

> Just as kids begin to get competent in printing their thoughts, we come along and teach them cursive—and what a curse it is! Now they devote more of their energy to joining all the letters together than to thinking about what they're trying to communicate, so that it's a total loss: It's impossible to make out their scribbles; but even if you can, it's impossible to figure out what they're trying to say. It's a plot to keep elementary schoolteachers in a state of permanent distress.

> *—Submitted by Erin Driedger of Osgoode, Ontario.*

why do starving children have bloated stomachs?

How often have we seen pictures of young children, near death from starvation, with emaciated faces and bloated stomachs? Why do these children, desperately in need of food, have such protruding abdomens?

Bloated abdomens are a symptom of protein calorie malnutrition (PCM). Many of these youths are starving from a generally inadequate calorie consumption and concomitant insufficient protein. But others are suffering from "kwashiorkor," a condition in which children who consume a proper amount of calories are not eating enough protein. Kwashiorkor is most common among many of the rice-based cultures in the third world, where traditional sources of protein (meat, fish, legumes) are uncommon or too costly for the average citizen.

Insufficient protein consumption can lead to severe problems—it produces the lack of energy reflected in the passive, affectless expression of these PCM children. PCM can affect every organ in the body, but it is particularly devastating to the pancreas, liver, blood, and lymphatic system.

A healthy person's blood vessels leak a little fluid, which collects outside of the vessels. Ordinarily, the lymphatic vessels remove this liquid. But when the lymphatic system malfunctions, as it does in PCM children, the fluid builds up in the skin, causing a condition known as edema.

In these children, a particular type of fluid accumulation, ascites (the fluid buildup in the abdominal cavity), accounts for much of the bloated stomach. A little fluid in the abdominal cavity is a desirable condition, because the fluid helps cushion organs. Ascites in isolation may not be dangerous, but they are often a symptom of liver damage. Don Schwartz, a pediatrician at Philadelphia's Children's Hospital, told *Imponderables* that membranes often weaken during protein calorie malnutrition, which only adds to the leakage of body fluids into the abdominal cavity.

Dysfunctional livers often swell. The liver is one of the largest organs in the body and usually constitutes 2 to 3 percent of one's entire body weight. According to Dr. Schwartz, an enlarged liver can contribute to a swollen belly.

Of course, not only small children are subject to this condition. Bloated stomachs are common in any individuals suffering malnutrition, and are most often seen in Western countries among sick people who have experienced sudden weight loss. Hospitals are alert to the problem of PCM among adults—one estimate concluded that about 25 percent of hospitalized *adults* in the United States have some form of PCM.

—Submitted by Candace Adler of La Junta, Colorado.

why do kids get more runny noses than adults?

The most common causes of runny noses are nasal infections, allergies, and the common cold. Kids tend to suffer from these conditions more than adults. As Dubois, Wyoming, ear, nose, and throat specialist Keith M. Holmes wrote:

> Perhaps it is safe to say that children are more susceptible to nasal infections. This susceptibility gradually clears as the child ages.

Stephen C. Marks of the American Rhinologic Society notes that research shows that

> the average child contracts up to six colds per year, while the average adult has only two colds per year.
> The reason for this may be that children have a less well developed immune system than adults. Alternatively, it may be that each time a person gets a cold, he or she develops some degree of immunity toward a subsequent infection by the same virus. Therefore, as time goes on, the immunity to different viruses becomes greater and greater,

WHY ARE JITTERS CALLED THE *HEEBIE JEEBIES*?

Heebie jeebies is a coined expression first written in 1910 by a man with an unusual distinction. Cartoonist Billy de Beck, creator of Barney Google, coined two other slang expressions that, though they now sound quaint, have survived for more than half a century: *hotsy totsy* and *horse feathers*. Few novelists or essayists have coined more than one enduring expression; de Beck, with the assistance of Mr. Google, originated three.

leading to fewer episodes of infection. A third possibility is that due to the close interpersonal relationships of children compared with adults, viral infections tend to be passed from child to child more readily.

Dr. Ben Jenkins, an ENT specialist from St. Mary's, Georgia, notes that many serial runny nosers suffer from problems with adenoids, an affliction adults are spared.

But we cast our lot with Richard O'Brien, an osteopath from Berkeley, California, who observes that children don't have the same obsessions about hygiene and aesthetics that their elders do. Although he concedes all the foregoing, he reminds us that kids have less awareness of their runny noses than adults. Smaller kids haven't learned that they are supposed to blow their noses when they start running. And children, who are prone to assorted high jinks and hyperactivity, often don't feel the drip on their faces. Or they do feel the drip, and they just don't care.

—Submitted by Jennifer Martz of Phoenixville, Pennsylvania.

why is the "I" in the word *I* capitalized?

After all, the "m" in *me* is not capitalized, and isn't it impolite to capitalize *I* when the "y" in *you* is stuck in lowercase?

Ego turns out not to be the original reason for the capitalized *I*. In Middle English, the first person singular was expressed with *ich*, eventually shortened to *i* in lowercase. But printers encountered difficulties setting the lowercase *i*. The letter would be dropped unintentionally or run together with the words that followed or preceded it. So the original purpose of capitalizing the *I* was to make it stand out from other single letters and provide it with the status as a whole word.

Now the rock star Prince has extended this principle by capitalizing the word *you*, although his spelling, *U,* is a little eccentric. Despite constantly being accused of narcissism, Prince should be commended for his altruistic and egalitarian philosophy of elevating the second person singular to the prestige of first-person-singular capitalization.

—Submitted by Sheila Reiss of St. Petersburg, Florida.

why are the toilet seats in public restrooms usually split open in the front?

This has become one of our most frequently asked Imponderables on radio shows. So for the sake of science and to allay the anxiety of unspoken millions, here's the, pardon the expression, poop on a mystery whose answer we thought was obvious.

Try as they might, even the most conscientious janitors and bathroom attendants know it is impossible to keep a multiuser public toilet stall in topnotch sanitary condition. Let's face it. Pigs could probably win a slander suit from humans for our comparing our bathroom manners to theirs. Too many people leave traces of urine on top of toilet seats. Men, because of a rather important physiological distinction from women, particularly tend not to be ideally hygienic urinators, but most sanitary codes make it mandatory that both male and female toilets contain "open-front" toilet seats in public

WHY ARE SISSIES CALLED *PANTYWAISTS?*

Until the 1920s in America, they weren't, but then a type of children's underwear was introduced in which underpants were buttoned to the undershirt. Pantywaists were intended as unisex underwear, but they proved much more popular for girls than for boys. The inevitable result in a sexist society: Boys who wore pantywaists were mocked as effeminate by their peers.

restrooms. In fact, at one time, "open back" seats were mandated as well, but the public wouldn't stand (or sit) for them.

If they are more hygienic, why not use open-front toilet seats at home? The answer is psychological rather than practical. An open-front seat would imply to the world that one's bathroom habits were as crass as those employed by the riffraff who use public restrooms. Still, we would think that open-front toilet seats in home bathrooms might lessen the number of divorce-causing arguments about men keeping the toilet seats up.

—Submitted by Janet and James Bennett of Golden, Colorado. Thanks also to Tom Emig of St. Charles, Missouri; Kate McNeive of Scottsdale, Arizona; and Tina Litsey of Kansas City, Missouri.

why do we say an outlaw is *beyond the pale?*

In the twelfth century, the Norman conquerors of England decided to set their sights on neighboring Ireland. They managed to capture much of the area around Dublin and some other coastal cities. For protection from Irish attacks, the Normans (later, the English) fenced off their property with *pales* (from the Latin *palus*) or "stakes."

The region around Dublin became known as "the pale," and *pale* became a noun signifying any territory. The expression *beyond the pale* was originally applied to an untamed Irishman but was clearly popularized by the Rudyard Kipling story of the same name.

why do you say that someone who isn't worthy *can't hold a candle* to a worthy person?

This cliché always struck me as strange. If you can't hold a candle to someone, aren't you doing him a favor? Holding a candle to him could be—well, rather painful. And who would want to hold a candle to someone, and why is someone inferior if he can't?

Note that this phrase always is expressed in the negative. We don't say, "Don Mattingly CAN hold a candle to Wade Boggs." Perhaps this is because at one time there were people who literally "held candles to," and they were far from equal to the people whom they held candles to.

In the sixteenth century, before the advent of streetlights, a common undertaking for servants was to help wealthy Britishers traverse darkened streets. These servants, called *linkboys,* followed their masters on foot while they walked down the street, holding a candle, or more often a *link* ("a torch") to light the way. Linkboys also held candles for their masters in theaters and other public places.

Obviously, the job requirements for linkboys did not include much education or intellectual capacity, so if someone couldn't hold a candle, they were considered to be below the depth of a servant. When we use this cliché in the twentieth century, though, we are left with the original conundrum. Somebody who can't *hold a candle* (i.e., isn't forced to act in a servile role) is deemed, in our language, inferior to the person who can.

why is someone who escapes penalty or punishment said to have gotten off *scot-free?*

Although we are not above dabbling in ethnic stereotypes, this expression has nothing whatsoever to do with Scots' supposed propensity for getting something for nothing (or as close to nothing as possible). *Scot-free* isn't even Scottish, but an Old English expression that, according to the *Oxford English Dictionary,* originally meant "an amount one owed for entertainment." If you went out with friends, your share of the food and drink would be your *sceot.*

Eventually, the meaning of *sceot* was broadened to include taxes, particularly a tax paid to a local sheriff. So the earliest beneficiaries of being

WHY ARE THE ELITE CALLED THE *UPPER CRUST?*

In the Middle Ages, bread was dispensed, even at formal meals, by diners tearing off chunks from a big loaf. Heaven forbid that the bread of an aristocrat might be touched by the hands of a commoner! So it became the custom to slice off the upper crust of the loaf and present it to royalty (or whoever was the most distinguished person at the table), both as a way of honoring the elite and of keeping out the potential germs of the hoi polloi.

scot-free were citizens who were exempt from paying local taxes or who circumvented paying them.

why are constantly fighting people said to be *at loggerheads?*

In the warm waters of the Atlantic Ocean, one can find snapping turtles called *loggerheads,* so named because they have big, knobby heads. But they are not responsible for this phrase. In fact, the turtles are named after the same weapons that generated *at loggerheads.*

Medieval navies carried long-handled sticks with a solid ball of iron at the end. The iron end was heated and used to melt tar, which was then flung at the enemy. If the tar supply was depleted, the combatants would bash each other with the sticks.

At loggerheads was recorded as early as 1680 in England. Its original meaning was "obstinate or ignorant blockhead," a clearly pejorative sentiment that lives on today. People who are *at loggerheads* are not only feuding but also are unable and unwilling to compromise or to seek a reasonable solution to their problems.

why do people look up when thinking?

Medical doctors have a nasty habit. You pose them a particularly tough Imponderable and they answer, "I don't know." Most medical and scientific research is done on topics that seem likely to yield results that can actually help clinicians with everyday problems. Determining why people look up when thinking doesn't seem to be a matter of earth-shattering priority.

Ironically, some serious psychologists *have* decided that this question is important, have found what they think is a solution to the Imponderable and, most amazingly, found a very practical application for this information. These psychologists are known as neurolinguists.

Neurolinguists believe that many of our problems in human interaction stem from listeners not understanding the frame of reference of the people speaking to them. Neurolinguists have found that most people tend to view life largely through one dominant sense—usually sight, hearing, or touching. There are many clues to the sensory orientation of a person, the most

obvious being his or her choice of words in explaining thoughts and feelings. Two people with varying sensory orientations might use totally different verbs, adjectives, and adverbs to describe exactly the same meaning. For example, a hearing-oriented person might say, "I hear what you're saying, but I don't like the sound of your voice." The visually oriented person might say, "I see what you mean, but I think your real attitude is crystal clear." The touch-dominant person (neurolinguists call them kinesthetics) would be more likely to say, "I feel good about what you are saying, but your words seem out of touch with your real attitude."

Neurolinguistically trained psychologists have found that they can better understand and assist clients once they have determined the client's dominant sense (what they call the client's representational system). All three of the above quotes meant the same thing: "I understand you, but your words belie your true emotions." Neurolinguists adapt their choice of words to the representational system of the client, and they have found that it has been a boon to establishing client trust and to creating a verbal shorthand between psychologist and patient. Any feeling that can be expressed visually can be expressed kinesthetically or auditorily as well, so the psychologist merely comes to the patient rather than having the patient come to the psychologist—it helps eliminate language itself as a barrier to communication.

When grappling with finding the answer to a question, most people use one of the three dominant senses to seek the solution. If you ask people what their phone number was when they were twelve years old, three different people might use the three dominant senses of vision, hearing, and feeling. One might try to picture an image of the phone dial; one might try to remember the sound of the seven digits, as learned by rote as a small child; and the last may try to call the feeling of dialing that phone number. Notice that all three people were trying to remember an image, sound, or feeling from the past. But some thoughts involve creating new images, sounds, or feelings. Neurolinguists found they could determine both the operative representational system of their clients and whether they were constructing new images or remembering old ones before the clients even opened their mouth—by observing their eye movements.

These eye movements have now been codified. There are seven basic types of eye movements, each of which corresponds to the use of a particular sensory apparatus. Please note that these "visual accessing cues" are for the average right-handed person; left-handers' eyes ordinarily move to the opposite side. Also, "left-right" designations indicate the direction from the point of view of the observer.

DIRECTION	THOUGHT PROCESS
up-right	visually remembered images
up-left	visually constructing [new] images
straight-right	auditory remembered sounds or words
straight-left	auditory constructed [new] sounds or words
down-right	auditory sounds or words (often what is called an "inner dialogue")
down-left	kinesthetic feelings (which can include smell or taste)

There is one more type of movement, or better, nonmovement. You may ask someone a question and he will look straight ahead with no movement and with eyes glazed and defocused. This means that he is visually accessing information.

Try this on your friends. It works. There *are* more exceptions and complications, and this is an admittedly simplistic summary of the neurolinguists' methodology. For example, if you ask someone to describe his first bicycle, you would expect an upward-right movement as the person tries to remember how the bike looked. If, however, the person imagined the bike as sitting in the bowling alley where you are now sitting, the eyes might move up-left, as your friend is constructing a new image with an old object. The best way to find out is to ask your friend how he tried to conjure up the answer.

Neurolinguistics is still a new and largely untested field, but it is fascinating. Most of the information in this chapter was borrowed from the work of Richard Bandler and John Grinder. If you'd like to learn more about the subject, we'd recommend their book *frogs into Princes* [*sic*].

To get back to the original Imponderable—why do people tend to look up when thinking? The answer seems to be, and it is confirmed by our experiments with friends, that most of us, a good part of the time, try to answer questions by visualizing the answers.

why do we feel warm or hot when we blush?

We blush—usually due to an emotional response such as embarrassment (we, for example, often blush after reading a passage from our books)—because the blood vessels in the skin have dilated. More blood flows to the surface of the body, where the affected areas turn red.

We tend to associate blushing with the face, but blood is sent to the neck and upper torso as well. According to John Hertner, professor of biology at Nebraska's Kearney State College,

> This increased flow carries body core heat to the surface, where it is perceived by the nerve receptors. In reality, though, the warmth is perceived by the brain in response to the information supplied by the receptors located in the skin.

Because of the link between the receptors and the brain, we feel warmth precisely where our skin turns red.

—Submitted by Steve Tilki of Derby, Connecticut.

2

ANIMALS

Did we say people are confusing? Our apologies—what we really meant to say was cats. And dogs. Cows too—and elephants, snakes, penguins, and lobsters. We love our pets, and wild animals as well, but they *do* do the strangest things. They can't tell us why, but we've figured out a few answers.

when did wild poodles roam the earth?

The thought of wild poodles contending with the forbidding elements of nature makes us shudder. It's hard to imagine a toy poodle surviving torrential rainstorms or blistering droughts in the desert, or slaughtering prey for its dinner (unless its prey was canned dog food). Or even getting its haircut messed up.

For that matter, what animal would make a toy poodle its prey in the wild? We have our doubts that it would be a status symbol for one lion to approach another predator and boast, "Guess what? I bagged myself a poodle today."

If something seems wrong with this picture of poodles in the wild, you're on the right track. We posed our Imponderable to the biology department of UCLA, and received the following response from Nancy Purtill, administrative assistant:

> The general feeling is that, while there is no such thing as a stupid question, this one comes very close. Poodles never did live in the wild, any more than did packs of roving Chihuahuas. The present breeds of dogs were derived from selective breeding of dogs descended from the original wild dogs.

Sally Kinne, corresponding secretary of the Poodle Club of America, Inc., was a little less testy:

> I don't think poodles ever did live in the wild! They evolved long after dogs were domesticated. Although their exact beginnings are unknown, they are in European paintings from the fifteenth century [the works of German artist Albrecht Dürer] on to modern times. It has been a long, LONG time since poodles evolved from dogs that evolved from the wolf.

Bas-reliefs indicate that poodles might date from the time of Christ, but most researchers believe that they were originally bred to be water retrievers much later in Germany. (Their name is a derivation of the German word *pudel* or *pudelin,* meaning "drenched" or "dripping wet.") German soldiers probably brought the dogs to France, where they have traditionally been treated more kindly than *Homo sapiens.* Poodles were also used to hunt for truffles, often in tandem with dachshunds. Poodles would locate the truffles and then the low-set dachshunds would dig out the overpriced fungus.

Dog experts agree that all domestic dogs are descendants of wolves, with whom they can and do still mate. One of the reasons it is difficult to trace

WHY IS THE MIDDLE OF SUMMER CALLED THE *DOG DAYS?*

No, *dog days* is not an invention of the greeting card industry to create a phony holiday for your canine pets. Nor is it an ironic reference to the fact that midsummer isn't exactly Bowser's favorite time of year.

Dog days goes back to the Romans, who believed that in the hottest part of the summer, Sirius (the "dog star" and the brightest star in its constellation) lent its own heat to the heat of the sun (*sirius* means "scorching" in Greek). The Roman *dog days,* which they called *caniculares dies* ("days of the dog"), lasted from approximately July 3 to August 11, when Sirius is ascending. Over time, *dog days* has come to mean any expected long streak of heat.

---

the history of wild dogs is that it is hard to discriminate, from fossils alone, between dogs and wolves. Most of the sources we contacted believe that domesticated dogs existed over much of Europe and the Middle East by the Mesolithic period of the Stone Age, but estimates have ranged widely—from 10,000 to 25,000 B.C.

Long before there were any "manmade" breeds, wild dogs did roam the earth. How did these dogs, who may date back millions of years, become domesticated? In her book, *The Life, History and Magic of the Dog,* Fernand Mery speculates that when hunting and fishing tribes became sedentary during the Neolithic Age (around 5000 B.C.), the exteriors of inhabited caves were like landfills from hell—full of garbage, animal bones, mollusk and crustacean shells and other debris. But what seemed like waste to humans was an all-you-can-eat buffet table to wild dogs.

Humans, with abundant alternatives, didn't consider dogs as a source of food. Once dogs realized that humans were not going to kill them, they could coexist as friends. Indeed, dogs could even help humans, and not just as companions—their barking signaled danger to their two-legged patrons inside the cave.

This natural interdependence, born first of convenience and later affection, may be unique in the animal kingdom. Mery claims our relationship to dogs is fundamentally different from that of any other pet—all other animals that have been domesticated have, at first, been captured and taken by force:

The prehistoric dog followed man from afar, just as the domesticated dog has always followed armies on the march. It became accustomed to living nearer and nearer to this being who did not hunt it. Finding with him security and stability, and being able to feed off the remains of man's prey, for a long time it stayed near his dwellings, whether they were caves or huts. One day the dog crossed the threshold. Man did not chase him out. The treaty of alliance had been signed.

Once dogs were allowed "in the house," it became natural to breed dogs to share in other human tasks, such as hunting, fighting, and farming. It's hard to imagine a poofy poodle as a retriever, capturing dead ducks in its mouth, but not nearly as hard as imagining poodles contending with the dinosaurs and pterodactyls, or fighting marauding packs of roving Chihuahuas.

—Submitted by Audrey Randall of Chicago, Illinois.

why do dogs have black lips?

You would prefer mauve, perhaps? Obviously dogs' lips have to be some color, and black makes more sense than most.

According to veterinarian Dr. Peter Ihrke, pigmentation helps protect animals against solar radiation damage. Because dogs don't have as much hair around their mouths as on most parts of their bodies, pigmentation plays a particularly important role in shielding dogs against the ravages of the sun.

According to Dr. Kathleen J. Kovacs of the American Veterinary Medical Association, the gene for black pigment is dominant over the genes for all other pigments, so the presence of black lips is attributable to hereditary factors. If two purebred dogs with black lips breed, one can predict with confidence that their puppies will have black lips too.

Not all dogs have black lips, though. Some breeds have nonpigmented lips and oral cavities. James D. Conroy, a veterinary pathologist affiliated with Mississippi State University, told *Imponderables* that some dogs have a piebald pattern of nonpigmented areas alternating with pigmented areas. The only breed with an unusual lip color is the Chow Chow, which has a blue color. Conroy says that "the blue appearance of the lips and oral cavity is related to the depth of the pigment cells within the oral tissue."

—Submitted by Michael Barson of Brooklyn, New York.

IMPONDERABLES

when and where do police dogs urinate and defecate?

Our fearless correspondent, Eric Berg, notes that he trains his eyes for police dogs whenever he is in a big city and has yet to see nature call one of our canine protectors. "Have the police bred some sort of Bionic Dog?" Eric wonders.

Natural urges dog police dogs just as often as any Fido or Rover, but the difference is in the training; police dogs are much more disciplined than other dogs, or for that matter, most dog owners. Before the animals go on duty, trainers allow police dogs to run and go to the bathroom (well, not literally a bathroom) in the area where they are kept.

Part of the training of police dogs involves teaching the dog to control itself while on patrol and when in front of the public. The dog is taught to signal when it has to "go," but is trained to keep itself under control in all circumstances.

Gerald S. Arenberg, editor of the official journal of the National Association of Chiefs of Police, alludes to the fact that "the dogs are given walks and care that is generally not seen by the public," the only hint we received that occasionally a dog might relieve itself while on duty.

Let's end this discussion here, before we run out of euphemisms.

—Submitted by Eric Berg of Chicago, Illinois.

why do owners or handlers use the word "sic" to instruct a dog to "get him"?

Dog World magazine was kind enough to print our query about this Imponderable in their June 1990 issue. We were soon inundated with letters from dog lovers, the most comprehensive of which came from Fred Lanting of the German Shepherd Dog Club of America:

> The command "sic" comes from a corruption of the German word *such*, which means to seek or search. It is used by Schutzhund [guardian and protection] and police trainers as well as by people training dogs for tracking. If the command "sic" is issued, it means that the dog is to find the hidden perpetrator or victim. In German, *sic* is pronounced "sook" or "suk," but like many foreign words, the pronunciation has been altered over time by those not familiar with the language.

"Sic" has developed from [what was originally] a command to find a hidden bad guy, who [in training exercises] is usually covered by a box or hiding in an open pyramidal canvas blind. Because in police and Schutzhund training the bad guy is attacked if he tries to hit the dog or run away, the word has become associated with a command to attack.

Lanting's answer brings up another Imponderable: If "sic" is a misspelling of the German word, should it be printed as "'sic' [*sic*]"?

—Submitted by Annie Lloyd of Merced, California.

why do dogs love to put their heads out the windows of moving cars? But then hate to have their ears blown into?

Most of the people who have asked this Imponderable connect these two questions, wondering why a dog loves speeding down a freeway at 65 mph (with its head totally exposed to the wind) when it balks at a little playful ear blowing. But dog authorities insisted the two Imponderables we were talking about mixed apples and oranges.

Of course, nobody has been able to interview canines on the subject, but the consensus is that dogs like to put their heads out of car windows because they are visually curious. Many dogs are not tall enough to have an unobstructed view of the outside world from the front seat, and most dogs are too short to have any forward or rearward view from the back seat. Poking their head out of the window is a good way to check out their surroundings and enjoy a nice, cool breeze sat the same time.

But blowing in a dog's ear, even gently, can hurt it, not because of the softness of the skin or the sensitivity of the nerves, but because of the sound of the blowing. Veterinarian Ben Klein told *Imponderables* that one of the ways a dog is tested for deafness is by the vet blowing into the ear through a funnel; if the dog doesn't get upset, it's an indication of deafness. So while we may associate blowing into the ear of a dog as playfulness or to a human mate as a sexual overture, to the dog it is the canine equivalent of scratching a blackboard with fingernails. The frequency of the sound drives them nuts.

Dr. William E. Monroe, of the American College of Veterinary Internal Medicine, adds that the external ears of dogs are full of sensory nerves that help to prevent trauma injuries and preserve hearing:

By preventing debris (sand, wood chips, etc.) from entering the ear canal, damage to the ear and hearing is prevented. Thus, avoiding air in the ear could have survival advantage.

The ear can't trap all the debris a dog must contend with. In fact, Dr. Klein mentioned that sticking their heads out of car windows is one of the major causes of ear infections in dogs.

Next thing we know, we'll have to install seat belts for dogs.

Submitted by Frederick A. Fink of Coronado, California. Thanks also to Allison Crofoot of Spring Valley, New York; Rich Williams of San Jose, California; Candace Savalas of New York, New York; Douglas Watkins, Jr., of Hayward, California; Melanie Jongsma of Lansing, Illinois; Jacob Schneider of Norwalk, Ohio; David Hays and Paul Schact of Newark, Ohio; and Roseanne Vitale of Port St. Lucie, Florida.

why do dogs walk around in circles before lying down?

The most common and logical explanation for the phenomenon is that in the wild, circling was a method of preparing a sleeping area or bed, particularly when it was necessary to flatten down an area among tall grass, leaves, and rocks.

Some experts also believe that circling is a way for dogs to map territory, to define an area of power. Dog writer Elizabeth Crosby Metz explains the habit this way:

> I believe it also has to do with spreading their proprietary scent around their nesting site, to say: "Keep away, this is MY nest!"
> In fact, as a breeder I know that mother dogs will circle many times before lying down to feed their sightless, deaf newborns as a way of spreading her scent and indicating to them exactly where she is and how far they have to go to reach her. Think about it: How else can blind, deaf newborns so surely find the milk bar?

—Submitted by Daniel M. Keller of Solana Beach, California. Thanks also to Joanna Parker of Miami, Florida.

Why do dogs eat standing up, while cats often eat sitting down?

No dog or cat would volunteer to answer this Imponderable, so we were forced to consult human experts. All agreed that the answer goes back to the ancestors of our pets, who lived in the wild.

Our most interesting response came from Dr. James Vondruska, research veterinarian and senior developmental scientist for pet food giant Quaker Oats Company. Vondruska reminds us that dogs are by nature pack animals. In the wild, they hunted in packs. In homes, they adopt the household as their pack and their owners as dominant members:

> In their prehistoric years, dogs lived with others of their type, and hunted or scavenged for food together. Many of their type, such as the African Cape Hunting Dog and the hyenas, still do. Scavenging dogs must compete with the pack members for their food, which often leads to fighting. For this reason, dogs will eat standing up, so that they can better protect their food. Even though they usually don't have to fight over their food anymore, the behavior persists in modern dogs.

Vondruska contrasts the dog's behavior in the wild with that of our house cat's ancestors. Most cats, even in the wild, are solitary creatures, and are hunters rather than scavengers. Susie Page of the American Cat Association compares the eating posture of cats to that of other hunting predators who "hunch" over their prey while devouring it.

With the exception of African lions, who live in prides, cats rarely had to contend with eating companions/rivals in the wild. This probably explains not only why cats today would feel secure eating in a more relaxed crouched or sitting position but also why cats eat languorously, while dogs eat at a pace that suggests that any meal might be their last.

Of course, cats as well as dogs often eat standing up, even while eating in comfortable surroundings from a bowl. Vondruska points out one big advantage to eating in a crouched position for both cats and dogs: "This is the only way in which they can use their paws to hold their food, and this is sometimes necessary when chewing bones."

—Submitted by a caller on the Ray Briem Show, KABC-AM, Los Angeles, California.

why do dogs smell funny when they get wet?

Having once owned an old beaver coat that smelled like a men's locker room when it got wet, we assumed that the answer to this Imponderable would have to do with fur. But all of the experts we spoke to agreed: the funny smell is more likely the result of dogs' skin problems.

First of all, not all dogs do smell funny when they get wet. Shirlee Kalstone, who has written many books on the care and grooming of dogs, says that certain breeds are, let us say, outstanding for their contribution to body odor among canines. Cocker spaniels and terriers (especially Scotties) lead the field, largely because of their propensity for skin conditions. (Cockers, for example, are prone to seborrhea.) Jeffrey Reynolds of the National Dog Groomers Association adds that simple rashes and skin irritations are a common cause of canine body odor, and that water exacerbates the smell. In his experience, schnauzers are particularly susceptible to dermatological irritations.

Of course, dogs occasionally smell when they get wet because they have been rolling in something that smells foul. Gamy smells are usually caused by lawn fertilizer, for example.

Regular grooming and baths can usually solve the odor problem, according to Kalstone. Don't blame the water, in other words—blame the owner.

—Submitted by Robert J. Abrams of Boston, Massachusetts.

there are many miniature dogs. Why aren't there any miniature house cats?

Our correspondent, Elizabeth Frenchman, quite rightly points out that there are legitimate breeds of dogs that resemble rodents more than canines. If poodles can be so easily downsized, why can't Siamese or Oriental cats? If dogs can range in size between the pygmyesque Pekingese or a sausage-like dachshund to a nearly three-foot-high borzoi or a lineman-shaped Saint Bernard, why is the size variation so small in cats?

According to Enid Bergstrom, editor of *Dog World,* the answer is in the genes. Bergstrom says that dogs are the most genetically variable mammals, the easiest to breed for desired characteristics. The genes of cats, on the other

hand, are much less plastic. If you try to mix two different breeds of cats, the tendency is for the offspring to look like an Oriental tabby. Of course, as dog breeder Fred Lanting points out, domestic breeds are miniature cats of sorts, the descendants of the big cats found in zoos.

Helen Cherry of the Cat Fanciers Federation told *Imponderables* that felines could be reduced somewhat in size by interbreeding small cats, but she, as well as all of the cat experts we spoke to, insisted that they had never heard of any interest expressed in trying to miniaturize cats. A representative of the American Cat Association remarked that a cat is small enough already.

Cat associations and federations are conservative by nature. Helen Cherry predicted that miniature cats would not be allowed to register or show or be "acknowledged in any way." It isn't easy being small.

—*Submitted by Elizabeth Frenchman of New York, New York.*

does catnip "work" on big cats like lions and tigers?

Catnip (or *Nepeta cataria*, as scientists so eloquently call it) is a perennial herb that drives many house cats wild with delight. It was probably first noticed as an attractant when big cats swarmed around withered or bruised plants growing in the wild.

A full response to catnip involves four actions, usually in this order:

1. Sniffing

2. Licking and chewing with head shaking

3. Chin and cheek rubbing

4. Head-over rolling and body rubbing

The full cycle usually lasts under fifteen minutes. Some cats will also vocalize after the head-over rolling, presumably a response to hallucinations. Although the cats exposed to catnip mimic their behavior when in heat, catnip does not increase sexual interest or activity and doesn't seem to affect cats in heat more perceptibly.

Scientists know quite a bit about how domestic cats react to catnip. Most cats do not begin responding to the plant until they are six to eight weeks of age, and some may not respond until they are three months of age. All of the research provided by the Cornell Feline Health Center indicates that cats'

reaction to catnip is independent of sex or neutering status. Susceptibility is inherited as an autosomal dominant trait—about a third of domestic cats have no reaction to catnip.

Two-legged mammals have not been immune to the charms of catnip. Veterinarian Jeff Grognet cites the historical use of catnip by humans; the versatile herb was used to make tea, juice, tincture, poultice, and infusions. Catnip was also smoked and chewed for its reputed therapeutic, hallucinogenic, or euphoria-inducing properties.

Scientists, like our reader, have also been curious about the effect of catnip on other cats, and other types of animals. In the largest study of catnip's effect on a wide range of animals, Dr. N. B. Todd's conclusion was clear: Although a few individual animals of almost every type reacted in some way to catnip, cats responded most often and most intensely.

Out of sixteen lions tested, fourteen had full household cat-type responses. Almost half of twenty-three tigers tested had no response at all, but many had incomplete responses: Some sniffed; fewer licked; only a couple chin-rubbed; and none exhibited head-over rolling. But young tigers had violently strong reactions to catnip. Most leopards, jaguars, and snow leopards had strong, full-cycle reactions to catnip. We know that bobcats and lynx love catnip, for the herb is sold commercially to lure these cats for trapping purposes.

Noncats, such as civets and mongooses, were mostly indifferent to catnip, although a few exhibited sniffing reactions. An earlier study that predates Todd's concluded that dogs, rabbits, mice, rats, guinea pigs, and fowls were indifferent to a powdered form of catnip that seduced domestic cats. Yet many dog owners report that their pets respond to catnip.

For some anecdotal evidence, we contacted several of the largest American zoos to see if they exposed their big cats to catnip. We found cat keepers almost as curious about catnip as the cats themselves.

We spoke to one cat keeper who fed jaguars catnip directly. "They like it," he said. "They get goofy." But the same keeper reported that a snow leopard wasn't interested. Another keeper reported that tigers responded "to some extent."

Rick Barongi, director of the Children's Zoo at the San Diego Zoo, reports that although most pet owners usually spray catnip scent on a favorite toy of their cat, zoo keepers cannot. A jaguar or lion will simply rip apart and then eat the toy, so instead they spray a piece of wood or a log that a big cat can claw or scratch. Barongi shares the belief that all cats respond to catnip to some extent but that younger cats respond more than older cats, and that all cats react more on first exposure to catnip than in subsequent encounters.

After a thrill or two with catnip, the San Diego Zoo keepers have found that big cats are more entertained in the long run by scratch posts, boomer balls, larger cages, or—most expensive, but most satisfying of all—the pleasure of the company of a cage mate.

—Submitted by Dave Williams of Ithaca, New York.

why are all calico cats female?

Not quite all. According to Judith Lindley, founder of the Calico Cat Registry International, approximately one male calico is born for every 3,000 females.

The occurrence of male calico cats is theoretically impossible. Ordinarily, male cats have XY sex chromosomes, while females have XX. The X chromosomes carry the genes for coat colors. Therefore, female cats inherit their coat color from both their queens (XX) and their toms (XY). To create a calico (or tortoise-shell) pattern, one of the X chromosomes must carry the black gene and the other the orange gene. If a black male and an orange female mate, the result will be a half-black and half-orange female offspring, a calico. A black female and an orange male will also produce a calico female.

WHY DOES IT RAIN *CATS AND DOGS?*
WHY NOT *OSTRICHES AND YAMS?*

We cast our lot, on circumstantial evidence, for the consensus view that this phrase goes back to Norse legends, which contended that animals had specific magical powers. Cats were reputed to have the ability to conjure up storms (visual representations of storms show witches taking the form of cats), and dogs were symbolic of wind. To Scandinavians, then, *raining cats and dogs* meant a violent storm with wind and rain, pretty much what it means to us today.

Holt argues that the phrase probably stems from seventeenth-century England, when Jonathan Swift, in *Polite Conversation,* described the city's gutters as full of debris—including cats and dogs.

Usually, the male kitten inherits its coat color from the queen alone, since the Y chromosome determines its sex but has nothing to do with its coat color. A male black cat mating with an orange female will produce an orange male; a male orange cat and black female will produce a black male kitten.

Geneticists have discovered that only one of the two X chromosomes in females is functional, which explains why you usually can make a blanket prediction that any male offspring will be the color of the queen. But occasionally, chromosomes misdivide, and a male calico is born with an extra chromosome—two X chromosomes and one Y chromosome. If one of the X chromosomes carries the orange gene and the other the nonorange, a calico will result.

Note that the presence of the extra X chromosome doesn't in itself create the calico. If both chromosomes are coded for orange or black, the offspring will be that color rather than a combination.

Abnormal chromosome counts are unusual but not rare. Most cat cells contain nineteen pairs of chromosomes, but sometimes a mutation will yield one extra chromosome or double or triple the normal number.

Although male calicoes are oddities, the cat experts we consulted indicated that they are normally healthy and have excellent life expectancies. But, unlike their female counterparts, male calicoes do tend to have a common problem—their sexual organs are often malformed, so they are usually sterile.

—Submitted by Stacey Shore of West Lafayette, Indiana.

why are horses' heights measured to the shoulder rather than to the top of the head?

David M. Moore, Virginia Tech University's veterinarian and director of the Office of Animal Resources, compares measuring a horse to trying to measure a squirming child. At least you can back a child up to a wall. If the child's legs, back, and neck are straight, the measurement will be reasonably accurate:

> But with a horse, whose spinal column is parallel to the ground (rather than perpendicular, as with humans), there is no simple way to assure that each horse will hold its head and neck at the same point. Thus, measurements to the top of the head are too variable and of little use.

Dr. Wayne O. Kester of the American Association of Equine Practitioners told *Imponderables* that when a horse is standing squarely on all four feet, the top of the withers (the highest point on the backbone above the

shoulder) is always the same *fixed* distance above the ground, thus providing a consistent measurement for height. Kester estimates that "head counts" could vary as much as two to six feet.

—Submitted by Gavin Sullivan of Littleton, Colorado.

why are cows usually milked from the right side?

Although this subject is usually not part of the veterinary school curriculum, we went right to the organization best suited to answer the Imponderable: the American Association of Bovine Practitioners and its officer Dr. Harold E. Amstutz. Although Dr. Amstutz said he had never considered this question before we posed it, he was ready with a sensible explanation:

> Since most people are right-handed, it is more logical to sit down on the right side of the cow and have more room to maneuver the milk bucket with the right hand between the cow's front and rear legs. There would not be nearly as much room to maneuver the bucket with the right hand if a right-handed person were to sit on the left side.
>
> In general, we think of "right" as correct and "left" as being wrong. Cows have no preference, since we milk them from either side in today's milking parlors. The only ones that would have a preference are those that were trained to be milked on one side and then someone tried to milk them from the other side. The milker would probably be kicked in that case.

—Submitted by Marci Perlmutter of Warren, New Jersey.

why do bulls in cartoons have nose rings? And why don't cows have them?

You give cartoonists far too much credit for imagination, David and Valerie. Long before there were punk rockers, bulls sported genuine brass rings.

The expression "bull-headed" wasn't pulled out of thin air. Bulls are among the most stubborn and least accommodating of farm animals. When a human wants a bull to move and a bull wants to sit for a spell, verbal commands are unlikely to work. Neither will a friendly little shove on the rear. Bulls' hooves have been known to crush the feet of owners who made them "see red," and they love to kick, too. Those rings are inserted to allow owners to "lead them around by the nose." As Richard Landesman, a University of Vermont

HOW AND WHY DO HORSES SLEEP STANDING UP?

Horses have a unique system of interlocking ligaments and bones in their legs, which serves as a sling to suspend their body weight without strain while their muscles are completely relaxed. Thus, horses don't have to exert any energy consciously to remain standing—their legs are locked in the proper position during sleep.

Most horses do most of their sleeping while standing, but patterns differ. Veterinarians we spoke to said it was not unusual for horses to stand continuously for as long as a month, or more. Because horses are heavy but have relatively fragile bones, lying in one position for a long time can cause muscle cramps.

While one can only speculate about why the horse's body evolved in this fashion, most experts believe that wild horses slept while standing for defensive purposes. Wayne O. Kester, D.V.M., executive director of the American Association of Equine Practitioners, told us that in the wild, the horse's chief means of protection and escape from predators was its speed. "They were much less vulnerable while standing and much less apt to be caught by surprise than when lying down."

—Submitted by Karole Rathouz of Mehlville, Missouri.

---

zoologist, puts it, "Any tension on the ring will produce pain, and this can be used as a means either to train or restrain the bull."

Most bulls are "ringed" before they are a year old, in a procedure that isn't as delicate as a human ear piercing. For some reason, bulls don't welcome a veterinarian driving a steel rod through their septum, so they are given a local anesthetic and placed in a "head bail" to keep them from moving.

Nose rings come in various sizes, and it is not uncommon for bulls to graduate to a larger-sized ring (as big as three inches in diameter) as they grow. Dan Kniffen of the National Cattlemen's Association told *Imponderables* that there are even temporary clip-on rings, called "bugs," the bovine equivalent of clip-on ties, that don't pierce the nostrils. Bugs can be used to shepherd the recalcitrant bull that needs to be moved occasionally.

It behooves the prudent farmer not to make permanent enemies of five-or six-ton creatures. Once the ring is inserted, vets urge owners to restrain the bull with a halter around his head, with a lead rope fed through the ring. Yanking on the ring directly is quite painful, and bulls have been known to carry a grudge. Hudson, New York, veterinarian Andrew S. Ritter also warns of the dangers of tethering a bull by the ring, lest it rip through the cartilage of the nose attempting to get free.

Why don't cows have nose rings? Although the occasional delinquent cow (and horse) sports a nose ring, the distaff bovines generally have a sunnier, more docile disposition than their bull-headed mates.

—Submitted by David Ng of Capiague, New York.
Thanks also to Valerie Valenzo of Chicago, Illinois.

do elephants jump?

We talked to a bunch of elephant experts and none of them has ever seen an elephant jump. Most think it is physiologically impossible for a mature elephant to jump, although baby elephants have been known to do so, if provoked. Not only do mature elephants weigh too much to support landing on all fours, but their legs are designed for strength rather than leaping ability. Mark Grunwald, who has worked with elephants for more than a decade at the Philadelphia Zoo, notes that elephants' bone structure makes it difficult for them to bend their legs sufficiently to derive enough force to propel the big lugs up.

Yet there are a few sightings of elephants jumping in the wild. Veterinarian Judy Provo found two books in her college library that illustrate the discrepancy. S. K. Ettingham's *Elephant* lays out the conventional thinking: "Because of its great weight, an elephant cannot jump or even run in the accepted sense since it must keep one foot on the ground at all times." But an account in J. H. Williams's *Elephant Bill* describes a cow elephant jumping a deep ravine "like a chaser over a brook."

Animals that are fast runners or possess great leaping ability have usually evolved these skills as a way of evading attackers. Elephants don't have any natural predators, according to the San Diego Wild Animal Park's manager of animals, Alan Rooscroft: "Only men kill elephants. The only other thing that could kill an elephant is a fourteen-ton tiger."

Most of the experts agree with zoologist Richard Landesman of the University of Vermont, that there is little reason for an elephant to jump in

its natural habitat. Indeed, Mike Zulak, an elephant curator at the San Diego Zoo, observes that pachyderms are rather awkward walkers, and can lose their balance easily, so they tend to be conservative in their movements.

But that doesn't mean that elephants are pushovers. Why bother jumping when you can walk through or around just about everything in your natural habitat? In India, trenching has been the traditional way of trying to control movements of elephants. Veterinarian Myron Hinrichs of Petaluma, California, notes that the traditional trench has to be at least two meters deep, two meters across at the top, and one and one-half meters across at the bottom to serve as a barrier for elephants:

> That tells us that they can't or won't try to jump a distance of 6.5 feet. But these trenches have a high failure rate, for elephants can fill them in, especially in the rainy season, and then walk across the trough they have made. And larger bull elephants can go down through and up even a trench that size.

Why leap when you can trudge?

—*Submitted by Jena Mori of Los Angeles, California.*

how do they get rid of the remains of dead elephants in zoos?

When an elephant in a zoo dies, a necropsy must be performed. In most cases, the necropsy is conducted by a licensed veterinarian or veterinary pathologist from tissue and blood samples extracted from the carcass.

Most zoos we contacted remove selected organs from the dead elephant, pack them in ice or Formalin, and ship them to various research institutions for reproductive or physiological studies. Typical is the response of San Francisco Zoo's Diane Demee-Benoit. She reports that her zoo has a binder full of requests from universities, zoos, and museums for various animal parts. Forensic labs might need DNA to help identify other creatures. A natural history museum might want skulls or a particular set of bones to perform comparative studies. Zoos make sure that all animal parts are used for research and educational purposes only and are not permitted to sell or donate parts to private individuals.

After organs and other body parts are removed, the least pleasant task is performed—cutting the elephants into smaller pieces, for even elephant *parts* are heavy. The parts are carried by forklifts and cranes and placed on flatbed trailers, dump trucks, or whatever vehicles are available.

Where do the trucks take the remains? That depends upon the zoo. The preference is always for burying animals on the premises. Alan Rooscroft, manager of animals at the San Diego Wild Animal Park, said that out of respect for the animals, their elephants are buried on the grounds of the zoo. But not all zoos have room enough for this "luxury."

Many zoos, such as the San Francisco Zoo, incinerate or cremate elephants. Ed Hansen, president of the American Association of Zoo Keepers, indicated that in areas where such disposal is legal, some elephants are buried in licensed landfills.

Some elephants, particularly those from circuses, meet a more ignoble fate—they are sent to rendering plants. Mark Grunwald of the Philadelphia Zoo told *Imponderables* that such boiled elephants end up as an ingredient in soap.

—Submitted by Claudia Short of Bowling Green, Ohio.
Thanks also to Richard Sassaman of Bar Harbor, Maine;
and David Koelle of North Branford, Connecticut.

why is an unwanted or useless possession called a *white elephant?*

The quintessential *white elephant* has several qualities in common: It is large and unwieldy; it is expensive (or at least extravagant for its category); it is a gift; and it is a gift that can't be refused in the first place and then can't be returned or destroyed for some reason. (Otherwise, who would want to keep a white elephant around the house?)

All of these connotations stem from the original *white elephants,* a strain of albino (actually whitish-gray) pachyderms that were considered sacred by the Siamese. Any captured white elephant, became, by law, property of the emperor. Under no circumstances could white elephants be destroyed without royal permission.

Any monarch worth his salt is besieged by assorted hangers-on, and a Siamese emperor devised an ingenious method to punish particularly obnoxious courtiers. He bestowed upon them the gift of one of the sacred white elephants.

Unsuspecting courtiers probably could think only about the good news: the tremendous honor they had received. Rather soon, however, they recognized the bad news: They were saddled with a literal and metaphorical *white elephant.* At least that awful vase that your boss brought you when you invited him over for dinner is an inanimate object, one that can be dragged out of the basement or a closet if he should by some miracle ever be reinvited back. But real elephants do annoying things like eating and defecating and running around and tearing down fences.

Recipients of the white elephants were not allowed to work the elephants. They couldn't even ride them. Only the emperor was allowed to ride the white elephant, and the recipient was always aware that he must keep the elephant on hand in case the emperor decided he felt like a trot.

But the recipients had a more pressing problem: They simply could not afford the upkeep of the elephant. So although the contemporary recipient of a white elephant is only emotionally scarred, the earliest victims were inevitably financially ruined.

why do deer stand transfixed by the headlights of oncoming cars?

Although no zoologist has ever interviewed a deer, particularly a squashed one, we can assume that no animal has a death wish. In fact, instinct drives all animals to survive. We asked quite a few animal experts about this Imponderable, and we received three different theories, none of which directly contradicts the others.

1. **The behavior is a fear response.** University of Vermont zoologist Richard Landesman's position was typical:

> Many mammals, including humans, demonstrate a fear response, which initially results in their remaining perfectly still for a few seconds after being frightened. During this time, the hormones of the fear response take over and the animal or person then decides whether to fight or run away. Unfortunately, many animals remain in place too long and the car hits them.

The self-defeating mechanism of the fear response is perpetuated because, as Landesman puts it, "these animals don't know that they are going to die

as a result of standing still and there is no mechanism for them to teach other deer about that fact."

2. Standing still isn't so much a fear response as a reaction to being blinded. Deer are more likely to be blinded than other, smaller animals, such as dogs and cats, because they are much taller and vulnerable to the angle of the headlight beams. If you were blinded and heard the rumble of a car approaching at high speed, would you necessarily think it was safer to run than to stand still?

3. The freeze behavior is an extension of deer's natural response to any danger. We were bothered by the first two theories insofar as they failed to explain why deer, out of all disproportion to animals of their size, tend to be felled by cars. So we prevailed upon our favorite naturalist, Larry Prussin, who has worked in Yosemite National Park for more than a decade. He reports that deer and squirrels are killed by cars far more than any other animals, and he has a theory to explain why.

WHY CAN SOME PEOPLE *GET YOUR GOAT* INSTEAD OF *GETTING YOUR MYNAH BIRD* OR *GETTING YOUR BASSET HOUND?*

Although there is some dispute about how this colorful term for the uncanny ability of some people to rile us, annoy us, irritate us, vex us, and get under our skin, most lexicographers attribute the origins of *get your goat* to the world of thoroughbred horse racing. Horse trainers have long put a companion in stalls with high-strung thoroughbreds, particularly volatile stallions.

Putting a horse of the same sex in the stall would lead to territorial battles; putting a horse of the opposite sex in the stall might, to put it politely, distract the stallion from the task at hand. Goats, among the most boring and least demanding of animals, soothed horses effectively.

Horses tended to become attached to their goat roommates, so much so that rival barns sometimes would steal the goat of a rival the night before a race. The horse would become upset and presumably underperform the next day. So someone whose goat has been gotten is actually being compared to a horse rather than a goat.

What do these two animals have in common? In the wild, they are prey rather than predators. The natural response of prey animals is to freeze when confronted with danger. Ill-equipped to fight with their stalkers, they freeze in order to avoid detection by the predator; they will run away only when they are confident that the predator has sighted them and there is no alternative. Defenseless fawns won't even run when being attacked by predators.

The prey's strategy forces the predator to flush them out, while the prey attempts to fade into its natural environment. Hunters similarly need to rouse rabbits, deer, and many birds with noises or sudden movements before the prey will reveal themselves.

Prussin notes that in the last twelve years, to his knowledge only one of the plentiful coyotes in Yosemite National Park has been killed by an automobile, while countless deer have been mowed down. When confronted by automobile headlights, coyotes will also freeze but then, like other predators and scavengers, dart away.

Although deer may not be genetically programmed to respond to react one way or the other to oncoming headlights, their natural predisposition dooms them from the start.

—Submitted by Michael Wille of Springhill, Florida. Thanks also to Konstantin Othmer of San Jose, California; and Meghan Walsh of Sherborn, Massachusetts.

why do beavers build dams?

Watch any nature documentary about beavers, and you'll see the giant rodents working furiously to construct their dams. Of course, if they weren't working furiously, they wouldn't deserve their hard-earned sobriquet. No one wants to be as busy as a sloth.

Beavers are industrious creatures, and we don't want to belittle their achievements, but we also don't want to fall into the trap of assuming that beavers cogitate deeply about how to solve their problems and build dams as a result. On the contrary, Dr. Peter Busher, professor of biology at the Center for Ecology and Conservation Biology at Boston University, told us:

> Most (if not all) beaver scientists would say that construction behavior is instinctual and not learned behavior. Thus construction behavior appears to be hard-wired into the beaver genome.

By damming small rivers and streams, beavers create ponds, still and deep bodies of water. Beavers create the pond by amassing dams with bases of

mud and stones, and piling up branches and sticks. Beavers reinforce the dam by using mud, stones, and vegetation from the water as "plaster."

Scott Jackson, a wildlife biologist at the Department of Natural Resources Conservation at the University of Massachusetts, Amherst, told *Imponderables* that while some dams are less than 100 feet long, others have been recorded at over 1,500 feet in length. According to Jackson, beavers are constantly on the lookout for leaks, and will fix any defect by plugging leaks with mud and sticks.

Why do these rodents, who are not fish, after all, bother constructing ponds? Ponds help provide beavers with three of the necessities of life:

1. Food. Beavers are PETA-friendly strict vegetarians. Not only do they not eat other mammals, but they disdain fish and insects, as well. They do eat leaves, barks, and twigs of trees, and make meals from the vegetation that grows around the ponds they construct. By creating a pond, beavers increase the supply of aquatic vegetation, such as water lilies, that they prefer. As Dr. Busher notes,

> The higher water table favors plants that are water tolerant (many of which are eaten by beavers) and drowns species that are not water tolerant. Beavers "feel" safer in water and the dams create ponds that allow them to have better access to food without leaving the water.

Why might beavers feel safer in the water? Because ...

2. Protection. Most of beavers' predators, such as wolves, coyotes, and occasionally bears, are more comfortable on land than water (young beavers, called "kits," are also vulnerable to owls and hawks). Beavers are adept in the water: With their webbed hind feet and large paddle tails, beavers are built for swimming. Beavers are awkward on land, and most of their forays onto terra firma are to chew down trees and bushes both to eat and to use as construction materials. They are unlikely to wander far afield from the shoreline, where they are prone to be attacked by land-based predators.

3. Shelter. Obviously, beavers can't sleep under the water, so it is necessary for them to build a place to sleep safely atop the water. A family of beavers will frequently build a "lodge," a tepee-like structure usually made from tree branches, twigs, and aquatic vegetation sealed together with mud. Usually, lodges feature a bed of grass, leaves, and wood chips on which the beavers sleep and their young are raised—it's not Martha Stewart, but it's home.

The upper part of the lodge is built above the water line, and there is an opening at the top, so that breathing air and ventilation are available. According to Jackson, these lodges may be fifteen to forty feet across at the base and protrude three to six feet above the water. To stabilize the lodge, the beavers anchor the sides deep into the water and attach them to a solid structure such as an island in the water, a large underground branch, or sometimes even the side of the river. Beavers build tunnels from the air chamber of the lodge down to the water. These tunnels provide the only entrances to the lodge, as the thick walls of sticks and mud provide protection from both predators and the weather. By damming the river so that the pond is sufficiently large, the beavers create a sort of moat around the visible, above-water part of the lodge.

In the winter, if the pond freezes, the mud on the lodge freezes as well, providing more resistance to predators and bad weather. Even if a wolf were to walk on the frozen pond, it would struggle to penetrate the lodge, and beavers usually have plenty of time to swim through one of the tunnels to escape.

Even after a lodge is built, beavers must often perform repair work on the dams, as the water level of the pond is crucial to the safety of the lodge. If the water level gets too high, the lodge can submerge; if it gets too low, the lodge would become exposed at the bottom and predators could infiltrate the lodge more easily.

Whole families live in these lodges. Beavers are monogamous (they're too busy being busy as beavers to be promiscuous, we surmise), usually "marrying" for life barring the death of a mate. Females give birth inside of a lodge, usually producing four kits, but occasionally as many as nine. One family unit, called a "colony," usually consists of the two parents, that year's kits, plus the young from the previous year. As beavers are far from petite (North American adult beavers range in weight from thirty-five to eighty pounds), there's plenty of tail staying in one lodge at any given time.

Most animals adapt to their surroundings, but except for humans, no animal alters its habitat to suit its needs more than the beaver. The beaver may be able to convert part of a flowing stream into a still pond and base for its home, but it can't keep the same pond forever. Eventually, the beavers plunder the vegetation on the shoreline—what they don't eat, they use for building materials. If dams break, ponds can drain off. Where beavers live, silt tends to form, rendering the ponds too shallow. Any of these problems can cause beavers to abandon their lodges and seek other opportunities.

But all is not lost, as Scott Jackson reassures:

> In the nutrient-rich silt, herbaceous plants flourish, forming beaver meadows. Over time, shrubs and trees eventually come to dominate these areas, setting the stage for the beavers' return.

> —*Submitted by Nathan Trask of Herrin, Illinois.*

why did the rabbit die when a pregnant woman took the "rabbit test"?

Ever since we were babes (as in "babes in the woods," not as in "hot babes," of course), popular culture, especially bad jokes, has informed us that "the rabbit died" meant "pregnant." But we always wondered why a rabbit had to die in order to diagnose a pregnancy. So we were gratified when this Imponderable was sent in by a reader who happens to be a physician. If he didn't know, maybe we weren't so dim-witted for not knowing ourselves.

At its height of popularity, the rabbit test would be administered to women after they missed two consecutive menstrual periods. A small sample of urine was injected into a female rabbit. But why urine? Why a rabbit?

Urine has been used to diagnose pregnancies as far back as the fourteenth century B.C. by the Egyptians. They poured urine on separate bags of barley and wheat. If either grain germinated, the woman was pregnant. They believed that if the wheat germinated, it would be a boy; the barley, a girl. There were probably a lot of unused cribs and miscolored baby clothing in ancient Egypt.

The early Greek physicians also dabbled in urine analysis for the detection of pregnancy. In his book *Obstetric and Gynecologic Milestones,* Dr. Harold Speert notes that urine analysis was a particular favorite of medieval English quacks, often called "piss-prophets," who claimed to diagnose just about any malady from indigestion to heartache. Reaction against these charlatans was so strong that urinary diagnosis was rejected during most of the eighteenth and nineteenth centuries by reputable physicians.

But in 1928, two German gynecologic endocrinologists, Selmar Ascheim and Bernhard Zondek, announced a urinary test that could be replicated easily throughout the world. They injected urine into five infant mice. Ascheim and Zondek explained why they needed five mice:

> Five infantile mice are used for each urine examination. The urine must be tested on several mice because an animal may die from the injection, but more important because not all animals react alike.... *The pregnancy reaction is positive if it is positive in only one animal and negative in the others.*

The A-Z test, as it has become known, is still the basis for all urine-based pregnancy exams, including the rabbit test.

So why the switch from mice to rabbits? Dr. T. E. Reed of the American Rabbit Breeder's Association explained the advantages of rabbits, and we promise to get through this discussion with no cheap "breeding like rabbits" jokes.

Most mammals have "heat" cycles, when females are receptive to the male. These cycles are physiologically based and are accompanied by changes in hormonal levels. The ovary is affected by the estrogenic hormone, the animal ovulates, and then is receptive to the male for breeding.

But the domestic rabbit is different, as Reed explains:

> The rabbit does not ovulate until it has been mated with the buck. The rabbit then ovulates ten hours later and the sperm that was deposited during the copulation process will fertilize the ovum.
>
> The uniqueness of domestic rabbits' physiology of reproduction is what allowed the pregnancy tests for humans to be utilized. Virgin does were used in the "rabbit test." Because researchers used does that had not been mated, the ovaries of the animal had never produced follicles from the ovaries.

Rabbit tests proved to be faster and more reliable than the original A-Z test.

But why did a pregnant woman's urine kill the rabbits? Ah, the nasty little secret: The test itself did not kill the rabbits, as Reed explains:

> The rabbit does not die of natural causes. The rabbit is euthanized after a specific amount of time [usually forty-eight hours after the first injection] has passed after being inoculated and the ovaries observed by the diagnostician. When the woman is pregnant, the follicles, which look like blisters on the ovary, would be present. If the woman was not pregnant, the ovary would be smooth as in virgin does.

The inventor of the rabbit test, Maurice Harold Friedman, injected the rabbits three times a day for two days, but later practitioners simplified the procedure to one injection and a twenty-four-hour waiting period. Through trial and error, researchers later found that it was not necessary to kill the rabbit at all, and one rabbit was used for several tests, after allowing the ovaries to regress after a positive result.

Although the theory behind the rabbit test was perfectly sound, one problem in reliability persisted: The rabbits chosen weren't always virgins, resulting in false positives. More sophisticated tests were developed without needing animals at all. But even modern laboratories, like the home pregnancy kits, measure the same hormone levels that Friedman, Ascheim and Zondek, and maybe even the piss-prophets and ancient Egyptians predicted pregnancy by.

—Submitted by Dr. Ray Watson of Shively, Kentucky.

do skunks think skunks stink?

Skunks can dish out a foul scent. But can they take it?

If, like us, most of our education about skunks comes from animated cartoons, you might be surprised to learn that skunks don't spray their noxious scent cavalierly. According to Skunks Scentral's counselor Nina Simone,

> Skunks only spray as a form of defense. It is the last action they will take when frightened. Each skunk has its own level of what degree of fear will trigger a spray. Some will stomp three times as a warning before "firing," which will give the "perpetrator" a chance to depart.

What exactly happens when a skunk sprays? We asked Jerry Dragoo, interim curator of mammals at the Museum of Southwestern Biology in Albuquerque, who is quite the mephitologist (an expert on bad smells):

> A skunk's scent glands are at the base of the tail on either side of the rectum. The glands are covered by a smooth muscle layer that is controlled by a direct nerve connection to the brain. The decision to spray is a conscious one. The smooth muscle makes a slight contraction to force the liquid through ducts connected to nipples just inside the anal sphincter, which is everted [turned inside out] to expose the nipples. The nipples can be aimed toward the target.
>
> When a skunk is being chased by a "predator" and is not exactly sure where the pursuer is located, the skunk, while running away will emit a cloud of spray in an atomized mist. The mist is light and takes a while to settle to the ground. A predator would run through this cloud and pick up the scent and usually stop pursuit. I call this the "shotgun approach."
>
> When the skunk is cornered or knows exactly where the predator is located, it emits the liquid in a stream that usually is directed toward the face. This intense spray will sting and temporarily blind the predator. I call this the ".357 Magnum approach."

Perhaps cartoons aren't far off the mark. Dragoo's description of the "shotgun approach" is not unlike Pépé le Pew's "cloud of stink bomb" method of foiling enemies.

But does the spray repulse other skunks? Our experts agree: "Yes." Simone mentioned that when other skunks smell a whiff, they become agitated. It is unclear whether this is a chemical reaction to the smell, or if it signals danger to them. She compared skunks' uneasy behavior when they smell other skunks' sprays to "a dog before an earthquake."

Considering that skunks don't like the smell of other skunks, it's surprising that they don't use their "weapon" more often during "intramural" battles.

One skunk expert e-mailed us:

> Skunks actually don't like the smell of skunk, either, and unless one is accidentally in the line of fire, it would never get sprayed by another skunk. It's kind of like a skunk pact that they won't spray each other.

If only humans were as accommodating!

But seriously, folks, we must delve into the seamier side of skunk behavior, for internecine spraying isn't that unusual. The most common perpetrators of skunk-on-skunk abuse are juveniles. Janis Grant, vice president of North Alabama Wildlife Rehabilitators, wrote us:

> The only situation in which I have observed skunks exchanging liquid insults has been when I have mixed different litters of young skunks together. They proceed to have a "fire-at-will stink-off" for about four to six minutes, including growls, chirps, and foot stomping, then gradually settle down to cohabitation. I can't say if this is to establish alpha status or just to make everybody smell the same, but none of them runs away from the encounters—they just spray a few times, retire to their corners, and let it go.

Dragoo notes that just as juveniles display the stomp, chirp, and spray behavior, sometimes a weaker skunk will spray a stronger young rival "if it feels it is being bullied." But they have been known to spray unknown adult skunks, too, "because adult males are known to kill young skunks."

Dragoo describes skunks' reaction to being sprayed as "the same behavior as other animals when they are sprayed":

> They will slide their face on the ground to attempt to wipe the odor off. They will also groom themselves [lick hands and rub face] to help remove the odor.

Are skunks, like humans, more tolerant of their own stench than others? According to Dragoo, skunks are not as egocentric:

> The skunk can spray without getting a drop on itself. Skunks are actually clean-smelling animals. It is what they hit that smells, well, like "skunk."
>
> If a skunk is in a situation where it would get its own spray on itself, the skunk's chances of survival are usually low. An animal hit by a car will often get the liquid on itself, but usually after death. If a skunk is caught by a predator and in the midst of a fight, it can get some of the liquid on itself. But in those situations the predator likely has already been sprayed and has not been deterred. The skunk will spray to defend itself even if it gets spray on itself.
>
> The chemical composition of the spray is the same from one animal to another with some potential individual variation, but the "smelly"

components are the same. Their own spray is as offensive as another's. The difference is that they are likely not to get their own spray near their face, whereas they would aim for the face of a "rival."

I have approached live, trapped animals and covered the trap with a plastic bag. This usually keeps the animal calm. However, on a few occasions, I have approached high-strung animals that spray multiple times at the bag. They are then covered by the same bag. They are still agitated when covered, but this may be a result of their already being wired.

On one occasion, I peeked under the bag and did observe the animal rubbing its face along the bottom of the trap as if it were trying to "get the odor off." Then it sprayed me ... in the face.

—Submitted by Robert Brown of Millerton, New York.

why don't penguins in the Antarctic get frostbite on their feet?

The yellow-necked emperor penguin, the largest species of penguin, spends its entire life resting on snow or swimming in water at a below-freezing temperature. A penguin's dense feathers obviously provide insulation and protection from the cold, but how can it withstand the cold on its feet, when humans won't put their limbs into the ocean when water is in the sixties?

Penguins' feet are remarkable creations. They are set back much farther than other birds, so that penguins walk upright, but this conformation's main attribute is to help them swim. Next to the dolphin, the penguin is the fastest swimmer in the ocean. When swimming, a penguin's foot trails behind in the water, acting as a rudder and a brake.

During their hatching season, mother and father alternate diving into the ocean for food. *Encyclopedia Britannica* estimates that the cooling power of the sea water to which they are exposed is the equivalent to the temperature of -4 degrees Fahrenheit with a wind of seventy miles per hour. Add the 10 or 20 mph speed at which the penguin typically swims, and you have rather uncomfortable conditions. The penguin's skin is protected by a layer of air trapped under its feathers—only the feet directly touch the water.

When the penguin finds food, returns to the mate, sits on the chick and watches the mate leave to find more food, it has gone from the frigid water to standing directly on snow that is, needless to say, freezing temperature. How can the feet withstand such punishment?

Penguins' feet do get very cold. They have been measured at exactly freezing, in fact. If their feet stayed at a warmer temperature, they would lose heat through convection or conduction.

The low temperature is maintained by penguins' unique circulatory system. As arteries carry warm blood toward the toes, penguins have veins right next to them carrying cold blood back in the opposite direction. In effect, the two bloodstreams exchange heat so that the circulation level can remain low enough to conserve heat and just high enough to prevent tissue damage and frostbite. Penguins' feet have very few muscles. Instead, their feet possess a vast network of tendons, which do not become as painful as muscles when cold.

Of course, there is another explanation for why penguins don't exhibit foot pain. They are not crybabies, and they are tougher than humans.

do penguins have knees?

They sure do, although they are discreetly hidden underneath their feathers. Anatomically, all birds' legs are pretty much alike, although the dimensions of individual bones vary a great deal among species.

Penguins, like other birds, have legs divided into three segments. The upper segment, the equivalent of our thigh, and the middle segment, the equivalent of our shinbone, or the drumstick of a chicken, are both quite short in penguins.

When we see flamingos, or other birds with long legs, they appear to possess a knee turned backwards, but these are not the equivalent of a human knee. Penguins, flamingos, and other birds do have knees, with patellas (knee caps) that bend and function much like their human counterparts.

We spoke to Dr. Don Bruning, curator of ornithology at the New York Zoological Park (better known as the Bronx Zoo), who told us that the backwards joint that we perceive as a knee in flamingos actually separates the bird equivalent of the ankle from the bones of the upper foot. The area below the backwards joint is not the lower leg but the upper areas of the foot. In other words, penguins (and other birds) stand on their toes, like ballet dancers.

Penguins are birds, of course, but their element is water rather than sky. Penguins may waddle on land, but their legs help make them swimming machines. Penguins use their wings as propellers in the water, and their elongated feet act as rudders.

So rest assured. Even if you can't see them, penguins have legs (with knees). And they know how to use them.

—Submitted by John Vineyard of Plano, Texas.
Thanks also to Ruth Vineyard of Plano, Texas.

why do birds bother flying back north after migrating to the south?

Why bother flying so many miles south, to more pleasant and warmer climes, only to then turn around and trudge back to the only seasonally hospitable northeastern United States? Come to think of it, are we talking about birds here or half the population of Miami?

We're not sure what motivates humans to migrate, but we do have a good idea of what motivates birds to bother flying back north again. Of course, birds probably don't sit around (even with one leg tucked up in their feathers) thinking about why they migrate; undoubtedly, hormonal changes caused by natural breeding cycles trigger the migration patterns. After speaking to several bird experts, we found a consensus on the following reasons why birds fly back to the North:

1. Food. Birds fly back north to nest. Baby birds, like baby humans, are ravenous eaters and not shy about demanding food.

As Todd Culver of the Laboratory of Ornithology at Cornell University put it, "The most likely reason they return is the super abundant supply of insects available to feed their young." The more food the parents can raise, the healthier the offspring will be and the lower the babies' mortality rate.

2. Longer daylight hours. The higher the latitude, the longer period of daylight parents have to find food and feed it to their babies. Some birds find food sources solely by using their vision; they cannot forage with any effectiveness in the dark.

3. Less competition for food and nesting sites. If all birds converged in the southern latitudes when nesting, it would be as easy to find a peaceful nest and plentiful food sources as it would be to find a quiet, pleasant, little motel room in Fort Lauderdale during spring break.

4. Safety. Birds are more vulnerable to predators when nesting. In most cases, there are fewer mammal predators in the North than in the South. Why? Many mammals, who don't migrate, can't live in the North because of the cold weather.

5. Improved weather. Some birds migrate south primarily to flee cold weather in the North. If they time it right, birds come back just when the weather turns pleasant in the spring, just like those humans in Florida.

—Submitted by Michael S. Littman of Piscataway, New Jersey. Thanks also to Jack Weber of Modesto, California; Lori Tomlinson of Newmarket, Ontario; and Saxon Swearingen of La Porte, Texas.

has anyone ever seen a live Cornish game hen?

We've seen a few dead Cornish game hens in our time, usually on a plate in front of us—and always when we are ravenously hungry at a formal dinner, surrounded by folks we don't know. So we feel we have to eat it with a knife and fork. Without picking up the dead hen and eating it with our fingers, we are capable of extracting a good two or three mouthfuls' worth of edible meat before we give up on meeting our protein requirements for the day.

As you can see, we have more than a little hostility toward these little bitty particles of poultry, so we are going to expose a nasty scandal about Cornish game hens (aka Rock Cornish game hens): They are nothing more than chickens—preadolescent chickens, in fact.

That's right. Cornish game hens, despite their highfalutin moniker, are nothing more than immature versions of the same broilers or fryers you buy in the supermarket. A Rock Cornish game hen could theoretically grow up to be a Chicken McNugget. (At least a Chicken McNugget gets eaten.) We have *all* seen a live "Cornish game hen."

Federal regulations define a Rock Cornish game hen or Cornish game hen as

> a young immature chicken (usually 5 to 6 weeks of age) weighing not more than 2 pounds ready-to-cook weight, which was prepared from a Cornish chicken or the progeny of a Cornish chicken crossed with another breed of chicken.

In practice, most Cornish fowls are crossbred with Plymouth Rock fowls.

Dr. Roy Brister, director of research and nutrition at Tyson Food, Inc., told *Imponderables* that all the chicken we eat has the Cornish White Rock as one of its ancestors. Cornish fowl are prized because they are plump, large-breasted, and meaty. Other breeds are too scraggly and are better suited for laying eggs. Most of the Cornish game hens now sold in the United States are actually less than thirty days old and weigh less than one pound after they are cooked.

According to the USDA's *Agriculture Handbook,* Cornish game hens are raised and produced in the same way as broilers. But because they are sold at a smaller weight, the cost per pound to process is higher for the producer and thus for the consumer.

But let's face it. It's a lot easier to get big bucks for a product with a tony name like "Rock Cornish game hen" than it is for "chick" or "baby broiler." If veal were called "baby cow," its price would plummet overnight.

Dr. Brister speculates that the creation of "Cornish game hens" was probably a marketing idea in the first place.

While we are pursuing our literary equivalent of *A Current Affair*, one more scandal must be unleashed. Not all those Cornish game hens are really hens. Legally, they can be of either sex, although they are usually females, because the males tend to be larger and are raised to be broilers. In fact, if immature chicks get a little chubby and exceed the two-pound maximum weight, they get to live a longer life and are sold as broilers.

—Submitted by an anonymous caller on the Mel Young Show, KFYI-AM, Phoenix, Arizona.

why do roosters crow in the morning?

Because there are humans around to be awakened, of course. Does anyone really believe that roosters crow when they are by themselves? Nah! Actually, they speak perfectly good English.

Ornithologists don't buy our commonsense answer. They insist that crowing "maps territory" (a euphemism for "Get the hell out of my way and don't mess with my women—this is my coop"). In the spirit of fair play, we'll give the last word to one of those nasty ornithologist types (but don't believe a word she says), Janet Hinshaw of the Wilson Ornithological Society:

> Most of the crowing takes place in the morning, as does most singing, because that is when the birds are most active, and most of the territorial advertising takes place then. Many of the other vocalizations heard throughout the day are for other types of communication, including flocking calls, which serve to keep members of a flock together and in touch if they are out of sight from one another.

—Submitted by Rowena Nocom of North Hollywood, California.

why have so many pigeons in big cities lost their toes?

The three main dangers to pigeons' toes are illnesses, predators, and accidents. Pigeons are susceptible to two diseases that can lead to loss of toes: avian pox—a virus that first shrivels their toes to the point where they fall off, and eventually leads to death—and fungal infections, the price that pigeons pay for roaming around in such dirty environments.

Nonflying predators often attack roosting pigeons, and the toes and lower leg are the most vulnerable part of pigeons' anatomy. Steve Busits of the American Homing Pigeon Fanciers told *Imponderables* that "Rats or whatever mammal lives in their habitat will grab the first appendage available."

Accidents will happen, too. Busits says that toes are lost in tight spaces, namely "any cracks or crevices that their toes can become stuck in." Bob Phillips of the American Racing Pigeon Union adds that toes get lost while pigeons are in flight, with television antennas and utility wires being the main culprits.

—Submitted by Nancy Metrick of New York, New York.
Thanks also to Jeanna Gallo of Hagerstown, Maryland.

why don't birds tip over when they sleep on a telephone wire?

A telephone wire, of course, is only a high-tech substitute for a tree branch. Most birds perch in trees and sleep without fear of falling even during extremely windy conditions.

WHY IS A PEDESTRIAN VIOLATION CALLED *JAYWALKING?*

When the colonialists first came to America, blue jays abounded along the Eastern Seaboard. As more and more immigrants settled, the jays retreated to the countryside, until eventually *jay* became synonymous with "hick" in the mid-eighteenth century.

Rural dwellers were often dumbfounded by the chaos of big-city traffic. They crossed in the middle of the street, crossed intersections on red lights after traffic signals were invented, and darted out on the street without looking for cross traffic. *Jaywalking* meant "hick-walking." Today we need an antonym for *jaywalking*, a word to express the ruthlessly efficient kamikaze tactics of pedestrians exhibited by big-city urban dwellers.

—Submitted by Cynthia King of Morgan Hill, California.
Thanks also to Sharon M. Burke of Los Altos, California.

The secret to birds' built-in security system is their specialized tendons that control their toes. The tendons are located in front of the knee joint and behind the ankle joint. As it sits on its perch, the bird's weight stretches the tendons so that the toes flex, move forward, and lock around the perch.

Other tendons, located under the toe bones, guarantee that a sleeping bird doesn't accidentally tip over. On the bottom of each tendon are hundreds of little projections. These fit perfectly into other ratchetlike sheaths. The body weight of the bird pressing against the telephone wire (or tree branch) guarantees that the projections will stay tightly locked within the sheaths.

Barbara Linton of the National Audubon Society adds that while this mechanism is most highly developed in perching birds and songbirds, many other birds do not perch to sleep. They snooze on the ground or while floating on water.

—Submitted by Dr. Lou Hardy of Salem, Oregon.
Thanks also to Jann Mitchell of Portland, Oregon.

why do geese honk furiously while migrating? Doesn't honking squander their energy on long flights?

Unlike humans, geese and other migrating birds don't have car radios and Stuckey's to keep them occupied on long trips. Honking allows geese to maintain communication during long flights. Most importantly, it helps them to avoid midair collisions. As Todd Culver, education specialist at the Cornell Laboratory of Ornithology, succinctly states, "Honking is cheap compared to crashing."

Culver adds that the call and response of birds is the main reason for flying in "V-formation." *Imponderables* has no desire to enter this raging debate, which we get asked about frequently. But our province is questions that aren't so well traveled. We have read theories about the etiology of V-formations ranging from greater aerodynamics to superior defense against predators and from facilitation of vision to Culver's theory about better auditory communication.

Janet Hinshaw of the Wilson Ornithological Society assures us that honking doesn't sap geese of vital energy: "They honk while exhaling, which they obviously have to do anyway."

—Submitted by Steve Acheson of New Berlin, Wisconsin.

why do "sea" gulls congregate in parking lots of shopping centers where there is little food or water?

The reason why "sea" is in quotation marks above is that there are many different species of gull, and quite a few of them spend little time near the sea. Several species live inland and survive quite easily.

Nancy Martin, naturalist at the Vermont Institute of Natural Science, told *Imponderables* that ring-billed gulls, the most common inland species, display great affection for fast-food restaurant Dumpsters as a feeding site. Ring-billed gulls are happy to leave wide-open landfills to the more aggressive herring and great black-backed gulls.

But even gulls who normally feed at the shore might have reason to visit the local mall parking lot. Little-used areas of parking lots are safe and warm. And don't assume there is nothing to eat or drink there. Humans, whether the intentional bread crumb tossers or the unintentional litterers, leave a veritable smorgasbord for the birds, and gulls can take advantage of puddles on the surface of the pavement to take a drink or a quick bath. Martin adds that near the ocean, "hard pavement is good for dropping clams or mussels onto to break them open, although gulls will usually choose an area away from other gulls to carry on this activity."

Tim Dillon, researcher at the Cornell Laboratory of Ornithology, speculates that the open space of a parking lot provides "sea" gulls a terrain "similar to a sandbar or beach where they naturally congregate in large numbers." Just as we may occasionally go to the beach as a break from the dull routine of parking lots and shopping, so might gulls take a spiritual retreat to the natural glories of the shopping center parking lot.

—Submitted by Marilyn Chigi of Clarkstown, Michigan. Thanks also to Doc Swan of Palmyra, New Jersey; Annie Bianchetti of East Brunswick, New Jersey; Melanie Jongsma of Lansing, Illinois; and Tim Poirier of Silver Spring, Maryland.

ANIMALS

why do snakes dart out their tongues?

Although snake watchers at zoos love to see the reptiles flick their tongues, imagining they are getting ready to pounce on some unsuspecting prey, the tongues are perfectly harmless. Snakes don't sting or use their forked tongues as weapons.

The tongue is actually an invaluable sensory organ for the snake. It enables the reptile to troll for food (just as a fisherman sticks his line out in the water and hopes for the best), while feeling its way over the ground. It does this by bringing in bits of organic matter that it can smell or taste, alerting it to a potential food source. Some evidence suggests that a snake's tongue is equally sensitive to sound vibrations, warning it of potential prey or predators.

why don't lizards get sunburned? Why don't other animals get sunburned?

Look down on lizards if you want, but you must admit that they sure know how to cope with the sun better than we do. We stay out too long at the beach and our skin starts peeling and falling off. Next thing we know, our bodies look like a map on the Weather Channel (and not on a sunny day).

All mammals shed skin as soon as their outer layer of skin (epidermis) dies.

WHY IS THERE A BLACK DOT IN THE MIDDLE OF OTHERWISE WHITE BIRD DROPPINGS?

An important question, one that philosophers throughout the ages have pondered. Luckily, ornithologists know the answer.

That black dot is fecal matter. The white stuff is urine. The urine and fecal matter of birds collect together and are voided simultaneously out of the same orifice. Feces tend to sit directly in the middle of droppings because the urine, slightly sticky in consistency, clings to them.

—Submitted by Ann Marie Byrne of Queens, New York.

But reptiles can hang out on rocks all day, basking in the sun. Reptiles, clearly, are different. As Dr. Norman J. Scott, Jr., of the Society for the Study of Amphibians and Reptiles told *Imponderables,*

> Reptiles keep the outer layer of dead cells on their skin until the next layer is ready. Then it is shed.

Scott also points out that a lizard's epidermis, both the living and dead layers, is thick and cornified, making it far harder for ultraviolet rays to penetrate.

And as in humans, the pigment melanin helps protect lizards from harmful rays. Dr. R. Anderson, of the American College of Veterinary Dermatology, notes that heavily pigmented animals are protected from the sun, much as darker-complected humans are partially safeguarded. But many animals do exhibit ill effects from the sun, even critters with fur.

Just like us, many animals are subject to skin cancer. Dogs can and do get carcinomas, even ones with heavy fur. White-eared cats often develop carcinomas at the ends of the ears. "For some reason," Anderson observes, "bull terriers seem to love to sunbathe and can contract solar-induced lesions on their undersides."

Are we sensing a potentially booming market for "Sunblock for Pets"?

—Submitted by Julie Peterson of North Carolina State University.

do snakes sneeze?

Norman J. Scott, Jr., zoologist and past-president of the Society for the Study of Amphibians and Reptiles, told *Imponderables,* "As far as I know, snakes don't sneeze with their mouths shut, but they do clear fluid from their throat with an explosive blast of air from the lungs."

Snakes don't sneeze very often, though. In fact, a few herpetologists we contacted denied that snakes sneeze at all. But John E. Simmons, of the American Society of Ichthyologists and Herpetologists Information Committee, insisted otherwise:

> Snakes sneeze for the same reason as other vertebrates—to clear their respiratory passages. Snakes rarely sneeze, however, and people who keep them in captivity know that sneezing in snakes is usually a sign of respiratory illness resulting in fluid in the air passage.

—Submitted by Sue Scott of Baltimore, Maryland.
Thanks also to June Puchy of Lyndhurst, Ohio.

why do bees buzz? Do they buzz to communicate with one another?

Most of the bee buzzing that we hear is nothing other than the vibrations of their flapping wings during flight. When bees are flying, their wings are usually cycling more than two hundred times per second. Entomologist Lynn Kimsey of the Bohart Museum of Entomology in Berkeley, California, notes:

> In my experience, even a bee flying slowly makes a buzzing sound. However, many bees are small enough that the human ear simply isn't capable of hearing the sound they generate. The speed that a bee is flying does alter the sound quality to the human ear to some extent.
> The buzzing sound in bees is generated by the architecture and deformation of the thorax by the flight muscles. Because of this, larger bees produce a lower-pitched sound than smaller ones. Needless to say, the buzzing sound continues as long as a bee flies.

Before we generalize about bees, entomologists tend to get a tad waspish when the term is thrown around indiscriminately. The "bee" is actually a member of a superfamily (Apoidea) of the order that includes many other insects, including wasps. Only approximately five hundred species of the twenty thousand or so bees are the social bees (e.g., honeybees, bumblebees) that form colonies and seem to have a fifty-fifty chance of being followed by camera crews from documentary nature shows.

As Kimsey puts it:

> You have to realize that 90 percent of the bee species are solitary and have no reason to communicate with other individuals except to find a mate. Only the social bees (honeybees, stingless bees, and bumblebees) need any kind of specialized communications among individuals. In all bees, mating "communication" is done either using visual or olfactory cues.

Leslie Saul-Gershenz, insect zoo director of the San Francisco Zoological Society, adds that bees are also capable of other forms of nonvocal communication, including creating vibrations by tapping a substrate, and touch or tactile signals (honeybees use their antennae to communicate with one another).

Bees can't hear the way we do (if they could, they'd probably knock off that annoying buzzing) for one simple reason—they don't have ears. They detect sound by "feeling" the vibration through their antennae or feet.

Nowhere is the bees' potential for using vibrations from buzzing to communicate more evident than in their "waggle dance." In 1973, Karl von Frisch

won the Nobel Prize for unlocking the mystery of how worker honeybees "tell" their companions at the hive about nectar sources. Frisch discovered that bees perform two distinct dances. One is a "circle dance," which seems to indicate a food discovery, but not its specific location; and a tail-wagging dance, which pinpoints the treasure. While the dancer is tail-wagging, the bee is also madly beating its wings, generating a distinctive buzzing sound.

Although the other bees can't hear the buzz, they can feel the vibration through their feet. Successors to von Frisch have confirmed the validity of his discovery by creating a "robot bee" that is capable of transmitting information that other bees can successfully interpret. Kimsey reports that the vibrating wings of the dancer also help to disperse the aroma of the flowers visited by the worker, which helps the other bees locate the same resource.

According to Mark Winston, associate professor of biological sciences at Simon Fraser University, the beating of the wings during the waggle dance is considerably slower than during flight, so the buzz would be at a much lower pitch, more like a "low-pitched drone":

> The tone would be comparable to that produced by the lowest notes on a piano. Most of the bee buzzing that we hear is certainly at much higher tones.

The other most common form of buzzing is what Doug Yanega of the Illinois Natural History Survey refers to as "body-buzzing." Unlike wing-buzzing, body-buzzing is executed with the wings folded, with the bees using their thoracic muscles to produce the vibrations. Whereas wing-buzzing seems to be merely a coincident byproduct of flight (although it might, possibly, scare off potential nonbee predators), body-buzzing, according to Yanega,

> can be relevant in a number of biological contexts, depending on which bees are involved. Virtually all bees will buzz while they are in burrows (bear in mind that most of the thirty thousand bee species live in burrows in soil or twigs) or when held.
> Bumblebees will buzz to warm up their bodies, and to produce heat to warm young brood. Male bees of many species will vibrate during mating, and presumably the buzzing is part of the ritual, performed in a species-specific manner.

We have heard of only one other use of buzzing in bees, and from a far-flung place. Pia Bergquist, a graduate student in chemical ecology at Göteborg University in Sweden, is currently researching bumblebees and pollination. Bergquist told *Imponderables* that while most flowers' anthers (the part of the stamen that contains pollen) open longitudinally and are relatively easy for bees to extract nectar from, some flowers have only tiny holes or channels. Bees have found an extraordinary way, though, to bring home their equivalent of the bacon:

> In these flowers, the bees can't just brush and groom to get pollen, so they use the buzzing technique. Usually, the bees hang from the flower holding on to the anther with all six legs. While hanging like this, the bee buzzes. This causes vibrations, which sonicate the flower and cause the pollen to fall out from the anther and onto the bee's belly.

> *—Submitted by Amy Bagshaw of Las Vegas, Nevada.*
> *Thanks also to Scott Robinson of Bay City, Michigan.*

where do houseflies go during the winter?

To heaven, usually. Some flies survive winter, but only under extremely favorable conditions, when they can take shelter in barns or inside human residences where they can find enough organic matter and warmth to eat and breed.

Even under the best of circumstances, the normal life-span of a housefly north of the equator is approximately seven to twenty-one days. The most important variable in the longevity of these insects is the ambient temperature—they die off in droves when it falls below freezing or becomes excessively hot.

Although they actually live longest in cool temperatures, because they are less active, flies breed most prolifically when temperatures are warm, food is abundant, and humidity is moderate. Winter tends to deprive them of all of these favorable conditions, so that they not only die off themselves, but do so without having been able to breed successfully. The U.S. Department of Agriculture claims that no housefly has been proved to live from autumn to spring (which answers another Imponderable: why do we see so few houseflies in the spring?).

So how can they regenerate the species? Most people believe that flies hibernate or become dormant, like some other insects, but this theory has proved to be untrue. The few flies that we find in the spring are mainly the descendants of the adult flies that managed to find good hiding places during the previous winter. These spring flies breed their little wings off, just in time to harass you on your picnics when the weather gets good.

Some of the flies that survive winter are not adults, but rather flies in their earlier developmental stages. Fly eggs are usually deposited in the ground, in crevices, in wood, or in a particular favorite, cow manure. These eggs hatch, literally, in a few hours, and turn into larvae, a phase that can last anywhere from one to four days. Larvae feed on decaying plant or animal matter (such as other insect larvae). As the fly larva grows, it undergoes pupation, a phase that lasts about five days, in which the fly rests as its larval features are transformed into adult ones. Many entomologists used to answer this Imponderable by speculating that most flies that survive the winter do so in the form of larvae or pupae, but scientists now believe that adult flies have a much better chance of surviving the winter than their younger brethren, who have a hard time coping with cold weather. Still, some larvae and pupae do stay alive during the very end of winter and develop into adults in the spring.

The fecundity of the *Musca domestica* is truly awesome. One scientist estimated that a single mating pair of houseflies could generate as many as 325,923,200,000,000 offspring in one summer. One-sixth of a cubic foot of soil taken in India revealed 4,024 *surviving* flies. Maybe the Imponderable should read: why isn't the entire world overcome with flies?

Any notion that flies migrate south during the winter is easily dispelled. The average flight range of a housefly is a measly one-quarter of a mile. Scientists have tracked the flight of flies: they rarely go beyond a ten-mile radius of their birthplace during their entire lifetime.

when a fly alights on the ceiling, does it perform a loop or a roll in order to get upside down?

The problem, as David Bodanis states it in *The Secret House,* is that "Flies, like most airplanes, lose their lift when they try to go through the air bottom-side up, and become not flies, but sinks."

We would not venture an uninformed opinion on such a weighty subject. When confronted with a fly question, we of course immediately think of contacting the Canada Biting Fly Centre (or as Maurice Chevalier preferred to call it, Centre Canadien sur les Insectes Piqueurs). Its director, Dr. M. M. Galloway, was bold enough to offer a definitive answer: "A fly lands by raising the forelegs above its head, making contact with the ceiling and then

bringing its second and hind legs forward and up to the ceiling. The fly thus flips with a landing."

Bodanis points out the extraordinary efficiency of this technique: "As soon as these two front legs contact the ceiling the fly will acrobatically tuck up the rest of its body and let momentum rotate it to the ceiling. The manoeuver leaves the fly's body suspended upside down, without it ever having had to do a full roll, a remarkable piece of topological extrication."

—Submitted by W. A. Nissen of Visalia, California.

why do crickets chirp at night? What are they up to during the day? And why does it seem that crickets chirp more in the summer?

The answer seems obvious: Crickets chirp at night because that's when we're trying to sleep. But perhaps our application of Murphy's Law (the Imponderables Corollary: "All acts of nature can be explained by their ability to annoy us to the maximum extent") isn't what is uppermost in crickets' minds. Come to think of it, very little is likely to be uppermost (or bottommost) in crickets' minds.

Crickets chirp at night because that's when they are most active. Most cricket species—and there are about 100 just in North America—are nocturnal. They come out at night to find their two most pressing needs: food and crickets of the opposite sex.

During the day, crickets are relatively dormant, hiding from predators beneath rocks, in the grass or trees, or in soil crevices. By lying low when the sun shines, they are hoping to avoid confrontations with small owls, snakes, mice, frogs, raccoons, opossums, and other creatures that might try to hunt them for food.

Most entomologists believe that only male crickets chirp. They chirp by rubbing the two covers over their long wings together by using what is usually called the "scraper and file" technique. The cricket lifts one wing cover to a forty-five-degree angle (the scraper) and rubs the front end of it against the other wing cover (the file). Specialized veins in the wing covers make this possible: the file surface is rough while the scraper is relatively sharp. Crickets are "ambidextrous chirpers"—each wing can serve as both the scraper and file, and commonly crickets will switch off, presumably to prevent fatigue and excess wear on the file. The chirping sound will be the same regardless of which wing cover is used, but different species can be

identified by slight differences in their "songs." The cricket is so famed for chirping that its name is of "echoic" origin (*cricket* is derived from the Old French *criquet,* an attempt to echo the chirping sound of the insect).

The primary purpose of chirping seems to be to attract female crickets. As Blake Newton, an entomologist at the University of Kentucky put it:

> Only males chirp, and they do so to attract females. This helps the females find the males. It is a big world out there for dating crickets!

Since each species creates a slightly different song, a female cricket of one species will not be attracted to a cricket from the wrong side of the tracks. Females are more active at night. Like their male counterparts, they are hiding from male predators during the day, and according to David Gray, biologist at California State University, Northridge, they are also busy laying most of their eggs in the daytime.

But sex isn't the only thing on a chirping cricket's mind. David Pickering, owner and webmaster of Chamowners Web, a site devoted to chameleons and crickets, wrote to *Imponderables:* "There are special songs for courtship, fighting, and sounding an alarm."

Chirping in the nighttime confers several other advantages to crickets regardless of what they are seeking when they sing, as Blake Newton elaborates:

> I can speculate that the special calmness of the night would allow the sounds of a chirping male cricket to emanate equally without distortion from the source. The chirps of the males not only attract females of the same species, but repel other males, thus resulting in distributing males in a way that would increase the mating success of females in the population.

Sound travels best when the air is calm, so nighttime is the right time for crickets. As anyone trying to sleep when crickets are chirping can attest, they can be quite loud. Cricket chirps have been known to travel over a mile in ideal conditions, but some crickets aren't content to leave their range to the vagaries of weather. In some cricket species, the wing itself acts as an amplifier; others burrow into long holes in the ground and chirp while inside, creating the kind of tunnel effect that echoes and augments the volume.

Entomologists used to believe that chirping was crickets' only way of communicating with one another, but we know now that they are capable of vocalizing. The sound generated is so high-pitched that humans are incapable of hearing it. The vocalizations seem to be some form of male bonding (female crickets don't seem to "talk"), perhaps a way of one male to tell another male of an impending predator.

Blake Newton mentions that the time of day or night that crickets chirp seems to be species-specific: Some species of crickets do chirp primarily when the sun shines. Captive crickets, such as those studied by entomologists in laboratories, are apt to chirp at any time, but with a definite bias toward the nighttime.

And yes, crickets do have a preference for hot weather. They *do* chirp more in the summer. When the weather gets cold, crickets not only stop chirping, they stop moving! Like other insects, crickets are cold-blooded. When the temperature rises, their metabolism increases, and the scraping of their wing covers is faster—so they chirp faster on hotter nights than cooler ones.

The relationship between chirping rate and temperature is so established that it is common folk wisdom to count chirps in lieu of consulting a thermometer. Just count the number of chirps from a cricket in fifteen seconds, and then add forty to that number. The sum is supposedly the current temperature in degrees Fahrenheit!

—Submitted by Alexei Baboulevitch of Mountain View, California.

why do some insects fly in a straight line, while others tend to zigzag?

As entomologist Randy Morgan of the Cincinnati Insectarium puts it, "Flight behavior is an optimization of the need to avoid predators while searching for food and mates." Gee, if Morgan just eliminated the word "flight" and changed the word "predators" to "creditors," he'd be describing *our* lives.

Notwithstanding the cheap joke, Morgan describes the problems of evaluating the flight patterns of insects. An insect might zigzag because it is trying to avoid an enemy or because it doesn't have an accurate sighting of a potential food source. A predatory insect might be flying in a straight line because it is unafraid of other predators or because it is trying to "make time" when migrating; the same insect in search of food might zigzag if its target wasn't yet selected.

Leslie Saul, Insect Zoo director at the San Francisco Zoological Society, wrote *Imponderables* that the observable flying patterns of different insects can vary dramatically:

Can a spider get caught in the web of another spider?
And would it be able to navigate with the skill of the spinner?

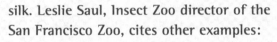

Yes, spiders get caught in the webs of other spiders frequently. And it isn't usually a pleasant experience for them. Theoretically, they might well be able to navigate another spider's web skillfully, but they are rarely given the choice. Spiders attack other spiders, and, if anything, spiders from the same species are more likely to attack each other than spiders of other species.

Most commonly, a spider will grasp and bite its intended victim and inject venom. Karen Yoder of the Entomological Society of America explains, "Paralysis from the bite causes them to be unable to defend themselves and eventually they succumb to or become a meal!"

Different species tend to use specialized strategies to capture their prey. Yoder cites the example of the Mimetidae, or pirate spiders:

> They prey exclusively on other spiders. The invading pirate spider attacks other spiders by luring the owner of the web by tugging at some of the threads. The spider then bites one of the victim's extremities, sucks the spider at the bite, and ingests it whole.
>
> The cryptic jumping spider will capture other salticids or jumping spiders and tackle large orb weavers in their webs. This is called web robbery.

Other spiders will capture prey by grasping, biting, and then wrapping the victim with silk. Leslie Saul, Insect Zoo director of the San Francisco Zoo, cites other examples:

> Others use webbing to alert them of the presence of prey. Others still have sticky strands such as the spiders in the family Araneidae. Araneidae spiders have catching threads with glue droplets. The catching threads of Uloborid spiders are made of a very fine mesh ("hackel band"). *Dinopis* throws a rectangular catching web over its prey item and the prey becomes entangled in the hackle threads.

Saul summarizes by quoting Rainer F. Foelix, author of *Biology of Spiders*: "The main enemies of spiders are spiders themselves."

Not all spiders attack their own. According to Saul, there are about twenty species of social spiders that live together peacefully in colonies.

—Submitted by Dallas Brozik of Huntington, West Virginia.

Flight paths are usually determined by visual, auditory, or olfactory stimulation. For example, bees and butterflies orient to the color and size of flowers; dragonflies orient to their prey items; moths orient to a wind carrying a specific smell, usually a "pheromone."

—Submitted by Dallas Brozik of Huntington, West Virginia.

what do mosquitoes do during the day? And where do they go?

At any hour of the day, somewhere in the world, a mosquito is biting someone. There are so many different species of mosquitoes, and so much variation in the habits among different species, it is hard to generalize. Some mosquitoes, particularly those that live in forests, are diurnal. But most of the mosquitoes in North America are active at night, and classified as either nocturnal or crepuscular (tending to be active at the twilight hours of the morning and/or evening).

Most mosquitoes concentrate all of their activities into a short period of the day or evening, usually in one to two hours. If they bite at night, mosquitoes will usually eat, mate, and lay eggs then, too. Usually, nocturnal and crepuscular female mosquitoes are sedentary, whether they are converting the lipids of blood into eggs or merely waiting to go on a nectar-seeking expedition to provide energy. Although they may take off once or twice a day to find some nectar, a week or more may pass between blood meals.

If the climatic conditions stay constant, mosquitoes tend to stick to the same resting patterns every day. But according to Charles Schaefer, director of the Mosquito Control Research Laboratory at the University of California at Berkeley, the activity pattern of mosquitoes can be radically changed by many factors:

1. **Light.** Most nocturnal and crepuscular mosquitoes do not like to take flight if they have to confront direct sunlight. Conversely, in homes, some otherwise nocturnal mosquitoes will be active during daylight hours if the house is dark.

2. **Humidity.** Most will be relatively inactive when the humidity is low.

3. **Temperature.** They don't like to fly in hot weather.

4. **Wind.** Mosquitoes are sensitive to wind, and will usually not take flight if the wind is more than 10 mph.

Where are nocturnal mosquitoes hiding during the day? Most never fly far from their breeding grounds. Most settle into vegetation. Grass is a particular favorite. But others rest on trees; their coloring provides excellent camouflage to protect them against predators.

A common variety of mosquito in North America, the anopheles, often seeks shelter. Homes and barns are favorite targets, but a bridge or tunnel will do in a pinch. Nocturnal or crepuscular mosquitoes are quite content to rest on a wall in a house, until there is too much light in the room. In the wild, shelter-seeking mosquitoes will reside in caves or trees.

We asked Dr. Schaefer, who supplied us with much of the background information for this Imponderable, whether mosquitoes were resting or sleeping during their twenty-two hours or so of inactivity. He replied that no one really knows for sure.

—Submitted by Jennifer Martz of Perkiomenville, Pennsylvania.
Thanks also to Ronald C. Semone of Washington, D.C.

why do only female mosquitoes eat human blood? What do male mosquitoes eat?

No, the mosquito menfolk aren't out eating steak and potatoes. Actually, the main food of both male and female mosquitoes is nectar from flowers. The nectar is converted to glycogen, a fuel potent enough to provide their muscles with energy to fly within minutes of consuming the nectar.

IF MOTHS ARE ATTRACTED TO LIGHT, WHY DON'T THEY FLY TOWARD THE SUN?

There is one little flaw in the premise of this Imponderable. Even if they were tempted to fly toward the sun, they wouldn't have the opportunity—the vast majority of moths are nocturnal animals. When's the last time you saw one flitting by in daylight? Actually, though, the premise of this question isn't as absurd as it may appear. For details, see the Imponderable on page 112.

—Submitted by Joel Kuni of Kirkland, Washington.
Thanks also to Bruce Kershner of Williamsville, New York.

Mosquitoes also possess an organ, known as the fat-body, that is capable of storing sugar for conversion to flight fuel.

Male mosquitoes can exist quite happily on a diet of only nectar, and nature makes certain that they are content—males don't have a biting mouth part capable of piercing the skin of a human. But females have been anatomically equipped to bite because they have an important job to do: lay eggs. In some species, female mosquitoes are not capable of laying any eggs unless they eat a nutritional supplement of some tasty, fresh blood. Their organs convert the lipids in blood into iron and protein that can greatly increase their fecundity.

A mosquito that would lay five or ten eggs without the supplement can lay as many as 200 with a dash of Type O. Although we don't miss the blood sucked out of us, this is quite a feast for the mosquito; many times, she consumes more than her own body weight in blood.

But let's not take it personally. Some studies have indicated that given a choice, mosquitoes prefer the blood of cows to humans, and in the jungle are just as likely to try to bite a monkey or a bird as a human.

—Submitted by Carolyn Imbert of Yuba City, California.

why are moths attracted to light? And what are they trying to do when they fly around light bulbs?

Moths, not unlike humans, spend much of their time sleeping, looking for food, and looking for mates. Most moths sleep during the day. Their search for dinner and procreation takes place at night. Unlike us, though, moths are not provided with maps, street signs, or neon signs flashing "EAT" to guide them to their feeding or mating sites.

Over centuries of evolution, moths have come to use starlight, and particularly moonlight, for navigation. By maintaining a constant angle in reference to the light source, the moth "knows" where to fly. Unfortunately for the insects, however, humans introduce artificial light sources that lull the moths into assuming that a light bulb is actually their natural reference point.

An English biologist, R. R. Baker, developed the hypothesis that when moths choose the artificial light source as their reference point, and try keeping a constant angle to it, the moth ends up flying around the light in ever-smaller concentric circles, until it literally settles on the light source. Baker even

speculates that moths hover on or near the light because they are attempting to roost, believing that it is daytime, their regular hours. Moths have been known to burn themselves by resting on light bulbs. Others become so disoriented, they can't escape until the light is turned off or sunlight appears.

So don't assume that moths are genuinely attracted by the light. Sad as their fate may be, chances are what the moth "is trying to do" isn't to hover around a porch light—the only reason the moth is there is because it has confused a soft white bulb with the moon. The moth would far rather be cruising around looking for food and cute moths of the opposite sex.

—Submitted by Charles Channell of Tucson, Arizona.
Thanks also to Joyce Bergeron of Springfield, Massachusetts;
Sara Anne Hoffman of Naples, Florida; Gregg Hoover of Pueblo, Colorado;
Gary Moore of Denton, Texas; Bob Peterson, APO New York;
and Jay Vincent Corcino of Panorama City, California.

what happens to an ant that gets separated from its colony? Does it try to find it? Can it survive?

As we all learned in elementary school, ants are social animals, but their organization doesn't just provide them with buddies—it furnishes them with the food and protection they need to survive in a hostile environment.

All the experts we consulted indicated that an isolated worker ant, left to its own devices, would likely die a week or two before its normal three-week lifespan. And it would probably spend that foreshortened time wandering around, confused, looking for its colony.

Ants help each other trace the path between food sources and the colony by laying down chemical trails called pheromones. Our hypothetical solitary ant might try following pheromone trails it encounters, hoping they will lead it back home. Worker ants in a given colony are all the daughters of the original queen and can't simply apply for admission to a new colony.

Three dangers, in particular, imperil a lost ant. The first, and most obvious, is a lack of food. Ants are natural foragers but are used to receiving cues from other ants about where to search for food. A single ant would not have the capacity to store enough food to survive for long. Furthermore, ants don't always eat substances in the form they are gathered. Cincinnati naturalist Kathy Biel-Morgan provided us with the example of the leaf-cutter ant. The leaf-cutter ant finds plants and brings leaves back to the nest, where the material is ground up and used in the colony's fungus garden. The ants then eat the fruiting body of the fungus. Without the organizational assistance of the colony, a leaf does nothing to sate the appetite of a leaf-cutter ant.

The second danger is cold. Ants are ectotherms, animals that need heat but are unable to generate it themselves. When it is cold, ants in colonies will seek the protective covering of the nest. If left to its own devices, a deserted ant would probably try to find a rock or the crack of a sidewalk to use as cover, which may or may not be enough protection to keep it from freezing.

The third problem our lonesome ant would encounter is nasty creatures that think of the ant as their dinner fare. Collectively, ants help protect one another. Alone, an ant must fend off a variety of predators, including other ants. Biel-Morgan compared the vulnerability of the ant, on its own, to a single tourist in New York City. And that is vulnerable, indeed.

—Submitted by Cary Hillman of Kokomo, Indiana.

do fish sleep? If so, when do they sleep?

Our trusty *Webster's New World Dictionary* defines sleep as "a natural, regularly recurring condition of rest for the body and mind, during which the *eyes are usually closed* and there is *little or no conscious thought or voluntary movement.*" Those strategically placed little weasel words we have italicized make it hard for us to give you a yes or no answer to this mystery. So as much as we want to present you with a tidy solution to this Imponderable, we feel you deserve the hard truth.

Webster probably didn't have fish in mind when he wrote this definition of "sleep." First of all, except for elasmobranchs (fish with cartilaginous skeletons, such as sharks and rays), fish don't have eyelids. So they can't very well close them to sleep. No fish has opaque eyelids that block out vision, but some have a transparent membrane that protects their eyes from irritants.

Pelagic fish (who live in the open sea, as opposed to coasts), such as tuna, bluefish, and marlins, *never* stop swimming. Jane Fonda would be proud. Even coastal fish, who catch a wink or two, do not fall asleep in the same way humans do. Gerry Carr, director of Species Research for the International Game Fish Association, wrote us about some of the ingenious ways that fish try to catch a few winks, even if forty winks are an elusive dream:

Some reef fishes simply become inactive and hover around like they're sleeping, but they are still acutely aware of danger approaching. Others, like some parrot fishes and wrasses, exude a mucous membrane at night that completely covers their body as though they've been placed in baggies. They wedge themselves into a crevice in the reef, bag themselves, and remain there, semicomatose, through the night. Their eyes remain open, but a scuba diver can approach them and, if careful, even pick them up at night, as I have done. A sudden flurry of movement, though, will send them scurrying. They are not totally unaware of danger.

In many ways, fish sleep the same way we plod through our everyday lives when we are awake. Our eyes are open but we choose, unconsciously, not to register in our brains most of the sensory data we see. If a crazed assassin burst into the room, we could rouse ourselves to attention, but if someone asked us to describe what fabulous tourist attraction we were watching, we couldn't say whether it was Stonehenge or the Blarney Stone.

If you accept that a fish's blanking out is sleeping, then the answer to the second part of the mystery is that fish sleep at night, presumably because of the darkness. Anyone with an aquarium can see that fish can float effortlessly while sleeping. They exude grace—which is more than we can say for how most humans look when they are sleeping.

—Submitted by Karole Rathouz of Mehlville, Missouri. Thanks also to Cindy and Sandor Keri of Woodstock, Georgia; and Heather Bowser of Tulsa, Oklahoma.

do fish pee?

You don't see them swimming in your toilet, do you? Yes, of course, fish urinate.

But not all fish pee in the same way. Freshwater fish must rid themselves of the water that is constantly accumulating in their bodies through osmosis. According to Glenda Kelley, biologist for the International Game Fish Association, the kidneys of freshwater fish must produce copious amounts of dilute urine to prevent their tissues from becoming waterlogged.

Compared to their freshwater counterparts, marine fish, who lose water through osmosis, produce little urine. For those readers who have asked us if fish drink water, the surprising answer is that saltwater fish do, because they need to replenish the water lost through osmosis, as Kelley explains:

> This loss of water is compensated for largely by drinking large amounts of sea water, but the extra salt presents a problem. They rid

themselves of this surplus by actively excreting salts, mainly through their gills.

Dr Robert R. Rofen of the Aquatic Research Institute told *Imponderables* that fish are able to excrete liquids through their gills and skin as well, "the counterpart to humans' sweating through their skin."

—Submitted by Billie Faron of Genoa, Ohio.

how do fish return to a lake or pond that has dried up?

Our correspondent, Michael J. Catalana, rightfully wonders how even a small pond replenishes itself with fish after it has totally dried up. Is there a Johnny Fishseed who roams around the world restocking ponds and lakes with fish?

We contacted several experts on fish to solve this mystery, and they wouldn't answer until we cross-examined you a little bit, Michael. "How carefully did you look at that supposedly dried-up pond?" they wanted to know. Many species, such as the appropriately named mudminnows, can survive in mud. R. Bruce Gebhardt of the North American Native Fishes Association suggested that perhaps your eyesight was misdirected: "If there are small pools, fish may be able to hide in mud or weeds while you're standing there looking into the pool." When you leave, they re-emerge. Some tropical fish lay eggs that develop while the pond is dry; when rain comes and the pond is refilled with water, the eggs hatch quickly.

For the sake of argument, Michael, we'll assume that you communed with nature, getting down on your hands and knees to squeeze the mud searching for fish or eggs. You found no evidence of marine life. How can fish appear from out of thin air? We return to R. Bruce Gebhardt for the explanation:

> There are ways in which fish can return to a pond after total elimination. The most common is that most ponds or lakes have outlets and inlets; fish just swim back into the formerly hostile area. They are able to traverse and circumvent small rivulets, waterfalls, and pollution sources with surprising efficiency. If they find a pond with no fish in it, they may stay just because there's a lot of food with no competition for it.

—Submitted by Michael J. Catalana of Ben Lomond, California.

why are saltwater fish more colorful than freshwater fish?

When we posed this Imponderable to R. Bruce Gebhardt, past president of the North American Native Fishes Association (NANFA), he was quick to say: "Whoa! Not so fast!":

> Some of the marine fish in a tropical fish store are outstandingly colorful. They're more striking than freshwater fishes in the store from the same latitudes. I think part of the answer may be the particular environments some of those saltwater fishes come from rather than the colorful effects of sodium. If you compare fishes from other parts of the world, the balance might tip the other way.
>
> If you go fishing the bays and ocean within 100 miles of New York, most of the fish you catch will be silver and bluish; if you go fishing in the creeks and streams within the same radius, especially in spring, you'll come up with a variety of colorful trout, green and yellow pickerel and perch with orange fins, and brilliant sunfish, not to mention the non-game fish like the common shiner that color up for a few months in spring and summer.

NANFA'S Robert E. Schmidt concurs with Gebhardt that many freshwater fish, such as the redbelly dace or *Notropis cardinalis,* both from North America, or the brilliantly colored South American tetras, display "incredible" colors:

> Our perception is that saltwater *coral reef* fish (note that it is not *all* saltwater fish that are considered colorful) are more brilliant—that is, the colors are more striking and the patterns tend to be bolder than freshwater fishes. Also, coral reef fish are colorful all the time, whereas our native fishes are colorful only during breeding season, and then usually just males.

Both sources have alluded to the changeability of fish coloration. Many males adopt brilliant colors during mating season—presumably, flashy colors attract mates in the same way that a shiny red Corvette is intended to do for lucky owners. Some fish even vary colors from hour to hour, sometimes using the bright hues to attract breeding companions, at other times displaying duller colors to avoid predators.

When trying to figure out why tropical fish are more colorful than those from other climes, we have to contend with this very paradox: At times, colors seem to be used to blend in with other fish or the plant life; at other times, they are meant to attract other fish.

Other than luring mates, why would it be an advantage for fish to display bright colors? Glenda Kelley of the International Game Fish Association told *Imponderables* that the bright colors displayed by schools of foraging fish are a way of keeping individuals in contact with one another. Bright coloration can also function as a way of fish mapping territories or warning predators that they won't be easy or digestible prey. Some of the most brightly colored tropical fish are never eaten, which leads some researchers to believe that potential prey remember the colors of poisonous or spiny fish that aren't worth the effort to kill and eat.

But the coloration of just as many fish seems designed to allow them to blend in with their surroundings. The most obvious example of this principle is "countershading." Many of the fish that live near the top layers of the sea have dark coloring on their tops, with white or silver stomachs. The dark top helps shield them from potential predators from above, while the light coloration on the bottom helps them to blend in with the light from below. Bottom fish tend to have even more complicated countershading patterns, with their bottoms often matching the vegetation on the sea floor.

All these trends hold true for both saltwater and freshwater fish, as well as tropical and nontropical fish, so we can assume that the key to the answer to this Imponderable lies in the more complex nature of saltwater ecosystems compared to their freshwater equivalents. Tropical reefs, in particular, support even greater biodiversity, as Doug Olander of *Sport Fishing* magazine explains:

> More numerous types of fishes and more complex species interrelationships seem to require more intricate schemes for interspecies identification (e.g., cleaner wrasse, with their bold blue-white striping to signal predators to open their mouths).

Kelley concurs with this thesis, noting that

> striking colors and patterns have evolved particularly in environments where there are many species living side by side (e.g., coral reefs)— perhaps recognizing and being recognized by one's own species is especially important there.

Coral reefs also tend to have ample supplies of warmth, hiding places, and food. The ecosystem is so benign that, again, biologists disagree about whether the main purpose of their vivid coloration is to blend in with the vivid hues of the plant life, or to draw attention to themselves.

As Bruce Gebhardt puts it,

> They're colorful because they can get away with it. There's so much life, further, that bright advertising is almost a necessity to tell one's fellows and prospective mates from other species.
>
> Moreover, many of these areas are very well sunlit, and sand and coral are white or multicolored; there's less of an advantage to being dark colored; though species that live in and on light substrates are liable to be sand colored.
>
> Tropical saltwaters are less turbid and that clarity may play some role in encouraging species' differentiation by colors. Many freshwater environments that produce tropical fish, by contrast, such as shady swamps and weedy banks, are sunless, and the substrates are muddy, which means they are dark. There's more of a survival incentive to have a dark coloration.

Several of our fish experts wanted to inform *Imponderables* readers that many of us have an unrealistic conception of the coloration of most tropical fish. We have a distorted viewpoint because most fish stores and aquariums we visit have no incentive to stock drab-looking fish.

—Submitted by Karen Langley of Germantown, Tennessee.
Thanks also to Nora Corrigan of Reston, Virginia; Anne Francis of Pittsburgh,
Pennsylvania; and Andrew Cahill of parts unknown.

are lobsters ambidextrous?

Have you ever noticed, while digging into a lobster, that one claw is significantly larger than the other, as if one claw was pumping iron and taking steroids, while the other claw was used only for riffling the pages of library books? The large claw is called the "crusher" and the smaller one the "cutter" (terms that sound like the members of a new tag team in the World Wrestling Federation). The crusher has broader and bigger teeth but moves relatively slowly. The cutter has tiny, serrated teeth and moves swiftly.

The two claws do not start out distinctly different. Lobsters shed their shells more often than Cher has plastic surgery—they undergo three molts in the larval stage alone. When lobsters are first hatched, the two claws look identical, but with each successive stage in their development, the differences become more pronounced. It isn't until their fifth molt, and second postlarval molt, that the two claws are truly differentiated.

As you may have guessed, the crusher claw is important for the defense of lobsters against predators, and the cutter particularly useful in eating.

Claws of lobsters are often torn off in accidents and in fights. Although there are some differences among species of lobsters, most lobsters will regenerate severed claws.

Most bizarre of all, if the remaining claw of an injured lobster is a cutter, many species with "plastic dimorphism" will change the function of that claw from cutter to crusher, presumably because the crusher is more essential for survival. The next regenerated claw of that lobster is capable itself of shifting to the cutter function, so that the positions of the two claws are reversed.

According to Darryl Felder, chairman of the University of Louisiana, Lafayette, biology department, lobsters are not always right- or left-"handed." The crusher may be on the right or left side of a lobster.

The ultimate answer to this Imponderable depends upon how you define ambidextrous. Certainly, lobsters can use either cheliped (the scientific name for claw) with equal ease. Although their regenerative powers give lobsters a certain flexibility, the versatility of each claw is not as great as that of a switch hitter in baseball, who can swing the bat equally well from both sides, or the pickpocket who can pilfer skillfully with either hand.

—Submitted by Danny Kotok of New York, New York.

why do worms come out on the sidewalk after it rains?

What do you think the worms are coming out for? Their health? In fact, they are. Except for those that live as parasites, most worms live by burrowing little holes in the ground. When it rains, those little holes fill with water. If the worms didn't get out of the holes, they'd drown. Worms may be creepers, but they're not dolts.

Why do they congregate on the sidewalk after a rain? Sidewalks provide more solid support than dirt or grass during a rainstorm. If you investigated the grass adjacent to the sidewalk, you would find many worms trying to stay above water, wishing they had made it to the sidewalk.

Submitted by Mike Arnett of Chicago, Illinois. Thanks also to Karole Rathouz of Mehlville, Missouri; John P. Eichman of Yucaipa, California; Willard Wheeler of Upland, California; and Tom Trauschke of Whitehall, Pennsylvania.

3 FOOD

How are animals different from people? Simple: When animals see food, they just eat it. We people farm, process, package, name, refrigerate, and cook our food; we decorate it and put it on pretty plates—and then talk endlessly about it. We even put on funny hats when we cook. Why? Here are some answers.

what are the little white particles found on the bottom half of English muffins?

The particles are farina. Farina helps add to the taste of the product, but the main function of farina particles, and the reason why they are placed only on the bottom half of the muffin, is to prevent the ball of dough from sticking to the oven plate during cooking.

—Submitted by Jessica Ahearne of Madawaska, Maine.

why can't you find English muffins in England?

Probably for the same reason you can't find French dressing in France or Russian dressing in Russia. Or why you're more likely to encounter a New York steak in Kansas City than in New York City. Locales mentioned in food names are more often marketing tools than descriptions of the origins of the product.

At least Samuel Thomas, the inventor of the English muffin, was actually born in England. Thomas emigrated to the United States in 1875 and opened his own bake shop in New York City in 1880. According to Kari Anne Maino of Best Foods Baking Group, the division of CPC International that markets Thomas' English Muffins, Thomas was probably inspired by the crumpets, scones, and cakelike muffins that were popular in England when he left the country. And he was smart enough to realize that the word "English" would lend his product a certain panache in the United States.

Maino says that her company knows of no "English muffins" that are marketed in England today, but "We have learned that a product very similar to our Thomas' English Muffins did exist in England until about 1920." Why an item would fade in popularity in England while gaining popularity in the United States is anybody's guess. An explanation of the gustatory preferences of the English—a culture that deems baked beans on white toast a splendid meal—would require an exegesis far beyond our mortal powers.

—Submitted by Rosemary Bosco of the Bronx, New York.

why is cheddar cheese orange?

Unless they've been breeding some pretty strange cows in Wisconsin, we would expect cows to produce white milk. All the folks in the dairy industry assured us that they haven't bred a mutant race of cows just to produce orangeish cheddar cheese.

Cheddar cheese is artificially colored with natural ingredients, most commonly annatto, a seed obtained from the tropical annatto tree, found in Central America. Kraft, the largest seller of cheese in the United States, uses a combination of annatto and oleoresin paprika, an oil extraction of the spice paprika, to color its cheddar cheese. Depending upon the natural color of the milk and the amount of annatto added, cheese can be turned into a bright orange color or a more natural-looking yellow shade.

The only reason why cheesemakers color their product is because consumers seem to prefer it. Regional tastes differ, though. Some areas of the eastern United States prefer white cheese, while most of the rest of the country favors yellow. Kraft even makes white "American Singles," although the artificially colored yellow slices far outsell them.

—Submitted by Christopher S. von Guggenberg of Alexandria, Virginia.

WHAT CAUSES THE HOLES IN SWISS CHEESE?

The cheese industry prefers to call these openings eyes rather than holes. The eyes are created by expanding gases that are emitted by a bacterium known as the eye former. The eye former is introduced during the early stages of Swiss cheese production. The bacterium forms the holes, helps ripen the cheese, and lends Swiss cheese its distinctive flavor.

The eyes, then, are not there for cosmetic reasons. Still, some domestic "Swiss" cheesemakers mechanically "add" holes to already formed cheese produced without the eye-former bacterium. This shortcut is what robs some domestic varieties of the mature flavor of genuine Swiss cheese.

why do cookbooks often recommend beating egg whites in a copper bowl?

We don't know whether any cookbook writers have received kickbacks from copper bowl manufacturers, but this advice always struck us as unnecessary and fussy. But then again, our cakes compare unfavorably to the offerings of school cafeterias.

We consulted our pals at the American Egg Board and United Egg Producers, and we learned there really is something to this copper bowl theory. The copper in the bowl reacts to a protein (the conalbumin, to be precise) in the egg whites, and helps stabilize the eggs and may actually increase their volume when whipped. Cream of tartar combines with egg whites in a similar fashion, working to keep the whites from separating from yolks. One reason why some cooks prefer to stabilize the whites with cream of tartar rather than the "no-cost" copper bowl is that if you leave the egg whites in the bowl for too long (sometimes, for as little as five minutes), the whites will turn pink.

Cooking is an art rather than a science, and we seem to see the prescription for the copper bowl less often these days. Kay Engelhardt, test kitchen supervisor for the American Egg Board, waxes philosophical:

HOW DO THEY PUT THE POCKETS IN PITA BREAD?

Who would have ever thought that the pocket is created without human hands intervening? Bakery engineer Simon S. Jackel, director of Plymouth Technical Services, explains,

"Pita bread is placed in the oven as a thin, solid piece of dough. There is no pocket in the dough when it goes into the oven. But the oven temperature is so high, about 900 degrees Fahrenheit, that there is a rapid, explosive expansion of the water in the dough, causing the formation of a pocket by literally ripping the bottom part of the dough piece from the top dough piece. Total baking time at this high temperature is only one and one-half to two minutes."

—Submitted by James Frisch of Great Neck, New York.

Perception of the copper bowl's merits varies considerably among various experts. The Strong Armed swear by it. The punier among us are willing to settle for an electric mixer and a bit of cream of tartar.

—Submitted by Merilyn Trocino of Bellingham, Washington.

why do Kellogg's Rice Krispies "Snap! Crackle! and Pop!"?

Kellogg's Rice Krispies have snapped, crackled, and popped since 1928. Kellogg's production and cooking process explains the unique sound effects.

Milled rice, from which the bran and germ have been removed, is combined with malt flavoring, salt, sugar, vitamins, and minerals and then steamed in a rotating cooker. The rice, now cooked, is left to dry and temper (i.e., sit while the moisture equalizes). The rice is then flattened and flaked as it passes through two cylindrical steel rollers. The Krispies are left to dry and temper for several more hours.

The cereal then moves to a toasting oven. The flattened rice is now exposed to hot air that puffs each kernel to several times its original size and toasts it to a crisp consistency. This hot air produces tiny air bubbles in each puff, crucial in creating the texture of Rice Krispies and their unique sound in the bowl.

When milk is added to the prepared cereal, the liquid is unevenly absorbed by the puffs, causing a swelling of the starch structure. According to Kellogg's, "This swelling places a strain on the remaining crisp portion, breaking down some of the starch structure and producing the famous 'Snap! Crackle! and Pop!'"

—Submitted by Kevin Madden of Annandale, New Jersey.

how do they keep all the raisins in cereal boxes from falling to the bottom?

The Rule of Popcorn Physics, which states that unpopped popcorn kernels fall to the bottom of the bowl, has saved many a tooth for generations. The explanation for this immutable law is easy enough to comprehend: unpopped kernels fall to the bottom both because their density is greater than expanded popcorn and because our handling of the corn creates crevices for the unpopped kernel to slide down.

Many inquisitive types have searched for corollaries to the Popcorn Physics rule. For example, the tenet of Slithery Sundaes posits that regardless of how much syrup or toppings one puts atop ice cream in a sundae, it will all fall to the bottom of the bowl anyway, collecting in a pool of glop.

So it was not without a feeling of reverence and awe that we approached the subject of raisins in cereal boxes, tiny dried grapes that seem to defy the usual laws of food gravity. Linda E. Belisle, at General Mills, supplied the simple but elegant solution.

Raisins are added to boxes only after more than half of the cereal has already been packed. The cereal thus has a chance to settle and condense. During average shipping conditions, boxes get jostled a bit (the equivalent of our stirring the contents of a popcorn bowl while grabbing a fistful), so the raisins actually sift and become evenly distributed throughout the box.

The tendency of cereal to condense within the package is responsible for the warning on most cereal packages that the contents are measured by weight rather than volume. Little did you know that this condensation was also responsible for the Law of Rising Raisins.

—Submitted by James A. Hoagland of Stockton, California.

who was the Benedict that *eggs Benedict* were named after?

Rest easy. You aren't unpatriotic if you enjoy this brunch specialty. It wasn't named after Benedict Arnold.

However, *eggs Benedict* were named after a more benign person, a ne'er-do-well member of New York café society who made few, if any, other contributions to our culture.

One morning in 1894, Samuel Benedict staggered into the Waldorf-Astoria and ordered an antidote for his hangover. Charles Earle Funk reports that he ordered "bacon, buttered toast, two poached eggs, and a hooker of hollandaise." The maître d' hôtel, the renowned Oscar, decided to improve on this new dish by substituting ham for bacon, and an English muffin for toast. Oscar honored Benedict by naming the new breakfast after good old Sam.

WHAT LETTERS DOES CAMPBELL'S INCLUDE IN ALPHABET SOUP IN COUNTRIES THAT DON'T USE OUR ALPHABET (E.G., GREECE, ISRAEL, EGYPT)?

And what about France? Does Campbell's include an accent mark over the *e*?

The media relations representatives at Campbell's aren't exactly inundated with this question, but they researched it for us and graciously responded with the disappointing answer: Campbell's Alphabet Soup is sold only in North America. We urge reconsideration. Contemplate the potential of Campbell's Cyrillic Soup!

—Submitted by David Faucheux of Lafayette, Louisiana.

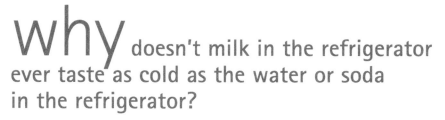

why doesn't milk in the refrigerator ever taste as cold as the water or soda in the refrigerator?

Actually, milk *does* get as cold as water or soda. If you are having a particularly boring Saturday night, you might want to stick a thermometer into the liquids to prove this.

Milk at the same temperature as water or soda just doesn't taste as cold to us because milk contains fat solids. We perceive solids as less cold than liquids. Taste experts refer to this phenomenon as "mouth feel."

If the milk/water/soda test wasn't exciting enough for you, run a test in your freezer compartment that will demonstrate the same principle. Put a pint of premium high-butterfat ice cream in the freezer along with a pint of low-fat or nonfat frozen yogurt. Consume them. We'll bet you two to one that the yogurt will taste colder than the ice cream. For the sake of research, we recently performed this experiment with due rigor, and because we wanted to go out of our way to assure the accuracy of the experiment, we conducted the test on many different flavors of ice cream and yogurt. Oh, the sacrifices we make for our readers!

—*Submitted by Pat O'Conner of Forest Hills, New York.*

why does milk obtain a skin when it is heated, while thicker liquids, like gravy, lose their skin when heated?

Proteins and starch react differently to heat. When heated, the protein in milk coagulates; the fat globules no longer can be suspended in water and, being lighter than water, float to the top. Bruce V. Snow, a dairy consultant, told us that the fat globules "adhere and form a surface skin when the liquid ceases to boil or simmer heavily."

But when gravy is heated, the starch, which has formed the skin in the first place, breaks down. Since starch is more soluble than protein, the result is that the ex-skin is reabsorbed into the rest of the gravy. The same process can be seen when soup is reheated after a skin has "grown" in the refrigerator.

—Submitted by Beth Oakley of Ishpeming, Michigan.

why is frozen orange juice just about the only frozen product that is cheaper than its fresh counterpart?

Our correspondents reasoned, logically enough, that since both fresh and frozen orange juice are squeezed from oranges, and since the frozen juice must be concentrated, the extra processing involved would make the frozen style more expensive to produce and thus costlier at the retail level. But according to economists at the Florida Department of Citrus, it just ain't so.

Although the prices of fresh fruit, chilled juice, and frozen concentrate are similar at the wholesale level (within two cents of the fresh fruit equivalent per pound), they depart radically at the retail level. In the period of 1987-1988, frozen concentrated orange juice cost 24.6 cents per fresh pound equivalent; chilled juice was 35 cents per fresh pound equivalent; and the fruit itself a comparatively hefty 58.5 cents per pound. Why the discrepancy?

In the immortal words of real estate brokers across the world, the answer is: location, location, location. Chilled juice (and the fresh fruit itself, for that matter) would cost less than frozen if it didn't need to be shipped long distances. But it does. The conclusion, as Catherine A. Clay, information specialist at the Florida Department of Citrus, elucidates, is clearly that the costs at the retail level are due to distribution rather than processing costs.

> One 90-pound box of oranges will make about 45 pounds of juice. Concentrating that juice by removing the water will reduce the weight by at least two-thirds, so the amount of frozen concentrate in one box would be about 15 pounds.
>
> So you can ship three times as much frozen concentrated juice in one truck than you can chilled juice, and twice as much chilled juice as fresh oranges. In the space in which one 90-pound box of oranges is shipped, you could ship six times as much frozen concentrated orange juice.
>
> In addition, fresh fruit can begin to decay or be damaged during transit to the retailer. So while the retailer may have paid for the entire truckload, he may have to discard decayed or damaged fruit. Yet his cost for that load remains the same regardless of how much actual fruit he sells.
>
> Frozen concentrated juice does not spoil, so there is no loss. The higher price for fresh fruit would compensate the retail buyer for the cost of the lost fruit.

Clay didn't add that many juice distributors who use strictly Florida oranges for their chilled juice use cheaper, non-American orange juice for their concentrated product. Why don't they use the cheaper oranges for their chilled juices? Location, location, location. It would be too expensive to ship the heavier, naturally water-laden fruits thousands of miles.

—Submitted by Eugene Hokanson of Bellevue, Washington.
Thanks also to Herbert Kraut of Forest Hills, New York.

how do they measure
the vitamin content of foods?

Some vitamins are present in such small concentrations in food that there are only a few micrograms (millionths of a gram) of the vitamin per hundred grams of food, while other vitamins might constitute ten milligrams per hundred grams of food. The techniques that work to measure the abundant vitamin often won't work to evaluate the presence of the other.

Jacob Exler, nutritionist for the Nutrient Data Research Branch of the Human Nutrition Information Service, told *Imponderables* that there are two types of analytical procedures to measure the vitamin content of foods, chemical and microbiological:

The chemical procedures measure the actual amount of a vitamin or a derivative of the vitamin, and the microbiological procedures measure the biological activity of the vitamin on some selected organism.

Today, chemical procedures are in vogue. In the past, microbiological studies were more common, and researchers tested not only on bacteria but also on live rats. In fact, as late as the 1970s, the FDA used approximately twenty thousand rats a year just to test foods for vitamin D content! Roger E. Coleman of the National Food Processors Association explains the theory behind microbiological studies:

> An older, but still very acceptable method for vitamin assay is to measure the amount of microbiological growth a food supports. There are certain bacteria that require an outside source of one or more vitamins to grow. The growth of these bacteria is proportional to the amount of the required vitamin in the food.

But microbiological work is extremely sensitive. If conditions are not perfect, results can be skewed. As an example, an article in *FDA Papers* states that "the organism used for measuring vitamin B_{12} activity will show a measurable response when dosed with less than one ten-billionth of a gram of the vitamin." Microbiological assays work more effectively than chemical methods for measuring B_{12} levels (and some other vitamins, such as biotin, B_6) because chemical analysis isn't sensitive enough to respond to the minute amounts of the vitamin contained in food.

WHY IS "GOOD MONEY FOR LITTLE WORK" CALLED THE *GRAVY TRAIN*?

A literal representation of a *gravy train* conjures up an unappetizing picture; gravy would be most unmanageable cargo, yet the expression has pleasant connotations. *Gravy train* was first recorded in the 1940s in the United States, but as early as the 1930s, *gravy* was slang for "easily obtained money."

Gravy train was borrowed directly from railroad terminology. A *gravy train* was an easy run with decent pay. Like extra, unearned money, gravy isn't necessary to survive, but it sure makes life more pleasurable.

In a chemical analysis, each vitamin in a given food must be measured separately. There are many chemical procedures to choose from, with catchy names like "gas-liquid chromatography" and "infra-red spectroscopy." Coleman explains a few different types of chemical analysis that are a little more comprehensible:

> Each measuring technique is based on a property of the vitamin. For example, riboflavin fluoresces [produces light when exposed to radiant energy] and is measured by a fluorometer or fluorescence detector. Vitamin C combines with a certain purple dye and makes it colorless. By measuring the amount of this dye that is changed from purple to colorless, we can calculate the amount of vitamin C present.

Despite the high-tech names, chemical analysis tends not to be as sensitive as old-fashioned microbiological methods, but it is cheaper and faster—and doesn't necessitate twenty thousand rats a year sacrificing their life for vitamin D.

—Submitted by Violet Wright of Hobbes, New Mexico.
Thanks also to Todd Grooten of Kalamazoo, Michigan.

what do coffee companies do with the caffeine left over from making decaffeinated coffee?

You wouldn't want them to throw away the caffeine, would you? If they flushed caffeine down the drain, it could end up in the ocean, and we wouldn't want to see the effect of a caffeine jolt upon killer sharks. It might be enough to turn a blowfish into a slayfish. If they discarded caffeine in the trash, could the caffeine wake up organic garbage in landfills?

We'll never have to worry about these contingencies, for the decaffeination process used in coffee yields pure caffeine, a marketable commodity. Coffee companies sell caffeine to soft drink companies (who need a little less now that many of them are selling caffeine-free sodas) and pharmaceutical companies.

When coffee companies justify the higher cost of decaf by citing processing costs, they rarely add the information that *they* get reimbursed on the back end for the caffeine they "eliminate."

—Submitted by Glenn Eisenstein of New York, New York.

what ingredient in diet drinks provides the one calorie? Why do some diet drinks have one calorie and some have none?

Let's solve the second part of this Imponderable first. Most diet drinks, ones containing aspartame or saccharin, contain less than one calorie per twelve-ounce can but more than one half-calorie. Whether or not the drink gets promoted as "zero calories" or "one calorie," then, usually depends upon how the marketer defines a serving size. Six ounces is the most popular serving size in the soft drink industry. If a twelve-ounce can of diet soda contains .66 of a calorie, then a six-ounce serving would contain .33 of a calorie. Because all figures are rounded off on nutritional labels, this soft drink can be advertised as containing zero calories.

A few soft drinks with mostly artificial sweeteners contain some natural flavorings, such as fruit juice, that contribute a meaningful number of calories (the flavored ginger ales marketed by Canada Dry and Schweppes contain a whopping two calories per six-ounce serving). But for the most part, the contributors to any caloric content in artificially sweetened drinks come from trace carbohydrates and other elements in flavorings.

So don't blame the sweetener if you binge on one of those fattening one-calorie diet drinks. NutraSweet brand, the most popular artificial sweetener for soft drinks, is made of two amino acids, which are, technically, protein components. So aspartame has the same caloric count, per gram, as the protein in a T-bone steak—four calories per gram. Fortunately for the dieter, the amount of aspartame in a soft drink doesn't compare to the weight of the protein in a steak. Phyllis Rosenthal, consumer affairs analyst for NutraSweet, explains:

> Since NutraSweet is 200 times sweeter than sugar, only a small amount is needed to sweeten products. Therefore, it contributes negligible calories to a product. A level teaspoon of sugar has 16 calories while the amount of NutraSweet with equivalent sweetness has 0.007 calories.
>
> One 12-ounce carbonated beverage contains approximately 180 mg of NutraSweet, a very small amount, which provides a negligible amount of calories.

Negligible, yes. But sometimes enough to push a drink over the precipice into one caloriedom. Of course, then the soft drink company can decide that

a serving size should really be three ounces, and the product magically becomes zero calories all over again.

—Submitted by Barry Long of Alexandria, Virginia.

how did Dr Pepper get its name?
Was there ever a real Dr. Pepper?

Yes, there was a real one, although he had a period after the "r" in "Dr." Dr. Charles Pepper owned a drugstore in Rural Retreat, Virginia, and employed a young pharmacist named Wade Morrison.

Unfortunately for Wade, Dr. Pepper wasn't too happy when a romance blossomed between the young pharmacist and his attractive daughter. Pepper nixed the relationship, and the dejected Morrison moved to Waco, Texas, and opened Morrison's Old Corner Drug Store.

Morrison hired Charles Alderton, a young English pharmacist, whose duties included tending the store's soda fountain. Alderton noted the waning interest of his customers in the usual fruit-flavored soft drinks and decided to blend several fruit flavors himself. Alderton finally hit upon a concoction that satisfied Morrison and his taste buds.

Word of mouth spread about Alderton's new creation, and in 1885, what we now know as Dr Pepper became a popular item at the Corner Drug Store. But what would they call the new drink? The Dr Pepper Company supplied the answer:

> Morrison never forgot his thwarted romance and often spoke fondly of Dr. Pepper's daughter. Patrons of his soda fountain heard of the affair, and one of them jokingly suggested naming their new fountain drink after the Virginia doctor, thinking it would gain his favor. The new drink became known as Dr Pepper. It gained such widespread favor that other soda fountain operators in Waco began buying the syrup from Morrison and serving it.

Even certified Peppers might not realize that Dr Pepper is the oldest major soft-drink brand and was introduced to a national constituency at the 1904 World's Fair Exposition in St. Louis, a conclave which was to junk food what Woodstock was to the musical counterculture. (The St. Louis Fair also featured the debut of the ice cream cone, as well as hamburgers and hot dogs served in buns.)

Morrison made a fortune and in that sense wreaked some revenge on the real Dr. Pepper, but he never regained the attentions of Miss Pepper. Alderton,

---

the actual originator of the drink, was content to mix pharmaceutical compounds, and was never involved in the operation of the Dr Pepper Company.

—Submitted by Barth Richards of Naperville, Illinois. Thanks also to Kevin Hogan of Hartland, Michigan, and Josh Gibson of Silver Spring, Maryland.

how and why did 7UP get its name?

7UP (a.k.a. Seven-Up) was the brainchild of an ex-advertising and merchandising executive, C. L. Grigg. In 1920, Grigg formed the Howdy Company in St. Louis, Missouri, and found success with his first product, Howdy Orange drink.

Intent upon expanding his empire, Grigg spent several years testing eleven different formulas of lemon-flavored soft drinks. In 1929, he introduced Seven-Up, then a caramel-colored beverage.

So where did the "7" and "UP" come from? Despite its identification as a lemon-lime drink, 7UP is actually a blend of seven natural flavors. According to Jim Ball, vice-president of corporate communications for Dr Pepper/Seven-Up Companies, Inc., all of the early advertisements for the new drink described a product that was uplifting and featured a logo with a winged 7. Long before any caffeine scares, 7UP was promoted as a tonic for our physical and emotional ills:

> Seven-Up energizes—*sets you up*—dispels brain cobwebs and muscular fatigue.

> Seven-Up is as pure as mountain snows ...

> Fills the mouth [true, but then so does cough syrup]—thrills the taste buds—cools the blood—energizes the muscles—soothes the nerves—and makes your body alive—glad—happy.

7UP's advertising has improved and changed markedly over the years, but its name has proved to be durably effective, even if customers don't have the slightest idea what "Seven-Up" means. Grigg could have chosen much worse. Contemplate sophisticated adults sidling up to a bar and ordering a bourbon and Howdy Lemon-Lime drink.

—Submitted by Richard Showstack of Newport Beach, California. Thanks also to Roya Naini of Olympia, Washington; Brian and Ingrid Aboff of Beavercreek, Ohio; and Jason M. Holzapfel of Gladstone, Missouri.

how do they keep soda in soft-drink machines from freezing in the winter?

You will be pleased to know that the soda companies have resisted the urge to solve this problem by inserting a little antifreeze in their concoctions. Instead, they keep their drinks fluid by controlling the temperature inside of vending machines.

According to Larry M. Eils, director of health, safety, and technical standards for the National Automatic Merchandising Association,

> The cabinet [that] is so well insulated to keep it cold also prevents the soda from freezing under certain conditions.

And what are those conditions? Coca-Cola's senior consumer affairs specialist, Melissa Packman, estimates that only in locations where the average temperature stays below twenty degrees Fahrenheit for weeks at a time is the insulation unlikely to keep the beverages stable, and she adds that along with the excellent insulation,

> the small amount of heat generated by the fan that circulates the air in the vendor will prevent product from freezing.

But if you encounter a soda machine outside a gas station in Montana, you'd be right to assume that insulation and a little fan wouldn't be enough to keep the beverage flowing. That's why in such cold locations, machines with two different systems are installed: a refrigeration unit to keep the sodas cold in warm or moderate weather; and a heating system to warm the drinks in cold weather.

Of course, "heating systems" can be high- or low-tech. In some cold-weather machines, the heaters are wired to a temperature sensor. When the electronic thermostats "tell" the heating unit that the temperature is below freezing, the heater is turned on, and cold, but not frozen, soda is available for guzzlers.

But our trusty representative from Pepsi-Cola, Chris Jones, told us that some vending-machine heating "systems" are not that elaborate, to say the least:

In extreme conditions, such as Montana, a sixty-watt lightbulb is often placed inside the insulated compartment. The heat from the bulb is often sufficient to maintain temperatures in the machine above freezing. The heat from the sign light ballasts and electronics in the coin mechanism and bill validator is sufficient to keep these systems functioning properly except in the most extreme conditions. These kits have thermostats and can control temperatures very accurately, but most operators prefer the less costly and simpler lightbulb. Sugared products freeze at around 23 to 26 degrees Fahrenheit, depending on the sugar content, while diet products freeze at 32 degrees.

—Submitted by Terry Newhouse of Downers Grove, Illinois.
Thanks also to Craig Townsend of Brooklyn, New York.

why is there an expiration date on many bottled waters?

Pepsico recently attracted much media attention when it announced that it was going to start putting expiration dates on its soft drinks. Consumers, who have been scared repeatedly by warnings from health officials about the dangers of virtually everything in the supermarket, suddenly had a new anxiety to confront: Is there something dangerous about "old" soft drinks?

There is no health hazard in an old Pepsi-Cola, let alone in bottled water. Pepsi chose to stamp expiration dates on its drinks to assure consumers that the product they purchase is wholesome (and, no doubt, to gain a competitive edge versus its main rival, Coca-Cola), and the same is true for the bottled-water industry. As C. E. Gostisha, corporate manager of packaging services at G. Heileman Brewing Company, put it, the expiration date is there to designate that the purchaser has bought a "fresh-tasting product."

In reality, the only serious degradation in water is likely to be the loss of carbonation in fizzy water. Sally Berlin, in quality control at Perrier, told *Imponderables* that most bottled water is given a two-year expiration date because some containers "break down" at that time. The water doesn't deteriorate so much as that the container itself, especially plastic bottles, will lend an off-taste.

A secondary advantage of expiration dates is to assure consumers that carbonated water will not be flat when opened. Plastic containers also allow carbonation to migrate through the container wall, reports Ruth A. Harmon, consumer affairs representative at Miller Brewing Company, and this problem is one of the key reasons why beer is sold in aluminum cans and glass bottles rather than plastic.

Some local regulations have led to expiration date stamping, too. Lisa Prats, vice president of the International Bottled Water Association, told *Imponderables* that New Jersey requires that all bottled waters, whether carbonated or still, must be stamped with an expiration date (two years after the bottling) in order to be sold in the state. Prats considers the regulation to be arbitrary and contends that if kept away from extreme temperatures, bottled water has an indefinite shelf life.

You'll find "Registered by the Pennsylvania Department of Agriculture" on virtually every prepackaged baked good sold in the U.S., because Pennsylvania doesn't allow any product sold in the state without such an inspection and this notice on the label. It's cheaper for national bakery and snack-food chains to include the notice on all their products than to make separate packages for Pennsylvania.

Although New Jersey doesn't demand credit on the label, the effect is the same. Any bottled-water company that intends to distribute its product in New Jersey will stamp all its bottles with an expiration date, as it is not feasible to separate out Jersey-bound bottles from the others.

—Submitted by Mark Kramer of San Diego, California.
Thanks also to James Marino of New York, New York.

why do chickens, unlike other fowl, have white meat and dark meat?

Other birds that we eat, such as quail, duck, or pigeon, have all dark meat. Chickens and turkeys are among a small group of birds with white flesh on the breasts and wings.

Birds have two types of muscle fibers: red and white. Red muscle fibers contain more myoglobin, a muscle protein with a red pigment. Muscles with a high amount of myoglobin are capable of much longer periods of work and stress than white fibers. Thus, you can guess which birds are likely to have light fibers by studying their feeding and migration patterns.

Most birds have to fly long distances to migrate or to find food, and they need the endurance that myoglobin provides. All birds that appear to have all white flesh actually have some red fibers, and with one exception, all birds that appear to be all dark have white fibers. But the hummingbird, which rarely stops flying, has pectoral muscles consisting entirely of red fibers because the pectoral muscles enable the wings to flap continuously.

The domestic chicken or turkey, on the other hand, lives the life of Riley. Even in their native habitat, according to Dr. Phil Hudspeth, vice president

of Quality and Research at Holly Farms, chickens are ground feeders and fly only when nesting. Ordinarily, chickens move around by walking or running, which is why only their legs and thighs are dark. They fly so little that their wings and breasts don't need myoglobin. In fact, the lack of myoglobin in the wing and breast are an anatomical advantage. Janet Hinshaw of the Wilson Ornithological Society explains why chicken and turkey musculature is perfectly appropriate:

> They spend most of their time walking. When danger threatens they fly in a burst of speed for a short distance and then land. Thus they need flight muscles that deliver a lot of power quickly but for a short time.

Next time you fork up an extra fifty cents for that order of all-white meat chicken, remember that you are likely paying to eat a bird that racked up fewer trips in the air than you have in an airplane.

—Submitted by Margaret Sloane of Chapel Hill, North Carolina. Thanks also to Sara Sickle of Perryopolis, Pennsylvania, and Annalisa Weaver of Davis, California.

why doesn't ham change color when cooked, like other meats?

Let's answer your Imponderable with a question. Why isn't ham the same color as a pork chop, a rather pallid gray?

The answer, of course, is that ham is cured and sometimes smoked. The curing (and the smoking, when used) changes the color of the meat. You don't cook a ham; you reheat it. According to Anne Tantum of the American Association of Meat Processors, without curing, ham would look much like a pork chop, with perhaps a slightly pinker hue.

Curing was originally used to preserve meat before the days of refrigerators and freezers. The earliest curing was probably done with only salt. But salt-curing alone yields a dry, hard product, with an excessively salty taste.

Today, several other ingredients are added in the curing process, with two being significant. Sugar or other sweeteners are added primarily for flavor but also to retain some of the moisture of the meat that salt would otherwise absorb. Sugar also plays a minor role in fighting bacteria.

For our purposes, the more important second ingredient is nitrites and/or nitrates. Sodium nitrate is commonly injected into the ham, where it turns into nitrite. Nitrite is important in fighting botulism and other microorganisms that spoil meat or render it rancid. Nitrites also lend the dominant taste we associate with cured meat (bacon wouldn't taste like bacon without nitrites).

WHY ARE THE EDGES ON THE LONG SIDE OF LASAGNA USUALLY CRIMPED?

Farook Taufiq, vice-president of quality assurance at The Prince Company, had no problem answering this Imponderable:

> The curls at the edge of lasagna strips help retain the sauce and the filling between layers. If the lasagna strips are flat, the sauce and the filling will slip out from between layers while cooking as well as while eating.

Now if someone will only invent a method of keeping lasagna (and its sauce) on our fork while it makes the arduous journey from the plate to our mouths, we would be most appreciative.

—Submitted by Sarah Duncan of Mars, Pennsylvania.

Unfortunately, for all the good nitrite does in keeping ham and other meats from spoiling, a controversy has arisen about its possible dark side. When nitrites break down, nitrous acid forms. Combined with secondary amines (an ammonia derivative combining hydrogen and carbon atoms), nitrous acid creates nitrosamines, known carcinogens. The debate about whether nitrosamines develop normally during the curing process is still swirling.

But nitrite was used to cure pork even before these health benefits and dangers were known, because it has always been valued as an effective way to color the meat. Nitrites stabilize the color of the muscle tissues that contain the pink pigment we associate with ham, as do some of the other salts (sodium erythorbate and/or sodium ascorbate) that help hasten the curing process.

Most curing today is done by a machine, which automatically injects a pickle cure of (in descending order of weight) water, salt, sweetener, phosphate, sodium erythorbate, sodium nitrate, and sodium nitrite. Usually, multiple needles are stuck in the ham; the more sophisticated machines can inject even bone-in hams. After this injection hams are placed in a cover pickle, where they sit for anywhere between a few days and a week. Hams that sit in cover pickle sport rosier hues than those that are sent directly to be cooked.

Hams are smoked at very low temperatures, under 200 degrees Fahrenheit, usually for five to six hours. Some cooked hams ("boiled ham" is a misnomer, as few hams are ever placed in water hotter than 170 degrees

Fahrenheit) are cooked unsmoked in tanks of water and tend to be duller in color. These hams are usually sold as sandwich meat.

One of the reasons why hams are beloved by amateur cooks is that, like (cured) hot dogs, they are near impossible to undercook or overcook. More than a few Thanksgiving turkeys have turned into turkey jerky because cooks didn't know when to take the bird out of the oven. Luckily, hams are precooked for us. We might have to pay for the privilege, but it is hard for even noncooks to ruin their texture or tarnish their pinkish color.

—Submitted by Dena Conn of Chicago, Illinois.

what are the skins of hot dogs made of?

Our correspondent wondered whether hot dog skins are made out of the same animal innards used to case other sausages. We recollect when we sometimes used to need a knife to pierce a hot dog. Don't hot dog skins seem a lot more malleable than they used to be?

Evidently, while we were busy chomping franks down, manufacturers were gradually eliminating hot dog skins. Very few mass-marketed hot dogs have skins at all anymore. Thomas L. Ruble of cold-cut giant Oscar Mayer explains:

> A cellulose casing is used to give shape to our hot dogs and turkey franks [Oscar Mayer owns Louis Rich] during cooking and smoking, but it is removed before the links are packaged. What may have seemed like a casing to you would have been the exterior part of the link that is firmer than the interior. This texture of the exterior of a link could be compared to the crust on a cake that forms during baking.

—Submitted by Ted Goodwin of Orlando, Florida.

why do lobsters turn bright red when boiled?

Wouldn't you get flushed if you were dumped into a vat of boiling water?

But seriously, folks, before the lobster gets boiled, it has a dark purplish-bluish color. But hidden in the exoskeleton of the lobsters (and shrimp) is a pigment called astaxanthin, in a class of compounds called carotenoids.

We spoke to Robert Rofen of the Aquatic Research Institute, and Ray Bauer of the biology department at the University of Louisiana at Lafayette, who explained that astaxanthin is connected to a protein. When you boil lobsters, though, the pigment separates from the protein and returns to its "true color," which is the bright red associated with drawn butter, white wine, and hefty credit-card bills.

—Submitted by Douglas Watkins, Jr., of Hayward, California. Thanks also to Laura Cannano of Englewood, Colorado; Kathleen Beecher of Naples, Maine; Jay Vincent Corcino of Panorama City, California; Emily Durling of Glens Falls, New York; Melissa and Dan Morley of Yelm, Washington; and Louis Lin of Foster City, California.

why does a loud bang or opening and closing the oven door sometimes make soufflés and cakes fall in the oven?

Tom Lehmann, bakery assistance director at the American Institute of Baking, told *Imponderables* that while a cake is being baked, the batter rises to a point slightly higher than its fully baked height. The baking powder in the batter produces gas that causes the leavening effect. "At a time when the batter is at its maximum height, but has not 'set' due to starch gelatinization and protein coagulation, the batter is very unstable." The cake is at its most fragile and delicate because, according to bakery consultant Dr. Simon S. Jackel, "the air cells holding the entrapped gases are very thin and weak."

Not all cakes will crash if confronted with a loud noise. But most will fall during this vulnerable time during the cooking process, and soufflés are always in danger. Joe Andrews, publicity coordinator for Pillsbury Brands, explains:

> The basic structure of a soufflé is developed by egg proteins, which are whipped into a foam and then set by baking. When whipping of the egg whites occurs, large pockets of air are trapped by the albumen, and in the process, this protein is partially denatured. The denaturation (or setting) continues (along with the expansion of the air bubbles) when the proteins are heated in the oven. If the oven is opened while this expansion is taking place, the air pressure change and temperature change can cause the whole structure to collapse.

The most common bang, of course, is the opening and closing of the oven door. Anyone near a loudspeaker at a rock concert knows that sound vibrations can be felt; a soufflé or cake can be pummeled by a nearby noise. Although cakes are usually hardier than soufflés, Andrews indicates the same problems that afflict soufflés also make cakes fall, especially if the primary source of leavening for the cake is beaten egg whites (e.g., angel food or chiffon cakes). Layer cakes contain more flour and the structure is formed

as much by starch gelatinization as egg denaturation, so they would not be as susceptible to falling when the door is opened—unless the door is opened too early in the baking process (during the first twenty minutes), before the cake structure has set.

Only when the internal temperature of the cake reaches a range of 160 to 180 degrees Fahrenheit is the cake out of the woods, because, as Jackel puts it, "the liquid batter is now converted to a solid cake structure."

—Submitted by Sherry Grenier of Amos, Quebec.

why do baked goods straight from the oven often taste (sickeningly) richer than after they are cooled?

When you ponder this Imponderable for a while, you realize there are only two approaches to the answer: one, the baked item really is different straight from the oven than it is ten or twenty minutes later, or two, that for some reason, the taster perceives the same item differently depending upon when it is consumed. It turns out there are some experts who subscribe to each explanation.

Bakery engineer Simon S. Jackel assures us that items really do change in structure after being cooled because of a process called "starch retrogradation." In raw flour, starch exists in a coiled, closed structure. When flour is baked into bread or cakes, the starch uncoils and opens up when exposed to the water in the dough and the high temperature of the oven.

When the product comes out of the oven, it starts to cool down, and the starch begins to revert or "retrograde" to a partially coiled structure. Most importantly for our purposes, when the starch retrogrades, it absorbs some of the flavors and locks them up in the coiled starch so that the taste buds cannot process them. In other words, less flavor is available to the consumer as the product cools. Jackel states that retrogradation continues until the product is stale.

Two other baking experts lay the "blame" for the noxiousness of just-baked products on our noses. Joe Andrews, publicity coordinator for Pillsbury Brands, explains:

> A great deal of taste perception is determined not only by the taste buds, but also by the olfactory senses.... When a food is hot, it releases many volatiles that the nose may perceive as sweet. Thus a cake may

seem sweeter when it is warm than when it is cold. The volatiles are perceived by the nose, both by sniffing through the nostrils and by the aromatics released in the mouth that make their way to the nose via a hole in the back of the mouth, the nasopharynx. We say we "taste" these, but in actuality we are smelling them.

Andrews believes that the "richness" our correspondent complains about may actually be sweetness.

Tom Lehmann of the American Institute of Baking also emphasizes the importance of volatiles in taste perception. Many aromatics, including spices, are simply too powerful when hot. Lehmann blames egg whites as particular culprits in making hot bakery items smell vile and taste noxious. Angel food cake, a dessert with a high concentration of egg whites, is particularly lousy hot, Lehmann says, because egg whites are volatiles that are released in heat and have to cool completely in order to avoid producing an unpleasant smell.

Of course, there is nothing mutually exclusive about the retrogradation and volatiles theories. Unlike arguments about genetic versus environmental factors in deviant behavior, or creationism versus evolution, the theories can coexist peacefully and respectfully. After all, bakers are engaged in an important and soul-lifting pursuit; it's hard to get bitter and angry when your life revolves around a task as noble as trying to concoct the perfect doughnut.

—Submitted by Connie Kuhn of Beaumont, Texas.

IS IT *KETCHUP* OR *CATSUP?*

It's *ketchup,* even though the English sailors who brought the condiment back from Singapore in the seventeenth century didn't have the slightest idea how the word should be spelled.

The original ketchup was the Chinese *ke-tsiap,* a pickled fish sauce. The Malays stole the name *(kechup)* but not the base—they used mushrooms instead of fish.

Americans added the tomatoes, and Heinz's first major product, tomato ketchup, was launched in 1876. Since the Chinese, Malay, English, and American incarnations all began with the "ke" sound, most word purists would rather say "hopefully" indiscriminately than be caught dead spelling the word *c-a-t-s-u-p*.

Why do ketchup bottles have necks so narrow that a spoon won't fit inside?

Heinz has had a stranglehold on the ketchup business in the Western world for more than a century, so the story of ketchup bottle necks is pretty much the story of Heinz Ketchup bottle necks. Ironically, although Heinz ads now boast about the *difficulty* of pouring their rather thick ketchup, it wasn't always so.

When Heinz Ketchup was first introduced in 1876, it was considerably thinner in consistency. It came in an octagonal bottle with a narrow neck intended to help impede the flow of the product. Prior to the Heinz bottle, most condiments were sold in crocks and sharply ridged bottles that were uncomfortable to hold.

Over the last 130 years, the basic design of the Heinz Ketchup bottle has changed little. The 1914 bottle looks much like today's, and the fourteen-ounce bottle introduced in 1944 is identical to the one we now use. Heinz *was* aware that as their ketchup recipe yielded a thicker product, it poured less easily through their thin-necked bottle. But they also knew that consumers preferred the thick consistency and rejected attempts to dramatically alter the by-now-familiar container.

Heinz's solution to the problem was the marketing of a twelve-ounce wide-mouth bottle, introduced in the 1960s. Gary D. Smith, in the communications department of Heinz USA, told *Imponderables* that the wide-mouth bottle, more than capable of welcoming a spoon, is the "least popular member of the Heinz Ketchup family." He added, though, that "its discontinuance would raise much fervor from its small band of loyal consumers who enjoy being able to spoon on" their ketchup.

In 1983, Heinz unveiled plastic squeeze bottles, which not only solved the pourability problem but also solved the breakability problem. The sixty-four-ounce plastic size, while mammoth, still has a relatively thin neck.

Until 1888, Heinz bottles were sealed with a cork. The neckband at the top of the bottle was initially designed to keep a foil cap snug against its cork and sealing wax. Although it was rendered obsolete by the introduction of screw-on caps, the neckband was retained as a signature of Heinz Ketchup.

—Submitted by Robert Myers of Petaluma, California.

why do onions make us cry?

Let's look at it from the point of view of the onion. An onion is perfectly polite to us until we start hacking at it with a knife. Alas, the act of cutting enlivens a gas, propanethiol S-oxide, which works in tandem with the enzymes in the onion to unleash a passive sulfur compound found within the onion. The result: As you cut, the gas moves upward and, combined with the water in your eyes, creates sulfuric acid.

Your eyes aren't happy, even if you are, and react in the only way they know how when irritated by a foreign substance—they start tearing. Rubbing your eyes with your hands is about the worst way to alleviate the problem, since your hands are likely full of the tear-inducing agent, too.

We've heard all kinds of folk remedies for onion tears, ranging from rubbing the onion with lemon to wearing gloves as you cut to donning scuba masks while performing surgery. But we're of the old school: no pain, no gain.

—Submitted by Jonathan Greenberg of Cedarhurst, New York. Thanks also to Candice Ford of Stanton, California; Jason Martin of Aiken, South Carolina; Megan Lavaty of Eden Prairie, Minnesota; Mindy Townsend of Aiken, South Carolina; Mike Wood of Sunset, Vermont; Greg Herr of Fremont, New Hampshire; Brian Dunne of Indianapolis, Indiana; Shira Ovidé of Dayton, Ohio; Andrew Bushard of Garretstown, South Dakota; and many others.

why is salt sold in round containers?

If the more specific question, "Why is Morton Salt sold in round containers?" is answered, all will be revealed, for Morton has always dominated the sales of household table salt. Until the twentieth century, Morton sold its salt in cloth bags. Moisture infiltrated the bags with ease, leading to hard lumps. Consumers had to break up the caked salt (pounding the bag on countertops and pummeling the lumps with mallets were two preferred methods), and then put the salt into their own glass jars.

Morton experimented with square cartons at the turn of the century, which were more durable than cloth, but still didn't solve the caking problem. Plus, salt stuck to the corners of the square box. The first round carton was introduced in 1900, but it had its own nuisance—a wooden spout that had to be plugged in between uses. Not until 1911 did Morton's research discover the wonders of adding a smidgen of magnesium carbonate, which

absorbed moisture and allowed the free flow of salt even in humid conditions (Morton now uses calcium silicate for the same purpose).

The only downside to the spiffy round container was that it cost more to manufacture than square ones, and the expense had to be passed on to consumers. The solution? Advertising.

The Morton Salt Girl, complete with umbrella, was introduced in a 1914 *Good Housekeeping* ad trumpeting the company's primary product benefit ("When it rains it pours"), and consumers proved willing to spend more money for free-flowing salt in the spiffy blue round containers that Morton calls "cans" internally. Morton has held on to a dominant market share, the slogan, and a similar-looking container ever since. The shape has become so identified with table salt that other brands, including generic and store-brand competitors, have copied the packaging.

But there's no inherent advantage to the round shape. In fact, Morton representative Don Monroe told *Imponderables* that the company still sells bales and bags of salt for institutional uses. For example, a pickler might buy a twenty-five-pound bale of salt and dump the whole bag into a vat to brine cucumbers. Morton and other companies sell specialty products, such as kosher, pickling, and tenderizing salt in rectangular packages.

—Submitted by Venia Stanley of Albuquerque, New Mexico. Thanks also to Ronald C. Semone of Washington D.C., and Kathy Farrier of Eugene, Oregon.

why can't you buy macadamia nuts in their shells?

Macadamia nuts do have shells. But selling them in their shells would present a serious marketing problem. Only Superman could eat them. According to the Mauna Loa Macadamia Nut Corporation, the largest producer of macadamias in the world, "It takes 300-pounds-per-square-inch of pressure to break the shell."

After macadamias are harvested, the husks are removed, and then the nuts are dried and cured to reduce their moisture. The drying process helps separate the kernel from the shell; without this separation, it would be impossible to apply the pressure necessary to shatter the shell without pulverizing the contents. The nuts then pass through counter-rotating steel rollers spaced to break the shell without shattering the nutmeat.

Of course, one question remains. Why did Mother Nature bother creating macadamias when humans and animals (even raging rhinos) can't break open the shells to eat them without the aid of heavy machinery?

—Submitted by Herbert Kraut of Forest Hills, New York.

what causes the green-tinged potato chips we sometimes find? Are they safe to eat?

Potatoes are supposed to grow underground. But occasionally a spud becomes a little more ambitious and sticks its head out. Nature punishes the potato by giving it a nasty sunburn.

But why do potatoes turn green rather than red? No, it's not out of envy. The green color is chlorophyll, the natural consequence of a growing plant being exposed to light. According to Beverly Holmes, a public relations representative of Frito-Lay, chip producers try to eliminate the greenies. But a few elude them:

> We store our potatoes in dark rooms and have "pickers" on our production lines who attempt to eliminate [green] chips as they move along on the conveyers because of their undesirable appearance. However, a few chips can make their way through the production process.

Is it harmful to eat a green-tinged chip? Not at all. Chlorophyll stains are as harmless as the green beer or green bagels peddled on St. Patrick's day, and chlorophyll contains no artificial ingredients.

—Submitted by Dr. John Hardin of Greenfield, Indiana.
Thanks also to Ed Hirschfield of Portage, Michigan.

why aren't there plums in plum pudding? And why is it called a pudding rather than a cake?

Even though it contains flour and is as sweet and rich as any cake, plum pudding cannot be classified as a cake because it contains no leavening and is not baked, but steamed.

Besides flour, plum pudding contains suet, sugar, and spices and is studded with raisins and currants. In early America, both raisins and currants were referred to as "plums" or "plumbs." And presumably because the raisins and currants were the only visually identifiable ingredients in the dessert (which traditionally was served after the pumpkin pie at Thanksgiving), the nickname stuck.

Come to think of it, plum pudding isn't the only weirdly named dessert served at Thanksgiving. We used to ask our parents where the meat was in mincemeat pie. Give us an honest pumpkin pie any day.

—Submitted by Bert Garwood of Grand Forks, North Dakota.

how do they print the "M&M" on M&M's chocolate candies?

While doing the radio promotional blitz for the first volume of *Imponderables,* we were inundated by questions about M&M's. Don't Americans have something less fattening to worry about?

We contacted the consumer affairs division of Mars Incorporated, and although they were as helpful and friendly as could be, mere flattery, bribery, and appeals to humanitarian instincts were not sufficient to pry away a definitive answer.

Despite wild theories to the contrary, the "M&M" *is* printed on each candy by machine, but the process is proprietary. The "M&M" insignia separates the Mars product from present and future knock-offs, so the company is understandably sensitive about guarding its technological secrets. Mars did reveal that the process is similar to offset printing, from which one could infer that the stamper does not strike the sugar coating of the candy directly. Many pill manufacturers print their logos with a similar offset technique.

We might as well take this opportunity to unburden our readers of some of the other weighty M&M Imponderables.

what does M&M stand for?

Two names—Mars and Murrie, the head honchos at M&M Candies in the early 1940s.

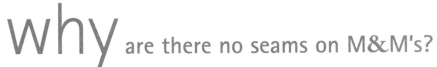

HAS ANYONE EVER LITERALLY *EATEN HUMBLE PIE?*

Yes—and voluntarily, too. In the sixteenth century, huntsmen ate more than their pride when they consumed *humble pie. Humble pie* was originally *umble pie,* a pastry made out of the heart, liver, and entrails of wild animals, usually deer. After a deer hunt, while the nobility enjoyed filets of venison in the master dining rooms of their palaces, the huntsmen had to content themselves with the more "umble" offering.

By the nineteenth century, *umble* became *humble.* James Rogers speculates that the transformation was self-conscious wordplay "on the humble station of people who ate umble pie."

why are there no seams on M&M's?

M&M's are coated by a process called "panning." After the individual pieces of chocolate are assembled, they are placed in a revolving pan that looks like a clothes dryer. As they rotate, the chocolates are sprayed with colored sugar. Cool air is blown into the pan to harden the coating. After evaporation, an even layer of dry shell is formed. The process is repeated several times to achieve the thickness that Mars desires. No seam shows because the coating is uniform and no cutting or binding of any kind was necessary to form the shell.

why are Oreos called "Oreos"?

Although the world's most popular cookie recently celebrated its seventy-fifth anniversary, the origin of its name is shrouded in mystery. It was first marketed in Hoboken, New Jersey, on March 6, 1912, as the Oreo Biscuit. In 1921, the name was changed to the Oreo Sandwich. In 1948, the same cookie was renamed the Oreo Creme Sandwich. Ultimately, in 1974, the immortal Oreo Chocolate Sandwich Cookie was born, a name that should last forever or until it is changed again, whichever comes first.

Of course, the lack of definitive facts has not deterred Oreo scholars from speculating on why those four magic letters were thrown together, Michael Falkowitz, a representative of Nabisco Brands Customer Relations, offers two of the more popular theories:

1. Mr. Adolphus Green, first chairman of the National Biscuit Company (founded in 1898 from the consolidation of the American Biscuit Co., the New York Biscuit Co., and the United States Baking Co.) was fond of the classics. The name "Oreo" is Greek for "mountain." It was said in early testing that the cookie resembled a mountain.

2. The name was derived from *or,* the French word for "gold." The original Oreo label had scrollwork in gold on a pale green background, and the product name was also printed in gold.

We have received several letters from Greek readers indicating that the Greek word for "mountain" is not *oreo* but *oros.* Furthermore, a Greek word that, phonetically, sounds like *oreo,* means "nice," "attractive," and even "delicious." Could this, and not Nabisco's "mountain theory," be the real answer to the origins of our number one cookie?

—Submitted by Ronald C. Semone of Washington, D.C.

how did chocolate bunnies for Easter come about?

No doubt, the chocolate bunny was introduced for the same reason that candy corn was introduced for Halloween—in order to make more money for the candy industry. Purveyors of nonessential gift items (flowers, greeting cards, candy) are always looking for new reasons to compel customers to buy their products. If one were inclined toward conspiracy theories, one could look on everything from Mother's Day to National Secretary's Week as nothing but blatant attempts to pry discretionary dollars from hapless citizens.

Chocolate bunnies date back to the 1850s in Germany. Along with bunnies, chocolatiers sold chocolate eggs and chickens. Switzerland, France, and other European chocolate producers followed soon after. Most of the chocolate companies we contacted felt that the bunnies symbolized renewal and rejuvenation, and were intended to symbolize the "Rites of Spring," not strictly Easter. As Charlotte H. Connelly of Whitman's Chocolates told us, the chocolate bunnies spread rapidly to the United States from Europe.

At present, chocolate eggs and bunnies help bridge the "chocolate gap" that befalls the confectionary industry between St. Valentine's Day and Mother's Day.

why are the sprinkles put on ice cream and doughnuts also called jimmies?

Do you call Coca-Cola "soda" or "pop"? Do you call those overstuffed sandwiches "hoagies" or "submarines" or "torpedoes" or "grinders"? The answer depends upon where you're from. Although we've received this "sprinkles" versus "jimmies" Imponderable before, we weren't too excited about researching another question about regional differences in food names until we received this e-mail from reader Netanel Ganin:

> I work at an ice cream store where there is currently a hot debate that has spread to most of my friends. Is the term "jimmies" for those sprinkles that people put on ice cream a racist term? What are its origins?

We had never considered "jimmy" to have racist connotations, so we decided to do some research. Dictionaries weren't of any help. The *American Heritage Dictionary's* definition was typical: "Small particles of chocolate or flavored candy sprinkled on ice cream as a topping. Etymology: origin unknown."

But quickly we could pinpoint the epicenter of jimmydom to the Mid-Atlantic and lower northeast United States. While ice cream parlors in San Francisco or Atlanta offer "sprinkles," in Boston or Providence, you are likely to be proffered "jimmies." You can buy jars of the cylindrical candy today, but most manufacturers hedge their bets, describing the product as "sprinkles/jimmies." Clearly, the terms are used interchangeably, although in some localities, "sprinkles" is used to describe all flavors but chocolate, and "jimmies" for chocolate sprinkles.

There might be confusion about what to call the darn things, but we can trace their history to one man—Samuel Born. A Russian immigrant, Born settled in San Francisco and within a few years made his first contribution to culinary culture—the Born Sucker Machine, which mechanically inserted sticks into hard candies—and lollipops entered the twentieth century.

In 1917, Born opened a candy store in Brooklyn, New York. He trumpeted the freshness of his confections by using the slogan "just born." Along the way, Born invented the chocolate coating for ice cream (the kind used to

**WHY WOULD ANYONE WANT TO CALL AN
EDIBLE SUBSTANCE *SHOOFLY PIE*?**

Because they are trying to shoo away flies, which are
inordinately attracted to the stuff, from messing with their
open pie made of a sugar and molasses filling.

—Submitted by Maurice H. Williams of Stewartstown, Pennsylvania.

enrobe soft ice cream at Dairy Queen, Carvel, Foster's Freeze, etc.). But for our
purposes, the key invention of Sam Born was the chocolate jimmy.

Nearly a century later, the grandchild of Sam Born and his cousin are co-
presidents of the company, now called Just Born. Janet Ward of Just Born
proudly proclaims:

> Yes, jimmies were invented at Just Born and we have in our archives
> some of the advertisements from that time period and containers with
> the word "jimmies" and the Just Born logo on them. Although there is
> nothing in writing to confirm it, it is commonly known here that the
> chocolate sprinkles were named after the Just Born employee who
> made them.

According to some sources, that employee was Jimmy Bartholomew, who
went to work at Just Born in 1930 and labored at the machine that produced
the chocolate pellets that have blanketed many an ice cream and doughnut
ever since, but the current co-president of the company, Ross Born, can't
positively confirm "Jimmy's" last name. Back then, most ice cream parlors
offered jimmies for free, so they proved most popular with customers who
wanted an extra sugar rush without springing for the cost of a sundae.

Just Born has gone on to sell many well-known products, including
Marshmallow Peeps, Mike and Ike, Hot Tamales, and Goldenberg's Peanut
Chews. But sadly, Ross Born told us: "We stopped producing jimmies in the
late 1960s; it wasn't one of our leading items."

The jimmies produced by Just Born were always brown, but not necessarily
chocolate—perhaps "chocolate-looking" would be more accurate. We've noticed
that most of the jimmies we've tasted have a waxy, gummy consistency and an
off-taste that doesn't resemble chocolate. Ross Born reveals a little-known secret about jimmies—they were probably never made from real chocolate:

> The forerunner of jimmies was a product called "chocolate grains,"
> which was a chocolate product. As I understand it, jimmies were non-

chocolate, at least the formula that I recall and is stated on the container we have in our archives. However, jimmies look like chocolate, and most people would call it that.

Assuming that jimmies were named after Mr. Bartholomew, we can assume he was of Irish descent. So then why is there a fear that "jimmy" is a slur against African Americans? Some etymologists speculate that "jimmy" is a variant of Jim Crow, the title character in a famous minstrel song performed by black performers (and white performers in blackface) in the 1830s. The song became so popular that anything that pertained to African Americans was dubbed "Jim Crow," especially in racist contexts. Later, "Jim Crow" came to refer to segregation of blacks from whites, including the infamous Jim Crow Laws, which were enacted in the South to preserve segregation after the Civil War.

But this theory seems lame to us. Although "jimmy" has many slang connotations in American English, from a crowbar to an engine made by General Motors, none of them refer specifically to blacks. We subscribe to a much simpler explanation. In most, although admittedly not all, places where sprinkles are called "jimmies," the reference is only to chocolate candies. Since their color resembles the complexion of many African Americans, it's easy to see how jimmies might have picked up the racist connotations, even if the inventor of jimmies intended only to honor his Irish American employee.

—Submitted by Kendra Delisio of Chelsea, Massachusetts. Thanks also to Rick Kot of New York, New York, and Netanel Ganin of Sharon, Massachusetts.

why doesn't sugar spoil or get moldy?

Virtually all living organisms can digest sugar easily. So why isn't sugar prone to the same infestation as flour or other kitchen staples?

Because sugar has an extremely low moisture content—usually about 0.02 percent—it dehydrates microorganisms that might cause mold. As John A. Kolberg, vice-president of operations at the Spreckels Division of Amstar Corporation, explains it, "Water molecules diffuse or migrate out of the microorganism at a faster rate than they diffuse into it. Thus, eventually the microorganism dies due to a lack of moisture within it." Sugar's low moisture level also impedes chemical changes that could cause spoilage.

All bets are off, however, if sugar is dissolved in water. The more dilute the sugar solution, the more likely yeasts and molds will thrive in it. Even exposure to high humidity for a few days will allow sugar to absorb enough moisture to promote spoilage and mold.

Storing sugar in an airtight container will retard the absorption of moisture even in humid conditions. If stored in an atmosphere unaffected by swings in temperature and humidity, sugar retains its 0.02 percent moisture level and has an unlimited shelf life.

—Submitted by Joel Kuni of Kirkland, Washington.

why is somebody who abstains from alcohol called a *teetotaler?*

Teetotal cropped up in England and the United States at about the same time, and it's impossible to discern who first coined it. Dick Turner, an Englishman, felt so strongly that *teetotal* was "his" word that his epitaph commemorates it:

> Beneath this stone are deposited the remains of Richard Turner, author of the word *teetotal* as applied to abstinence from all intoxicating liquors, who departed this life on the twenty-seventh day of October 1846, aged fifty-six years.

The early temperance movement in the United States didn't ask members to abstain from all liquor. Hard-drinking Americans were asked to forsake all but beer and wine. But as the movement progressed, it got more militant. *Teetotal,* whether first coined in England or the United States, was almost certainly a play on words, emphasizing the *t* in *total.* Somebody who signed up as a *teetotaler* gave up all alcohol, as opposed to the wishy-washy O.P. ("Old Pledge") members, who promised to abstain only from hard liquor.

why does a drunk person have *three sheets to the wind?*

Stuart Berg Flexner points out that whoever first coined this expression was undoubtedly a landlubber who mixed up his terminology. A "sheet" is not a sail but is the rope or chain attached to the lower corner of the sail. By shortening or extending the sheet, one can determine the angle of sail. If one loosens the sheet completely, the sail flaps and careers. If one loosens all three sheets, the ship would reel like a drunk person. Since "in the wind" had long referred to a ship out of control, *three sheets to the wind,* first in print in 1821, was the perfect way to describe the fool who has imbibed two too many.

Why do some tequila bottles have a worm on the bottom?

Because worms aren't good swimmers?

Those worms are a marketing concept designed to demonstrate that you've bought the real stuff. In order to research this topic with the rigorousness it deserves, we recently undertook a worm-hunting expedition to our local liquor store but found no tequila bottles with worms. We had heard about the worm-filled tequila bottles for years but had never found one ourselves.

So we beseeched one of our favorite liquor authorities, W. Ray Hyde, to help us. As usual, he knew the answer immediately.

We couldn't find worms in tequila bottles because they are included only in bottles of mescal, as he explains:

> Tequila and mescal are related beverages. Both are distinctive products of Mexico. While mescal is any distillate from the fermented juice of any variety of the plant *Agave Tequiliana Weber* (also known as *maguey*), tequila is distilled from the fermented juice of only one variety of this plant and only in one restricted area of Mexico. Therefore, all tequila is [technically] mescal but not all mescal is tequila.
>
> The worm is placed in bottles of mescal as an assurance that the beverage is genuine since the worm used lives only in the *Agave Tequiliana Weber* plant.

The worm is found only in the agave cactus in Oaxaca province. Natives of Oaxaca consider the worm a delicacy and believe that the agave possesses aphrodisiac powers.

Lynne Strang, of the Distilled Spirits Council of the United States, adds that the United States Food and Drug Administration approved the practice of allowing the worm in imported bottles of mescal and tequila in the late 1970s. Although actual worms were once the rule, most are now replicas, made of plastic or rubber.

—Submitted by Suzanne Bustamante of Buena Park, California.
Thanks also to Teresa Rais of Decatur, Georgia; Dianna Love of Seaside Park, New Jersey; Richard T. Rowe of Sparta, Wisconsin; Dana Patton of Olive Branch, Mississippi; Tim Langridge of Clinton Township, Michigan; Mary J. Davis of El Cajon, California; and Aaron Edelman of Jamesburg, New Jersey.

what did liquor distilleries do during Prohibition?

During the nearly fourteen years of Prohibition (the Eighteenth Amendment went into effect on January 17, 1920), most of the distilleries in the United States were put out of business. Many distilleries were small, family-run operations with colorful names that were forced to shutter their operations: The Chickencock distillery was converted into a seed company; Rolling Fork became a stockyard.

Some distilleries were a little luckier. According to Matthew J. Vellucci, library director of the Distilled Spirits Council of the United States, some distilleries were given reprieves by the federal government—they were licensed to produce industrial alcohol or whiskey for medicinal purposes.

But enterprising entrepreneurs found all kinds of ways to get booze to a parched America. The government demanded that industrial alcohol be denatured so that citizens would not drink what could easily blind or cripple them. Industrial alcohol was usually mixed with soap or lavender, but many included more dangerous agents, such as wood alcohol or carbolic acid. Some thrill-seeking alcohol cravers still bought the smuggled, adulterated liquor, and many paid for it with their lives.

The larger bootlegging outfits hired chemists to remove the poisons from industrial alcohol, according to Lynwood Mark Rhodes, who wrote "That Was Prohibition" for the August 1974 *American Legion* magazine. After the toxins were removed, to form a substance called "washed alcohol," the bootleggers added caramel for coloring and oil of rye or bourbon for flavoring. With luck, the final product tasted not unlike real whiskey:

> All such mixtures were offensive to the taste, but so what? They had
> unmistakable wallop. The thumbnail test was devised. Stick your thumb
> in your drink and if the nail stayed on it was safe. If you think I am
> being flip, this is exactly how those who drank the stuff spoke of it.

Obviously, alcohol consumers could not be fussy during Prohibition. Indeed, several large distilleries tried to make the best of a bad situation by producing new, nonalcoholic or low-alcoholic drinks. Many breweries tried to market "near beer," with only occasional success. Anheuser-Busch was forced to diversify out of the beer business during Prohibition but also foisted a legal, nonalcoholic drink called "Bevo" on the public as a way of utilizing its otherwise moribund breweries. Another company produced "wort," the cooled boiled mash that would ordinarily be the stage of the brewing process before the beer became alcoholic. The company was kind enough to package the wort with a cake of yeast, which promptly turned the wort into a spirit, but of course such a suggestion was not stated on the label.

Another alternative for lucky distilleries was to manufacture "medicinal spirits." Sean Thomas of the Seagram Museum wrote:

> Some companies, such as the Frankfort Distillery, remained open to produce medicinal spirits, which were available by prescription to treat various illnesses.

Suddenly, Americans were beset with maladies that could be treated only by a nip or two. And of course, the poor sufferer wasn't consuming illegal liquor to obtain a cheap high—it was medicine.

According to Rhodes, doctors wrote eleven million prescriptions for alcohol per year ("for medicinal purposes") during Prohibition. Theoretically, a "patient" was only allowed one half-pint every ten days, but drugstores became havens for the dispensing of spirits. Counterfeiters produced fake prescription pads and sold them for two dollars apiece, while motivated "sufferers" learned the fine art of forgery.

Even though the production of spirits by big distilleries was severely curtailed during Prohibition, Americans, displaying characteristic Yankee ingenuity, found ways to consume the stuff.

—Submitted by David Bang of Los Angeles, California.

why is 40 percent alcohol called 80 proof?

Before the nineteenth century, the technology wasn't available to measure the alcohol content of liquids accurately. The first hydrometer was invented by John Clarke in 1725 but wasn't approved by the British Parliament for official use until the end of the century. In the meantime, purveyors of spirits needed a way to determine alcohol content, and tax collectors demanded a way to ascertain exactly what their rightful share of liquor sales was.

So the British devised an ingenious, if imprecise, method. Someone figured out that gunpowder would ignite in an alcoholic liquid only if enough water was eliminated from the mix. When the proportion of alcohol to water was high enough that black gunpowder would explode—this was the *proof* of the alcohol.

The British proof, established by the Cromwell Parliament, contained approximately eleven parts by volume of alcohol to ten parts water. The British proof is the equivalent of 114.2 U.S. proof. More potent potables were called "over proof" (or o.p.), and those under 114.2 U.S. proof were deemed "under proof" (or u.p.).

The British and Canadians are still saddled with this archaic method of measuring alcohol content. The United States' system makes slightly more sense. The U.S. proof is simply double the alcohol percentage volume at 60°F. For once, the French are the logical nation. They recognize the wisdom in bypassing "proof" and simply stating the percentage of alcohol on spirits labels. The French method has spread to wine bottles everywhere, but hard liquor, true to its gunpowder roots, won't give up the "proof."

—Submitted by Robert J. Abrams of Boston, Massachusetts.

why hasn't beer been marketed in plastic bottles like soft drinks?

Now that the marketing of soda pop in glass bottles has pretty much gone the way of the dodo bird, we asked several beer experts why the beer industry hasn't followed suit. The reasons are many; let us count the ways:

1. Most beer sold in North America is pasteurized. According to Ron Siebel, president of beer technology giant J. E. Siebel Sons, plastic bottles cannot withstand the heat during the pasteurization process. Plastics have gained in strength, but the type of plastic bottle necessary to endure pasteurization would be quite expensive.

John T. McCabe, technical director of the Master Brewers Association of the Americas, told *Imponderables* that in the United Kingdom, where most beer is not pasteurized, a few breweries are marketing beer in plastic bottles. Siebel indicated that he would not be surprised if an American brewer of nonpasteurized (bottled) "draft" beer doesn't try plastic packaging eventually.

2. Breweries want as long a shelf life as possible for their beers. According to Siebel and McCabe, carbon dioxide can diffuse through plastic and escape into the air, while oxygen can penetrate the bottle, resulting in a flat beverage. Glass is much less porous than plastic.

3. Sunlight can harm beer. Siebel indicates that beer exposed to the sun can develop a "skunky" taste and smell; this is why many beers are sold in dark and semi-opaque bottles.

4. Appearance. We have no market research to support this theory, but we wouldn't guess that beer would be the most delectable looking beverage to the consumer roving the supermarket or liquor store aisle.

One might think that breweries would kill to package their product like soft drinks. Could you imagine the happy faces of beer executives as they watched consumers lugging home three-liter plastic bottles of suds?

—Submitted by John Lind of Ayer, Massachusetts.

how did they keep beer cold in the saloons of the Old West?

Just about any way they could. In the nineteenth century, guzzlers didn't drink beer as cold as they do now (the English often imbibed pints of ale warm, for goodness' sake, and still do—as do the Chinese) but even grizzled cowboys preferred their brew cool.

In colder areas of the West, saloons used to gather ice from frozen lakes in the winter. John T. McCabe, technical director of the Master Brewers

---

WHY DO WE CALL A GLASS OF LIQUOR A *HIGHBALL?*

Most likely, *highball* derived from late-nineteenth-century bartenders' lingo that called glasses *balls*. *Highball* replaced another expression, *long drink*, which at first referred to Scotch and soda and later applied to any whisky and soda served in a tall glass.

For the record, Charles Earle Funk believed *highball* was a signal to the locomotive engineer that it was safe to bypass a station without stopping. The signal was a large ball that would be hoisted to the top of a mast to indicate that there were no passengers, freight, or connecting trains awaiting it. Funk had a harder time explaining how the expression switched from the railroads to the barroom. Funk's best speculation was that a drunk train passenger might have noticed the resemblance between the floating ice atop a high glass and the ball atop the train signal. Not likely.

Association of the Americas, says that the harvest was stored in ice houses, "where the blocks of ice were insulated with sawdust. This method would keep ice for months."

Even where it wasn't cold enough for ice to form, many saloons in the Old West had access to cool mountain streams. Historical consultant William L. Lang wrote *Imponderables* that saloon workers would fill a cistern with this water to store and cool barrels of beer.

And if no cold mountain stream water was available? Phil Katz of the Beer Institute says that up until about 1880, many saloons built a root cellar to house beer. Usually built into the side of a hill, root cellars could keep beer below 50 degrees Fahrenheit.

And what if you wanted cold beer at home? According to Lang, "Beer was served in buckets or small pails, and often kids delivered the beer home from the saloons." Consumers in the mid-nineteenth century thought no more of bringing home "take-out beer" than we would think of ordering take-out Chinese food.

Beer expert W. Ray Hyde explains that we needn't feel sorry for the deprivation of Old Westerners before the days of refrigeration. In fact, those might have been the "good old days" of American beer:

> Beer in the Old West wasn't cold in the modern sense of the word—but it was refreshingly cool. Evaporation kept it that way. Beer in those days was packaged in wooden barrels, and the liquid would seep through the porous wood to the outside of the barrel, where it would evaporate. And basic physics explains the cooling effect of evaporation.
>
> Also, it should be noted that beer then was not artificially carbonated. The slight natural carbonation required only that it be cool to be refreshing and tasty. Modern beer, with its artificial carbonation, needs to be very cold to hide the sharp taste of the excess carbon dioxide.

—Submitted by Dr. Robert Eufemia of Washington, D.C.

why do beer steins have lids?

When we first started researching this Imponderable, we posed the mystery to the partisans of "rec.beer," the Internet newsgroup devoted to the love of lager. Soon we were offered all sorts of plausible theories. These are the four we liked the most. Which do you think makes the most sense?

1. **The lids keep the beer from overflowing.** As Tim Harper put it: "A good hearty pour down the middle, as you know, often results in suds runneth over. A quick capping, however, would keep all the nectar in the stein, to settle back down without a drop being wasted."

Ray Shea added that light, "hoppy" beers have a particular penchant for overflowing.

2. It keeps insects out of the beer. Bernie Adalem wrote: "Without a lid, you'd be picking flies off the top of the rich, creamy, foamy head of your favorite beer. Drinking a full glass on a hot day outdoors in the farm country will attract all manner of flying vermin that are drawn by the sweet malt aromas of a fine beer."

3. The lid helps keep the beer cool.

4. The lid keeps the beer fresher longer, and helps retain its head.

So, what do you think?

Believe it or not, the correct answer is number two. Although all the theories *might* have helped explain why lids were put on steins, the precipitating event was a law passed in Germany in the late nineteenth century that mandated that manufacturers put lids on all steins. Fred Kossen, a collector of steins, wrote *Imponderables:*

> I asked the same question when I first got into stein collecting more than twenty years ago. I found out that it was because of lack of sanitary conditions of the time and the common belief that insects, predominately flies, caused disease. After Europe experienced the plague, many steps were taken to minimize the spread of diseases.
>
> Germany had many drinking establishments, a good portion of them outdoors, especially during the Oktoberfest in Munich. Therefore, Germany passed a law prohibiting stein makers from producing them without lids.

Another cyberspace beer expert, John Lock ("The Beer Info Source" at http://www.beerinfo.com), notes that folks often enjoyed their beer outdoors in gardens, under the shade of a nearby tree. Unfortunately, Murphy's Law seemed to dictate that various flora and fauna floated straight into the suds. Lids proved to be effective in eliminating problems with plant, as well as insect, infestation.

The German law mandating lids caught stein makers unprepared. Most manufacturers were not equipped to make their own lids. Even the most renowned stein maker, Villeroy & Boch of Mettlach, Germany, realized that stoneware was their specialty and chose local pewterers to furnish their lids. Villeroy & Boch and most stein manufacturers offered consumers a choice of lids at many different price ranges. But even the humblest of lids did a fine job of keeping thirsty flies at bay.

—Submitted by Marie Beekley of Casper, Wyoming.
Thanks also to Myron Meyer of Sioux Falls, South Dakota.

Why is a diversion or distraction called a "*red* herring"?

The cliché "neither fish nor fowl" is actually shortened from another expression, "neither fish nor fowl nor good red herring." William and Mary Morris attribute the earlier expression to the dietary caste system of the Middle Ages. It was then believed that only the clergy were worthy of eating fish. The masses should be happy with fowl. And paupers would have to be happy with red herring. (Royalty, of course, could eat whatever they damn pleased.) *Neither fish nor fowl nor good red herring*, then, referred to something that wasn't suitable for anybody.

But why a *red* herring? Refrigeration was nonexistent in the Middle Ages, so paupers sun-dried and salted herring, and the fish turned dark. But those who also smoke-cured the herring found that the fish turned a bright red color. Hence, the red herring.

Smoked herring was popular among a few other groups as well. Sailors found smoked herring the perfect food to carry on long voyages (much as American cowboys relied on beef jerky), for it would remain edible long after fresh meat or fish.

But another, more elite group also found a valuable use for red herring: hunters. Smoked herring has a strong odor, and hunters found that it was the perfect substance to train young bloodhounds. Before dogs were expected to follow the tracks of foxes, hunters would drag the herring along a trail. If the hound showed talent at discerning the "herring trail," it would advance to real chases.

Two other groups, with more complicated motives, also used red herring to promote their purposes. Criminal fugitives in the seventeenth century would drag red herring to divert the trail of bloodhounds in pursuit. And animal-rights groups would sabotage hunting expeditions by laying red herring along the path of the fox-chasers.

Fooling the fox became known as "faulting the hounds." If a hound was diverted from a trail by a false clue, it would follow a real red herring. When we are distracted by a deliberately laid trap, we follow a metaphorical red herring.

why are nonsweet wines called "dry"?

"Sweet" makes sense. Sweet wines *do* have more sugar in them than dry ones. The main purpose of the sugar is to combat the acidity of the tannic and other acids found in wine.

Consumers may disagree sharply about how much sugar they prefer in wines, but can't we all agree that "dry" wine is just as wet as sweet wine?

Surprisingly, few of our wine experts could make any sense of "dry" either, but two theories emerged. Spirits expert W. Ray Hyde argues that the terminology stems from both the sensory experience of tasting and more than a little marketing savvy:

> Sugar stimulates the saliva glands and, leaves the mouth wet. Acids, on the other hand, have an astringent quality that leaves the mouth feeling dry. Winemakers know that the consumer prefers a "sweet" wine to a "wet" wine and a "dry" wine to an "acidic" wine.

But Irving Smith Kogan, of the Champagne News and Information Bureau, wrote *Imponderables* about an intriguing linguistic theory:

> ... the explanation is in the French language. *"Sec"* is a synonym of lean, and means *peu charnu* (without flesh), without softness or mellowness. This image appears in the English expression "bone-dry." *"Sec"* also means neat, as in undiluted, pure, bare, raw (*"brut"* in French), i.e., unsweetened.
>
> The issue of "dry" versus "sweet" is not the same for Champagne as for still wines. In the case of Champagne, the wine was originally labeled *"doux,"* which is the French word for sweet. But in the mid-nineteenth century a Champagne-maker named Louise Pommery decided to make a less-sweet blend and called it *"demi-sec"* (half-dry), which is still quite sweet but less so than the *doux.*
>
> Since her day, Champagnes have been blended progressively dryer (i.e., less and less sweet). So, today we have a range of Champagnes in ascending order of dryness, demi-sec, sec, extra-dry, brut, and extra-brut. The doux is no longer commercially available.

Kogan adds that the above etymology of "dry" does not apply to still wines, for which "dry" simply means not sweet. Notice our current bias for dry champagne. Now the "driest" champagne you can buy is half-bone-dry.

—Submitted by Bob Weisblut of Wheaton, Maryland.

how did the toque become the traditional chef's hat? Does it serve any functional purpose?

Most men, in their daily lives, wear neither rags nor haute couture. We don a pair of pants and a shirt—maybe a sports coat or suit and tie if the occasion warrants it. But in the kitchen, headwear has always been schizophrenic. Cooks wear either ugly but functional hair nets or *toques blanches* ("white caps"), smart-looking caps with tops long enough to camouflage the heads of the entire Conehead family. Isn't there a middle ground? Why can't a chef wear a baseball cap or a derby? Can there possibly be a logical function for the shape of toques?

As early as the Roman and Greek empires, master chefs were rewarded for their achievements by receiving special headwear. For the ancients, laurel-studded caps were the honor.

In France up until the seventeenth century, chefs were awarded different colored caps depending upon their rank. Apprentices wore ordinary skull caps. During the early eighteenth century, Talleyrand's chef required his entire staff to don the toque blanche for sanitary reasons. The toque blanche was designed not only to keep the chef's hair from entering food but to register any stains upon the white background.

But this original cap was flat. The high hat gradually gained popularity not as a fashion statement, not to hide Mohawk hairdos, but to provide some ventilation for the head, as chefs frequently work under extremely hot conditions.

Viennese chef Antonin Careme, not willing to leave well enough alone, decided that the toque blanche needed still more oomph. He put a piece of round cardboard inside his toque to give the cap a stiffer, more dashing appearance. The cardboard has been replaced today by starch.

The toque blanche is no more functional than a hair net, and almost as silly looking. But as Shriners or Mouseketeers can testify, any hat bestowed upon someone as an honor is likely to be worn proudly by the recipient, regardless of how funny it looks.

—Submitted by William Lickfield of Hamburg, New York.

why does the ice found in restaurants often have holes in the cubes? Why do they sometimes have dimples?

With few exceptions, restaurants can't charge for ice, yet many restaurants use hundreds or even thousands of pounds of the stuff per day. Cubes with holes cost less to manufacture because, as restaurant consultant Henry Verden points out, the majority of time and energy required to freeze an ice cube is spent freezing its center.

The commercial ice machines that create "holey" ice can make anywhere from 400 to 24,000 pounds in twenty-four hours. With the help of Verden and James S. Boardman of the Packaged Ice Association, we'll provide a simplified explanation of how these machines work.

Inside a large metal cylinder with fittings along the top, bottom, and sides, lie many vertically inclined tubes that are open at the top and bottom. Water is pumped to the top of the cylinder and allowed to flow inside the tubes. At first, the water drops to the bottom, returning to an open tank only to be pumped up again.

But a refrigerant, usually freon or ammonia, is introduced so that the water forms as ice and sticks to the interior surfaces of the tube. The thickness of the ice can be adjusted by how long the water is allowed to run; on a timing cycle, the water pump and refrigerant are stopped, and the sides of the tube are heated sufficiently to cause the ice to drop out of the cubes. The portions of the tubes that were not filled become "the holes."

Occasionally, you will find finger-shaped cubes in restaurants. The machines that manufacture these cubes contain a grid of finger-shaped metal protrusions. These are lowered repeatedly into water-building layers of ice much as a hand-dipped candle is made. When sufficient ice has built up, heating elements in the protrusions warm, melting the ice closest to the metal, causing the ice to drop down and leaving the hole intact.

Dimpled ice cannot be manufactured as quickly or in as much quantity as ice with holes, so the dimples are there more for aesthetics than economy. Instead of water being sprayed into tubes, here it is placed on a plate that looks like an upside-down waffle iron. The liquid refrigerant is placed on the top while water is sprayed into the "pits," which are upside down. The water

freezes to the sides and top of the small chambers. When heat is introduced into the chamber where the refrigerant was, the ice melts away, falls onto a screen, and is moved away from the water. The dimple is formed at the center and bottom because this is the place where the water is always flowing; thus, it will always be the last to freeze.

—Submitted by Charles Myers of Ronkonkoma, New York. Thanks also to Karen Fraser of Merritt, British Columbia, and Michael Hamm of Brooklyn, New York.

4

PROCEDURES AND TRADITIONS

Why are there 21 guns in a military salute? Why do auctioneers talk so rapidly? Why do cowboy hats have a dent in the top? Why is a blue ribbon used to designate first prize? Sometimes there are wonderful stories behind the rituals of life. And sometimes traditions take hold for no good reason at all.

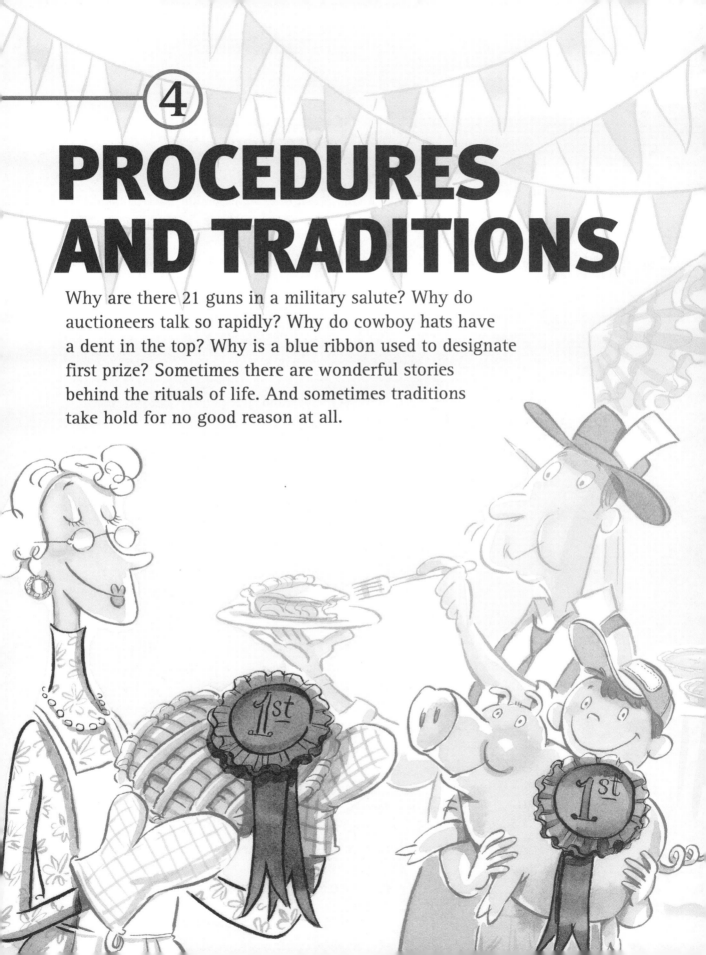

If the ZIP code defines the city and state, why do we have to include both on envelopes? Or do we?

Jack Belck, the true zealot who posed this Imponderable, gave as his return address his full name, a street number, and 48858, with this note: "The above address is guaranteed to work."

Evidently it did. He received a letter we wrote to him in that lovely town, 48858.

But the question is a good one, so we asked our friends at the USPS to respond. And they were a tad cranky.

Yes, they will deliver letters addressed by the Belcks of the world, but they aren't too happy about it for a couple of reasons. First of all, many people inadvertently transpose digits of the ZIP code. The city and state names then serve as a cross check. Without the city and state names, the letter would be returned automatically to the sender. Even if it is delayed, the postal service will reroute a letter with an incorrect ZIP code.

Second, Mr. Belck isn't quite right about one of his premises. In rural areas, more than one municipality might share the same ZIP code. City names can thus be of assistance to the local post office in sorting and delivering the mail.

—Submitted by Jack Belck of 48858.

do the digits in a Social Security number have any particular meaning?

Now that the Social Security number has become a virtual citizenship identification number, paranoid types have become convinced that each digit is another way for Uncle Sam to poke into our private lives. No, the government can't tell by looking at our Social Security number whether we are registered Democrats or Republicans, whether we are in the highest income-tax bracket or are on welfare, or even whether we have committed a crime.

Under the current system, the first three digits of a Social Security number indicate the state of residence of the holder at the time the number was issued. The remaining digits have no special meaning.

Before 1973, Social Security numbers were assigned by local Social Security offices. The first three digits were assigned based on the location of the Social Security office rather than the residence of the issuee. Opportunists used to scoop up several different Social Security numbers by applying for cards at several different offices, which led to the current practice of issuing all numbers from the central Social Security office in Baltimore. According to Dorcas R. Hardy, commissioner of Social Security, the first three digits of a person's Social Security number are now determined by the ZIP code of the mailing address shown on the application for a Social Security number.

Although the first three digits of the Social Security number do not correspond exactly to the first three digits of that state's ZIP codes, the lowest Social Security numbers, like their ZIP code counterparts, start in New England and then get progressively larger as they spread westward. Numbers 001-003 are assigned to New Hampshire, and the highest numbers assigned to the 50 states are New Mexico's 585. The Virgin Islands (580), Puerto Rico (580-584, 596-599), Guam (586), American Samoa (586), and the Philippine Islands (586) are also assigned specific three-digit codes.

Until 1963, railroad employees were issued a special series of numbers starting with the digits 700-728. Although this practice is now discontinued, these numbers remain the highest ever issued. No one has ever cracked the 729-plus barrier.

—Submitted by Douglas Watkins, Jr., of Hayward, California. Thanks also to Jose Elizondo of Pontiac, Michigan; Kenneth Shaw of San Francisco, California; and Rebecca Lash of Ithaca, New York.

WHAT HAPPENS TO YOUR SOCIAL SECURITY NUMBER WHEN YOU DIE? HOW AND WHEN, IF EVER, IS IT REASSIGNED?

You don't need to be a hall-of-famer to get this number retired. John Clark, regional public affairs officer of the Social Security Administration, explains:

> Each number remains as unique as the individual it was first assigned to. When someone dies, we retire the number.
>
> The first number was issued in 1936. The nine-digit system has a capacity for creating nearly one billion possible combinations. A little more than a third of the possible combinations have been issued in the fifty-five years since the first number was issued.

It's comforting to know that you can take *something* with you.

—Submitted by Albert Mantei of Crystal, Minnesota.

why was April 15 chosen as the due date for taxes?

It wasn't ever thus. In fact, the original filing date for federal taxes, as prescribed in the Revenue Act of 1913, was March 1. A mere five years later, the deadline moved back; until the Internal Revenue Code of 1954 was approved on August 16, 1954, midnight vigils were conducted on *March* 15. Taxpayers who paid on a fiscal year were also given a month's extension in 1954, so that they now filed on the fifteenth day of the fourth month, instead of the third month, after their fiscal year was over. In fact, all federal returns, with the exception of estates and trusts, are now due on April 15, or three and one-half months after the end of the fiscal year.

Were these dates plucked out of thin air? Not really. The IRS wants to process returns as early in the year as possible. In the 1910s, when most tax returns were one page long, it was assumed that after a wage earner totaled his or her income, the return could be filled out in a matter of minutes. Why wait until after March 1? As anyone who now is unfortunate enough to make a so-called living knows, the IRS form isn't quite as simple as it used to be. The 1040 is no easier to decipher than the Dead Sea Scrolls.

Kevin Knopf of the Department of the Treasury was kind enough to send us transcripts of the hearings before the House Ways and Means Committee in 1953 pertaining to the revision of the Internal Revenue Service Code. Now we don't necessarily expect the contents of all hearings in the legislature to match the Lincoln-Douglas debates in eloquence and passion, but we were a little surprised to hear the original impetus for the legislation cited by a sponsor of the 1954 IRS revision, the Honorable Charles E. Bennett of Florida, who argued for changing the due date from March 15 to April 15:

> The proposal to change the final return date from March 15 to April 15 was first called to my attention by the Florida Hotel Association. They advised that many taxpayers must cut their winter vacations short to return to their homes and to prepare their tax returns for filing before March 15. They pointed out that changing the deadline to April 15 would help their tourist trade as well as that of other winter tourist areas in the United States such as California, Arizona, Maine, and Vermont.

This is why we changed the tax code? Probably not. A succession of witnesses before the House Ways and Means Committee—everybody from the Georgia Chamber of Commerce to the American Federation of Labor to

the American Cotton Manufacturers Institute—argued for moving back the date of tax filing. In descending order of importance, here were their arguments.

1. Taxpayers need the extra time to compile their records and fill out the tax forms.

2. The IRS needs more time to process returns efficiently. If the date were moved back to April 15, the IRS could rely more on permanent employees rather than hiring temporary help during the crunch. Perhaps so many taxpayers wouldn't file at the deadline date if they had an extra month.

3. An extension would also ease the task of accountants and other tax preparers.

4. It would make it easier for people who have to estimate their tax payments for the next year to make an accurate assessment.

5. It would allow businesses that have audits at the end of the year time to concentrate on their IRS commitments.

The 1954 bill passed without much opposition. The April 15 date has proved to be workable, but it is no panacea. Any fantasy that most taxpayers wouldn't procrastinate until the last minute was quickly dispelled.

This drives the IRS nuts, because most taxpayers receive refunds. The basis of the free-market economic system is supposed to be that people will act rationally in their economic self-interest. If this were true, taxpayers with refunds would file in January in order to get their money as fast as possible, since the IRS does not pay interest on money owed to the taxpayer.

The IRS would love to find a way to even out its workload from January through April. In reality, most returns are filed either in late January and early February or right before the April 15 deadline. A 1977 internal study by the IRS, investigating changing the filing dates, said that "These peaks are so pronounced that Service Centers frequently have to furlough some temporary employees between the two workload peaks."

Before the code changed in 1954, the IRS experienced the same bimodal pattern—the only difference was that the second influx occurred in mid-March instead of mid-April. If the due date was extended a month, the second peak would probably occur in mid-May.

The IRS has contemplated staggering the due dates for different taxpayers, but the potential problems are huge (e.g., employers would have to customize W-2s for employees; single filers who get married might end up

with extra-short or extra-long tax years when they decided to file a joint return; if a change in the tax rate occurs, when does it take effect?; would states and cities conform to a staggered schedule?) and probably not worth the effort. The same study contemplated extending the filing date (while offering financial incentives for filing early) but also concluded that the potential traps outweigh the benefits.

The IRS knows that many taxpayers deliberately overwithhold as a way to enforce savings, even though they will not collect any interest while the government holds their money. These overwithholders, flouting the advice of any sensible accountant, are most unlikely to be tempted to file early because of a possible $10 bonus from the IRS.

Now that the IRS grants an automatic two-month extension on filing to anyone who asks for it, even tax preparers are generally against changing the April 15 deadline. Henry W. Bloch, the president of H&R Block, has penetrated the very soul of his customer, and in 1976 offered this appraisal in the *Kansas City Times:*

> We get people in our office at 10 or 11 the night of April 15 and then they run down to the post office. If you extended that April 15 deadline to June 30, in my opinion, all they're going to do is wait until June 30 instead of April 15.... The reason for that is simply the old American habit of putting things off.

—Submitted by Richard Miranda of Renton, Washington.
Thanks also to Edward Hirschfield of Portage, Michigan.

how did the expression "two bits" come to mean 25 cents? How did "two-bit" come to mean "cheap"?

"Bit," which has long been English slang for any coin of a low denomination, derived from the Old English word, *bite,* which meant a small bit or morsel. Before the American Revolution, English money was in short supply, so coins from all over Europe, Mexico, and South America were equally redeemable. Sailors and new immigrants assured a steady stream of non-English coins into the new country. Because there were so many different denominations, coins were valued by their weight and silver and gold content.

Spanish and Mexican coins were especially popular in early America. "Bit" became a synonym for the Spanish and Mexican coin, the *real.* The real was equivalent to one-eighth of a peso, or twelve and one-half cents. Particularly in the southwestern United States, where the Mexican influence was most strongly felt, Americans rarely called a quarter anything else but "two bits." Recognizing that U.S. coinage had no equivalent to one bit, Southwesterners usually referred to ten cents as a "short-bit" and fifteen cents as a "long-bit," and occasionally still do so today.

In Spain, a bit was an actual coin. Pesos were manufactured so that they could literally be cut apart. A peso, which equaled eight bits, could be cut in half to become two four-bit pieces. Cut in fourths, a peso became four two-bit pieces.

How did the term "two-bit" become synonymous with cheapness and tackiness (especially because, obviously, one bit is cheaper than two)? The first known use of this meaning, according to word whiz Stuart Flexner, was in 1856, referring to a saloon that was so cheap that a good, stiff drink could be had for ... two bits.

—Submitted by John A. Bush of St. Louis, Missouri.
Thanks also to Tom and Marcia Bova of Rochester, New York.

why is "$" the symbol for the U.S. dollar?

We remember reading a numismatics book thirty years ago that stated the $ was derived from a stylized version of an "S" super-imposed on a "U." We never understood this explanation, because we could never see the "U" in the dollar sign. A professor of the history of mathematics at the University of California, Dr. Cajori, spent decades researching this Imponderable in the 1910s and 1920s. He concluded:

> The American dollar sign, popularly supposed to be derived from the letters U and S, is, instead a lineal descendant of the Spanish abbreviation "ps" for "pesos."

Cajori pored through hundreds of early colonial manuscripts and could find no proof of the "US" theory.

So, the official position of the Department of Treasury is that the "S" gradually came to be written over the "P" in the "pesos" abbreviation,

> developing a close equivalent of the $ mark, which eventually evolved [into our current mark]. The $ was widely used before the adoption of the United States dollar in 1785.

Indeed, Spanish and Mexican coins were the main currency in many parts of the United States in the eighteenth and much of the nineteenth centuries.

We're still not sure if the $ looks any more like a P and an S than a U and an S, but at least the abbreviation of "pesos" makes more sense than a shortening of "United States."

—Submitted by Ed Booth of Chico, California. Thanks also to Ken Shafer of Traverse City, Michigan; Josh Siegel of Fountain Valley, California; and Barry Kaminsky of Brooklyn, New York.

why do mayors hand out keys to their city?

We've all seen those silly ceremonies on TV where a grinning mayor hands a three-foot-long key to a minor celebrity as flashbulbs pop. But we have always wondered: Why does the recipient need a key to the city? He's already *in* the city.

Actually, this ceremony has legitimate historical antecedents. In the Middle Ages, most large cities were walled. Visitors could enter and exit only through gates that were locked at sundown and reopened at dawn.

Mike Brown of the United States Conference of Mayors told *Imponderables* that gatekeepers used keys to open and close the gates. These keys were closely guarded, for they were crucial in preventing military attacks. If a key was passed to an honored visitor, it indicated total trust in him.

Today, a mayor no longer threatens the security of her domain by handing out the key to the city, and the honor is more likely a public relations stunt than in gratitude for service or accomplishment. But the meaning is the same. By handing out the key to the city, the mayor says, "Come back anytime and you don't even have to knock. We trust you."

who decides where the boundary line is between oceans? If you're on the ocean, how do you know where that line is?

Much to our shock, there really is a "who." The International Hydrographic Organization (IHO) is composed of about seventy member countries, exclusively nations that border an ocean (eat your heart out, Switzerland!). Part of their charter is to assure the greatest possible uniformity in nautical charts and documents, including determining the official, standardized ocean boundaries.

All of the oceans of the world are connected to one another—you could theoretically row from the Indian Ocean to the Arctic Ocean (but, boy, would your arms be tired). No one would dispute the borders of the oceans that hit a landmass, but what about the 71 percent of the earth that is covered by sea?

The IHO issues a publication, "Limits of Oceans and Seas," that determines exactly where these water borders are located, but is used more by researchers than sailors. Michel Huet, chief engineer at the International Hydrographic Bureau, the central office of the IHO, wrote to *Imponderables* and quoted "Limits of Oceans and Seas":

> The limits proposed ... have been drawn up solely for the convenience of National Hydrographic Offices when compiling their Sailing Directions, Notices to Mariners, etc., so as to ensure that all such publications headed with the name of an ocean or sea will deal with the same area, and they are not to be regarded as representing the result of full geographic study; the bathymetric [depth measurements of the ocean floor] results of various oceanographic expeditions have, however, been taken into consideration so far as possible, and it is therefore hoped that these delimitations will also prove acceptable to oceanographers. These limits have no political significance whatsoever. Therefore, the boundaries are established by common usage and technical considerations as agreed to by the Member States of the IHO.

Essentially, a committee of maritime nations determines the borders and titles for the oceans.

How would the IHO decide on the border between the Atlantic and Pacific? A somewhat arbitrary man-drawn line was agreed upon that extends from Cape Horn, on the southern tip of South America, across the Drake Passage to Antarctica. A specific longitude was chosen, so the border goes exactly north-south from the cape to Antarctica.

Of course, there are no YOU ARE LEAVING THE PACIFIC OCEAN, WELCOME TO THE ATLANTIC OCEAN signs posted along the longitude. But a sailor with decent navigational equipment could determine which ocean he was in—likewise with the boundaries between other oceans.

Unlike the United Nations, most of the time the IHO does not become embroiled in political disputes, presumably because the precise location of the oceans' borders has no commercial or military implications. Disputes are not unheard of, though. For example, Korea and Japan recently tussled about

the designation of the sea that divides their countries. Traditionally, the body of water has been called the Sea of Japan, but Korea wanted it changed to "East Sea."

Perhaps we were dozing during some of the year 2000 hoopla, but much to our surprise, the IHO was involved with a rather important event in that year—the debut of a new ocean. The southernmost parts of the Pacific, Atlantic, and Indian oceans (including all the water surrounding Antarctica), up to 60 degrees south, were dubbed the "Southern Ocean." The name was approved by a majority of the IHO and went into effect in 1999, with Australia among the dissenters. Why wasn't this a bigger deal than Y2K?

−Submitted by Bonnie Wootten of Nanaimo, British Columbia.
Thanks also to Terry Garland, via the Internet.

if all time zones converge at the North and South Poles, how do they tell time there?

Imagine that you are a zoologist stationed at the South Pole. You are studying the nighttime migration patterns of emperor penguins, which involves long periods observing the creatures. But you realize that while you watch them waddle, you are in danger of missing a very special episode of *The Bachelor* on television unless you set that VCR for the right time. What's a scientist to do?

Well, maybe that scenario doesn't play out too often, but those vertical line markings on globes do reflect the reality. All the time zones do meet at the two poles, and many *Imponderables* readers wonder how the denizens of the South Pole (and the much fewer and usually shorter-term residents of the North Pole) handle the problem.

We assumed that the scientists arbitrarily settled on Greenwich Mean Time (the same time zone where London, England, is situated), as GMT is used as the worldwide standard for setting time. But we found out that the GMT is no more! It is now called UTC (or Coordinated Universal Time—and, yes, we know that the acronym's letter order is mixed up). The UTC is often used at the North Pole as the time standard, and sometimes at the South Pole.

We veered toward the humanities in school partly because the sciences are cut and dried. If there is always a correct answer, then teachers could always determine that we came up with the wrong answer. Science students were subjected to a rigor that we were not.

But when it comes to time zones, the scientists at the poles are downright loosey-goosey: They use whatever time zone they want! We spoke to Charles Early, an engineering information specialist at the Goddard Space Flight Center in Greenbelt, Maryland, who told us that most scientists pick the time zone that is most convenient for their collaborators. For example, most of the flights to Antarctica depart from New Zealand, so the most popular time at the South Pole is New Zealand time. The United States' Palmer Station, located on the Antarctic Peninsula, sets its time according to its most common debarkation site, Punta Arenas, Chile, which happens to share a time zone with Eastern Standard Time in the United States. The Russian station, Volstok, is coordinated with Moscow time, presumably to ease time-conversion hassles for the comrades back in Mother Russia.

We researched this subject earlier to answer a question from a child who wondered what time Santa Claus left the North Pole in order to drop off all

HOW DO YOU TELL DIRECTIONS AT THE NORTH AND SOUTH POLES?

You think time zones are a problem, how about giving directions to a pal at the South Pole. By definition, every direction would start with "Head north."

In practical terms, though, the distances aren't great at the science stations, and it's not like there are suburbs where you can get lost. But scientists do have a solution to this problem, as Nathan Tift, a meteorologist who worked at the Amundsen-Scott South Pole Station explains:

> If someone does talk about things being north or south here, they are most likely referring to what we call "grid directions," as in grid north and grid south. In the grid system, north is along the prime meridian, or 0 degrees longitude, pointing toward Greenwich, England, south would be 180 longitude, east is 90 degrees, and west is 270 degrees. It's actually quite simple. Meteorologists like myself always describe wind directions using the grid system. It wouldn't mean much to report that the wind at the South Pole always comes from the north!

—Submitted by Michael Finger of Memphis, Tennessee.

his presents around the world. Based on our lack of goodies lately, we think Santa has been oversleeping big time, and now we know that time-zone confusion is no excuse.

—Submitted by Thomas J. Cronen of Naugatuck, Connecticut.
Thanks also to Christina Lasley of parts unknown; Jack Fisch of Deven, Pennsylvania;
Dave Bennett of Fredericton, Ontario; Paul Keriotis, via the Internet;
Peter Darga of Sterling Heights, Illinois; Marvin Eisner of Harvard, Illinois;
Jeff Pontious of Coral Springs, Florida; and Dean Zona, via the Internet.

do the police really make chalk outlines of murder victims at the scene of the crime? Why do they use chalk?

As soon as law enforcement officials descend upon a murder scene, a police photographer takes pictures of the corpse, making certain that the deceased's position is established by the photographs. The medical examiner usually wants the body as soon as possible after the murder; the sooner an autopsy is conducted, the more valuable the information the police are likely to obtain.

Right before the body is removed, the police do indeed make an outline of the position of the victim. More often than not the body is outlined in chalk, including a notation of whether the body was found in a prone or supine posture.

A police investigation of a murder can take a long time, too long to maintain the murder site as it appeared after the murder. Forensic specialists cannot rely on photographs alone. Often, the exact position of the victim can be of vital importance in an investigation. By making an outline, the police can return to the murder scene and take measurements which might quash or corroborate a new theory on the case. Outline drawings may also be used in the courtroom to explain wound locations, bullet trajectories, and blood trails.

Herbert H. Buzbee of the International Association of Coroners and Medical Examiners told *Imponderables* that chalk is not always used to make outlines. Stickum paper or string are often used on carpets, for example, where chalk might be obscured by the fabric. Carl Harbaugh of the International Chiefs of Police says that many departments once experimented with spray paint to make outlines, but found that paint traces were occasionally found on the victim, confusing the forensic analysis.

The ideal outline ingredient would be one that would show up, stay put, and do no permanent damage to any surface. Unfortunately, no such ingredient exists. Chalk gets high marks for leaving no permanent markings, but is not easily visible on many surfaces. Tape and string (which has to be fastened with tape) have a tendency to mysteriously twist out of shape, especially if they get wet.

None of these flaws in the markers would matter if murder victims were considerate enough to die in sites convenient to the police. Harbaugh says that on a street or highway any kind of outline will do. But what good is a chalk outline on a bed covered with linens and blankets?

—Submitted by Pat O'Conner of Forest Hills, New York.

why do police officers hold flashlights with an overhand grip?

Reader Raphael Klayman writes:

> I've noticed that police (real ones as well as those who play them on TV) hold their flashlights the way one might hold a knife to stab someone in the chest. We civilians tend to hold our flashlights from underneath, in a kind of semi-bowling or fishing rod grip. With both methods, you can shine the flashlight from floor to ceiling, but the police style feels a lot more awkward. Yet they must have their reasons. What are they?

Although few of the police officers we contacted have ever received formal training in flashlight "gripology," the overhand style was the favored position for two main reasons. The most often cited rationale was alluded to in our reader's letter: The overhand grip allows the officer to use the flashlight as a weapon. One Tennessee officer wrote us:

> The way we hold a flashlight gives you a tactical advantage against the person that you are encountering in case of a use-of-force situation. Your arm is already in a raised or almost a defensive position against an attack, not to mention you have something in your hand that can strike a pressure point.

With just the quick flick of a wrist, an officer might be able to stop an unruly perpetrator; if the flashlight were held straight in front, the hand would have to be drawn back first.

The second reason for the "police grip" is that perhaps its most common use is to survey the occupants and contents of motor vehicles. In conventional cars, the officer is above the level of the driver and the car, and it is simply more comfortable to beam the flashlight downward in the overhand grip. As one cop put it:

When I am walking up to the car, I don't think I ever make eye contact for more than a few seconds at a time. I'm looking through the car, at hands, containers, etc. You cannot see those things well by holding the flashlight at waist level.

What about when an officer is searching a darkened house? We finally found one officer who preferred the underhand grip for this purpose, with his arm out in front of him, "like I would when I'm holding a gun." But most officers sided with this viewpoint:

I never extend my arms out unless I intend on shooting someone. If I'm moving through a house with my arms extended and a burglar is around the corner, and he sees my arms and flashlight, there is a pretty good darn chance he might grab me. If your arms are already extended out, they are bound to get tired. There is no strength in those arms if they are extended; the closer the hands and arms are to the body, the stronger they are going to be.

Once firearms are added to the mix, flashlight position can become a matter of life and death. An Arizona police officer wrote:

We are trained to hold our flashlights in a specific way when firing our weapons. I was taught many years ago to always place your flashlight in your "weak hand" so that you would be able to pull your weapon quickly if needed. The reason that we hold them in a "stabbing" type manner is that they are easier to bring up to the firing position if needed. By holding the flashlight in a "stabbing" position by the switch, the officer is able to bring the flashlight up toward the target, and it allows the officer to use the back of his or her strong hand against the back of his or her weak hand in order to support the proper alignment in case of need to fire the weapon.

Many police departments use lightweight Maglite flashlights, and many companies that manufacture firearms for law enforcement agencies provide mounts for putting the Maglites directly on the weapon, as one officer explained:

I have a tactical flashlight attached to the Mag tube of my Mossberg that comes in handy for investigating suspicious noises around the barn and workshop at night. The light also makes a good aiming guide, because the shot is centered on the circle of light.

And with the light source attached to the firearm, all those nasty decisions about how to grip the flashlight are moot.

—Submitted by Raphael Klayman of Brooklyn, New York.

how was 911 chosen as the uniform emergency telephone number?

Old-timers like us will remember when the codes for telephone services were not uniform from city to city. In one town, "information" could be found at 411; in another, at 113. The Bell system needed to change this haphazard approach for two reasons. Making numbers uniform throughout the country would promote ease of use of their services. And reclaiming the 1 as an access code paved the way for direct dialing of long-distance calls.

Most of AT&T Bell's service codes end in "11." 211, 311, 411, 511, 611, 711, and 811 were already assigned when pressure accumulated to create a uni-

WHY IS A BRUTAL INTERROGATION CALLED THE *THIRD DEGREE?*

The "third degree" is neither a reference to a third-degree burn nor to third-degree murder, even though the phrase conjures up both a criminal interrogation and the possibility of pain and torture. A misunderstanding of the Freemasons is to blame for the frightening connotations stirred up when one contemplates receiving the third degree.

Masons must take examinations before ascending the ranks of the organization. The first and second stages require little in preparation or performance. The third degree (Master Mason) is achieved only after passing a slightly more elaborate test. Because Freemasons were secretive about their customs, rumors circulated that the ritual required to achieve the third degree involved arduous mental gymnastics and brutal physical punishment. Although this allegation was totally unfounded, the Masons' exam was compared to the interrogation and physical badgering of a suspected criminal by the police.

Criminals sometimes refer to their arrest as the *first degree;* the escorted trip to the jail as the *second degree;* and, of course, their questioning as the *third degree.*

form, national number for emergencies. According to Barbara Sweeney, researcher at AT&T Library Network Archives, all the numbers up to 911 had already been assigned. So 911 become the emergency number by default.

Think of how sophisticated the automated routers of the phone system are. When you dial 411 for directory assistance, each digit is crucial in routing the call properly. The first digit, 4, tells the equipment that you are not trying to obtain an operator ("0") or make a long-distance call. The second and third digits, 11, could be used in an area code as well as an office code, so the equipment has to be programmed to recognize 211, 311, 411, 511, 611, 711, 811, and 911 as separate service codes and not "wait" for you to dial extra digits before connecting you with the disconnected recording that will tell you the phone number of Acme Pizza.

—Submitted by Karen Riddick of Dresden, Tennessee.

why is a marshal's or sheriff's badge traditionally a five-pointed star but a deputy's six-pointed?

The five-pointed pentacle is the symbol of the United States Marshals Service. In ancient times, the pentacle was used by sorcerers and believed to impart magical powers. As late as the sixteenth century, soldiers wore pentacles around their necks in the belief that they made them invulnerable to enemy missiles.

But it turns out that even early American lawmen forged a new tradition of forsaking old traditions at the drop of a hat. It just isn't true that sheriffs always wore five-pointed stars and their deputies six-pointed ones. Charles E. Hanson, Jr., director of the Museum of the Fur Trade in Chadron, Nebraska, wrote *Imponderables* that one could despair of trying to find logic to the patterns of badges:

> There seems to be no fixed protocol on five- and six-pointed badges. In America, the five-point star has been preeminent from the beginning. It is the star in the flag, in the insignia of an army general, and on the Medal of Honor. It was obviously the logical choice for the first sheriffs' badges.
>
> When other shapes began to be used for badges, it seemed right that circles, shields, and six-pointed stars would be used for lesser legal representatives than the top lawman.

This didn't hold true indefinitely. Our library has a 1913 supply catalog which offers five-point stars engraved "City Marshal" or "Chief of Police" and six-point stars engraved, "City Marshal," "Sheriff," "Constable," "Detective," etc.

Historian Charley Eckhardt has even developed a theory to explain why the five-point might have been inflated to six points: It was simply too hard to make a five-pointed star.

> The five- and six-pointed star "tradition" seems to be purely a twentieth-century one. I've seen hundreds of badges from the nineteenth century, and they ranged from the traditional policeman's shield to a nine-pointed sunburst. Five- and six-pointed stars predominated, but in no particular order—there was no definite plurality of five points in one group and six points in another. I have noticed, however, that the majority of the *locally* made star-shaped badges produced outside of Texas were six-pointed. There may be a reason for that.
>
> When you cut a circle, if you take six chords equal to the radius of the circle and join them around the diameter, you will find that the chords form a perfect hexagon. If you join alternate points of the hexagon, you get two superimposed equilateral triangles—a six-pointed star. In order to lay out a pentagon within a circle—the basic figure for cutting a five-pointed star—you have to divide the circle into 72-degree arcs. This requires a device to measure angles from the center—or a very fine eye and a lot of trial and error. Since many badges, including many deputy sheriff and marshal badges, were locally made, it would have been much easier for the blacksmith or gunsmith turned badgemaker for a day to make a six-pointed star.

Who says that the shortage of protractors in the Old West didn't have a major influence on American history?

—Submitted by Eugene S. Mitchell of Wayne, New Jersey.
Thanks also to Christopher Valeri of East Northport, New York.

why is the lowest-ranked admiral called a *rear* admiral?

If you think that we are going to joke about the fact that a rear admiral is the lowest-ranked admiral because he tends to sit on his duff all day, you severely underestimate us. Puns are the refuge of the witless.

Dr. Regis A. Courtemanche, professor of history at the C. W. Post campus of Long Island University, wrote to *Imponderables* that the term originally referred to the admirals who commanded English naval fleets in the seventeenth-century Dutch Wars. The fleets were divided into three segments: the vanguard (the ships in front), the center, and the rear. "So," Courtemanche concludes, "the term lies in the fact that the *lowest* ranking admiral controlled the *rear* of the fleet at sea."

—Submitted by Peter J. Scott of Glendale, California.

why are military medals worn on the left?

Military historians generally trace the custom of wearing military decorations on the left breast to the Crusaders, who wore the badge of honor over the heart. Whether this spot was chosen for its symbolic purpose or to use the badge as a shield for the heart is unclear. We do know that the Crusaders carried their shields in their left hands, freeing the right hand for manipulating a weapon. (This poses an ancient Imponderable: did left-handed Crusaders carry their shield in their right hand, exposing their heart to the enemy?)

Military decorations are a relatively recent phenomenon and were originally worn at the neck or from a sash. According to S. G. Yasnitsky of the Orders and Medals Society of America, the practice changed in the first decades of the nineteenth century. During the Napoleonic campaigns, many awards were given to and by the different governments that participated in these wars. More and more orders were created for the lower classes, as well as medals given to all classes of the military and civil participants, with the proviso that they were to be worn "from the buttonhole."

Many fighting alliances between countries were forged during the Napoleonic period, and decorations were exchanged frequently. Medal inflation was rampant. A good soldier could expect to be decorated not only by his own country but by an ally or two as well. Buttonholes were bursting. Only tailors were happy. What could be done about this crisis?

As Yasnitsky told us:

> Common sense prevailed. No one wanted to hide his gorgeous accumulation of gold and enameled awards, so several methods were tried out. Some had their jewelers make smaller copies of these medals, so that they would all fit into one prescribed space on their uniforms. Others—and this became the more popular method—would display their own country's decoration from the buttonhole, but mount the other awards so that they extended in a line from that buttonhole, from left to right.

Why do all the armed forces start marching with the left foot?

Is there a practical reason? Is this custom the same all over the world?

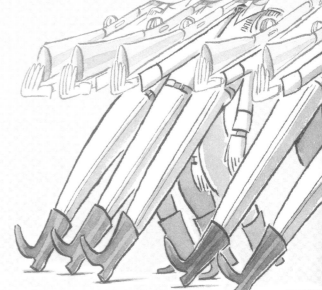

Bottom line: We can only answer the third question with any confidence. As far as we can ascertain, soldiers all over the world step off on the left foot.

We contacted many of our trusty military sources about why the practice spread. They collectively shrugged their shoulders.

Imponderables has been besieged by questions about the origins of left/right customs (e.g., why we drive on the right side of the road, why the hot water faucet is on the left, why military medals are worn on the left) and found that usually the practices stem from a technical advantage.

What possible advantage could there be in starting a march with the left foot? We received a fascinating speculation on the subject by Robert S. Robe, Jr., president of the Scipio Society of Naval and Military History, which may not be definitive but is certainly more sensible and interesting than anything else we've heard about the subject.

> When warfare was institutionalized in prebiblical times so that trained armies could fight one another on a battlefield, the evolution of infantry tactics in close formation required regimented marching in order to effectively move bodies of heavy and light infantry into contact with an enemy.
>
> I am hypothesizing that some long forgotten martinet discovered by accident or otherwise that a soldier advancing at close quarters into an enemy sword or spear line could, by stepping off on his foot in unison with his fellows, maintain better balance and sword contact to his front, assuming always that the thrusting or cutting weapon was wielded from the right hand and the shield from the left. The shield would also protect the left leg forward in close-quarter fighting.

Robe's explanation echoes the usual explanation of why we mount horses from the left. The horse itself couldn't care less from what side its rider mounts it. But in ancient times, when riders wore swords slung along the left side of the body (so that the swords could be unsheathed by the right hand), riders found it much easier to retain their groin if they mounted on the left.

—*Submitted by John Williams of North Hollywood, California. Thanks also to Ann Czompo of Cortland, New York, and Sylvia Antovino of Rochester, New York.*

how do military cadets find their caps after tossing them in the air upon graduation?

Be it West Point, Annapolis, or Colorado Springs, the tradition is the same: at the end of graduation ceremonies, after the class is called to attention for the last time and the immortal words "You are dismissed" are uttered, the former cadets fling their caps in the air. Occasionally, hats will fly at sporting events as well. How are they retrieved?

The press and relatives grab a few. But the vast majority of the caps are claimed by children. Lieutenant Colonel James A. Burkholder, Commandant of Cadets at the U.S. Air Force Academy, wrote that after most, but not all, of the graduates throw their hats in the air, "children under 12 are allowed to scramble to get [the hats]. It becomes 'finders keepers.' Keeping the children off the field prior to that moment is also a sight to see. Thus, after graduation, you will see children with their 'treasures' and others, without hats, in all sorts of despair."

Could the cadets find their caps if they did want them? Possibly. Caps have a pocket with a piece of cardboard in the inside lining, on which cadets write their names with a felt pen. More often than not, however, the ink will have worn off or become smeared. As the graduating classes at West Point usually number about a thousand, the chances of someone actually finding his own hat are remote.

WHY DOES *HOODWINK* MEAN "TO FOOL" OR "TO BLINDSIDE"?

The original meaning of *wink* was "to close one's eyes," with no implication that the closing was voluntary or a kind of signal to another. In the sixteenth century, when cloaks were a fashion must, cowls or hoods were attached to the cloaks. When one was hoodwinked, then, one was literally blinded by the hood. Cognizant of the phenomenon, industrious thieves preyed upon unsuspecting suckers whose peripheral vision was extremely limited.

Is the hat tossing rehearsed? Choreographed? No. It is a spontaneous gesture, albeit a spontaneous gesture repeated yearly. Is it frowned upon? Not really. As Al Konecny, assistant public affairs officer at West Point, told us, there is nothing wrong with the graduates tossing away a part of their uniform—it's no longer their proper uniform, anyway. They've just been promoted!

—Submitted by Merry Phillips of Menlo Park, California.
Thanks also to Paul Funn Dunn of WSOY, Decatur, Illinois.

why are there twenty-one guns in a twenty-one-gun salute?

The original intention of gun salutes was probably to assure the royalty or nation being honored that they were physically secure—that the weapons that were meant to pay tribute could also be used to kill. Before any recorded history of formal gun salutes, many cultures were known to discharge ordnance indiscriminately at festivals and holidays. Some good old-fashioned noise, be it fireworks in China or cheering at football games, has always been an accompaniment to joyous rituals.

Twenty-one-gun salutes have existed since at least the sixteenth century (the final scene from *Hamlet* mentions one), but the number of guns fired evolved gradually and inconsistently from country to country. The English were the first to codify the practice. According to a study conducted in 1890 by C. H. Davis, a commander and chief intelligence officer in the U.S. Navy, the earliest English regulation, formulated in 1688, prescribed that the birthdays and coronations of royalty should be solemnized "by the Fleet, Squadrons, and every single ship of war, by the discharge of such number of their great guns," but allowed that the number of guns used should be decided upon by the chief officer. By 1730, the British Naval Regulations were amended so that the number of guns discharged was still at the discretion of the chief officer, but was not to exceed twenty-one for each ship.

The notion of twenty-one as the highest gun salute undoubtedly stems from this royal origin. Salutes were always in odd numbers in the British military, with lower-ranking officers receiving, say, a five-gun salute and each increasing rank offered two more guns. The 1730 regulation was probably a response to rampant inflation in gun salutes; the Navy wanted to assure that no one received more guns than the royalty. In 1808, twenty-one guns was mandated as the *only* proper salute for royalty.

Although the United States, in its infancy, adopted gun salutes, there were no specific regulations governing the practice. Until 1841, the U.S. Navy fired one gun for each state in the Union. As our nation grew, and what with the price of ammunition, we prudently decided to limit our salutes to twenty-one guns. This change was codified in 1865 and has remained the practice ever since. The establishment of a maximum standard was not arbitrary or capricious. Gun salutes were a form of international diplomacy, and any deviation from the norm had possible ramifications. Commander Davis stressed the importance of conforming to international practice: "According to the present regulations and long established custom, a vessel of war, on her arrival in a foreign port, salutes the flag of the nation to which that port belongs, after having ascertained that the salute will be returned, with 21 guns. The salute is immediately returned gun for gun. This rule is universal and invariable in all countries in the world."

Davis believed that if the United States had continued its practice of discharging one gun for each state, it could have had serious consequences. He feared that other countries would assume that by exceeding twenty-one guns, we were trumpeting our own power and superiority.

A last objection to the one gun/one state idea was that gun salutes have always involved an odd number. Even numbers have traditionally been fired in mourning and at funerals. While modern communications equipment has largely obviated the need to use gun salutes as a symbol of peace and goodwill, the twenty-one-gun salute is alive and well as a ritual to express celebration and honor. Although we can't pinpoint exactly why the British first arrived at twenty-one (some speculate that the combination of three multiplied by seven might have been adopted for mystical or religious reasons), we clearly owe our custom to the British military's desire to salute royalty with the utmost hoopla.

—Submitted by Debra Kalkwarf of Columbus, Indiana.
Thanks also to Douglas Watkins, Jr., of Hayward, California.

why were duels always fought at dawn?
Or is this depiction in fiction and movies not true?

Not true, we're afraid. Historians assured *Imponderables* that duels were fought at any time of the day. But dawn was definitely the preferred time; a duel fought in twilight could turn into more of a crapshoot than a gunshoot.

Doesn't make much sense to us. We might be convinced to get up at dawn to go fishing. But if we knew we had an approximately fifty-fifty chance of dying on a particular day, we'd at least want a decent night's sleep the night before and time for a doughnut or two before we fought.

Historian C. F. "Charley" Eckhardt speculates on this strange predilection of duelists to fight to the death at inconvenient hours:

> Just at sunrise, if the list [the technical term for a dueling ground] was oriented north-south, neither man got the sun-to-the back advantage. Also, either the local law was still abed or, if there was a regular police force in the area, the day watch and night watch were changing shifts. Fighting at dawn minimized the likelihood of interference by the law, the same reason many burglaries occur between 3 and 4 P.M. and 11 P.M. to midnight. Most police departments change shifts at 3 P.M., 11 P.M., and 7 A.M.

—*Submitted by Jan Anthony Verlaan of Pensacola, Florida.*

why did pirates bother making prisoners or enemies "walk the plank" instead of just chucking them overboard?

Try as we might, we couldn't find any pirates to talk to us, on or off the record. Instead, we had to rely on a librarian and historian, Toby Gibson (who has made a lifelong study of pirates, and maintains an entire Web site devoted to pirate lore at http://blindkat.hegewisch.net/pirates/pirates.html), and on more than twenty books about pirates. Pirates have always captured the imagination of writers, both nonfiction and storytellers, and it has become difficult to separate the myths about pirates from serious documentation.

The reader who posed this Imponderable rightly wondered why pirates would bother with the elaborate ritual of forcing a victim to walk on a wooden plank with eyes blindfolded and hands behind his back, when it would have been far easier simply to throw the poor guy overboard. Either way, the victim would end up as shark food.

The stories about "walking the plank" usually refer to the "Golden Age" of piracy, from approximately 1690 to 1720, when such legendary (but flesh-and-blood) pirates as Blackbeard, William Kidd, and Stede Bonnet terrorized the oceans. But accounts of piracy have been documented as long as there have been ships, including tales of skulduggery in the Mediterranean in ancient Roman and Greek times.

We are lucky that many contemporaneous accounts of piracy written in the seventeenth and eighteenth centuries still exist. Many purport to be first-hand reports, but unfortunately exaggerated and outright fabricated adventure stories often masqueraded as nonfiction in those days, so much of the information therein must be taken with more than a few grains of salt. Several pirates were tried and executed for their crimes, however, so court records exist, including minutes of the proceedings for many of them.

The bottom line: There is little, if any, proof that walking the plank existed. Three other forms of punishment are clearly documented:

Flogging. Miscreants were beaten with a whip, the dreaded cat-o'-nine-tails.

Marooning. Offenders of the worst variety (murderers, rapists, despised captains) were given the clothes on their backs (and sometimes were even stripped of those), a bottle of water, a pistol, a bottle of powder, and a handful of shot, and were abandoned on an inhospitable island. They were never left on a romantic island with abundant vegetation, as depicted in Robert Louis Stevenson's *Treasure Island*. Marooning was a nonviolent but nevertheless torturous death sentence.

Throwing Overboard. This form of punishment, while not common, *has* been amply documented.

Some historians maintain that walking the plank did exist. In his book, *The Age of Piracy,* Robert Carse claims:

> The story about prisoners being forced to walk the plank is almost complete fiction. Examination of the record gives only a single example. Men were thrown in over the side, though, and strung up from the yards for musket practice, pistoled point-blank.

Carse's "single example" is a reference to Major Stede Bonnet, a soldier rather than a seaman, who in the early eighteenth century forsook a comfortable life as a gentleman in the West Indies to become a pirate. Carse writes:

> Bonnet died with two distinctions as a pirate. He was the first man ever in recorded history to have bought a ship with his own funds and then to have gone forth deliberately on a piratical venture. He was also, by the record, the only captain of his kind to make his victims walk the plank.

Perhaps the most famous real-life pirate was Blackbeard, whose real name was Edward Teach. In his 1935 book, *Sinbad's Book of Pirates,* author A. E. Dingle claims that Teach tortured the skipper of a captured ship:

> Blackbeard laid a plank across the brig's open hatch, dragged the skipper toward it, and promised him that if he could walk across it blindfolded he would be set free and his brig given back to him. He was even

permitted to walk across the plank with his eyes unbound, and he performed this part of the task with agility. He was much astonished to land safely on the other side of the deck, unhindered, and submitted to the blindfolding with a little laugh of returning confidence.

But the pirates turned him about, shoving him here and there while the bandage was being tied, a dozen of them vowing that it was not well fastened, shifting him about until when at last he was set with his feet on the plank he never noticed that it now projected out through the gangway and over the sea instead of across the hatch.

The victim's wife, mad at her husband for surrendering to Blackbeard so easily, protested, and was sent below into the cabin:

> There she saw her husband tumble past her open window from the end of the plank.

Neither of these two stories is substantiated in any way, and the second, at least in the manner of expression, "feels" like fiction. Most of our sources discounted the reality of walking the plank. In his 1951 book, *The Great Days of Piracy in the West Indies*, George Woodbury argues that pirates' ferociousness has been greatly exaggerated. Pirates made most of their money from kidnapping and holding wealthy shipowners as hostage. There was every reason to keep such valuable booty alive. On the other hand,

> Those of poorer estate were usually invited to jump overboard, encouraged, and finally coerced, to do so.

In general, though, pirates did not injure, let alone kill their captives, unless the victims provided physical resistance. In fact, it was common for pirates to recruit their prisoners, often offering them equal rights, although some were forced into indentured servitude. Even if violence was a byproduct of their work, Woodbury describes pirates as less than bloodthirsty:

> Ordinarily, too, pirates did not scuttle or burn ships just for the fun of it. If they wanted the ship for their own use, they took it; if they didn't, they let it go. The mere fact that there are so many tales about pirates is pretty good evidence that they did not follow the practice of "Dead men tell no tales," generally ascribed to them.
>
> Only one atrocious practice, marooning, seems to be really characteristic of piracy. Marooning was a form of punishment usually meted out to backsliders from their own numbers.

Even stronger in his "defense" of pirates and the denial of the reality of walking the plank is perhaps the most prestigious historian to write

extensively about pirates, Patrick Pringle. In his 1953 book, *Jolly Roger, The Story of the Great Age of Piracy,* Pringle notes:

> I have ransacked official records, reports of trials, and much other documentary evidence without being able to discover a single case of walking the plank. I do not mean merely that I have not found an authenticated case. In all the documentary literature on pirates I could not find even an accusation or suggestion that the practice was ever used. The very expression seems to have been invented many years after the Age of Piracy.

Pringle argues that it was to the advantage of pirates to have potential victims fear them. And seamen of merchant ships had little reason to resist—who would want to risk their lives to protect the merchandise of the ship's owner?

And although Bonnet is the one famous pirate often "credited" with having prisoners walk the plank, Pringle discounts the contention:

> Bonnet's career is even more fully documented than Blackbeard's, for a full report of his trial has been preserved. The evidence against him was considerable, yet not one of the witnesses accused him of ill-treatment of prisoners. It seems as if this is another myth.

So then how did these myths begin? They began with early "classics" of pirate literature, such as *Bucaniers of America* (1679) and *A General History of the Robberies and Murders of the Most Notorious Pyrates* (1724), which contained facts mixed in with hyperbole. The latter book, written by "Captain Charles Johnson," is widely suspected to have been the work of Daniel Defoe, author of *Robinson Crusoe.* Pirate stories remained popular in the nineteenth century. Several of the most popular, Stevenson's *Treasure Island* and Gilbert and Sullivan's *Pirates of Penzance,* had no mention of walking the plank.

But Howard Pyle, a popular author and illustrator who worked in the last half of the nineteenth century into the beginning of the twentieth, used pirates as one of his most common subjects. And one of Pyle's most popular pictures depicted a man walking the plank, along with this commentary by the artist:

> With Blackbeard, we have a real, ranting, raging, roaring pirate who really did bury treasure, who made more than one captain walk the plank, and who committed more private murders than he could number on the fingers of both hands.

Probably totally untrue, but even folks in the nineteenth century needed goose bumps, too.

When we first asked Toby Gibson about walking the plank, he answered,

There's little doubt that pirates threw people overboard, especially enemies. We also know that Hollywood has turned walking the plank into a pirate tradition.

Perhaps no Hollywood rendition is more famous than in *Peter Pan,* in which the nefarious Captain Hook forces Wendy to walk the plank. Luckily for Wendy, Peter Pan just happens to be hiding under the plank, eager and able to snatch her and fly away, with Hook none the wiser.

Even if pirates were not the brutes they have been commonly depicted to be, they are without a lobbying organization to better their image. In cartoons, they remain evil and merciless. And even though they sing beautifully, a ride through the Magic Kingdom's "Pirates of the Caribbean" will try to convince you that forcing prisoners to walk the plank was part of the "pirate's life for me."

—Submitted by John Little of Coquitlam, British Columbia.

why are so many large national corporations incorporated in Delaware?

We blanched when we noticed that two of the largest New York banks, Citibank and Chase Manhattan, were incorporated in Delaware. Both banks' names betray their New York roots, so surely there must be some practical reasons why they chose to incorporate in another state.

Then we encountered a November 1986 *Forbes* article, which reported that Delaware houses more than thirty out-of-state banks. A call to the Delaware Chamber of Commerce yielded even more startling statistics. More than

WHY DOES *PIPE DOWN* MEAN "SHUT UP!"?

The original *pipe* in *pipe down* was a boatswain's whistle, and *pipe down* was a signal to sailors that they were dismissed for the day and could go belowdecks. By the late nineteenth century, the tattoo signal, usually sounded immediately before taps, explicitly meant to quiet down. Obviously the deck was quieter once the sailors went belowdecks. Eventually the boatswain's whistle was replaced by a bugle, but the meaning of the signal was the same.

170,000 companies are incorporated in Delaware, including more than one-half of all Fortune 500 companies, 42 percent of all New York Stock Exchange listees, and a similar proportion of AMEX companies.

How could Delaware, the home of fewer than 700,000 people, house so many corporations? The answer is a textbook illustration of the ways a small state can attract big business by changing its laws and tax structure to attract outsiders. One of the reasons that Delaware attracted so many banks, for example, is that it abolished usury ceilings, which are set by the state rather than by the federal government. Let's look at the other inducements that Delaware offers corporations seeking a home.

Favorable Tax Laws

1. No state sales tax.

2. No personal property tax.

3. No corporate income tax for corporations maintaining a corporate office in Delaware but not doing business in the state. If Chase Manhattan were incorporated in New York, New York State would demand a share of the income generated beyond its borders.

4. No corporate income tax for holding companies handling intangible investments or handling tangible properties located outside Delaware.

5. An extremely low franchise tax, based on authorized capital stock (the minimum is a staggeringly low $30; but there is also a maximum, $130,000 per year, that is very attractive to big corporations). Even with the low rate, the franchise tax generates 14 percent of the state's general fund revenues—Delaware collected over $126 million in 1986.

6. The corporate tax rate itself is a low 8.7 percent and is collected only on money generated inside Delaware. Compare this to the 10 percent New York State tax and the total burden of 19 percent for companies operating within New York City.

Favorable Corporation Law

1. Delaware's court of Chancery sets the nation's standards for sophistication and timeliness in shaping corporate law. Donald E. Schwartz, professor of law at Georgetown Law Center, says: "There is, by an order of several magnitudes, a larger body of case law from Delaware than there is from any other jurisdiction, enabling not only lawyers who

practice in Delaware, but lawyers everywhere who counsel Delaware corporations to be able to render opinions with some confidence." By quickly establishing precedents on the issues that confront corporate heads today, Delaware has defined the legal parameters for doing business faster and more comprehensively than any other state. Business leaders feel more secure in making decisions and planning for the future, because the law is set early; as Schwartz puts it, "Corporate managers and their lawyers seek predictability."

2. In Delaware, only a majority of shareholders of a company need agree to incorporate a company. Many states require a two-thirds majority.

3. Delaware allows mergers to proceed with less intrusion than just about any other state.

4. Once incorporated, a corporation can change its purpose of business without red tape from the state.

5. The corporation's terms of existence is perpetual in Delaware. Some states require renewals, which involve paperwork and extra expense.

Favorable Treatment of Corporate Leaders

Delaware has recently enacted several laws designed to make life easier for corporate heads, particularly boards of directors.

1. Delaware law allows corporations to indemnify directors, officers, and agents against expenses and often against judgments, fines, and costs of settlements incurred in suits against them filed by third parties.

2. Delaware law makes it difficult to unseat directors of a corporation.

3. Directors of a Delaware corporation do not necessarily have to meet in Delaware. Decisions can be made by conference call; the directors can even take an action without any meeting if there is unanimous written consent.

4. Perhaps most important in this category, Delaware passed an enabling act that allowed corporations to limit or eliminate outside directors' personal financial liability for violations of their fiduciary duty (including potential liability for gross negligence). This rule makes it much easier to attract directors to Delaware corporations; would-be directors in many states are forced to pay high liability insurance premiums to

protect themselves against just such lawsuits. Although Delaware law does not allow directors to escape unscathed for perpetrating fraud, the knowledge that they won't be held up for making a mistake (even a "gross" one) makes directors happy to work in the state.

Other factors also make Delaware attractive to corporations. Unions are not as entrenched in Delaware as they are in most other areas of the Mid-Atlantic and Northeast. Pay and cost-of-living scales are lower than in surrounding regions.

Perhaps the most enticing nontangible asset of Delaware in attracting business is the accessibility of government officials to business people. State Insurance Commissioner David Levinson was quoted in the *Forbes* article on this subject: "If you have a problem and you're operating a company in Delaware, within 48 hours you can have in one room the governor, the insurance commissioner, the president pro tem of the senate and the speaker of the house."

Delaware's pro-business slant has revived what was once a stagnant economy. But has this infusion of incorporations helped the average citizen of Delaware, when most companies do not relocate there? Evidence suggests that money has trickled down. Although there are pockets of poverty in Delaware, unemployment is now well below the national average.

The secret weapon of Delaware is its small size. A bigger state would need promises of a large number of jobs before offering financial concessions to corporations. But a small state like Delaware can siphon off the gravy and thrive. For example, Delaware offers some tax breaks to out-of-state banks if they incorporate in Delaware and maintain an office with at least one hundred employees. To a multinational bank, one hundred jobs is a drop in the bucket. To a state with fewer than twenty thousand unemployed people, one hundred jobs represents a substantial opportunity.

what do FedEx delivery people do after 10:30 A.M.?

FedEx is justly famous for its pledge to deliver Priority One packages before 10:30 A.M. the next business day. What, then, do delivery people do after the last priority package is delivered? Take a siesta? Smoke cigars? Play poker with U.S. Postal Service employees who haven't delivered their first-class mail yet?

Actually, FedEx keeps its employees hopping all day long. In some cities, packages are delivered as early as 7:30 A.M. (The pickup and delivery cycles of packages tend to be earlier in the West, because *all* packages are routed through FedEx headquarters in Memphis, Tennessee, prior to shipment to their eventual destinations.) Before any packages can be delivered, they must be sorted by routes; in smaller stations, the courier often does the sorting himself.

After all Priority One packages are delivered, the courier tries to drop off all second-day deliveries before noon. If he succeeds, he is likely to take a lunch break around midday.

After lunch, the pickup cycle begins. By the time the courier has gathered all the incoming packages, he has worked a full day. If there is any spare time at all, paperwork has a way of filling it.

In large stations, the process of sorting routes, delivering Priority One packages, delivering second-day packages, picking up all packages, and filling out paperwork can consume more than eight hours. For this reason, about 25 percent of all FedEx employees are part-timers, often used for sorting packages for delivery by couriers. When a FedEx courier drops off his last Priority One package before the 10:30 A.M. deadline, his workday has just begun.

—Submitted by Merle Pollis of Cleveland, Ohio.

why are the commercials louder than the programming on television?

Having lived in apartments most of our adult lives, we developed a theory about this Imponderable. Let us use a hypothetical example to explain our argument.

Let's say a sensitive, considerate yet charismatic young man—we'll call him "Dave"—is taking a brief break from his tireless work to watch TV late at night. As an utterly sympathetic and empathic individual, Dave puts the volume at a low level so as not to wake the neighbors who are divided from him by tissue-thin walls. Disappointed that *Masterpiece Theatre* is not run at 2 A.M., Dave settles for a rerun of *Hogan's Heroes*. While he is studying the content of the show to determine what the character of Colonel Klink says about our contemporary society, a used-car commercial featuring a screaming huckster comes on at a much louder volume.

What does Dave do? He goes up to the television and lowers the volume. But then the show comes back on, and Dave can't hear it. Ordinarily, Dave would love to forgo watching such drivel, so that he could go back to his work as, say, a writer. But he is now determined to ascertain the sociological significance of *Hogan's Heroes*. So for the sake of sociology, Dave gets back up and turns the volume back on loud enough so that he can hear but softly enough not to rouse the neighbors. When the next set of commercials comes on, the process is repeated.

Isn't it clear? Commercials are louder to force couch potatoes (or sociological researchers) to get some exercise! When one is slouched on the couch, the walk to and from the television set constitutes aerobic exercise.

Of course, not everyone subscribes to our theory.

Advertising research reveals, unfortunately, that while commercials with quick cuts and frolicking couples win Clio awards, irritating commercials sell merchandise. And it is far more important for a commercial to be noticed than to be liked or admired. Advertisers would like their commercials to be as loud as possible.

The Federal Communications Commission has tried to solve the problem of blaring commercials by setting maximum volume levels called "peak audio voltage." But the advertising community is way ahead of the FCC. Through a technique called "volume compression," the audio transmission is modified *so that all sounds, spoken or musical, are at or near the maximum allowable volume.* Even loud rock music has peaks and valleys of loudness, but with volume compression, the average volume of the commercial will register as loudly as the peaks of regular programming, without violating FCC regulations.

The networks are not the villain in this story. In fact, CBS developed a device to measure and counterattack volume compression, so the game among the advertisers, networks, and the FCC continues. Not every commercial uses volume compression, but enough do to foil local stations everywhere.

Of course, it could be argued that advertisers have only the best interests of the public at heart. After all, they are offering free aerobic exercise to folks like Dave. And for confirmed couch potatoes, they are pointing out the advantages of remote-control televisions.

—Submitted by Tammy Madill of Millington, Tennessee.
Thanks also to Joanne Walker of Ashland, Massachusetts.

in movies and television dramas, what is the purpose of boiling water when babies are delivered at home?

Considering the urgency with which characters in movies bark orders to boil water as soon as it becomes evident a woman is going to give birth at home, we assumed there *was* a better reason for the command than to rustle up some tea. But we've never seen the boiled water actually being used on-screen.

Most of the medical authorities we contacted echoed the sentiments of Dr. Steven P. Shelov, professor of pediatrics at the Montefiore Medical Center:

> This is an attempt to make as sterile an environment as possible, though clearly it is far short of inducing any sterility whatsoever. There might be some ability with hotter water to allow for a cleaner, more efficient cleansing of the baby and of the mother postpartum.

Obviously, it can't hurt to sterilize equipment that comes in contact with the mother or baby, such as scissors, cord clamps, white shoelaces (used in lieu of cord clamps), syringes, and tongs (used to lift the other sterile items), or even more importantly, to sterilize other household implements commandeered to act as sterilized medical equipment.

But boiling water isn't confined to emergency deliveries. Midwives have been boiling water for years for planned home deliveries. Most attempt to boil sterile equipment for thirty minutes and then place instruments in a covered dish (syringes are usually wrapped in a sterile cloth).

Dr. William Berman of the Society for Pediatric Research indicated that it couldn't hurt to sterilize water for washrags used to cleanse mother and baby, whether they are washcloths or ripped-up bed sheets. Actually, it *could* hurt—if they forget to let the boiled water cool down.

—Submitted by Scott Morwitz of Pittsburgh, Pennsylvania. Thanks also to Jil McIntosh of Oshawa, Ontario and Dr. John Hardin of Greenfield, Indiana.

in large shopping malls, why is the last door on both sides of the main entrance often closed?

The answer is, of course, laziness. Mark Weitzman posed this Imponderable in 1987, and ever since we've sought the solution, we have met with obfuscation worthy of politicians and beauty pageant contestants.

Fire codes mandate wide exits for malls. We've seen many with eight sets of double doors side by side. Barring an emergency, the main entrance/exit is rarely congested. Too often, security personnel at malls find it more convenient to not unlock some doors (usually the doors on the far left and right), so as not to have to lock them up again later. Some mall employees have tried to convince us that outer doors are closed to conserve energy or for security reasons, but the explanations ring hollow.

Our friend at the National Fire Academy, Bruce Hisley, told *Imponderables* that when he was a fire marshal, he often found that all but one set of a local mall's doors were locked shortly before closing time, in clear violation of fire codes. A little investigation yielded the discovery that this was the employees' less than subtle method of deterring customers from going into the mall at the last minute. Anyone who has ever entered a restaurant five minutes before the stated closing time and received less than stellar service will comprehend the operative mentality.

—Submitted by Mark Weitzman of Boulder, Colorado.

WHAT WAS THE FIRST STUFF TO BE *CUT AND DRIED*?

Herbs. Physicians in the sixteenth century were likely to prescribe herbs as treatment for most maladies. Although they also were used as cooking ingredients, much faith was put in herbs as "modern" remedies. Physicians preferred dispensing herbs that were already *cut and dried,* because dry herbs are both more concentrated and more uniform in strength.

While one batch of fresh thyme might vary in potency from another, dried thyme made the dosage routine, which, come to think of it, is pretty much our definition of *cut and dried* today.

why do phone companies charge customers extra for unlisted numbers?

Imponderables is pleased to announce a change in policy. As you know, we have always sent a free, autographed book to any reader who is the first to send in an Imponderable that we use. And we will continue to do so. However, because of added overhead costs, we have reluctantly decided that we will now charge all readers who haven't sent in an Imponderable that we use a small service fee of two dollars per month.

That's right! For less than the cost of buying a daily newspaper for a week, you can have all the privacy attendant on not being published in our books. You can hardly afford *not* to pay a mere twenty-four dollars per year for this luxury. Sorry, no credit card orders can be accepted. But for your convenience, we'll call you with this offer when we know you'll be home—dinnertime. There's no way you can afford not to avail yourself of this service, offered exclusively to *Imponderables* readers.

Well, we tried, anyway.

The phone company has been getting away with charging us for *not* being listed in the phone book (and directory assistance) for a long time. Do they have any rationalization for the practice?

Officials from phone companies were reticent about speaking on the record about this topic, but we've been able to piece together the story with off-the-record interviews and discussions with telephone consultants. Engineering consultant Douglas A. Kerr of Dallas, Texas, wrote us:

> The original rationale for this surcharge was that, first, the telephone company needed to take special clerical steps to keep that subscriber's entry out of the database system from which directories were compiled. Second, a person's having an unlisted number inflated the volume of inquiries made to directory assistance, which was a free service at the time.

Historically, unlisted numbers weren't handled the same way as listed numbers. Phone companies maintained an "unlisted number bureau" to provide access for police and fire departments.

But the bigger expense, as Kerr indicates, is the increased volume to directory assistance. A disproportionate percentage of "information" calls are for unlisted numbers. The calling party doesn't know that the number is unlisted but is more likely to call because the desired party is not listed in the

phone book. James Turner, who worked at Pacific Telephone from 1974 to 1983, explains the problem he faced when the company charged fifteen cents per directory assistance call (in the 1960s and before, it was *free*):

> I don't know if any studies were ever made about the true cost of an unlisted number to the telephone company, but I would suspect that it exceeds the revenue brought in. As a former service rep, I can tell you that we spent a great deal of time explaining to callers who wanted someone's unlisted number that we couldn't give it out.
>
> And I'm sure that operators had a much harder time with it than service reps ever did. Then there's always the customer who insists that it's an emergency, so the operator has to call the unlisted party and relay a message to call the party back.

Of course, providing unlisted numbers also lessens the total number of phone calls, for the few folks who can't find the phone number of the intended party will never make that revenue-generating call. The phone company also derives income from selling "names" to phone directories; every unlisted phone number is one entry "missing" from the White Pages.

Still, we think the most compelling explanation for the current policy was voiced by many of our sources: The phone company charges more for unlisted numbers because the phone company can get away with it! Steve Forrette of Seattle's Walker, Richer & Quinn, Inc., put it this way:

> Telephone services in many cases are not priced in relation to their cost, but rather the perceived value to the consumer. Take, for example, touch-tone dialing, which actually reduces the telco's cost, but is often surcharged because the customer perceives that they are getting an extra service.

Most telephone companies now offer "nonpublished" as well as unlisted numbers. Even though the term would seem to mean the opposite, other parties can obtain a nonpublished number, even if it doesn't appear in the phone directory.

With current technology, a few keystrokes by a service rep can process inquiries about listed, unlisted, or nonpublished numbers with ease. And with the current pricing for making directory assistance calls, the telcos might even be turning a slight profit on the service. We can think of no truer statement to close this chapter than the wisdom tendered by Douglas Kerr: "Telephone surcharges have a way of never evaporating."

—Submitted by William F. McGrady of Vallejo, California.
Thanks also to Curtis Kelly of Chicago, Illinois; Dennis David Thorpe of Appleton, Wisconsin; and Jeanie Vance of Hyannis, Massachusetts.

why do auctioneers talk funny? And why do auctioneers often speak unintelligibly?

Auctioneering dates back to Anglo-Saxon times, when all sorts of merchandise and commodities were sold in open markets. Bernard Hart, executive secretary of the National Auto Auction Association, wrote *Imponderables*:

> The reason for the talk by auctioneers is that before the advent of public-address systems, especially the portable type, an auctioneer had not only to be in good voice but to talk in a method that was pleasing rather than irritating to the ears of his audience of prospective buyers.

The modus operandi of the auctioneer has not changed much since its origins, as Peter Lukasiak, executive director of the National Auto Auction Association, explains:

> A typical auctioneer describes the products offered for sale; chants to find the lowest (or floor) price for the items being sold; acknowledges each bid received; and attempts to move bidders to the highest bid level possible. This results in a rolling, sonorous tone that actually builds competition among bidders and secures the highest market price for sale goods and the seller.

Although the "chant" might sound funny to the uninitiated, it's an essential element in the strategy of the auctioneer. The auctioneer usually must

WHAT ANGRY PERSON FIRST *READ THE RIOT ACT?*

George I of England gave new meaning to the words "law and order." In 1716 he instituted the Riot Act, which made it illegal for twelve or more people to congregate together and "disturb the peace." If the crowd did not disperse, they were subject to a minimum of three years in prison.

George put quite a burden on all public officials. If they encountered such a crowd, they were obligated to stand before the crowd and literally *read the Riot Act,* ticking off the provisions of the law, which undoubtedly must have endeared them to drunken revelers or political protesters.

try to sell as much merchandise as possible in the shortest amount of time (not only so that more goods can be sold but also so that buyers uninterested in the particular item on sale won't leave the premises before they have a chance to bid on later items). As Joseph Keefhaver, executive vice president of the National Auctioneers Association put it,

> Rhythm is as important as speed in developing an effective chant. Auctioneers will adjust their speed, depending on the bidding experience level of their crowd, and the numbers of a good chant will be readily understood.

Lukasiak indicates that some auctioneers have personal preferences for slow or fast paces, but conditions often dictate the chant speed. A wholesale tobacco buyer does not want a leisurely pace at an auction; and an auctioneer trying to sell a multimillion-dollar Monet at Sotheby's had better not carry off the bidding at a breakneck pace, as Keefhaver amplifies:

> The purpose of an auction is to sell items at a rapid and steady pace. Unlike other types of sales, an auction is a one-time event where all the customers are present at the same time. Thus, the auctioneer is responsible for selling all the items within a few hours, and his or her use of the chant helps keep the items moving.
>
> Since auctioneers have a limited amount of time to sell many items, they need to move at a rapid pace. At an average household estate auction, the auctioneer's chant uses speed and rhythm to sell an average of 60 items per hour. Certain types of auctions go even faster; wholesale automobile auctioneers frequently sell 125 to 175 cars per hour and tobacco auctioneers may sell 500 to 600 lots per hour.

Obviously, it is far more difficult for the uninitiated to understand what is going on at a tobacco auction. Many auctioneers pepper their chants with regional speech patterns or terms understood only by the cognoscenti within the field.

O.K. We've established that the form of the auctioneer's chant makes some sense, but why can't you understand them? When we've gone to auctions, a typical chant might sound to bidders something like this:

Hey, budda budda budda twenty-five, hey wonka wonka wonka thirty, got twenty-five, thirty, budda budda, twenty-five, thirty, hey thirty, budda budda budda, do I have a thirty? Budda budda.

Of course, that's not what the auctioneer is actually *saying*. More likely, he is using "real words." Joseph Keefhaver provides a classic, basic chant:

One-dollar bid, now two, now two, will you give me two?
Two-dollar bid, now three, now three, will ya give me three?

The culprits in misunderstanding the chants, in the previous example the "budda's" and "wonka's" are called "filler words" (or simply, "filler") by auctioneers. The purpose of filler is to give bidders a chance to think about bidding while keeping the momentum of the chant (and with luck, a frenzy of interest in the item) alive. Bernard Hart told *Imponderables* that a good auctioneer develops several different filler words and alternates them throughout an auction, to avoid the monotony of "budda budda budda":

In one of the auction schools where I worked, they trained the students to base their fillers on words that would encourage an increase in the bids such as "make," "bid," and "go." For example, "I have twenty-five, will you make it thirty?" This is a five-word filler and only a select few are able to handle that many words. It can be shortened in several ways such as "twenty-five go thirty," "twenty-five bid thirty," and so on.

We were shocked when every single one of the auctioneers we consulted insisted that the bidder should be able to understand every single word of the auctioneer, even the fillers. The comments of J. McBride, director of information at the Livestock Marketing Association, were typical:

Actually, if you can't understand what an auctioneer is saying, he or she is not doing their job, and we should know, because we sponsor the granddaddy of all auctioneer contests, the World Livestock Auctioneer Championship.

I direct your attention to the judging criteria for this year's contest. Under the section "Advancing to World Finals," you can see that "clarity of chant" is a major judging criterion. [Indeed, it is the first criterion mentioned, along with "voice quality," "bid-catching ability," "conduct of the sale," and "Would the judge hire this auctioneer?"]

Granted, it may take awhile for you as an auction observer to "pick up" on the auctioneer's particular chant. And the auctioneer may sometimes use patter or fill words that are not crystal clear. But to sell, you have to be understood—and that's true whether you're auctioning off cattle or fine crystal, ranch land or Rembrandts.

—Submitted by Morgan Dallman of Martin, South Dakota. Thanks also to Valerie Grollman of Kendall Park, New Jersey, and Myron Meyer of Sioux Falls, South Dakota.

how can owners of small cemeteries make money? How can they plan their finances when they have to wait for people to die before they derive income?

We were asked this Imponderable several times on radio talk shows. And we were stumped. The income of a small cemetery owner must be severely limited by the population the cemetery serves. In many cases, privately owned cemeteries and funeral homes even in the smallest towns must "compete" against their church-owned or municipal counterparts. Church-owned cemeteries often charge only for the cost of digging a grave; the privately owned cemetery charges Tiffany prices in comparison.

We found out that more than a few cemetery owners in small towns are not millionaires. Many funeral directors and a few cemeterians need second jobs to provide more income. How do the small cemeterians survive? Are there any (legal) ways of "drumming up" business?

We were lucky enough to find Howard Fletcher, the chairman of the Small Cemetery Advisory Committee of the American Cemetery Association. Mr. Fletcher, who owns a memorial park in Muscatine, Iowa, helps fellow small cemeterians contend with the very financial problems we have discussed. Despite all the jokes about the business (such as "*everybody is a potential customer*"), a small cemeterian must do more than sit around and wait for people to die in order to survive. Howard Fletcher is unusually frank and unsanctimonious about his profession, and unashamed about the methods he uses to maximize his income. He developed a pamphlet called "50 Sources of Income for Small Cemeteries," from which most of the material below was adapted.

Within Fletcher's fifty sources of income are at least five broad categories: preselling; upgrading; maximizing underutilized assets; creative financing; and expanding services and products.

Preselling

To Fletcher, this is the key ingredient in a successful small cemetery operation. Most funeral directors have to wait until a death before seeing any income. Fletcher tries to sell his community on the advantages of buying space, vaults, caskets, and even memorial markers "preneed" rather than "at

need." He has many arguments in his arsenal: a preneed purchase saves the bereaved family from the emotional strain of making funeral arrangements at the time a loss occurs; the decision can be made at the home of the buyer; prices will be lower now than when bought in the future; no cash is necessary right away, while most funeral directors would require some cash "at need"; making arrangements now will provide the buyer with peace of mind, not only for him or herself, but in knowing that the family will not be saddled with the unpleasant task; spouses can make decisions about funeral arrangements together; terms are negotiable–the buyer is likely to have more leverage when he or she is hale and hearty. To quote Mr. Fletcher: "It is not a question of if these arrangements will be made, it is only a question of who is going to make them and when!"

Here are some of the successful variations of preneed selling:

Sell child burial protection. Child protection doesn't cost much, but it does provide great cash flow. By the time the child is likely to die, compound interest has made this presell very profitable.

Presell grave opening and closing charges.

Offer one free burial space or two-for-one sales to married couples. Presumably, married couples want to be buried together, so the free space for one turns out to be the same deal as the two-for-one–these offers are always nonassignable and nontransferable (thus solving the possible divorce problem).

Upgrading

1. Sell marker refinishing kits. Bronze markers often tarnish because of oxidation.

2. Sell granite bases as upgrades from concrete bases.

3. Sell larger memorials.

4. "Reload." Use existing customers as a base to sell new or improved products. This is one reason cemeterians like to deliver by hand all deeds and official papers. They can discreetly get referrals or find family members who have not yet made funeral plans. Fletcher issues two newsletters per year with return cards and pitches for upgrading products.

5. Sell wreath and grave coverings for Christmas, Memorial Day, and other holidays.

6. Sell vesper lights.

7. Sell carillon chimes with the donor's name on plaque.

Maximizing Underutilized Assets

1. Launch a lawn-care business to more fully utilize landscaping equipment.

2. Sell double-depth privileges.

3. Grow and sell sod.

4. Raise and sell nursery stock from open land.

5. Cut and sell firewood from open land.

6. Sell excess trees on property.

7. Lease extra acreage to farmers.

8. Sell excess materials from graves as fill dirt.

Creative Financing

Many of these tips consist of charging separate fees for services that might or might not be included in the usual package deal:

1. Charge a filing and recording fee.

2. Charge for deed transfer and replacement.

3. Offer discount for cash payment of open accounts in order to generate cash flow.

4. Sell accounts receivable for cash flow.

5. Charge interest on house accounts.

6. Increase price of lots by having care charge paid separately.

7. Increase price of memorial by having installation and care charges paid separately.

8. Sell for allied businesses, such as monument dealers.

9. Sell extra-care charge for special care.

10. Where cemetery has historic value, apply for federal, state, or local registry in historical society for funding purposes.

11. Hire professional collectors for delinquent accounts.

12. Offer a discount on a new marker if purchased within one month of burial.

Expanding Services and Products

Here are some of the more creative ideas, all potentially practical:

1. Start a pet cemetery, with preneed and at need sales.

2. Manufacture vaults.

3. Build a funeral home that offers preneed as well as at need follow-up.

4. Start a trailer park on extra acreage where feasible.

5. Rent the chapel tent for weddings and lawn parties.

6. Raise and sell livestock.

7. Develop a flower shop.

8. Sell garden features and entrance features.

9. Sell trees—lining drives and/or walks.

10. Sell benches in cemetery.

11. Sell stained-glass windows.

12. Sell pews in chapel.

13. Sell furniture in mausoleum or committal area.

Some of these "money-making tips" might be offensive to your sensibilities. The image of a trailer park next to the memorial park is less than pleasing, and the thought of discussing preneed services at your kitchen table might dull the appetite a bit. The alternative, though, is usually a full-court press at the time of death.

Howard Fletcher is providing a service, but is also willing to admit that he is in business to make money. He wants the public to know what the business is like, so that the public can understand the industry's problems. Most small cemeteries make less than $100,000 in sales per year and conduct fewer than 150 burials. In order to survive, the small cemetery owner must often hustle as aggressively as any other salesperson.

how can "perpetual care" be assured in cemeteries after they run out of space for new plots?

The cemetery industry has long promoted perpetual care, the notion that your burial area will be tended, well, perpetually. But how can a cemetery continue to pay the expenses for perpetual care after its source of income, new burials, is eliminated?

Stephen L. Morgan, executive vice president of the American Cemetery Association, explained how perpetual care is supposed to work:

> By law, most private cemeteries operate as endowed care cemeteries and are statutorily required to invest a portion of the proceeds from the sale of a lot [and usually, mausoleum sales], frequently a minimum of ten percent in many states [the range is 5-30 percent], into an irrevocable trust fund. The principal of the trust cannot be spent but the trust income is used for cemetery maintenance and repairs. In this manner, income for care and maintenance will be available long after all lots have been sold. The obligation is continuing and literally perpetual, hence the term "perpetual care."

John R. Rodenburg, vice president of the Federated Funeral Directors of America, acknowledges that the principle often breaks down in practice, "as can be seen by looking at many inner-city and country cemeteries that have fallen into disrepair." In the past, small cemeteries were frequently abandoned

WHY DO WE SAY A SUDDEN ONSLAUGHT WAS EXECUTED IN *ONE FELL SWOOP?*

Fell and *swoop* are both Middle English words, and the two words were combined to describe how a bird dives to capture its prey. The graceful and skillful action of a bird seems to contradict the meaning of *fell,* but "fell" has more than one meaning. The *fell* in *one fell swoop* is derived not from the verb meaning "to fall," but from the same Middle English word, *fell,* that formed the root of *felon.*

Fell in Middle English meant "cruel" or "terrible." *Swoop* meant "snatch." *One fell swoop,* then, accurately described the ruthless proficiency of birds of prey.

after they stopped generating cash flow, which is why perpetual-care laws were established in the first place.

In many towns, the responsibility for maintaining cemeteries has fallen on churches, local civic groups, and associations of property owners. Church-owned cemeteries often hand over the tending of the cemetery to a nearby for-profit funeral director.

The standards of service provided by perpetual care vary from state to state, but are almost always minimal compared to the services rendered by active cemeteries or funeral parks. In most cases, perpetual-care statutes mandate that grass must be cut and rows plowed. There is no provision, necessarily, that the grass must be leveled or the grounds landscaped with plants or flowers. Nor do most states have a regulation insisting that snow be plowed away during the winter or even that the cemetery be passable for visitors. "Perpetual care" doesn't include the maintenance of markers or memorials, either.

One small-cemetery owner we talked to said that although the interest on his perpetual-care trust was significant (more than $10,000 annually), this money still represented less than what was needed to hire one full-time employee. How can anyone be expected to maintain a cemetery properly when the income generated by the perpetual-care trust doesn't pay for one maintenance worker?

when a body is laid out at a funeral home, why is the head always on the left side from the viewer's vantage point?

Why are so many readers obsessed with this Imponderable? And why are so many of them from Pennsylvania?

We found no evidence that any religion cares one iota about the direction in which a body is laid out at a viewing. Discussions with many funeral directors confirmed that the arrangement has become a custom not because of religious tradition but because of manufacturing practice.

Caskets can be divided into two types: half-couches, which have two separate lids, either or both of which can be opened; and full couches, whose lids are one, long unit. Full couches are designed to display the entire body at the viewing; half-couches are intended to show the head and upper torso of the deceased, with the option that, if the second lid is opened, the full body can be displayed.

The hinges of all caskets allow the lids to be opened only in one direction. When the lids are lifted, they move first up and then back away from the viewers, to allow an unobstructed view for the bereaved. In many viewing rooms, the raised lids rest against a wall during viewing, dictating the direction the casket will be placed in a viewing room.

According to Howard C. Raether, former executive director and now consultant to the National Funeral Directors Association, the half-couch caskets made in the United States are all manufactured so that "only the left side has an interior and pillow for positioning and viewing the body." The two sides of the half-couch are also not symmetrical and thus not totally interchangeable. The left side of the half-couch is shorter than the "leg side," and because it is not normally opened, the bottom of the right side of the casket is usually unfinished. The interiors of full-couch caskets are also designed for the head to be placed on the left side.

Occasionally, however, a funeral director may need to put the head on the right side of the casket, usually when an injury or disease has disfigured the "wrong" side of the deceased's face. Since American-made caskets are rarely tapered, it is easy to rearrange the pillows inside the casket and put the deceased in the opposite direction.

One of our sources, who has worked in the industry for over fifty years and has sense enough to want to remain anonymous, told *Imponderables* that more families are asking for full-body viewings these days. He singled out Pennsylvania (along with southern New Jersey and parts of Florida and Ohio) for special mention in their preference for full-couch caskets—everywhere else, half-couches predominate.

What's with these Pennsylvanians?

—Submitted by Barbara Peters of Norwood, Pennsylvania. Thanks also to Bridget Hahn of Conneaut Lake, Pennsylvania; Carol Haten of Monroeville, Pennsylvania; Earle Heffley of Springfield, Illinois; Sandy Zak of Pittsburgh, Pennsylvania; and Jason Humble of Starks, Louisiana.

why are barns red?

We first encountered this Imponderable when a listener of Jim Eason's marvelous KGO-San Francisco radio show posed it. "Ummmmm," we stuttered.

Soon we were bombarded with theories. One caller insisted that red absorbed heat well, certainly an advantage when barns had no heating system. Talk-show host and guest agreed it made some sense, but didn't quite buy it. Wouldn't other colors absorb more heat? Why didn't they paint barns black instead?

Then letters from the Bay Area started coming in. Donna Nadimi theorized that cows had trouble discriminating between different colors and just as a bull notices the matador's cape, so a red barn attracts the notice of cows. She added: "I come from West Virginia and once asked a farmer this question. He told me that cows aren't very smart, and because the color red stands out to them, it helps them find their way home." The problem with this theory is that bulls are color-blind. It is the movement of the cape, not the color, that provokes them.

Another writer suggested that red would be more visible to owners, as well as animals, in a snowstorm. Plausible, but a stretch.

Another Jim Eason fan, Kemper "K.C." Stone, had some "suspicions" about an answer. Actually, he was right on the mark:

> The fact is that red pigment is cheap and readily available from natural sources. Iron oxide—rust—is what makes brick clay the color that it is. That's the shade of red that we westerners are accustomed to—the rusty red we use to stain our redwood decks. It's obviously fairly stable too, since rust can't rust and ain't likely to fade.

The combination of cheapness and easy availability made red an almost inevitable choice. Shari Hiller, a color specialist at the Sherwin-Williams Company, says that many modern barns are painted a brighter red than in earlier times for aesthetic reasons. But aesthetics was not the first thing on the mind of farmers painting barns, as Ms. Hiller explains:

> You may have noticed that older barns are the true "barn red." It is a very earthy brownish-red color. Unlike some of the more vibrant reds of today that are chosen for their decorative value, true barn red was selected for cost and protection. When a barn was built, it was built to last. The time and expense of it was monumental to a farmer. This huge wooden structure needed to be protected as economically as possible. The least expensive paint pigments were those that came from the earth.

Farmers mixed their own paint from ingredients that were readily available, combining iron oxide with skim milk—did they call the shade "2% red"?—linseed oil and lime. Jerry Rafats, reference librarian at the National Agricultural Library, adds that white and colored hiding pigments are usually the most costly ingredients in paints.

K.C. speculated that white, the most popular color for buildings in the eighteenth and nineteenth centuries, was unacceptable to farmers because it required constant cleaning and touching up to retain its charm. And we'd like to think that just maybe the farmers got a kick out of having a red barn. As K.C. said, "Red is eye-catching and looks good, whether it's on a barn, a fire truck, or a Corvette."

—Submitted by Kemper "K.C." Stone of Sacramento, California.
Thanks also to Donna Nadimi of El Sobrante, California;
Jim Eason of San Francisco, California; Raymond Gohring
of Pepper Pike, Ohio; Stephanie Snow of Webster, New York;
and Bettina Nyman of Winnipeg, Manitoba.

why is a blue ribbon used to designate first prize?

Most sources we contacted give credit to the English for introducing the blue ribbon. In 1348, King Edward III of England established the Order of the Garter, now considered one of the highest orders in the world. Ribbons had traditionally been used as a badge of knighthood. Members of the Order of the Garter were distinguished by wearing their dark blue ribbon on their hip.

A second theory presented by S. G. Yasnitsky of the Orders and Medals Society of America was new to us:

> Another version of the blue ribbon as meaning the highest achievement may have originated among British soldiers who practiced abstinence by belonging to the various army abstinence groups, especially in India, in the latter part of the nineteenth century. Their basic badge for the first six years' total abstinence was a medal worn on a blue ribbon. Hence a "blue ribbon unit" was one which was comprised of all men who were sporting a blue ribbon in their buttonhole to denote their sobriety. "Blue ribbon panel" and "blue ribbon selection" followed this, I'm sure.

Yasnitsky and others have speculated that our ribbon color schemes might have had an astronomical basis. Blue, the highest award, represented the sky and the heavens, the highest point possible. Red (second prize) represented the sun, which was high up in the sky. Yellow (third prize) represented the stars, once thought to be lower than the sun. Yasnitsky mentions that runners-up in fairs and festivals are often given green ribbons as consolation prizes. The green color probably represents the lowly grass on the ground.

What is the difference between "flotsam" and "jetsam"?

Although they sound suspiciously like two of Santa's missing reindeer, flotsam and jetsam are actually two different types of debris associated with ships. We rarely hear either term mentioned without the other close behind (and saying "jetsam" before "flotsam" is like saying "Cher" before "Sonny"). When we talk about "flotsam and jetsam" today, we are usually referring metaphorically to the unfortunate (for example, "While visiting the homeless shelter, the governor glimpsed what it is like to be the flotsam and jetsam of our society").

At one time, however, "flotsam" and "jetsam" not only had different meanings, but carried important legal distinctions. In English common law, "flotsam" (derived from the Latin *flottare*, "to float") referred specifically to the cargo or parts of a wrecked ship that float on the sea.

"Jetsam" (also derived from Latin— *jactare*, "to throw") referred to goods purposely thrown overboard in order either to lighten the ship or to keep the goods from perishing if the ship did go under.

Although the main distinction between the two terms was the way the goods got into the water, technically, to become jetsam, the cargo had to be dragged ashore and above the high-water line. If not, the material was considered flotsam, which included all cargo found on the shore between the high- and low-water lines.

Actually, two more terms, "lagan" and "derelict," were also used to differentiate cargo. "Lagan" referred to any abandoned wreckage lying at the bottom of the sea; "derelict" was the abandoned ship itself.

While insurance companies today have to pay out for flotsam, jetsam, lagan, and derelict, the old distinctions once dictated who got the remains. Jetsam went to the owner of the boat, but flotsam went to the Crown. The personal effects of nonsurviving crewmen could become flotsam or jetsam—depending on how far the debris traveled and whether it floated.

why do we grow lawns around our houses?

At first blush, this Imponderable seems easily solved. Lawns are omnipresent in residential neighborhoods and even around multiunit dwellings in all but the most crowded urban areas. Lawns are pretty. Enough said.

But think about it again. One could look at lawns as a monumental waste of ecological resources. Today, there are approximately 55 million home lawns in the United States, covering 25 to 30 million acres. In New Jersey, the most densely populated state, *nearly one-fifth of the entire land area is covered with turfgrass,* twice as much land as is used for crop production. Although turfgrass is also used for golf courses and public parks, most is planted for lawns. The average home lawn, if used for growing fruits and vegetables, would yield two thousand dollars' worth of crops. But instead of this land becoming a revenue generator, it is a "drainer": Americans spend an average of several hundred dollars a year to keep their lawns short and healthy.

If the purpose of lawns is solely ornamental, why has the tradition persisted for eons, when most conceptions of beauty change as often as the hem length of women's dresses? The Chinese grew lawns five thousand years ago, and circumstantial evidence indicates that the Mayans and Aztecs were lawn fanciers as well. In the Middle Ages, monarchs let their cattle run loose around their castles, not only to feed the animals, but to cut the grass so that advancing enemy forces could be spotted at a distance. Soon, aristocrats throughout Europe adopted the lawn as a symbol of prestige ("if it's good enough for the king, it's good enough for me!"). The games associated with lawns—bowls, croquet, tennis—all started as upper-class diversions.

The lawn quickly became a status symbol in colonial America, just as it was in Europe. Some homeowners used scythes to tend their lawns, but most let animals, particularly sheep, cows, and horses, do the work. In 1841, the lawn mower was introduced, much to the delight of homeowners, and much to the dismay of grazing animals and teenagers everywhere.

Dr. John Falk, who is associated with the educational research division of the Smithsonian Institution, has spent more time pondering this Imponderable than any person alive, and his speculations are provocative and convincing. Falk believes that our desire for a savannalike terrain, rather than being an aesthetic predilection, is actually a genetically encoded preference. Anthropologists agree that humankind has spent most of its history roaming the grasslands of East Africa. In order to survive against predators, humans needed trees for protection and water for drinking, but also grass-land for foraging. If primitive man wandered away into rain forests, for example, he must have longed to return to the safety of his savanna home. As Falk commented in an interview in *Omni* magazine: "For more than ninety percent of human history the savanna was home. Home equals safety, and that information has to be fairly hard-wired if the animal is going to respond to danger instantaneously."

When we talked to Dr. Falk, he added more ammunition to support his theories. He has conducted a number of cross-cultural studies to ascertain the terrain preferences of people all over the world. He and psychologist John Balling showed subjects photographs of five different terrains—deciduous forest, coniferous forest, tropical rain forest, desert, and savanna—and asked them where they would prefer to live. The savanna terrain was chosen overwhelmingly. Falk's most recent studies were conducted in India and Nigeria, in areas where most subjects had never even seen a savanna. Yet they consistently picked the savanna as their first choice, with their native terrain usually the second preference.

Falk and Balling also found that children under twelve were even more emphatic in their selection of savannas, another strong, if inconclusive, indication that preference for savanna terrain is genetic.

In the *Omni* article, Falk also suggested that even the way we ornament our lawns mimics our East African roots. The ponds and fountains that decorate our grasses replicate the natural water formations of our

WHY IS SOMETHING GREAT, A "REAL KNOCKOUT," CALLED A *DOOZY?*

There is a quaint feel to the word *doozy,* perhaps because the object it was first created to describe has long vanished. The first *doozy* was the Duesenberg, an American car created by two brothers named Duesenberg. State of the art at the time it was produced (1921-37), the Duesenberg was considered more elite than the Cadillac. The engineer brother, Frederick, aimed so high that he installed the same high-performance engines in boats and airplanes as well as automobiles.

homeland, and the popularity of umbrella-shaped shade trees might represent an attempt to re-create the acacia trees found in the African savanna.

Of course, psychologists have speculated about other reasons why we "need" lawns. The most common theory is that lawns and gardens are a way of taming and domesticating nature in an era in which affluent Westerners are virtually divorced from it. Another explanation is that lawns are a way of mapping territory, just as every other animal marks territory to let others know what property it is ready to defend. This helps explain why so many homeowners are touchy about the neighborhood kid barely scraping their lawn while trying to catch a football. As Dr. Falk told *Imponderables*, "People create extensions of themselves. When people create a lawn as an extension of themselves, they see a violation of their lawn as a violation of their space."

Lawns are also a status symbol, for they are a form of property that has a purely aesthetic rather than economic purpose. Historically, only the affluent have been able to maintain lawns—the poor simply didn't have the land to spare. Fads and fashions in lawns change, but there are usually ways for the rich to differentiate their lawns from the hoi polloi's. Highly manicured lawns have usually been the preference of the rich, but not always. In the Middle Ages, weeds were considered beautiful. In many parts of the world, mixed breeds of turf are preferred.

American taste has become increasingly conservative. Ever since World War II, the "ideal" American lawn has been a short, monoculture, weed-free lawn, preferably of Kentucky bluegrass. Falk sees these preferences as carry-overs from the technology used by American agronomists to develop grass for golf courses. Americans always want to build a better mousetrap; our "ideal lawn" has become just about the only type.

Americans have largely resisted the inroads of artificial grass. Although many team owners endorse it, sports fans by and large recoil at artificial turf in sports stadiums—perhaps another genetically determined predisposition.

—Submitted by Rick Barber of Denver, Colorado.

what do all the chime signals on airlines mean? Are they uniform from airline to airline?

We might not be white-knuckle fliers anymore, but let's put it this way: We're closer to a pale pink than a full-bodied red. So we're not too happy when we find ourselves sitting next to fearful fliers. Why is our fate in life always to be seated alongside a middle-aged passenger taking his or her first flight? Invariably, our rowmates quake when they hear the landing gear go up. And more than one has reacted to the chime signals as if they were a death knell; one skittish woman knocked our Diet Coke off our tray when she heard the chimes. She assumed that the three-chime signal must signify that our flight was doomed. Actually, all that happened of consequence was that our pristine white shirt soon resembled the coat of a Dalmatian.

But we always have been curious about the meaning of these chime codes, so we contacted the three largest airlines in the United States—American, United, and Delta—to ask if they would decode the mystery. We were surprised at how forthcoming they were. Nevertheless, for the first time in the history of *Imponderables*, we are going to withhold some of the information our sources willingly provided, for two reasons. First, airline chime signals vary not only from airline to airline but from plane to plane within companies, and today's signals are subject to change in the future. Second, every airline *does* have a code to signify a true emergency, and the airlines aren't particularly excited about the idea of passengers decoding such a signal before the cockpit crew has communicated with flight attendants. Airlines are justifiably concerned about readers confusing emergency signals with innocuous ones and confusing one company's codes with another's. We agree.

Michael Lauria, an experienced pilot at United Airlines, told *Imponderables* that he has never had to activate an emergency chime signal. He is much more likely to sound one chime, to indicate that the cockpit wishes to speak to the first-class cabin attendant or (two chimes) to the coach flight attendants. Even if Lauria's passengers are enduring particularly nasty turbulence, chances are that the cry for help from the cockpit, expressed by the chimes, is more likely to be for a coffee or a soda than for draconian safety measures.

The number of chimes is not the only way of differentiating signals. Some United planes emit different tone frequencies: a lower-tone chime is heard for a passenger call than for a crew call, and a "bing bong" indicates a call from one flight attendant to another.

American Airlines uses different chime configurations to inform attendants when they should prepare for landing, remain seated with seat belts fastened, and call the cockpit crew. Although American does have a designated emergency signal, like other airlines' it is rarely used.

Delta Air Lines features an array of different chime signals, which specify events during a flight. For example, when the "fasten seat belt" signs are turned off, a double high-low chime marks the event. These chimes also tell the flight attendants what elevation the plane has attained. Even during uneventful flights, there are periods of "sterile cockpits," when attendants are not supposed to disturb the cockpit crew except in an emergency. Sterile cockpits occur during takeoff and landing, and even though domestic airlines no longer allow smoking anywhere on the plane, some airlines still use the turning off "no smoking" sign as the marker for when the pilots can be contacted freely.

On most Delta planes, each phone station has a select tone, so that on a widebody plane, the flight attendant can recognize who is calling, and the flight crew can call any one or all of the flight attendant stations at one time. Alison Johnson, manager of aircraft interiors for Delta, told *Imponderables* that during an emergency, it is important for the flight crew to be able to speak to flight attendants without causing panic among passengers. Obviously, if the entire staff is briefed, a game plan can be established before informing passengers about a potential problem.

—Submitted by Gabe Wiener of New York, New York.
Thanks also to Dr. Richard Presnell of Augusta, Georgia.

what good does a "Falling Rock" sign do? How are we supposed to adjust our driving when we see a "Falling Rock" sign?

We know what Laurie Hutler means. Driving along a mountain pass and seeing a "Falling Rock" sign always leaves us with free-floating anxiety. Are we supposed to crane our necks and look up at the mountain to spot tumbling rocks? If so, how are we supposed to keep our eyes on the road?

"Falling Rock" signs are usually placed on roadways adjacent to rocky cliffs. You are supposed to worry about rocks on the road, not rocks tumbling down slopes.

Of course, traffic engineers know that we are going to be more anxious once we see a "Falling Rock" sign, and that is one of the reasons the sign is there in the first place. Anxious drivers proceed more slowly than complacent drivers. The chief of the traffic engineering division of the Federal Highway Administration told *Imponderables*, "By alerting the motorist to the potential hazard, the motorist should be able to react more quickly if a rock is encountered." If the motorist slows down, he or she can choose to drive over small rocks; at faster speeds, accidents are created when drivers swerve to avoid such obstacles. At slow speeds, the option of driving around a larger rock is more feasible.

The "Falling Rock" sign is one of the few warning signs for which there are no federal standards. Some jurisdictions use more accurately worded signs, such as "Caution Rocks May Be on Road" or "Watch for Rocks on Road." New York State chooses to use the wording "Fallen Rocks," which manages to be briefer than these other alternatives while simultaneously making it clear that the greater danger is rocks on the road rather than rocks from above.

The state of New York's Department of Transportation indicated how important brevity is in the effectiveness of warning signs. After reiterating the greater semantic precision of "Fallen" over "Falling," the director of the traffic and safety division, R. M. Gardeski, elaborates:

> Naturally we want sign legends to be as precise as possible, but absolutely precise legends often would be too long and complicated to be effective. Drivers have only a few seconds to read, understand, and react to each sign. Precision has to be balanced with the length and size of the legend to produce signs that can be read and understood quickly and easily. Even if it were more grammatically correct to do otherwise, we might still have chosen "Fallen" over "Falling" so the legend could be larger and more readable.

That's right. New York's "Falling" vs. "Fallen" decision was made partly because "Fallen" contains one less letter than "Falling."

Donald L. Woods, a research engineer at the Texas Transportation Institute, has a refreshing perspective on the problems with warning signs:

Unfortunately, the public presses for warnings of all kinds and the tort liability situation forces government to install far too many warning signs. This results in far too many warning signs being used on our nation's street and highway system. My favorites are "Church" and "Slow Children."

The "Church" warning sign must mean to watch out because that church is really something. Possibly Brother Swaggart's church should have had such a sign. The "Slow Children" warning sign completely mystifies me. Why should folks want to advertise that their children were not too bright?

Obviously, Mr. Woods's tongue was planted firmly in cheek, but his point is well taken. By oversigning, traffic planners risk desensitizing motorists to the danger implicit in the sign.

—Submitted by Laurie Hutler of Boulder Creek, California.

why is there no apostrophe on the flashing "DONT WALK" traffic signal?

Because an apostrophe just uses up space. If you can believe that one of the main reasons New York uses "Fallen Rocks" rather than "Falling Rocks" is because "Fallen" is one letter shorter, why wouldn't you believe that an apostrophe is dead weight?

After all, traffic signs are designed for motorists in moving vehicles who are some distance away. Research has shown that punctuation marks aren't even perceived from a distance. If a punctuation mark isn't noticed, then it is redundant. Any word, mark, or even letter that doesn't add to the meaning of the sign will be eliminated. By using "PED XING" rather than "PEDESTRIAN CROSSING" on signs, the letters can be made larger without a lessening of motorist comprehension.

According to Victor H. Liebe, director of education and training for the American Traffic Safety Services Association, punctuation "is rarely used on any traffic sign or signal except for certain parking signs, which are usually read from a very slowly moving or stopped vehicle."

—Submitted by Bruce W. Miller of Riverside, Connecticut.

where does a new speed limit begin? At the speed limit sign, at some point beyond the sign, or where the sign becomes clearly visible?

If a speed limit drops from fifty-five miles per hour to thirty-five miles per hour, isn't it clearly legal to drive at fifty-five miles per hour until you pass the thirty-five miles per hour sign? But how are we expected to drop twenty miles per hour instantaneously? Is there a grace period, a distinct length of road on which we are exempt from the new speed limit?

No such luck. The speed-limit sign is posted precisely where the new limit takes effect. How you slow down to the new speed is your business, and your problem.

Of course, traffic laws are up to the individual states, but most legislatures rely on the provisions of the federal government's *Manual on Uniform Traffic Control Devices*. And the manual is unambiguous: "Speed limit signs, indicating speed limits for which posting is required by law, shall be located at the points of change from one speed limit to another.... At the end of the section to which a speed limit applies, a Speed Limit sign showing the next speed limit shall be erected." The one provision intended to help drivers slow down before a new speed limit is the "Reduced Speed Ahead" sign. These are placed primarily in rural areas where drops in speed limits can easily reach twenty to thirty-five miles per hour. But these warning signs must be followed by a speed-limit sign that marks precisely where the altered speed limit applies.

—Submitted by Glenn Worthman of Palo Alto, California.

why are covered bridges covered?

We have driven by stretches of rivers where, it seemed, about every third bridge we passed was a covered bridge. Why is one covered when the next two are topless?

The most obvious advantage to a covered bridge is that it blocks "the elements," particularly snow. Accumulated snow can render a bridge impassable, and it is true that covered bridges are found most often in cold climates. Of course, one could argue that engineers should design covers for all roadways. But bridges remain frozen long after adjacent road surfaces, primarily because bridge surfaces are exposed to the elements from all sides, the bottom as well as the top.

But then some folks believe that covered wooden bridges were originally constructed to ease the fears of horses, who were skittish about crossing bridges, particularly if they saw torrents of water gushing below. The fact that covered bridges resembled wooden barns supposedly also allayed the horses' anxiety.

The most likely answer is: to save wood from rotting. Alternate cycles of rain and sun play havoc on the wood. According to Stanley Gordon of the Federal Highway Administration's Bridge Division, an uncovered wooden bridge might last twenty years, while a covered bridge can last a century or longer.

–Submitted by Gary L. Horn of Sacramento, California.
Thanks also to Matthew Huang of Rancho Palos Verdes, California.

whatever happened to pay toilets?

Going to the bathroom is one of the few activities that has gotten cheaper of late. Pay toilets used to be the rule in airports and bus and train stations, and one would often encounter them in gas stations and restaurants.

Pay toilets were never meant to be profit-making enterprises, but merely a method to help defray the costs of cleaning the bathrooms. It was presumed that the dime or quarter "entrance fee" would motivate users to keep the pay stalls cleaner. It didn't work, though, for instead of encouraging users to exercise best behavior, bathrooms with pay toilets were often trashed by angry patrons.

WHY IS A LUCKY OR SPECIAL DAY CALLED A *RED-LETTER DAY?*

As early as the fifteenth century, ecclesiastical calendars designated religious holidays by printing them in red (and, less frequently, purple) letters. In England, saint's days and feast days were printed in red in the calendar of the Book of Common Prayer, indicating that special services were provided for these days. Many calendars distributed by churches and civic organizations still print holidays, and often Sundays, in red.

The vast majority of pay toilets in the 1950s and 1960s were operated by municipalities. According to Ben Castellano of the Federal Aviation Administration, the small amount of revenue generated by pay toilets in airports simply was not worth the attendant hassles: the numerous complaints about their presence and the constantly broken locks that rendered toilets unusable.

But the real death knell of the pay toilet came with several lawsuits filed against municipalities by women's groups. Pay toilets were sexually discriminatory, they argued, because women, unlike men, were forced to pay to urinate. Instead of putting women on the honor code or installing human or video monitors, most cities relented and abandoned the pay toilet. Even male chauvinists were forced to admit that the women's movement had struck a blow for humankind.

why is mincing around a subject called *beating around the bush?*

Medieval men may not have had the thrill of flinging Frisbees, but they had a worthy counterpart, the challenging sport of *batfowling*. A rare nocturnal sport, batfowling consisted of going into a forest or shrub-laden area and beating birds senseless with a bat.

Batfowlers sought sleeping birds for their prey, but being true sportsmen, they didn't want to kill a defenseless bird. So before whacking it with the bat, they were kind enough to wake the bird up first, by stunning it with a harsh light, rendering the bird blind and temporarily helpless. "Sensitive" batfowlers caught the birds in nets rather than using the Darryl Strawberry approach.

Sometimes, though, the birds proved to be uncooperative, selfishly sleeping in bushes where they were invisible, instead of marching forward and offering themselves as ritual sacrifices. So batfowlers engaged servants or boys, known as beaters, to literally beat adjacent bushes to rouse flocks of sleeping birds. As the stunned birds awakened and fled in panic, they would be attracted to the torch or lantern and be socked into unconsciousness by the batfowler.

Although the person today who beats around the bush might not have violence on his mind, he similarly conceals or avoids the real thing that concerns him. While he might pretend to be interested in the bush, he might be more interested in the bird, or worm, lurking inside.

what is the difference between a "kit" and a "caboodle"?

Anyone who thinks that changes in the English language are orderly and logical should take a look at the expression "kit and caboodle." Both words, separately, have distinct meanings, but the two have been lumped together for so long that each has taken on much of the other's meaning.

Both words have Dutch origins: "Kit" originally meant tankard, or drinking cup, while "Boedel" meant property or household stuff. By the eighteenth century, "kit" had become a synonym for tool kit. For example, the knapsacks carried by soldiers that held their eating utensils and nonmilitary necessities were often called "kits." "Boodle" became slang for money, especially tainted money. By the nineteenth century, "caboodle" had taken on connotations of crowds, or large numbers.

Yet the slurring of meanings occurred even before the two terms became inseparable. The *Oxford English Dictionary* quotes from Shelley's 1785 *Oedipus Tyrannus,* "I'll sell you in a lump the whole kit of them." In this context, "caboodle" would seem more appropriate than "kit."

By the mid-nineteenth century, "kit" had found many companion words in expressions that meant essentially the same thing: "kit and biling"; "whole kit and tuck"; "whole kit and boodle" and "whole kit and caboodle" were all used to mean "a whole lot" or "everything and everyone." The *Dictionary of Americanisms* cites a 1948 *Ohio State Journal* that stated: "The whole caboodle will act upon the recommendation of the *Ohio Sun.*"

The expression "kit and caboodle" was popularized in the United States during the Civil War. The slang term was equally popular among the Blue and the Gray. Although the expression isn't as popular as it used to be, it's comforting to know that old-fashioned slang made no more sense than the modern variety.

why is a final effort called *last ditch?*

Anyone who fought in a war has probably hoped that the trench he was in was the "last ditch" he would ever see. Most of us would guess that the *ditch* referred to in *last ditch* is a military trench rather than a farmer's irrigation ditch, but few realize that this expression predates the two world wars.

The first recorded use of *last ditch* was in Bishop Gilbert Burnet's memoirs, *History of My Own Time,* published in the early eighteenth century: "There was a sure way never to see it [Holland] lost, and that was to die in the last ditch." The earliest use of *last ditch* was a literal one, signifying a last stand, a last defense against an aggressive enemy.

The first American citation was in a proclamation issued by the citizens of Westmoreland, Virginia, in 1798: " ... but one additional Obligation, To Die in the Last Ditch or uphold our nation."

Thomas Jefferson was perhaps the first to use the phrase figuratively (1821): "A government ... driven to the last ditch by the universal call for liberty."

what exactly are the liberal arts, and who designated them so?

Our correspondent, Bill Elmendorf, contacted two four-year colleges and one two-year college for the answer to this question. Despite the fact that they were liberal arts colleges, none of the officials he spoke to could answer this question. Evidently, a good liberal arts education doesn't provide you with the answer to what a liberal art is.

Actually, a consultation with an encyclopedia will tell you that the concept of the liberal arts, as developed in the Middle Ages, involved seven subjects: grammar, logic, rhetoric, arithmetic, geometry, music, and astronomy. Why astronomy and not biology? Why rhetoric and not art? For the answers to this question, we have to delve into the history of the liberal arts.

Our expression is derived from the Latin *artes liberalis*, "pertaining to a free man." Liberal arts are contrasted with the "servile" arts, which have practical applications. As educator Tim Fitzgerald wrote *Imponderables*, "the liberal arts were considered 'liberating,' enabling the student to develop his or her potential beyond the mundane, to create, to be fully human, to (in the medieval mindset) believe."

The notion of seven ennobling arts emerged long before the Middle Ages. In Proverbs 9:1, the Bible says, "Wisdom hath built her house, she hath hewn out her seven pillars." Robert E. Potter, professor of education at the University of Hawaii at Manoa, wrote *Imponderables* a fascinating letter tracing the history of the liberal arts. Before the birth of Christ and into the first century A.D., Roman writers like Cicero and Quintilian discussed the proper curriculum for the orator and public leader. Varro (116-27 B.C.)

WHY DOES *HOBNOB* MEAN "TO MINGLE" OR "TO CHAT SOCIALLY"?

Hobnob goes back to the Middle English *habben* ("to have") and *ne habben* ("to have not"). *Hobnob* is a contraction of these two words.

In the twelfth century, when Chaucer used the word, *hobnob* meant "hit or miss" or "give and take" as well as "have and have not."

Hobnob eventually described the age-old custom of alternating purchasing rounds of drinks (literally "having" and then "not having" to buy the next drink). Although the use of *hobnob* is no longer confined to drinking, the conviviality and sociability conjured by *hobnob* resemble the interaction among a group of drinkers.

---

listed in his *Libri Novem Disciplinarum* the seven liberal arts but also included medicine and architecture.

Potter mentions that in the early Christian era, church elders opposed the classical liberal arts. Perhaps the most stirring condemnation was written in the Apostolic Constitutions in the third century:

> Refrain from all the writings of the heathen for what has thou to do with strange discourses, laws, or false prophets, which in truth turn aside from the faith for those who are weak in understanding? For if thou wilt explore history, thou hast the Books of the Kings; or seekest thou for words of wisdom and eloquence, thou hast the Prophets, Job, and the Book of Proverbs, wherein thou shalt find a more perfect knowledge of all eloquence and wisdom, for they are the voice of the Lord.

Later Christian scholars, including Augustine, embraced the study of the liberal arts.

Potter calls Martianus Capella of Carthage's *The Marriage of Philology and Mercury* the "definitive" work on the liberal arts:

> This fourth-century allegory had nine books. The first two described the wedding of the daughter of Wisdom, a mortal maiden who represented schooling, and Mercury, who, as the inventor of letters, symbolized the arts of Greece. The remaining seven books describe the bridesmaids. Apollo did not admit two other "bridesmaids," medicine

and architecture, "inasmuch as they are concerned with perishable earthly things."

Many people attack the modern liberal arts education, saying that little is taught that pertains to our actual lives now. Little do they know that this lack of "relevance" is precisely what characterized the liberal arts from their inception. In ancient times, servile folks had to sully themselves with practical matters like architecture, engineering, or law. Only the elite freemen could ascend to the lofty plateau of the contemplation of arithmetic.

Today, the meaning of liberal arts is murky, indeed. Art, other hard sciences besides astronomy, foreign languages, philosophy, history, and most social sciences are often included under the umbrella of liberal arts. Just about any school that *doesn't* train you for a particular profession is called a liberal arts institution.

—Submitted by Bill Elmendorf of Lebanon, Illinois.
Thanks also to Brianna Liu of Minneapolis, Minnesota.

has anybody ever been given *long shrift?*

How many times have you ever seen the word *shrift* without *short* preceding it? Never? *Shrift* is one of those words that I call an "inevitable." As soon as you see it, you know its partner *short* will be alongside it, just as surely as *ample* will be followed by *parking* (was *ample* coined simply as a way of describing large parking lots?).

Shrift has a long history of its own; *scrifan* was Anglo-Saxon for "to receive confession." *Shrift* is simply the noun form of *shrive*, which today means "confession to a priest." We use *shrive*, in particular, to describe the process of giving confession and receiving absolution upon one's deathbed, an important ritual of the Catholic faith.

Short shrift, then, refers to the inability to give a full confession or receive absolution, and the expression comes from the practice of not giving condemned prisoners enough time to shrive properly. Often they would be allowed only a few seconds to speak at the gallows before the executioner. In *Richard III*, Shakespeare alludes to the practice. The Duke of Gloucester, soon to become Richard III, has just sentenced Lord Hastings to death. The official in charge of the execution, Sir Richard Ratcliff, tells the wailing Hastings:

> Dispatch my lord; the duke would be at dinner:
> Make a short shrift; he longs to see your head.

So although we have seen many long shrifts in movies and soap operas, no such expression has evolved, and *short shrift* has broadened its meaning to any context in which we allow little time or give insufficient attention to the matter at hand.

why do we say that someone who is fired *gets the sack?*

The ancient Romans didn't believe in mollycoddling convicted felons. Rehabilitation wasn't their style. Those convicted of parricide or other heinous murders were tied in a sack and dumped into the Tiber River, instantly solving any potential recidivism problem.

The practice spread throughout many other European countries, and, as late as the nineteenth century, murderers in Turkey were tossed into the Bosporus in a sack. *To get the sack*, then, probably was used figuratively as a threat of any sort of punishment, such as losing one's job.

Another theory to explain how *get the sack* was recorded—as early as 1611 in France—is that it referred to craftsmen of the Middle Ages. Artisans carried their tools in sacks; while they worked, they handed the sacks to their employers. When a craftsman *got the sack*, it meant that his services no longer were required. He was left, literally, *holding the bag.*

why are there dents on the top of cowboy hats?

Of course, not *all* cowboy hats have dents. How about country and western star George Strait's? Or *Bonanza*'s Dan ("Hoss") Blocker's?

Yet the vast majority of cowboy hats do have dents, and no one we spoke to could give us any other explanation than that dents are there "for style." Ralph Beatty, director of the Western/English Retailers of America, theorizes that early cowboy hats may have acquired dents by wear, and later were intentionally added.

As one, better-to-be-kept-anonymous, western hat marketer put it, "Let's face it. Without the dent, you would look like a dork."

We wonder if he would have said that to Dan Blocker's face.

—*Submitted by Lisa R. Bell of Atlanta, Georgia.*

why do we say that someone who has appropriated someone else's ideas or future remarks has *stolen thunder* from the victim?

I had always assumed that this expression must have Greek mythological roots and perhaps was a reference to Zeus. The true story is much more prosaic.

John Dennis, an English poet and playwright, wrote a tragedy called *Appius and Virginia,* which was produced in 1709 to less than rousing commercial success. Only one element of the production stirred the audience: thunder sound effects more realistic than any heard before on the stage, effects that Dennis himself created.

The play failed, but the theater's next production didn't. Dennis went to check out a successful production of *Macbeth* and was more than a

---

WHY DOES *BACK AND FILL* MEAN "TO VACILLATE"?

Back and fill always sounded more like a disco step than its actual meaning, which has a long nautical tradition. In sailing, *backing* means to let the wind blow sails against the mast. *Filling* means to let the wind blow the sails toward the bow. *Backing and filling* means alternating having the sails "filled" with wind and then allowing the wind to escape by hauling "back" on the stays.

Yes, backing and filling impedes the movement of the ship, but sometimes this is necessary. When tacking a ship, a navigator might want to keep the boat in the same place. If the tide is running with the ship but the wind is against her, backing and filling is the usual tactic to steady the boat, even if this results in alternating movements forward and backward. Backing and filling is also a way to let the tide take control of the movement of a boat, especially when negotiating through narrow channels or rivers where banks, wharfs, or other objects stand as dangerous obstacles.

little upset to discover that his sound effects were used in the storm scenes of Shakespeare's tragedy.

Different sources vary slightly in describing what Dennis exclaimed upon hearing "his" thunder help promote the new production, but they are all variations of Stuart Berg Flexner's quote: "See how the rascals use me! They will not let my play run, and yet they steal my thunder!" I'm sure that Dennis would be even more embittered to learn that the only phrase of his that has gained immortality is his expression of sour grapes.

why is someone who surreptitiously listens to others' conversations called an *eavesdropper?*

Eavesdropping isn't exactly an endearing activity today, but from the sixteenth through the nineteenth centuries, eavesdropping was a crime in England. Back then, communities were not equipped with gutter systems, so houses were surrounded by eavesdrops, spaces all around a building

HOW DID *XMAS* COME TO STAND FOR *CHRISTMAS?*

The use of the colloquial "Xmas" has often been singled out as an example of how the holiday has been commercialized and robbed of its religious content.

The *X* in Xmas is actually the descendant of the Greek equivalent of *Ch,* as in "Christos," which means "Christ." The letter *X* has stood for Christ (look up *X* in any dictionary) since at least A.D. 1100, and the term "Xmas" was first cited in 1551. Word expert Eric Partridge points out that the scholarly abbreviation for "Christianity" is "Xianity."

So many people dislike "Xmas" for its supposed crassness that its use is now virtually confined to commercial literature and banners. The *New York Times Manual of Style and Usage,* for example, offers this simple recommendation for when "Xmas" is acceptable: "Never use."

—Submitted by Bobby Dalton of Maryland Heights, Missouri.
Thanks also to Andrew Neiman of Dallas, Texas.

where water dripped from the eaves. The purpose of the eavesdrop was to allow a wide overhang so that rain fell far enough from the house to safeguard the security of the foundation.

The first *eavesdroppers* were nefarious types who literally stood in the eavesdrops to overhear private conversations. Protected from the elements by the overhang, this low-tech espionage evidently faded as sewer systems rendered eavesdrops obsolete.

—Submitted by Patricia Fox-Sheinwold of New York, New York.

does anyone ever engage in *low jinks?* And what's a *jink?*

Originally a Scottish word, the primary meaning of *jink* has, for the past two hundred years, been "to move swiftly, especially with sudden turns." *High jinks* has existed just as long. Although we now use *high jinks* to refer to any prank or frolic, during the late seventeenth century and the eighteenth century, *high jinks* was a popular parlor game. A throw of dice would determine one "victim." He would have to embarrass himself by performing some prank for the amusement of the other revelers; if the victim refused or couldn't satisfactorily perform the task, he had to pay a forfeit, usually downing a hefty container of liquor.

If this is the origin of *HIGH jinks,* it is probably just as well that there is no *LOW jinks* in our lexicon.

why do Scotsmen wear kilts? And why didn't men in surrounding areas wear kilts?

Entire books have been written about the history of the kilt, so the first part of this question is hardly imponderable. Our reader's focus is on why this strange garment was a mainstay in the Highlands of Scotland and not in the rest of Scotland or surrounding countries.

Although we are most likely today to see a Scot in a kilt, inside or outside Scotland, only in a parade or on a formal occasion, its initial popularity was based on practical rather than ceremonial or aesthetic considerations.

Although the contemporary kilt resembles a skirt, early kilts covered not only the waist to knee region of the body but the upper torso as well. Essentially, the earliest kilts were huge blankets, which were wrapped around the body several times and draped over the shoulder. This one garment served as blanket, sleeping bag, cloak, and trousers.

The geography of the Highlands of Scotland was no doubt responsible for the kilt's longevity. The Highlands are mountainous and damp, with innumerable streams and rivers. Anyone traversing the countryside in long pants and shoes would quickly be wearing wet long pants and wet shoes. The kilt saved the wearer from continually rolling up his pants. By rearranging the kilt, he could shield himself from the cold and wind. Perhaps most importantly, shepherds could leave their home base for months at a time wearing one garment and no "extra" clothes. As kilts were constructed out of elements easily obtainable in the Highlands (wool from the omnipresent sheep, and the plaid prints from native vegetable dyes), even the poorest of Highlanders could afford one. And the poor wore the kilt the most: According to Steward MacBreachan, a Scottish historian, performer, and demonstrator of Highland games and ancient Scottish culture, the kilt was of special importance to those who had to spend most or all of the day outdoors. More affluent Highlanders could switch from kilts to pants once they returned home from a day's work.

We had a long talk with Philip Smith, Ph.D., one of thirteen fellows of the Scottish Tartan Society worldwide and an author of several books about Scotland. He informed us that kilts, or their equivalents, were worn in many parts of Europe in the ancient world. The Scottish kilt is not too different from the garb of the ancient Romans and the Portuguese.

Smith feels that the widespread use of the horse in other countries eventually led to the abandonment of kiltlike clothing. For rather obvious anatomical reasons, kilts and horse riding are, let us say, an uncomfortable fit for men.

After an unsuccessful Jacobean uprising in 1745, the English Prohibition Act of 1746 (more commonly known as the "Dress Act") banned the wearing of both the kilt and any tartan material by anyone except the Highlands regiment. Ironically, the prohibition is probably responsible for our current association of Scotsmen with kilts. Scotsmen kept their kilts during the ban and wore them surreptitiously at closed gatherings. Along with the tartan, which identifies the clan of the wearer, the kilt became a symbol of Scottish pride.

As Scotsmen needed the blanketlike garment less and less for practical reasons in the nineteenth and twentieth centuries, the kilt, if anything, gained in significance as a way for Scotland to carve its psychic independence from England. If proof of this were necessary, we need only point to the wearing of kilts in ceremonial occasions by Scotsmen from the south, who never wore them in the eighteenth century.

—Submitted by Yvonne Martino of LaVerne, California.

why do hospital gowns tie at the back?

It's bad enough being laid up in the hospital. Why do patients have to undergo the indignity of having their backsides exposed to all? This is a fashion statement that even sick people don't want to make.

We realize that hospital gowns aren't the first priority of hospital administrators, that items like nursing staffs, research budgets, and surgical care justifiably occupy much of their time. But while hospitals pursue the impossible dream of serving edible food, the eradication of the back-tied gown is possible right now.

The original justification for the back closure of hospital gowns was that this configuration enabled health care workers to change the gowns of the bedridden without disturbing the patients. If the gown tied in the front, the patients would have to be picked up (or lift themselves up) to remove the garment.

Perhaps it is growing concern for "patient modesty" (buzz words in the "patient apparel" industry), or perhaps it is jockeying for competitive advantage among hospitals, especially private, for-profit hospitals, but many health care administrators are starting to recognize the existence of alternatives to the back-tied gown. Scott Hlavaty, director of patient/surgical product management of uniform giant Angelica, told *Imponderables* that ties on the sides provide a maximum of patient modesty while requiring no more patient inconvenience to remove.

Angelica and other companies manufacture gowns for patients that minimize patient exposure and inconvenience when procedures are performed. Hlavaty explains:

> There are specialized gowns with "I.V. sleeves" that allow the gown to be removed by unsnapping the sleeves so that the I.V. tubes do not have to be removed from the patient in order to change a gown. Also, with the advent of pacemakers and heart monitors, "telemetry pockets"

have been placed in the center of gowns. These pockets have openings in the back to allow for the pass through of the monitoring device so that these do not have to be disconnected either.

Some nurses we spoke to commented that gowns with back closures make it more convenient to give shots (in the backside, of course). But many patients prefer to wear their own pajamas, and nurses always manage to administer the shot.

Even if a patient were so incapacitated that a back closure was deemed best, many improvements have been made in hospital uniforms to prevent patients from exposing themselves to roommates and passersby. Back-closure gowns wouldn't be such a problem if the closures were made secure. Uniforms are now available with metal or plastic grippers, as well as Velcro. And just as important, gowns are available with a "full overlap back," which provides enough material to overlap more like a bathrobe than a traditional hospital gown. At least with a full overlap gown, you have a shot at covering your rump if the closure unfastens.

Sure, these improvements in gown design cost a little more. But in times when a day in the hospital costs more than the weekly salary of the average person, who cares about a few more cents? After all, how can you encourage postsurgical patients to take a stroll around the hospital corridors when they're more concerned about being the objects of peeping Toms than they are about aches and pains?

—Submitted by Diane M. Rhodes of Herndon, Virginia.

why do nurses wear white? Why do surgeons wear blue or green when operating?

Florence Nightingale always wore a white uniform. White, of course, is a symbol of purity, and in the case of a nurse, an appropriate and practical one—white quickly shows any dirtiness.

Surgeons also wore white until 1914, when a surgeon decided that red blood against a white uniform was rather repulsive and needlessly graphic. The spinach green color he chose to replace it helped neutralize the bright red.

At the end of World War II, the lighting was changed in operating rooms, and most surgeons switched to a color called "misty green." Since about 1960, most surgeons have used a color called "seal blue," which contains a lot of gray. Why this latest switch? According to Bernard Lepper of the

Career Apparel Institute of New York City, seal blue shows up better on the TV monitors used to demonstrate surgical techniques to medical students.

—Submitted by Norman J. Sanchez of Baton Rouge, Louisiana. Thanks also to Lori Bending of Des Plaines, Illinois; Andrew Neiman of Dallas, Texas; and Reverend Ken Vogler of Jeffersonville, Indiana.

why did Pilgrims' hats have buckles?

Would you be heartbroken if we told you that just about everything they taught you in elementary school about Pilgrims was wrong? We at Imponderables Central remember being forced to draw pictures of Pilgrims during elementary school, presumably to obscure the food stains on our families' refrigerators during the Thanksgiving season. We remember not liking to draw Pilgrims, because they wore boring black and white clothing, and the men wore those long black steeple hats sporting a gold or silver buckle.

So it is with more than a little feeling of righteous vengeance that we report that we were sold a bill of goods. Pilgrims might have worn hats, and those hats might have even been tall. But they were rarely black and never had a buckle on them.

How were generations brainwashed into thinking that Pilgrims wore buckled hats? For many Americans, there is confusion between the Pilgrims and Puritans. The two groups weren't totally unrelated: Both were early settlers in America in the early seventeenth century, and both groups fled

WHY IS Rx THE SYMBOL FOR A PRESCRIPTION?

The *R* is the sign of the Roman god Jupiter (the patron of medicines). *Rx* was an abbreviation of *recipe* (from the Latin *recipere*—"to receive").

The reason that *R* was atop all prescriptions was that *recipe* meant "take" in Latin, so that "take" preceded all directions to the patient. Even the English word *recipe* originally referred to medical prescriptions, although the connection between formulas for medical purposes and formulas for cooking were then less farfetched, since both used many of the same herbs and spices.

—Submitted by Douglas Watkins, Jr., of Hayward, California.

England to escape what they considered to be an authoritarian and tyrannical Anglican Church, the state-sponsored religion of their government.

But in spirit, the two groups were far apart. The Pilgrims were separatists, who wanted to practice a simple religion without the rituals and symbolism that they felt had spoiled the "Protestant" church. Pilgrims first tried emigrating to Holland, but the poor economic conditions there, along with some religious intolerance, led one contingent to come to America. Approximately sixty of the one hundred passengers aboard the *Mayflower* were separatists (i.e., Pilgrims), and they settled in or near Plymouth, Massachusetts, in 1620.

Puritans, on the other hand, did not want to sever their relationship from the Anglican fold completely, but sought to "purify" the church. Puritans wanted to eliminate many of the reforms of the Protestant movement, and return the church to more traditional practices. Several hundred Puritans moved to America in 1629, and settled the Massachusetts Bay Colony in what is now Cape Cod.

Both Puritans and Pilgrims have reputations as authoritarian, humorless, and conformist in their beliefs, but this stereotype characterizes the Puritans (who later in the century went on to conduct the Salem witch trials) more than the Pilgrims, who were much more democratic and inclusive in style. For example, the Pilgrims did, indeed, befriend local Native Americans, although it is unclear whether this pact was motivated by feelings of brotherhood or an arrangement for mutual self-defense.

Both Pilgrims and Puritans would probably be appalled that they are lumped together in Americans' consciousness today. Puritans would probably consider Pilgrims to be hopeless idealists, and too tolerant of dissent; Pilgrims would probably have deemed Puritans intolerant of others, and too timid to sever their links to the Anglican Church.

The two groups' different attitudes toward religion and democracy were reflected in their apparel choices. It was the Puritans who dressed the way Pilgrims are often depicted—with dark, somber clothing. Pilgrims, on the other hand, dressed much like their counterparts in England at the time. They did not consider it a sin to wear stylish or colorful clothing—indeed, several of the men who made the original trip on the *Mayflower* were in the clothing or textile trade. Many dyes were available to the Pilgrims, and they favored bright clothing—wills, provisions lists, written inventories, contemporaneous histories, and even sparse physical evidence all indicate that male *Mayflower* passengers wore green, red, yellow, violet, and blue garments along with the admittedly more common white, gray, brown, and black ones. The Pilgrim men wore many different types of hats, including soft caps made of wool or cloth, straw hats, and felt hats with wide brims. Wealthier Pilgrims might have worn more elaborate silk hats with decorative cords or tassels—but nary a buckle in sight.

We contacted Caleb Johnson, a Mayflower descendant who has written the 1,173-page book *The Complete Works of the Mayflower Pilgrims* and hosts a Web site devoted to all things Pilgrim at www.mayflowerhistory.com. Johnson confirmed what we had read in other histories:

> The Pilgrims did not have buckles on their clothing, shoes, or hats. Buckles did not come into fashion until the late 1600s—more appropriate for the Salem witchcraft trials time period than the Pilgrims' time period.

So if Pilgrims didn't wear buckles, why have we always seen depictions of Pilgrims wearing what turns out to be nonexistent doodads on hats that they never actually wore? Johnson implicates writers:

> I am not sure I can pinpoint a specific reason as to why the popular image developed. I would suspect that authors and poets such as Nathaniel Hawthorne, Henry Wadsworth Longfellow, even Arthur Miller [in *The Crucible*], might have contributed to the "popular culture" image of a generic New England Puritan, which then got backward-applied to the early seventeenth-century Separatists—many not consciously realizing that 70 years separated the arrival of the Pilgrims and the more "traditional" Puritan we see portrayed at, say, the Salem witchcraft trials.
>
> It really wasn't until the mid-twentieth century that any serious scholarship into the archaeology, contemporary artwork, contemporary accounts, and analysis of historical records (such as probate estate inventories) of the Pilgrims enlightened us as to what they truly were wearing.

We also heard from Carolyn Freeman Travers, research manager and historian for the Plimoth Plantation, a "living-history museum" in Plymouth, Massachusetts ("Plimoth" was the preferred spelling of William Bradford, the first governor of the colony). The Plimoth Plantation boasts a replica of the *Mayflower,* a re-creation of a Pilgrim village, arts and crafts, and no buckles. She dates the buckle-obsession to the early twentieth century, and thinks artists were the key perpetrators:

> The popular image of the Pilgrim developed in America about 1900 to 1920 into the man with the bowl-shaped haircut; tall, dark hat with the prominent square buckle; and large square buckles on his belt and shoes as well. The square buckles on the belt and shoes actually appear very frequently, and seem to mean quaint and "old-timey"—popular depictions of eighteenth-century people have them. Mother Goose, Halloween witches, and leprechauns generally do. The last often have

the tall-crowned, narrow-brimmed hat with the buckle as well—it's the green color of the clothing that sets them apart.

Why turn-of-the-century artists chose the buckle as a hat ornament to mean the Pilgrims/Puritans, I don't know. Earlier historical paintings of the mid-nineteenth century often had hats with a strap and buckle for Puritan men of the English Civil War. The famous 1878 painting by William Yeames, *And When Did You Last See Your Father?*, has a hat of this style, known as a sugar-loaf from the shape, with a strap and a buckle for the Puritan interrogator. There is also a similar hat in *The Burial of Charles I* (1857) by Charles W. Cope. My guess is that American painters looked to these paintings for inspiration, and went on from there.

Buckles did adorn hats in the late seventeenth century, though. We corresponded with the manager and curator of Plymouth's Pilgrim Hall Museum, Peggy Baker. Her museum features a cool Pilgrim-era felt hat processed from beaver furs that can be seen at www.pilgrimhall.org/beav_hat.htm. Baker concurred with our experts that buckles weren't around in the early seventeenth century, but came into vogue later:

> Buckles on hats were a genuine style, however—just not for Pilgrims. It was a short-lived style in the later seventeenth century, a fad, if you will. Why would anyone put a buckle on his hat? Who can really understand the vagaries of fashion? Imagine trying to explain logically and rationally to an audience 300 years from now the costumes worn, for instance, by Britney Spears and her imitators?

Who could explain those costumes right now?

Peggy Baker agrees that artists are probably to "blame" for the buckle misconceptions:

> What happened, however, was that Victorian-era artists, illustrating the Pilgrims, were less interested in historical accuracy than in conveying the impression of "ye olde-timey." They used the buckled hat to convey that impression and the image became "stuck" in the popular imagination.

—Submitted by Michael Goodnight of Neenah, Wisconsin.

WHY IS SOMETHING DONE SECRETLY *ON THE Q.T.?*

This nineteenth-century expression comes from the first and last letters of "quiet."

why do sailors wear bell-bottom trousers?

Nobody knows for sure if there was one particular reason why this custom started, but three theories predominate:

1. The flared leg allows bell-bottoms to fit over boots easily. Sailors traditionally sleep with their boots at the side of the bed, so that, in case of emergency, they don't have to waste time trying to position their pants over their footwear. Once a sailor arrives on deck, having the trouser legs fully cover the top of the boot has practical advantages as well—it protects him from spray and rain entering his boots.

2. Bell-bottoms are easily rolled up. Because sailors often work with potentially harmful chemicals (scrubbing the deck with lye, for example), rolling up the cuffs prevents permanent damage to the pants. Also, if a sailor needs to wade ashore, bell-bottoms can easily be rolled up above the knee.

3. If a sailor is thrown overboard, bell-bottoms are also easier to remove than conventional trousers. And the loose fit of the bell-bottom also makes it easier to remove boots in the water.

Sailors in boot camp are taught another practical use for bell-bottom trousers. If the legs are tied at the ends, bell-bottoms can hold quite a lot of air; in a pinch, they can be used as flotation devices.

why do judges wear black robes?

American law is derived from English common law. English judges have always worn robes, so it follows logically that American judges would, too. But the road from English garb to American robes has been bumpier than you might expect.

Actually, there wasn't such a profession as judge in England until the last half of the thirteenth century. Before then, high-level clergymen, robe-wearers all, arbitrated disputes and expounded law. But the church eventually forbade its clergy from the practice, and a new job category was born. From the very start, judges, like most important people, wore robes.

Not too long after the first judge donned his robe, Parliament enacted several laws (between 1337 and 1570) dictating just who could wear what kind of robe. Judges' gowns were often elaborate affairs, usually made of silk and fur. (High judges wore ermine; sergeants, lambskin.)

Green was the most popular color for judges' robes at first; later, scarlet gowns and, to a lesser extent, violet gowns, predominated. Black robes did not appear until 1694, when all judges attended the Westminster Abbey funeral of Queen Mary II dressed in black, as a sign of respect for the queen. The mourning period went on for years, and some, but by no means all, lawyers and judges wore black gowns into the next century.

Our Founding Fathers actually argued over whether our justices of the Supreme Court should wear robes at all. Thomas Jefferson railed against "any needless official apparel," but Alexander Hamilton and Aaron Burr favored them and won the argument. At the first session of the court, Chief Justice Jay wore a robe of black silk with salmon-colored facing. By the early nineteenth century, Supreme Court justices donned black robes of the style worn today.

The solemn costumes of the Supreme Court were not necessarily mimicked by lower courts. Some colonial court judges in the eighteenth century, such as those in Massachusetts, wore gowns and powdered wigs. But in reaction to the Revolutionary War, most trappings of English aristocracy were banished. In fact, the wearing of robes was discontinued in Massachusetts until 1901.

Judges in the West and South tended to be a little less formal. In his book *The Rise of the Legal Profession in America,* Anton-Hermann Chroust described one of the first judges in Indiana as having a judicial costume consisting of "a hunting shirt, leather pantaloons, and a fox skin cap." Most legal scholars believe that the majority of judges in colonial and pre–Civil War times did not wear robes at all.

One reason why so little is known about the dress of judges in early America is that few laws or regulations govern what judges wear. Only Michigan prescribes a dress code ("When acting in his or her official capacity in the courtroom, a judge shall wear a black robe"), and nothing can stop judges from wearing a chartreuse robe if they desire, or none at all.

Still, the vast majority of judges do wear black robes today.

The only reason they aren't wearing more colorful attire is because Queen Mary II died three hundred years ago.

—Submitted by Susie T. Kowalski of Middlefield, Ohio.
Thanks also to Karen Riddick of Dresden, Tennessee.

why do priests wear black?

Imponderables readers are asserting their spiritual side. At least you seem to be curious about superficial questions about Catholic priests and the clothes they wear, and that's good enough for us. Most readers assume that every vestment was adopted for its symbolic meaning, but in reality many of the clothes priests wear reflect the everyday dress of nonreligious folks nearly two millennia ago.

As John Dollison, author of the whimsical but solidly researched book *Pope-Pourri,* put it:

> Because they believed the second coming of Christ was imminent, [early Christians] didn't bother to formalize many aspects of their new religion. Clerical dress was no exception—nobody gave any thought to what priests should wear during Mass; they just wore the same clothes that laypeople did....
>
> Fashions changed over time, but the priests didn't. They stuck with the same clothes they had always worn ... until their garments became so different from what everyone else was wearing that they were associated exclusively with religious life.

Not until the sixth century did the Church start to codify the dress of priests, and mandate that special garb be worn outside of the sanctuary. Even if most Catholics have no idea of the reasons for the uniforms, Dr. Brian Butler of the U.S. Catholic Historical Society feels: "The Church wants priests to be recognized easily by the laity. This is in the interest of both parties." You're unlikely to see priests in pastels soon.

Some priests started wearing black vestments in the early days of Christianity, as Father Kevin Vaillancourt of the Society of Traditional Roman Catholics explains:

> The practice of priests' wearing black originated in Rome centuries ago. Since the priesthood involves a renunciation of pleasures that the laity can practice, black was worn as a symbol of death—death to these desires, and death to slavish attachment to the fashions of the world. They were to concentrate solely on the service to God and others.

But by no means was there uniformity among priests in their garb until much later. Professor Marie Anne Mayeski of the theology department of Loyola Marymount University in Los Angeles points out that no specific color was required until after the Council of Trent (1545-1563), and that a

response to the Reformation might have been partly responsible for the codification of clerical garb:

> Perhaps Catholic and Anglican clerics did not want to appear less sober and upright than their Puritan challengers.

There are exceptions to the generalization that priests wear black vestments. Higher-ranking priests put a little color in their garb. Cardinals' cassocks feature scarlet buttons, trim, and inside hems; bishops and other higher officials don amaranth; and chaplains to the pope wear purple trim. During liturgical ceremonies, the cardinals wear all-scarlet cassocks, bishops wear purple, while parish priests wear black, although there are even exceptions here—a few dioceses, especially in warm-weather areas such as South America and Africa, allow priests to wear white cassocks, with trim indicating their rank.

—Submitted by Doug Ebert of San Bruno, California. Thanks also to Keith Cooper of Brooklyn, New York; Douglas Watkins, Jr., of Hayward, California; and Tony Dreyer and William Morales, Jr., of parts unknown.

since priests wear black, why does the pope wear white?

Blame it on Pius V, who assumed the papacy from 1566 until his death in 1572. For centuries before that, popes wore red. Why the change? Reverend Monsignor Dr. Alan F. Detscher, executive director of the Secretariat for the Liturgy, explains:

> Religious men who became bishops wore a cassock in the same color as the habit worn by their religious community. Pius V, being a [member of the] Dominican order, continued the practice of using the color of his religious habit, even after he was elected pope. The practice of the pope wearing white continued on after his papacy. On some occasions, the pope will wear a red cape over his white cassock, this a reminder that the more ancient papal color was not white, but red.

Like other religious traditions, what might have started as a personal predilection became codified to the point where now there are elaborate agreements about color codes—you'd think we were talking about battling VH-1 Divas who feared clashing outfits. For example, when the queen of England visits the Vatican, she wears black, as she is technically representing the Protestant Anglican church. But when the pope visits her at Buckingham Palace, she can wear chartreuse if that's what she fancies.

—Submitted by a caller on the Jim Eason Show, KGO-AM, San Francisco, California.

why does the pope change his name upon assuming his office?

The tradition of name changes for Church officials dates back to the beginnings of the Christian movement. In the Book of Matthew, Jesus appoints his disciple Peter to be the first head of the Church. Yet Peter's birth name was Simon.

According to Lorraine D'Antonio, the retired business manager of the Religious Research Association,

> Their names were changed to signify the change in roles, attitudes, and way of life. When the pope assumes his role as head of the Church, it is assumed that he will change his life as his name is changed when he dedicates his total being to the service of the Church. Quite often, when a person dedicates his or her life to the service of God (during ordination, confirmation, etc.), the person assumes a new name, as he or she assumes a new role and commitment.

The first pope who we know changed his name was John II, in A.D. 533. Presumably, his given name, Mercurio, a variation of the pagan god Mercury, was deemed unsuitable for the head of the Church. So Mercurio paid tribute to John I by adopting his name.

No other pope changed his name until Octavian chose John XII for his papal name in 955. A few decades later, Peter Canepanova adopted John XIV. Brian Butler, president of the U.S. Catholic Historical Society, told *Imponderables* that John XIV was the first of several popes with the given name of Peter to start a tradition—no pontiff has ever taken the name of the Church's first pope.

Butler notes that the last pope to keep his baptismal name was Marcellus II, born Marcello Cervini, who served in the year 1555.

—Submitted by David Schachow of Scarborough, Ontario.

5
MACHINES AND DEVICES

Right or wrong: engineering is ruled by logic and reason? You would think so. But if it were true, a toaster would last forever. Here we explore the often surprising world of marketing and manufacturing with profound questions, such as why are there 88 keys on a piano?

why do gas gauges in automobiles take forever to go from registering full to half-full, and then drop to empty at the speed of light?

On a long trek down our illustrious interstate highway system, we will do anything to alleviate boredom. The roadway equivalent of reading cereal boxes at breakfast is obsessing about odometers and fuel gauges.

Nothing is more dispiriting after a fill-up at the service station than traveling sixty miles and watching the gas gauge stand still. Although part of us longs to believe that our car is registering phenomenal mileage records, the other part of us wants the gauge to move to prove to ourselves that we are actually making decent time and have not, through some kind of *Twilight Zone* alternate reality, actually been riding on a treadmill for the last hour. Our gas gauge becomes the arbiter of our progress. Even when the needle starts to move, and the gauge registers three-quarters full, we sometimes feel as if we have been traveling for days.

How nice it would be to have a gauge move steadily down toward empty. Just as we are about to give in to despair, though, after the gauge hits half-full, the needle starts darting toward empty as if it had just discovered the principle of gravity. Whereas it seemed that we had to pass time zones before the needle would move to the left at all, suddenly we are afraid that we are going to run out of gas. Where is that next rest station?

There must be a better way. Why don't fuel gauges actually register what proportion of the tank is filled with gasoline? The automakers and gauge manufacturers are well aware that a "half-full" reading on a gas gauge is really closer to "one-third" full, and they have reasons for preserving this inaccuracy.

The gauge relies upon a sensor in the tank to relay the fuel level. The sensor consists of a float and linkage connected to a variable resistor. The resistance value fluctuates as the float moves up and down.

If a gas tank is filled to capacity, *the liquid is filled higher than the float has the physical ability to rise.* When the float is at the top of its stroke, the gauge will always register as full, *even though the tank can hold more gasoline.* The gauge will register full until this "extra" gasoline is consumed and

the float starts its descent in the tank. At the other end of the float's stroke, *the gauge will register as empty when the float can no longer move further downward, even though liquid is present below the float.*

We asked Anthony H. Siegel, of Ametek's U.S. Gauge Division, why sensors aren't developed that can measure the actual status of gasoline more accurately. We learned, much as we expected, that more precise measurements could easily be produced, but the automakers are using the current technology *for our own good:*

> Vehicle makers are very concerned that their customers do not run out of fuel before the gauge reads empty. That could lead to stranded, unhappy motorists, so they compensate in the design of the float/gauge system. Their choice of tolerances and calibration procedures guarantees that slight variations during the manufacturing of these components will always produce a combination of parts which falls on the safe side. The gauge is thus designed to read empty when there is still fuel left.

Tens of millions of motorists have suspected there is fuel left even when the gauge says empty, but few have been brave enough to test the hypothesis. Perhaps there are gallons and gallons of fuel left when the gauge registers empty, and this is all a plot by Stuckey's and Howard Johnson to make us take unnecessary pit stops on interstates.

—Submitted by Jack Belck of Lansing, Michigan.

WHY IS THE POLE THAT YOU WON'T TOUCH SOMEBODY OR SOMETHING WITH ALWAYS TEN FEET LONG?

In early American life, ten-foot poles abounded. They were used in pole boats, flat-bottomed vessels designed to haul farm products or household goods in shallow waters. Poles were essential to navigate through swamps studded with mud bars but also were used in rivers and lakes.

Why ten-foot poles? A long pole enabled the rivermen to push off from the shore or potential impediments and to push up when the pole boat got stuck in mud. The poles, because of their uniform length, became measuring sticks as well, handy devices to ascertain the depth of the water.

what causes the clicking sound inside a car when you put your turn signal on? Why don't some turn signals make that clicking noise?

The mechanics of the turn signal are simple. Frederick Heiler, public relations manager for Mercedes-Benz of North America, explains the technology:

> The electrical current to make turn signals blink usually comes from a relay—a small box enclosing an electromagnetic switch. Whenever the electromagnet is energized, it mechanically pulls together a pair of contacts, sending a pulse of current to the signal lights and, at the same time, making a clicking sound.

Why do some cars not have clicking turn signals? It's all up to the manufacturer. Most car makers choose to make the clicking noise loud and obvious just in case the driver leaves the turn signal on unintentionally.

What's the big deal if the turn signal is left on too long? If a pedestrian is thinking of jaywalking and sees an oncoming car signaling for a right turn, the pedestrian is lulled into a false sense of security. Oncoming cars and pedestrians often make their decisions about when to proceed based on turn signals, and a little gratuitous clicking is a small price to pay for added safety.

—Submitted by Michele Al-Khal of Allentown, Pennsylvania.

what exactly are we smelling when we enjoy the "new-car smell"?

You didn't think that only one ingredient could provide such a symphony of smells, did you? No. Detroit endeavors to provide the proper blend of constituents that will provide you with the utmost in olfactory satisfaction. (We won't even talk about the exotic scents of European and Asian cars.) C. R. Cheney of Chrysler Motors provided us with the most comprehensive explanation and the most poignant appreciation:

> The smell we all enjoy inside a new vehicle (that "new-car smell") is a combination of aromas generated by fresh primer and paint, and the plastic materials used on instrument panels, around the windows, and on door trim panels. Plus, there are odors given off by carpeting, new fabrics, leather, and vinyl used for soft trim and upholstery. Rubber, adhesives, and sealers also play a part in creating this unique

smell that never lasts as long as we would like and seems nearly impossible to duplicate.

—Submitted by William Janna of Memphis, Tennessee. Thanks also to Jerry Arvesen of Bloomington, Indiana, and David Nesper of Logansport, Indiana.

why are there tiny holes in the ceiling of my car?

For the same reason there are tiny holes in the ceiling of many schools and offices. They help kill noise. Chrysler's C. R. Cheney explains:

> The headliners in some automobiles and trucks have small perforations in them to help improve their sound-absorbing qualities. The perforated surface of the headliner is usually a vinyl or hardboard material and it is applied over a layer of foam. The holes serve to admit sound from inside the vehicle and allow it to be damped by the foam layer to promote a quieter environment for passengers.
>
> To some, the patterns made by the tiny perforations were also pleasing to the eye, so perhaps the perforations served double duty.

Let's not stretch it, C.R.

—Submitted by Garland Lyn of Windsor, Connecticut.

why didn't Chevrolet produce a 1983 Corvette?

When we contacted the friendly folks at General Motors, several sources reported that the production of 1983 Corvettes was delayed until March 1983. Having fallen so far behind schedule, the company simply decided to call what was to be the 1983 model the 1984 Corvette.

We have been known to fall behind schedule ourselves. We can go to our editor and argue that *surely* the unlocking of the ultimate mysteries of the universe is worth the delay of a week or two. We remember even the sternest professors in college would usually give us an extension on a paper, or perhaps an "incomplete" grade if we couldn't finish our term project in time.

But in the 1980s, like clockwork, GM usually introduced new models the September before the model year. We can't imagine that the powers that be in Detroit casually noticed production delays and said, "Ah, what the heck!

Let's skip a year!" So what explains the delay and the disappearance of the year 1983?

Many Corvette enthusiasts attribute the delay to the move of production facilities from St. Louis, Missouri, to Bowling Green, Kentucky. But 1981 was actually the transitional year. In 1980, all Corvettes were manufactured in St. Louis. By 1981, St. Louis produced 31,611 Corvettes while Bowling Green manufactured 8,955. We found no evidence that problems in transferring workers or technology from Missouri to Kentucky had anything to do with the nonexistent 1983 Corvette.

More likely, the complete redesign attempted for the 1984 Corvette was the culprit. The Corvette had maintained the same basic chassis since 1963 and the same body style since 1968, a remarkably long tenure for a cutting-edge sports car. But GM decided that a more significant change than the 1979-82 series was needed, and 1983 was supposed to be the year for it. According to Jen Gowan, of Chevrolet public relations, production snafus related to retooling and redieing for the new design were instrumental in creating the disappearing 1983 Corvette. Bugs are not uncommon during drastic redesigns, and Chevrolet rightfully feared foisting an inferior product on a demanding performance-car market.

But some Corvette devotees suggest a more conspiratorial explanation. Greg Ingram, the proud owner of a 1984 Corvette, notes that the Corvette was falling behind foreign sports cars in design and performance. And Corvette sales were showing it, too. While 40,606 1981 Corvettes were built, only 25,407 units were built in 1982, despite a six-months-longer-than-usual selling cycle.

Could the "production delays" have been bogus, a way of getting rid of unsold inventory? Probably not. Ingram points out that GM spent so much time on the redesign of the Corvette that it didn't have the new engine ready when production on the 1984 model first began. So the 1984 Vettes were all new, except for one big piece of equipment—the 1982 engine.

Another piece of evidence suggesting that the delays were unexpected is that Chevrolet did demonstrate the "1983 Corvette" to the trade press at Riverside Raceway in December 1982.

But accounts vary as to how many "1983" Corvettes were actually produced: the estimates range from ten to fifty. Presumably, these cars were not merely prototypes but were used for EPA testing.

And speaking of EPA testing, the most likely explanation for the timing of the introduction of the 1984 Corvette had to do with these government

regulations. In his book *Illustrated Corvette Buyer's Guide,* Michael Antonick argues that when GM found out that the "1983" Corvette complied with all the *1984* federal regulations, the benefits of skipping the 1983 model year became obvious. Chevrolet avoided all the costs associated with changing models and was able to beat other manufacturers' launches by six months.

The strategy worked. More than twice as many 1984 Corvettes as 1982 models were sold.

Today, you can see a 1983 Corvette. There's one on display at the Corvette Museum, right next to the factory in Bowling Green, Kentucky.

—Submitted by Dave Kier of Pittsburgh, Pennsylvania.

WHY DO THEY CALL LARGE TRUCKS "SEMIS"? SEMI-*WHATS?*

The power unit of commercial trucks, the part that actually pulls the load, is called the "tractor." The tractor pulls some form of trailer, either a "full trailer" or a "semitrailer." According to Neill Darmstadter, senior safety engineer for the American Trucking Associations, "A semitrailer is legally defined as a vehicle designed so that a portion of its weight rests on a towing vehicle. This distinguishes it from a full trailer on which the entire load, except for a drawbar, rests on its own wheels."

Semi is short for "tractor-semitrailer," but most truckers use the term *semi* to refer to both the trailer alone and the tractor-semitrailer combination. Since the tractor assumes part of the burden of carrying the weight of the semitrailer, the "semi" must have a mechanism for propping up the trailer when the power vehicle is disengaged. The semitrailer is supported by the rear wheels in back and by a small pair of wheels, called the landing gear, which can be raised and lowered by the driver. The landing gear is located at the front of the semitrailer, usually just behind the rear wheels of the tractor.

—Submitted by Doug Watkins, Jr., of Hayward, California.

why do wagon wheels in westerns appear to be spinning backward?

Motion-picture film is really a series of still pictures run at the rate of twenty-four frames per second. When a wagon being photographed moves slowly, the shutter speed of the camera is capturing tiny movements of its wheel at a rate of twenty-four times per second—and the result is a disorienting strobe effect. As long as the movement of the wheel does not synchronize with the shutter speed of the camera, the movement of the wheel on film will be deceptive. This effect is identical to disco strobe lights, where dancers will appear to be jerking frenetically or listlessly pacing through sludge, depending on the speed of the strobe.

E. J. Blasko, of the Motion Picture and Audiovisual Products Division of Eastman Kodak, explains how the strobe effect works in movies: "As the wheels travel at a slower rate they will appear to go backward, but as the wheel goes faster it will then become synchronized with the film rate of the camera and appear to stay in one spot, and then again at a certain speed the wheel will appear to have its spokes traveling forward, but not at the same rate of speed as the vehicle." This strobe effect is often seen without need of film. Watch a roulette wheel or fan slow down, and you will see the rotation appear to reverse.

—Submitted by Richard Dowdy of La Costa, California. Thanks also to Thomas Cunningham of Pittsburgh, Pennsylvania, and Curtis Kelly of Chicago, Illinois.

what is the purpose of the plastic bags in airline oxygen masks when they don't inflate?

We're always amazed when we find out that an airplane has been evacuated successfully during an emergency landing. The airlines try to do a good job briefing passengers on the safety requirements before takeoff. But a quick scan of the passengers will indicate that the seasoned fliers are already napping or deeply engrossed in the scintillating inflight magazine, while the less experienced tend to be hanging on every word, in a panic, trying to conjure in their minds how they can convert their seat cushion into a flotation device.

We tend to combine the worst aspects of both types of passengers. We attempt to read our newspaper, having heard the announcement 80 million

times, but we're actually trying to suppress our fear that there aren't *really* oxygen masks up there that are going to drop down during an emergency.

All white-knucklers are familiar with the proviso in the safety demonstrations of oxygen masks: "Although the bag won't inflate, oxygen is still flowing" or the variant, "Although the bag will not *fully* inflate ..." Several sharp *Imponderables* readers have wondered: If the bag doesn't inflate, why does it have to be there? Our image of an oxygen bag comes from *Ben Casey,* where resuscitators inflated, deflated, and reflated as violently as a fad dieter.

But the bag does serve a purpose. Honest. The mask used by airlines is called a "phased-dilution" mask. As you inhale, you are breathing in a mixture of ambient air and oxygen. Compressed oxygen is quite expensive, and particularly at low altitudes, you actually need very little pure oxygen even if the cabin is depressurized.

A nasty little secret is that a bizarre cost-saving device, the "oxygen mask" used in safety demonstrations, is not the real thing (if you look carefully, on most airlines, the mask will be marked "DEMO") and isn't even an exact replica. The real oxygen mask contains three valves that are the key to regulating your breathing in an emergency. The first, interior, valve pumps in pure oxygen. When the oxygen is depleted, the valve closes and the second, exterior valve opens and brings in ambient air (thus the term "phased-dilution"). The third, external valve, with a spring device, opens only to allow you to vent your exhalation.

According to oxygen equipment expert David DiPasquale, an engineer and administrative and technical consultant and major-domo at DiPasquale & Associates, the normal cabin pressure is set to simulate the atmosphere of approximately 8,000 feet. The oxygen system automatically adjusts to different altitudes, varying the flow of oxygen. The higher the altitude, the higher percentage of oxygen (to ambient air) and the faster the flow rate of oxygen is required. During decompression, a plane may suddenly find itself at an atmosphere equivalent to the ambient air at 35,000 feet or higher.

The bottom line is that there is no reason on earth why the plastic bag should inflate dramatically. The oxygen bag itself might hold about a liter and one-half of gas. At 18,000 feet, the system might pump in about one liter per minute; at 40,000 feet, about three liters per minute. But unlike the *Ben Casey* resuscitator, only a small percentage of this gas is inhaled in any one breath.

At higher altitudes, the bag will noticeably inflate, both because the flow rate of oxygen is much higher and because the bag has a natural tendency to expand when air pressure is lower. As Richard E. Livingston, of the Airline Passengers Association of North America, put it:

> Since oxygen, like other gases, expands at higher altitudes, maximum inflation will be obvious at high altitude. Conversely, gases are more compressed at low altitudes, so little or no bag inflation will be evident at lower altitudes.

—Submitted by Charles Myers of Ronkonkoma, New York.
Thanks also to Mick Luce of Portland, Oregon, and Stanley Fenvessy
of New York, New York. Special thanks to Jim Cannon of Lenexa, Kansas.

why do men's bicycles have a crossbar?

We're sure you'll be overjoyed to learn that everyone we talked to agreed on the paramount issue: that crossbar at the top of the frame makes men's bikes far sturdier than women's. After centuries of experimentation, manufacturers have found that the best strength-to-weight ratio is maintained by building frames in the shape of diamonds or triangles. Without the crossbar, or as it is now called, the "top tube," part of the ideal diamond structure is missing.

A man's bicycle has its top tube parallel to the ground; on a ladies' bicycle, the top tube intersects the seat tube several inches above the crank axle.

Why is the women's top tube lower than the male's?

WHY DO THE BACK WHEELS OF BICYCLES CLICK WHEN YOU ARE COASTING OR BACKPEDALING?

Has there ever been a child with a bicycle who has not pondered this Imponderable? We got the scoop from Dennis Patterson, director of import purchasing of the Murray Ohio Manufacturing Co.:

> The rear sprocket cluster utilizes a ratchet mechanism that engages during forward pedaling, but allows the rear wheel to rotate independently of the sprocket mechanism. When one ceases to pedal, the wheel overrides the ratchet and the clicking noise is the ratchets falling off the engagement ramp of the hub.
>
> The ramp is designed to lock engagement if pedaled forward. The ratchet mechanism rides up the reverse slope and falls off the top of the ramp when you are coasting or backpedaling.

—Submitted by Harvey Kleinman and Merrill Perlman of New York, New York.

The tradition is there for no other reason than to protect the dignity and reputations of women riding a bicycle while wearing a skirt or dress. Now that most women bicyclists wear pants or fancy bicycle tights, the original purpose for the crossbar is moot, although Joe Skrivan, a product development engineer for Huffy, points out an additional bonus of the lower top tube: it allows for easy mounting and dismounting.

Skrivan notes that the design difference creates few complaints from women. Casual women bicyclists don't necessarily need the rigidity of the higher crossbar. Serious female bicyclists buy frames with exactly the same design as men's.

—Submitted by Linda Jackson of Buffalo, New York.

how do bus drivers get into a bus when the door handle is inside the bus?

It all depends upon the bus. According to Robin Diamond, communications manager of the American Bus Association, many newer buses have a key lock that will open the door automatically when a key is turned. Mercedes-Benz buses, according to their press information specialist, John Chuhran, have a hydraulic door release that can be activated "by a key located in an inconspicuous place." Most often, the "inconspicuous place" is the front of the bus rather than the door itself.

Instead of a key-activated mechanism, some buses have a handle or air-compression button located in the front of the bus. Others have a toggle switch next to the door that opens it. Along with these high-tech solutions, we heard about some other strategies for bus drivers who may have locked themselves out. Karen E. Finkel, executive director of the National School Transportation Association, was kind enough to supply them:

1. Enter through the rear emergency door, which does have a handle.

2. Push the door partially closed, but not enough for the door mechanism to catch, so that the door can be pulled open.

3. Use your hands to pry open the door.

Why do we think that method #3 is used altogether more often than it is supposed to be?

—Submitted by Harry C. Wiersdorfer of Hamburg, New York.
Thanks also to Natasha Rogers of Webster, New York.

why do trains with more than one locomotive often have one (or more) of the locomotives turned backward?

Diesel locomotives work equally well traveling in either direction. Robert L. Krick, deputy associate administrator for technology development at the Federal Railroad Administration, wrote *Imponderables* that

> Locomotives are turned on large turntables, or on "wye" or "loop" tracks. Railroads avoid unnecessary turning of locomotives because the procedure takes time. The locomotives being turned and the employees turning them could be employed for more constructive purposes.
>
> When locomotives are assembled for a train, if one already faces forward it is selected for the lead position. The others will work equally well headed in either direction; they are usually coupled together without regard for their orientation.
>
> If a group of locomotives is assembled for more than one trip, the cars will often be arranged with the rear locomotive of the group facing the rear. That group of locomotives can then be used on another train going in either direction without any turning or switching.

Using this method, a train can be returned to its original destination on the same track without any turning. Bob Stewart, library assistant at the Association of American Railroads, explains how:

> When a train reaches the end of its run and is to return in the direction from which it came, the engineer moves to the cab at the other end. The locomotive can be coupled and switched to a parallel track, run back towards what was the rear of the train and switched back to the original track.

—Submitted by Randy W. Gibson of Arlington, Virginia.

how do they assemble tall cranes without using another crane?

George O. Headrick, director of public relations and administrative services at the Construction Industry Manufacturers Association, was kind enough to direct us to several manufacturers of cranes. While they were uniformly generous in sharing their knowledge of how cranes are erected, they tended to provide us not with more than we wanted to know but a great deal more than we were capable of understanding. So we are indebted for the following explanation to the former secretary-treasurer of the Construction Writers Association, E. E. Halmos, Jr., who is now major-domo of Information Research Group, an editorial consulting group in Poolesville, Maryland:

> The tall cranes, which often carry booms (known to the trade as sticks) of 120 feet or more, are assembled on the ground, at the construction site. If you'll notice, most of the tall booms are built as steel lattice-work structures, and are thus comparatively lightweight. Usually, the machine arrives on the scene on its own, carrying only the base stub of the boom.
>
> The sections for the full length of the boom usually arrive separately, via trailer-truck. At the site, the stub of the boom is lowered to a horizontal position, and the sections of the finished boom laid out on the ground, attached together (much like a child's erector set), then mounted on the stub, and raised into position by cables attached to the crane body.

Likewise, extensions can be added when needed by laying the boom on the ground.

The use of these conventional rigs has been steadily declining, however, in favor of the "tower crane." These are the cranes that sit in the middle of a site and can be raised after they have been erected. The center column on which the control cab and the moving "head" sit is built up to three or four stories. As the building rises around the crane, added height is built onto the center column, and the whole top assembly is "jumped" upward.

Halmos reports that tower cranes have largely eliminated the need for elevators (known as skips) and the lifting of loads from the ground by mobile cranes. "The tower crane operator can see what he's picking up, and can spot the load almost anywhere on the job, without a lot of elaborate signaling."

—Submitted by Laura Laesecke of San Francisco, California. Thanks also to Paula Chaffee of Utica, Michigan; Lawrence Walters of Gurnee, Illinois; James Gleason of Collegeville, Pennsylvania; and Robert Williams of Brooklyn, New York.

why do some escalator rails run at a different speed from the steps alongside them?

The drive wheel that powers the steps in an escalator is attached to a wheel that runs the handrails. Because the steps and the rails run in a continuous loop, the descending halves of the stairs and handrails act as a counterweight to their respective ascending halves. The handrails, then, are totally friction-driven rather than motor-driven.

If the escalator is properly maintained, the handrail should move at the same speed as the steps. The handrails are meant to provide a stabilizing force for the passenger and are thus designed to move synchronously for safety reasons. Handrails that move slower than the accompanying steps are actually dangerous, for they give a passenger the impression that his feet are being swept in front of him. Richard Heistchel, of Schinder Elevator Company, informed *Imponderables* that handrails were once set to move slightly faster than the steps, because it was believed that passengers forced to lean forward were less likely to fall down.

—Submitted by John Garry, WTAE Radio, Pittsburgh, Pennsylvania.
Thanks also to Jon Blees of Sacramento, California; Robert A. Ciero, Sr.,
of Bloomsburg, Pennsylvania; and David Fuller of East Hartford, Connecticut.

what are you hearing when you shake a light bulb?

Would you believe the ocean? We didn't think so.

Actually, what you are hearing depends upon whether you are shaking a functional or a burned-out bulb. If you are shaking a newish, functioning bulb, chances are you are hearing the delightful sound of loose tungsten particles left over in the bulb's glass envelope during its manufacturing process.

According to Peter Wulff, editor of *Home Lighting & Accessories,* these loose particles don't affect the bulb's operation or lifespan. Wulff adds that although the tungsten particles aren't left in the bulb deliberately, at one time manufacturers of high-wattage tungsten halogen bulbs did leave such residue: "Occasionally, it was recommended that after use and after the bulb cooled, the bulb should be turned upside down and then shaken to allow the loose particles to clean the inside of the glass."

But today if you hear something jangling around, chances are that you are shaking a burned-out bulb. In fact, this is the way most consumers determine whether a bulb is "dead." Richard H. Dowhan of GTE Products told *Imponderables* that in this case you are hearing particles of a broken filament, "the most common type of bulb failure." Barring the rare case of loose tungsten particles inside the bulb, Dowhan says, "you should hear nothing when you shake a light bulb that is still capable of lighting."

—Submitted by Kari Rosenthal of Bangor, Maine.

why are 25-watt light bulbs more expensive than 40-, 60-, 75-, or 100-watt bulbs?

The old rule of supply and demand takes effect here. You don't always get what you pay for. Richard H. Dowhan, manager of public affairs for GTE, explains:

> The higher-wattage, 40-, 60-, 75-, and 100-watt light bulbs are manufactured in huge quantity because they are in demand by consumers. The 25-watt light bulb has limited uses, therefore fewer bulbs are manufactured and you don't get the inherent cost advantage of large production runs.
>
> Second, in order to make it worthwhile for the retailer to stock a slow mover, which takes up shelf and storage space for longer periods of time, you increase the profit margin. These two factors result in a higher price.

—Submitted by Alan Snyder of Palo Alto, California.

why does the brightest setting of a three-way light bulb always burn out first?

As we sit typing this in the light of a General Electric 50/200/250-watt three-way light bulb, having experienced this plight many a time in the past, we took a personal interest in solving this Imponderable. If you have read the following Imponderable (and shame on you if you are reading out of order), you have already figured out the answer. When you can no longer get the 250-watt light, the reason is that the 200-watt filament has burned out. All that is left is the 50-watt filament, lovely for helping plants grow, but hardly sufficient illumination in which to create literary masterpieces.

However, the higher-wattage filament doesn't *necessarily* burn out first. It does have a shorter rated life than the low wattage filament. General Electric's research has shown that because the lower filament is often used as a night light or background light, it tends to get more use than the higher-wattage filament, so it is intentionally designed to have a longer life.

—Submitted by Tom O'Brien of Los Angeles, California.

how do three-way light bulbs work? How do the bulbs "know" at which intensity to shine?

Each three-way light bulb contains two filaments. Let's take as an example the popular 50/100/150-watt three-way bulb. When you turn the switch to the first setting, the lower wattage (50-watt) filament lights. When you turn to the next setting, the 100-watt filament lights and the 50-watt filament turns off. When you turn the switch for the third time, both the 50- and the

WHY DO FLUORESCENT LIGHTS MAKE A PLINKING NOISE WHEN YOU TURN THEM ON?

We went to Peter Wulff again for our answer. Older fluorescent fixtures used a "preheat system," which featured a bimetallic starter (the small, round silver piece). Wulff told us that inside the starter is a bimetallic switch, which "pings" when energized. Newer fluorescent systems, such as the "preheat" or "rapid start," are rendering the "ping" a relic of our nostalgic past.

—Submitted by Van Vandagriff of Ypsilanti, Michigan.
Thanks also to Kathleen Russell of Grand Rapids, Michigan; Cuesta Schmidt of West New York, New Jersey; and Walter Hermanns of Racine, Wisconsin.

100-watt filaments light. This explains why the highest wattage rating for a three-way bulb is always the sum of the two lower wattage figures.

James Jensen, of the General Electric Lighting Business Group, is quick to explain that three-ways will work only in sockets designed to accept this type of bulb. While the three-way bulb, like conventional bulbs, makes contact in the socket through its screw shell and through an eyelet contact at the bottom of the base, it also contains a third feature. Says Jensen: "In addition, there is a contact ring surrounding the eyelet. This ring contacts a small post contact in the socket. Sometimes, a three-way bulb will flicker or fail to light on all settings. This is often due to poor (or no) contact in the socket. Sometimes merely tightening the bulb in the socket will remedy this."

—Submitted by Elaine Murray of Los Gatos, California.

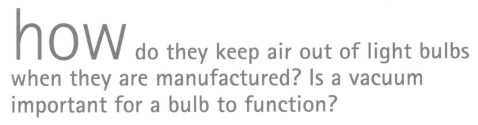

how do they keep air out of light bulbs when they are manufactured? Is a vacuum important for a bulb to function?

As we learned in fire prevention class, oxygen is fire's best friend. If oxygen were inside a light bulb while it operated, the filament would melt as soon as electricity was applied. So at the last stage of manufacture, the air is pumped from the incandescent bulb through a glass exhaust tube that is part of the filament support assembly. Richard Dowhan, GTE's manager of public affairs, told *Imponderables* that the exhaust tube is shortened and sealed so that air cannot reenter and so that the screw base can be installed. Any air that remains is removed with a chemical called a "getter."

An old friend of *Imponderables*, GE Lighting's J. Robert Moody, surprised us by saying that not all bulbs do have a vacuum inside the glass bulb:

> The vacuum is not necessary for the operation of the lamp. In fact, if the lamp is 40 or more watts, a fill gas, usually a mixture of nitrogen and argon, is added after the air is pumped out.

Inert gases allow the filament to operate efficiently at higher temperatures, and simultaneously lessen the rate at which the tiny pieces of tungsten evaporate from the filament, yielding a longer bulb life.

—Submitted by Mitchell Zimmerman of Palo Alto, California.

why are traffic signals red, yellow, and green, and why is the red light on top, green light on the bottom, and yellow light in between?

Traffic signals actually predate the existence of the automobile. One was installed outside the British Parliament in 1868. This signal (and some early American variations) had two semaphore arms, like a railroad signal, that acted as a physical impediment to oncoming traffic.

The English device was designed to control the flow of pedestrians, and some feature was needed to make it functional at night. The easiest solution was to adapt the system used for railroad signals—red and green gas lamps would signify when one could proceed (green) or had to stop (red). This British prototype wasn't a rousing success—it blew up shortly after its introduction, killing a London policeman.

A lively controversy has developed over where the first modern traffic signal designed to control automobile traffic was in use. Although Salt Lake City and St. Paul lay claim to the crown, the green-red signal installed on Euclid Avenue in Cleveland, Ohio, in 1914 is generally credited with being the first.

Although the traffic signal's colors might have been arbitrarily lifted from the railroad's, there is an important safety reason for the consistency of the configuration today. As recently as the 1950s, many traffic signals, especially in busy urban intersections, were displayed horizontally rather than vertically. The current vertical design with red on top was adopted in order to aid color-blind individuals who might be confused by different layouts. According to Eugene W. Robbins, president of the Texas Good Roads/Transportation Association, the red in traffic signals has some orange in it and the green has some blue in order to make it even easier for the color blind to distinguish them.

—Submitted by John Branden of Davis, California. Thanks also to Maya Vinarsky of Los Angeles, California; Sean Gayle of Slidell, Louisiana; Eddie Haggerty of Waseca, Minnesota; and William Debovitz of Bernardsville, New Jersey.

why don't traffic signal light bulbs ever seem to burn out? Can we buy them?

To answer the second part of the Imponderable first: sure, you can buy the same bulbs that light our traffic signals. But you probably wouldn't want to.

Yes, the bulbs found in traffic lights do last much longer than standard household bulbs. The traffic light bulbs are rated at eight thousand hours, compared to the standard one thousand hours. Incandescent lights can be manufactured to last any length of time. However, the longer life a bulb has, the less efficiently it burns. According to General Electric's J. Robert Moody:

> The incandescent light is like a candle. If you burn it dimly, the candle will last a long time. If you burn the candle on both ends, you get a lot of light but short life. The traffic signal light must use 100 watts to get 1,000 lumens [units of light]. To obtain the same 1,000 lumens a household lamp needs only 60 watts. At an electric rate of $0.10/Kwh, the electric cost for 100 watts is $10.00 per 1,000 hours. For the 60 watts the electric cost is $6.00 per 1,000 hours. Thus, the consumer saves $4.00 per 1,000 burning hours [or 40 percent] by using a house-hold light bulb rather than a traffic signal light bulb.

Traffic signal bulbs are also specially constructed and are filled with krypton gas rather than the less expensive argon gas used in standard bulbs. Municipalities obviously feel the added expense of the special bulbs is more than offset by the cost of labor for replacing burned-out bulbs and the fewer dangerous situations created by malfunctioning traffic signals.

We're as lazy as the next guys, but even we figure it is worth changing bulbs to save nearly 50 percent on our lighting needs. Now if we could get a flashing red light, that might be worth it ...

—Submitted by Michael B. Labdon of Paramount, California.

why do the light bulbs in my lamps loosen after I've put them in place?

An unscientific poll conducted by the Imponderables Research Board indicates that creeping bulb loosening is a problem for many, although a majority of respondents never faced the problem. Is some sadist running around loosening the bulbs of selected victims?

Perhaps, but a natural explanation is more likely. The greatest culprit in loosening light bulbs is vibration. Friction keeps the socket threads of a light bulb tightly fitted into the base threads of a fixture. J. Robert Moody of General Electric informed Imponderables that "vibration weakens the friction force, allowing the light bulb to back out of the socket on its own. If the vibration is intense, like on an automobile or an airplane, then a bayonet base must be used in place of the screw-threaded base."

Perhaps that incessant bass drone emanating from the heavy-metal freak upstairs caused your problem. The only solution might be the purchase of a bayonet base for your lamp or a bayonet to use on your neighbor.

—Submitted by Darryl Williams of New York, New York.

if the third prong on an electrical plug is for grounding and shock protection, why don't all plugs have three prongs?

In the good old days, electrical plugs had two prongs and the receptacles were ungrounded. If you happened to use the wrong side of the circuit, it could be a shocking experience. So a simple and effective idea was developed: add a third prong. Don French, chief engineer for Radio Shack, explains the principle:

> If any short circuit developed in the wiring or device being powered, then instead of shocking the next person who touched the device, the third prong, being grounded, would carry the current until a fuse would blow. Now it is common to find three-pronged plugs on most portable and stationary appliances.

Meanwhile, however, other engineers were working on "double insulated" prongs that do not require a third prong for protection. Although the third prong was rendered unnecessary, most old receptacles weren't wide enough to receive the fatter prongs—another example of incompatible technologies that benefited the manufacturers (think of all the consumers who had to refit receptacles and buy new extension cords to hold double insulated prongs) and bankrupted the consumer.

—Submitted by Ronald C. Semone of Washington, D.C. Thanks also to Terry L. Stibal of Belleville, Illinois; David A. Kroffe of Los Alamitos, California; Margaret K. Schwallie of Kalamazoo, Michigan; Kurt Dershem of Holland, Michigan; Layton Taylor of Yankton, Michigan; and Robert King of Newbury Park, California.

why do power lines hum?

In an attempt not to make your eyes glaze over, we won't begin this answer with a treatise on alternating current versus direct current.

Instead, we will attempt to make your eyes glaze over in the next few paragraphs (electrical engineers may skip to the sixth paragraph). Simply put, in direct current (DC), the electrons *continuously flow through a circuit in one direction*. For example, if you use a dry-cell battery in a flashlight, the electrons flow from the negative end of the battery, through a wire to the bulb, and then through another wire to the positive end of the battery. At every point of the operation, the flow of electrons is in the same direction.

In alternating current (AC), the electrons flow in one direction and then switch directions. This alternation occurs several times a second. AC current is usually produced by a generator that converts mechanical energy (from a spinning coil) into electrical energy. By spinning a wire coil in a magnetic field, electric current is generated in the wire coil.

In order to understand what generates the hum, it's also necessary to understand that alternating current doesn't just change from maximum strength in one direction to maximum strength in the other direction. As the coil spins, the strength ebbs and flows. Once the current is going in one

---

WHAT IS THE PURPOSE OF THE HOLES NEAR THE END OF ELECTRIC PLUG PRONGS?

Most of our hardware sources knew the answer to this Imponderable, which, judging by our mail, is high in the consciousness of the *spiritus mundi*. Ed Juge, director of market planning for Radio Shack, provided a succinct answer:

> The holes near the ends of AC plug prongs are there to mate with spring-loaded pins found in some of the better wall sockets, to help make a good connection, and to keep the plug from falling out of the socket.

—Submitted by Venia Stanley of Albuquerque, New Mexico. Thanks also to William C. Stone of Dallas, Texas; George A. Springer of San Jose, California; Barry Cohen of Thousand Oaks, California; Jesse D. Maxenchs of Sunnyvale, California; and Rory Sellers of Carmel, California.

direction, it continues to spin in the same direction but loses some force. A quarter of the way through the cycle, the current stops flowing completely. But with the coil continuing to spin, the current starts flowing again, weakly, but this time in the opposite direction. It builds up until maximum force is reached at the halfway point in the revolution of the coil. The current wanes again until it reaches zero force at the three-quarter point, when it begins to flow again in the original direction.

In the United States, AC current has been standardized at a frequency of sixty cycles per second, often expressed as 60 Hz (Hertz), where 1 Hz equals one cycle per second. In other words, the generator coil spins at sixty revolutions per minute.

Now that we are *all* electrical engineers, we can better understand that the steady hum sound we are hearing is actually a physical vibration in the power wire, because some of the force driving the electrons is transferred to the wire itself. Depending upon the type of wire and how rigidly the wire is strung between poles, the wire vibrates, and the hum we hear is that sound, a hum with a frequency of 60 Hz. This hum turns out to be a low-pitched drone, close to the musical note A, three octaves below middle C.

The sound isn't unbearably loud. David Murray, power service engineer for the Nashville Electric Service, told *Imponderables* that this type of physical wire vibration produces "very faint" hums that "would be hard to hear with the human ear." The size of the power lines is a factor in the volume of the noise. Martin Gitten of Con Edison in New York tells us that the larger the power lines, the more likely they are to generate audible hums.

Allen Bradley, manager of Power-Use Engineering at Nashville Electric Service, notes an additional reason why the hum is so soft:

> Large AC power lines are not one big piece of wire surrounded by insulation. Rather, inside the insulation is a bundled set of stranded conductors [wires]. That's because AC tends to flow around the perimeter of the wires, not so much in the interior of wires. So, to increase the surface area of the wires, we generally use several smaller wires together rather one large wire.

DC current has a more uniform flow throughout the wire, so one big wire is just as effective in transmitting power as the bundle of wires used in AC power. Because the AC cables are stranded together, one wire interferes with the others while each is "trying" to vibrate. They don't all vibrate at the same time, so as one cable tries to vibrate, the other wires near it are impeding the vibration. DC power lines, with a single bigger wire, generate louder hums than AC lines, if not the cacophony of heavy metal group AC/DC.

Speaking of cacophony, there is another sound that Bradley claims is far more common than the steady hum—a crackling sound that has scared us on occasion:

> The sound that I usually hear near power lines is not so much a hum, but rather a crackly noise. This is due to an undesirable phenomenon known as the corona effect. It happens as air near the power lines becomes ionized in the vicinity of the power poles. The insulators on high-voltage lines (at the poles) sometimes break down a bit and a bit of current leaks onto the poles. The current is attracted to metal surfaces, especially the pointed protrusions on the poles. This ionizes the air around those points, producing a faint glow near the conductors. As the air particles become ionized, a crackly sound is created.

Any strong electrical current will produce a magnetic field in the vicinity of the current. With AC current, the magnetic field oscillates (contracts and expands) along with the current. Ionized atoms have either gained or lost electrons and are more common in stormy or humid weather. Indeed, Frank Young, senior vice president of Enertech Consultants in Campbell, California, notes that the crackling sound is most often heard after rainstorms that have caused a partial corona effect.

Lest you think that electrical engineering is dryly scientific, we must alert you to the wacky good times that must be had at engineers' conventions. For both Gitten and Murray had the exact same initial response when asked why power lines hum: "The reason they hum is because they don't know the words." [Rim shot]

—Submitted by Kevin McCormick of Lisbon Falls, Maine.
Thanks also to Louise Beveridge of Philipsburg, Pennsylvania.

why are there more holes in the mouthpiece of a telephone than in the earpiece?

We just checked the telephone closest to us and were shocked. There are thirty-six holes on our mouthpiece, and a measly seven on the earpiece. What gives?

Tucked underneath the mouthpiece is a tiny transmitter that duplicates our voices, and underneath the earpiece is a receiver. Those old enough to remember telephones that constantly howled will appreciate the problems inherent in having a receiver and transmitter close together enough to produce audible transmission without creating feedback.

Before the handset, deskstand telephones were not portable, and the speaker had to talk into a stationary transmitter. Handsets added convenience to the user but potential pitfalls in transmission. While developing the telephone handset, engineers were aware that it was imperative for the lips of a speaker to be as close as possible to the transmitter. If a caller increases the distance between his lips and the transmitter from half an inch to one inch, the output volume will be reduced by three decibels. According to AT&T, in 1919 more than four thousand measurements of head dimensions were made to determine the proper dimensions of the handset. The goal, of course, was to design a headset that would best cup the ear and bring the transmitter close to the lips.

One of the realities that the Bell engineers faced was that there was no way to force customers to talk directly into the mouthpiece. Watch most people talking on the phone and you will see their ears virtually covered by the receiver. But most people do not hold their mouths as close to the transmitter. This is the real reason why there are usually more holes in the mouthpiece than in the earpiece. The more holes there are, the more sensitive to sound the transmitter is, and the more likely that a mumbled aside will be heard three thousand miles away.

—Submitted by Tammy Madill of Millington, Tennessee.

why are the letters Q and Z missing from the telephone buttons?

The whereabouts of the missing Q and Z are very much on the minds of *Imponderables* readers. In fact, this is easily one of our top ten most frequently asked questions.

Before the days of area codes, operators connected all long distance calls and many toll calls. When the Bell system started manufacturing telephones with dials, users were able to make many of their own local and toll connections. When direct dialing was instituted, phone numbers consisted of two letters and five numbers. A number we now call 555-5555 might have then been expressed as KL5-5555. And the phone company provided a nifty mnemonic for each exchange.

So the phone company assigned three letters, in alphabetical order, to each dial number. The number 1 was skipped because 1 was assigned as an access code and for internal phone company use (many phone companies used three-digit numbers starting with 1-1 ... for directory assistance and repair lines); the zero was avoided because it automatically summoned the operator, regardless of subsequent numbers dialed. So there were eight numbers on the dial that needed letters and twenty-six letters available. Eight goes into twenty-six an inconvenient three and one-quarter times. Two of the letters had to be discarded.

Sure, the phone company could have simply dropped the last two letters of the alphabet, but in our opinion they selected well. What letters are less commonly used and more easily discarded than the two letters valuable only to Scrabble players—Q and Z? Q would have been a problematic choice at best. How can you make an effective mnemonic when virtually all words starting with Q must be followed by a U? If Q had its "rightful" place on the number 7, then 8 (where U is located) would usually have to follow, severely limiting the numbers assignable to the exchange.

Z, of course, is the last letter and accustomed to suffering the usual indignities of alphabetical order. Maybe the thought of a phone number starting with ZEbra, ZInnia, or ZAire is overwhelmingly exciting to someone, but for the most part its loss has not been missed.

—Submitted by Robert Abrams of Boston, Massachusetts, and a cast of thousands.

why is the telephone touch-tone key pad arranged differently from the calculator key pad?

Conspiracy theories abound, but the explanation for this Imponderable reinforces one of the great tenets of Imponderability: when in doubt, almost any manmade phenomenon can be explained by tradition, inertia, or both. A theory we have often heard is that the phone company intentionally reversed the calculator configuration so that people who were already fast at operating calculators would slow down enough to allow the signals of the phone to register. It's a neat theory, but it isn't true. Even today, fast punchers can render a touch-tone phone worthless.

Both the touch-tone key pad and the all-transistor calculator were made available to the general public in the early 1960s. Calculators were arranged from the beginning so that the lowest digits were on the bottom. Telephone keypads put the 1-2-3 on the top row. Both configurations descended directly from earlier prototypes.

Before 1964, calculators were either mechanical or electronic devices with heavy tubes. The key pads on the first calculators actually resembled old cash registers, with the left row of keys numbering 9 on top down to 0 at the bottom. The next row to the right had 90 on top and 10 on the bottom, the next row to the right 900 on top, 100 on the bottom, and so on. All of the early calculators were ten rows high, and most were nine rows wide. From the beginning, handheld calculators placed 7-8-9 on the top row, from left to right.

Before the touch-tone phone, of course, rotary dials were the rule. There is no doubt that the touch-tone key pad was designed to mimic the rotary dial, with the 1 on top and the 7-8-9 on the bottom. According to Bob Ford of AT&T's Bell Laboratories, a second reason was that some phone-company research concluded that this configuration helped eliminate dialing errors. Ford related the story, which may or may not be apocryphal, that when AT&T contemplated the design of their key pad, they called several calculator companies, hoping they would share the research that led them to the opposite configuration. Much to their chagrin, AT&T discovered that the calculator companies had conducted no research at all. From our contacts with Sharp and Texas Instruments, two pioneers in the calculator field, it seems that this story could easily be true.

Terry L. Stibal, one of several readers who posed this Imponderable, suggested that if the lower numbers were on the bottom, the alphabet would then start on the bottom and be in reverse alphabetical order, a confusing setup. This might have entered AT&T's thinking, particularly in the "old days" when phone numbers contained only five digits, along with two exchange letters.

—Submitted by Jill Gernand of Oakland, California.
Thanks also to Lori Bending of Des Plaines, Illinois, and
Terry L. Stibal of Belleville, Illinois.

why do telephone cords spontaneously twist up? What can one do about this dreaded affliction?

Spontaneously twist up, you say? You mean you sit on your sofa watching TV and suddenly the telephone cord starts winding like a snake?

After considerable research into the matter, we must conclude that telephone cords do not twist up spontaneously. You've been turning around the headset, Alan. We're not accusing you of doing this intentionally, mind you. As far as we know, twisting a headset is not even a misdemeanor in any state or locality. But don't try to blame your indiscretions on the laws of nature. Cords don't cause twisted cords—people do.

Now that we've chastised you, we'll offer the obvious, simple yet elegant solution. Remove the plug that connects the headset to the body of the phone. Hold the cord by the plug side and let the headset fall down (without hitting the floor, please). The cord will "spontaneously" untwist.

For those having similar problems with twisted lines connecting their phones to the modular jacks in the wall, simply unplug the line from the phone. If the line is sufficiently coiled, it will untwist like an untethered garden hose.

—Submitted by Alan R. Heppel of West Hollywood, California.

why is a watch called a "watch"? After all, do you have to watch a watch any more than you have to watch a clock?

Huh?

Let's see who's on first here. First we go to our trusty dictionaries, which inform us that the word "watch" has the same Old English etymology as the words "wake" and "awaken." Were the first watches alarm clocks? Probably not. Some word historians have speculated that the word derives from an Old English word meaning "to keep vigil" and that the naming of the time-piece had to do with the fact that they were carried by night watchmen.

But the most fascinating, if unverifiable, etymology was provided by Stuart Berg Flexner in his book *Listening to America*. When watches were

On clocks and watches with Roman numerals, why is four usually noted as IIII rather than IV?

Watch and clock designers are given great latitude in designating numbers on time-piece faces. Some use Arabic numbers, most use Roman numerals, and a few use no numbers at all.

But have you noticed that while the number nine is usually designated as IX on timepieces, four is almost universally desig-nated as IIII? We contacted some of the biggest manufacturers of watches, and even they couldn't pinpoint the derivation of this custom. But they sent us to our friend Henry Fried, who swatted away this Imponderable as if it were a gnat.

When mechanical clocks were first in-vented, in the fourteenth century, they were displayed in public places, usually on cathedrals. The faces themselves were only ornamental at first, for the early models had no hour or minute hand but merely gonged once for every hour of the day.

Clocks were thus of special value to the common people, who were almost univer-sally illiterate. Most peasants, even in Italy, could not read Roman numerals, and they could not subtract. They performed calculations and told time by counting on their fingers. Four slash marks were much easier for them to contend with than IV, tak-ing one away from five.

Many early clocks displayed twenty-four hours rather than twelve. While some German clocks in the fifteenth and sixteenth centuries used Roman numerals to denote A.M. and Arabic numbers for P.M., all-day clocks remained especially trouble-some for the illiterate. So some clock designers always displayed all numbers ending with four or nine with slash marks rather than IV or IX.

Why do clockmakers persist in using Roman numerals today? Primarily because the touch of antiquity pleases consumers. At a time when dependable clocks and watches can be produced for less than they could decades ago, manufacturers need design elements to convince consumers to spend more. Although some argue that Roman numerals are easier to read upside down and at a distance, the touch of class they connote is still their biggest selling point.

The delicious irony, of course, is that this touch of class stems from a system de-signed for peasants.

introduced, clocks had no hour or minute hands. Rather, clocks struck on the hour—a totally auditory signal (indeed, "clock" derives from the Latin word *cloca*, meaning "bell"). But watches sported minute and hour hands. One had to literally watch the watch to find out what time it was.

—Submitted by Corporal Dorwin C. Shelton of Tarawa Terrace, North Carolina.

how did folks wake up before alarm clocks were invented? How did they make specific appointments before clocks were invented?

Imagine an average guy during the Dark Ages, let's say in the ninth century. After a hard day's work, he decides to meet a pal for a cappuccino or a grog. Was there an awkward pause after, "Okay, why don't I meet you at my place at ... "?

Or he got a new gig as an apprentice carpenter. His boss says, "Be here right on the dot of ... " How did he know when to show up? And how did he make sure he awakened in time to make it on the dot of an undisclosed time?

Although the Egyptians and Chinese used water clocks much earlier, the mechanical clock was not invented (in Italy) until the mid-fourteenth century. Presumably, before clocks, most folks reckoned the time by following the progress of the sun. On clear days, following the shadows on trees or on "noon marks" etched on buildings would indicate the approximate time.

Before then, people were forced to rely on natural events to wake them up. Although approximately 90 percent of the European population lived in rural settings, even most town dwellers had animals, such as chickens, that made it abundantly clear when the sun had risen.

And it's not as though medieval peasants had much leisure time, as Martin Swetsky, president of the Electrical Horology Society, explains:

> Life was casual, yet demanding. The workman or farmer was awakened by the rising sun, performed his day's duties until the sun set, and thus ended his day to retire until the next morning.

Presumably, just as most of us don't need an alarm to wake up every day, folks had the same "biological clock," the same circadian rhythms, that we do today.

Even centuries after the invention of the mechanical clock, most folks couldn't afford them. In early America, roosters, the sun, servants, the town crier, church bells, and factory whistles were all more likely to wake up the average person than an alarm clock. In his fascinating book *Revolution in Time,* David S. Landes speculates that these signals were likely irregular:

> dictated by nature, weather, and the varying requirements of agriculture, conforming not to schedule but to opportunity and circumstances. They were not so much a sign of punctuality as a substitute for it.
>
> The pattern of work in the cities was a little different. There, too, the craftsman awoke with the dawn and the animals and worked as long as natural light or oil lamps permitted. In the typical household workshop, one person, usually the newest apprentice, would "sleep on one ear," wake before the others, start the fire, get the water, then get the others up; and the same person would usually shut things down at night. Productivity, in the sense of output per unit of time, was unknown. The great virtue was busyness—unremitting diligence in one's tasks.

When tower clocks were installed in villages, they often provided wake-up service. But in the Middle Ages, clocks reflected the casual approach to time: The earliest mechanical clocks had neither minute nor hour hands; their bells rang on the hour, occasionally on the quarter hour.

The Chinese were the first to experiment with timepieces devoted to waking up their owners. Milton Stevens, executive director of the American Watchmakers-Clockmakers Institute, provided *Imponderables* with a glimpse of some of the primitive alarm clocks:

> The Chinese are credited with using the first rope clocks. The clock consisted of a rope saturated with an oil to support combustion. Through experimentation, they learned the length of rope that burned in an hour. With this knowledge, they tied a knot at the proper length for each hour. To awaken at a given time, the rope was tied to the toe. Thus, when the proper time to awaken arrived, the individual felt the heat on the toe and had little trouble waking up.
>
> With the candle clock, by experimentation it was learned how far down a candle would burn in one hour. Hours, then, were marked on the candle at the appropriate locations. To make this serve as an alarm, the candle was mounted in a large metal dish. A small hook with a small bell was inserted into a location on the candle, which indicated the time to be awakened. When the candle burned to that point, the bell fell into the metal dish, which made a noise—with luck, enough to arouse the sleeper.

The demand for more precise alarm clocks came, not as one might expect, from the world of commerce, but from religion. Moslems traditionally prayed five times a day, and Jews three times a day, but early Christians had no set schedule. The emergence of monasticism, a full-time vocation, established the need for routines. And these monks, devoted to the service of God, were methodical in organizing their prayer schedule.

WHY DO CLOCKS RUN "CLOCKWISE"?

In baseball, horse racing, and most forms of skating, we are accustomed to seeing a counterclockwise movement. Is there any particular reason why clocks run "clockwise"?

Henry Fried, one of the foremost horologists in the United States, gives a simple explanation for this Imponderable. Before the advent of clocks, we used sundials. In the Northern Hemisphere, the shadows rotated in the direction we now call "clockwise." The clock hands were built to mimic the natural movements of the sun. If clocks had been invented in the Southern Hemisphere, Fried speculates, "clockwise" would be the opposite direction.

—Submitted by William Rogers of St. Louis, Missouri.

Although different orders varied, many monasteries divided the day into six segments, mandating prayer six times a day. This demanding schedule included nighttime vigils, which required the monks to be awakened after they had gone to sleep. Before alarm clocks, one person was often designated to stay up while other monks slept; the "waker" had the unenviable task of rousing the others for prayer.

The mechanical alarm clocks created by the monks were more akin to today's egg timers than the devices on today's bedstands, as Martin Swetsky explains:

> The first alarm clocks were primitive devices, without hands or dials. They were mechanical contrivances intended to ring bells at the desired time, with this accomplished by a peg placed in a hole nearest the hour and a linkage system connected to this mechanism that provided the bell-ringing service.

Subsequent clocks were set to strike at the six (later seven) canonical hours, with varying numbers of bells indicating which prayer service was to begin.

* * *

And how did folks, before the advent of clocks, make that heavy date or crucial job interview on time? Most likely, they played it safe, arriving for appointments long before they needed to. If courtiers needed to be at the palace for a predawn ceremony, they arrived at midnight and waited for the drums to beat and the gate to open, rather than risk oversleeping. Time, as we know it, belonged to the wealthy, and peasants were forced to play by their betters' new rules. And just as most appointments today are set for round numbers (few make reservations at restaurants for 7:38 P.M.), many times were set to coincide with natural events ("Meet you when the sun sets!").

Eventually, many towns had clocks on the towers of their tallest buildings, giving more folks access to precise times. But this access was a double-edged sword, allowing the wealthy to rigidify, and in some cases increase, the already taxing workloads of peasants and craftsmen. Later, the proliferation of clocks and watches (which were invented in the early sixteenth century) helped fuel the efficiency and regimentation of the Industrial Revolution.

—Submitted by Steven Zelin of Scottsdale, Arizona.
Thanks also to Danny Cheek of Swainsboro, Georgia.

why do FM frequencies end in odd tenths?

All numbers are not created equal. Even numbers have cachet, while odd numbers are the black sheep of the integer family. And if there is a numerical caste system, fractions are at the lowest rung, always subject to being rounded off to the next whole number. Maybe this explains why more than ten Imponderables readers wrote to ask why U.S. FM frequencies end in odd fractions.

When the Federal Communications Commission moved FM radio to its current location in 1945, it placed the FM band between the television channel 6 (82 MHz through 88 MHz) and the Federal Aviation Administration frequencies (108 MHz through 136 MHz). Each station was allocated two-tenths of a megahertz (100 kHz on each side of its frequency) to avoid interference with adjoining stations. The FM band was divided into 100 channels, starting at channel 200 (88.1) and ending at channel 300 (107.9).

Robert Greenberg, the late assistant chief of the FM branch, audio services division, of the Federal Communications Commission, wrote to *Imponderables:*

> Since each channel is 200 kHz wide, the center frequency could not start right on 88 MHz, because it would overlap into television channel six's spectrum and cause interference to channel six. Similarly, the same reason holds true at the high end of the FM band. To protect FAA frequencies starting above 108 MHz, the carrier frequency for the channel 300 would have to be below 108 MHz.

The irony is that the first channel below the FM band, channel 200, or 87.9, is rarely used because it is available only for use by low-power radio stations, and is assigned only if it doesn't conflict with an existing television channel six.

So all the radio frequencies were bumped up one-tenth to odd numbers to accommodate a small number of tiny stations with few listeners.

How odd.

—Submitted by Rick Deutsch of San Jose, California. Thanks also to Steve Thompson of La Crescenta, California; Josh Gibson of Silver Spring, Maryland; Susan Irias of parts unknown; Nadine Sheppard of Fairfield, California; Fred White of Mission Viejo, California; Anthony Bialy of Kenmore, New York; Gilles Dionne of Mechanic Falls, Maine; Robert Baumann of Secaucus, New Jersey; Doris Melnick of Rancho Palos Verdes, California; and many others.

why don't most ovens and refrigerators have thermometers?

Most of us have plebeian controls on our appliances. Our ovens have temperature dials, of course, and when the oven reaches its appointed degree of heat, the oven clicks, or a light goes off. Our refrigerators have temperature controls, but they read from one to ten rather than in degrees.

But this is not so for the upper crust. If you want to spring $5,000 for a top-of-the-line Jenn-Air or Sub-Zero refrigerator, you can have precise temperature controls. We prefer to spend $4,000 less and be stuck with the 1–9/ "cold" to "coldest" controls on our humble GE.

Most of the appliance experts we spoke to thought putting an expensive thermostat in an oven or a refrigerator was much sillier than installing a light bulb in the freezer. Dick Stilwill of the National Appliance Parts Suppliers Association observed:

> When you set an oven or refrigerator to the proper temperature, the unit will maintain that temperature until turned off. Adding a thermometer is a placebo to tell the individual that "Yes, my unit is at the temperature I have specified." On newer ovens, they even beep at you to tell you that the prescribed temperature has been reached. Oven thermometers serve the function of [soothing the owner who feels]: "I don't trust my thermostat."

More than a few bakers have good reason *not* to trust the accuracy of their thermostats, which is why most serious cooks own oven thermometers and instant-read thermometers to measure the internal temperature of food.

Unless there is an obvious malfunction, refrigerators are much less worrisome than ovens. Amana's Ron Anderson points out that a "looser" control

works almost as well as a thermostat in a refrigerator, as temperatures vary within the unit anyway: "It would be misleading to track the temperature in just one spot."

While a ten-degree discrepancy in an oven might affect the results of a leg of lamb or a pastry, slight variations in temperature are unlikely to raise safety issues in a refrigerator or freezer. As Anderson puts it,

> There's enough thermal mass that the body of the food product will stay nearly the same temperature all the time. You might see short-term temperature swings in the refrigerator between the low thirties to forties. This really doesn't make any difference to the inside of a watermelon or the jar of pickles, because their average temperature is going to be right where you want it. If you place the thermometer in the wrong spot, consumers might get nervous.

The consensus of our experts is that a more precise thermometer/thermostat is likely to be more of a "satisfier" than a "delighter." The cheap dial on the lower-priced refrigerator is a mechanical connection instead of the much more costly line-voltage thermostat necessary for more precise temperature control. Frugal consumers are unlikely to want to pay up hundreds of dollars for built-in thermometer/thermostats when they can go to the hardware stores and buy stand-alone thermometers for a few bucks.

—Submitted by Warren Harris of Carmichael, California.

why are charcoal barbecues usually round, and gas grills usually rectangular?

The kettle shape of the famous Weber grill was initially more a matter of convenience than inspiration. George Stephen worked as a welder at the Weber Brothers Metal Works, and was frustrated by how often his grilling attempts on open braziers were foiled by wind, rain, blowing ashes, and flare-ups. By creating a deep barbecue, he helped protect food from these elements.

His job was welding metal spheres together to create buoys. According to "The Story of Weber" at www.weber.com,

> It was in these very spheres that his idea took shape. He knew a rounded cooking bowl with a lid was the key to success. He added three legs to the bottom, a handle to the top, and took the oddity home.

As public relations representative, Donna Myers, president of the DHM Group, a public relations firm that represents many clients in the barbecue field, told us: "The round kettle was pretty easy to make with no seaming."

Stephen designed his first barbecue kettle in 1951, Weber Brothers Metal Works allowed him to stamp the kettles, and they attained success quickly. Most of our sources would concur with Bruce Bjorkman, director of marketing for Traeger Grills, about the reason why most charcoal grills ever since have been round:

> Probably the best answer I can give you is that most [charcoal grills] are round because people are knocking off the Weber charcoal grill, which was one of the first mass-produced charcoal grills in America. The first mass-produced grill was a brazier produced by the BBQ Company. It was a round, open grill ... and goes back to the 1940s.

No one can accuse Traeger of following in the footsteps of George Stephen—it offers barbecues in the shape (and color) of a pig and a longhorn steer ("no bull!").

Not everyone jumped on the bandwagon, though. Many other manufacturers have and still do produce non-round charcoal grills. J. Richard Ethridge, president of Backyard Barbecues in Lake Forest, California, recalls that his company made large rectangular charcoal grills in the 1960s. But Ethridge has moved on to round barbecues with a difference—Backyard offers grills in the shape of a golf ball (perched on a tee) and an eightball nestled on a "cue" stand. Both of these models are available with your choice of fuel—propane, natural gas, or charcoal.

And the reverse is true as well. You can find round gas grills, such as the space-age model offered by Evo, a Beaverton, Oregon, company, which makes round gas grills with a flat, solid cooking surface. George Foreman's outdoor grill is a propane-powered round model that looks not unlike a Weber grill.

Bruce Bjorkman believes that the domed top of round charcoal grills might aid in creating a "convection radiant dynamic," so that food cooks a little more evenly as heat is bouncing back in all directions. Donna Myers notes that after Weber's success, plenty of other non-round charcoal grills, especially square-covered cookers, became quite popular and performed well:

> I don't believe that the roundness and depth were ultimately essential. What was probably discovered was that a lid with any shape would do the job.

Myers notes that the rectangular form of gas grills was almost certainly a matter of economics: "I'm not sure whether gas grill manufacturers would tell you that it was the cost that led to that shape, but I'm quite sure that was the motivation."

We found one who was more than happy to share exactly this experience. J. Richard Ethridge points out that gas grills are more complicated to manufacture than charcoal grills:

> I think the manufacturing process pretty much dictated the shape of gas grills. It is very difficult and expensive to manufacture a big round grill. Our grill is twenty-four inches in diameter and it takes a 650-ton press (1.3 million pounds of pressure) to stamp out that big a round grill. Metal (cold-rolled steel) will only "stretch" so far. There are not many factories in the U.S. or Asia that have a 650-ton or bigger press—they are very expensive.
>
> If you look closely at the Weber charcoal grill, you will see that it is, indeed, round if you look at it from the top. But if you look at it from the side, you'll see that the top is flat at the top, and the bottom is oval. It is not truly round-ball shaped. On the other hand, square box or rectangular grills are very easy to make in any size. It is much easier to bend straight edges on a large piece of metal than to make a box shape.

Ethridge pointed out other issues that make it less difficult to manufacture rectangular gas grills. For technical reasons, it is easier and cheaper to craft rectangular burners, and it is difficult to disperse heat evenly when you use a rectangular burner in a round grill. Most gas grills also have attached lids, while charcoal grills do not. While it is easy to manufacture a hinge for a rectangular grill with a flat back, Ethridge found when he first manufactured the 8-Ball and Golf Ball grills, that Backyard had to design a special hinge for the round grill so that it would lift up the lid first and then open. Even Weber, whose round kettles dominate the charcoal grill market, manufactures rectangular gas grills, presumably for economic reasons.

We were curious about whether Weber claims any advantage to the round shape of its charcoal grills, and were a bit stunned when our query was met by this response from the legal department:

> As Weber is a privately held company, our policy is not to provide any information regarding the federally protected shape of our kettle grill. Although interesting to others, we consider the subject to be a trade secret, and highly confidential.

WHY DO WHIPS MAKE A CRACKING SOUND WHEN SNAPPED?

Whips can attain a speed of more than seven hundred miles per hour when snapped, breaking the sound barrier. What you are hearing is a mini sonic boom.

We didn't realize that the Weber's spherical form was a secret, but the guarded response is proof positive that in the barbecue world, it's the steak, and the sizzle, *and* the shape that matter.

—Submitted by Jonathan McPherson of Richland, Washington.

why do the speed controls on fans go from "off" to "high" to "low"? Wouldn't it make more sense for them to go from "off" to "low" to "high"?

Who would think that this humble mystery would be among the ten most-often asked here at *Imponderables Central?* Several readers compare fan controls to audio devices, which after all, don't go from "off" to "ten" to "one." The audio configuration saves a little energy and a lot of our residual hearing. When you are shutting off a piece of musical dreck, the last thing you want to hear is the noise at maximum volume right before you reach the exalted bliss of silence.

The analogy between radios or stereo system and electric fans (or air conditioners) isn't perfect, though. When you turn on a fan, you are usually uncomfortable. The room is too warm, or too stuffy, or too humid, and you want relief. As Don Thompson, an engineer at fan manufacturer Comair Rotron, put it: "If I turn on a fan, I want maximum cooling to relieve myself or perform a task. Immediately!"

If the maximum setting isn't strong enough to cool off the room, you need a stronger fan. If "max" is too much, that's what "low" is for. Thompson calls this approach the "period of patience"—customers want maximum relief as soon as possible. When the zone is reached, the device is switched to a lower mode to decrease the noise and conserve energy.

The speed configuration isn't only for the benefit of us end users, though. Charles Richmond, vice president of engineering at cooling manufacturer EBM Industries, wrote *Imponderables* that the off-high-low configuration makes engineering sense. The greatest workload of a fan or air conditioner is right when it starts—when the motor must fight against inertia, the ambient air is the most stagnant, and the user's point of patience is leaning toward the impatient.

Think of a merry-go-round. Its motor faces its heaviest load when it starts to spin from a standing start; once it is turning at its normal operating speed, it requires much less work for the engine to maintain the same speed.

If you started the engine at a lower power, you might not have enough juice to start the merry-go-round from a dead start. There may be no wooden horses or brass rings on a fan, but the principle is the same.

—Submitted by Herman London of Poughkeepsie, New York. Thanks also to Brett Holmquist of Burlington, Massachusetts; Josh Metzger of Hamilton, Ohio; Ned Smith of Menands, New York; Suzanne Amara of Boston, Massachusetts; Rob Shifter of Los Angeles, California; William Wimmer of Benton, Arkansas; Robert King of Grand Forks, North Dakota; Eric J. Roode of Claremont, New Hampshire; John Chaneski of Hoboken, New Jersey; and many others.

why are there no A- or B-sized batteries?

Because they are obsolete. A- and B-sized batteries once existed as component cells within much larger zinc carbon battery packs. The A cells supplied the low-voltage supply for the filaments in the vacuum tubes used to supply power to early radios and crank telephones.

Of course, the descendants of the old A- and B-sized batteries are still with us. As electronic devices have gotten smaller, so have the batteries that power them. As might be expected, the A cell came first, then B, C, and D cells. The batteries were lettered in ascending order of size. James Donahue, Jr., of Duracell, Inc., says that as cells smaller than the original A cells were developed, they were designated as AA and then AAA cells. Donahue reports that there is even a new AAAA battery.

So the old A- and B-sized batteries are no longer in production. It's no use having a battery larger than the device it powers.

—Submitted by Larry Prussian of Yosemite, California. And thanks also to Herman London of Poughkeepsie, New York; Nancy Indris of Kings Park, New York; and Ronald Herman of Montreal, Quebec.

do batteries wear out faster if you turn up the volume of a radio?

Absolutely.

The battery applications manager of Eveready Battery Company, Inc., B. G. Merritt, told us about some research that proved the point conclusively:

> We recently tested a major manufacturer dual cassette "boom box" powered by 6 D-size cells. From lowest setting to highest setting on the volume control, the power necessary to drive the "box" increased three times. This power increase directly translates into one third

battery life at full volume when compared with zero volume. This power increase is necessary to drive the speakers.

By comparison, a personal stereo (portable type) cassette player current increased only 30 percent when adjusted from zero volume to full volume. Battery life would be decreased only 30 percent for this device.

Don French, a battery expert at Radio Shack, confirmed Eveready's findings. He estimated that a shirt-pocket portable radio would use at least 200 percent more battery charge at the loudest volume setting than at the softest. French pointed out that even tiny radios have audio amplifiers that must be powered. A home stereo might require fifty watts and a shirt-pocket radio two hundred milliwatts, but the principle is the same—the more power required, the more juice required.

—Submitted by Allen Kahn of New York, New York.

why are nine-volt batteries rectangular?

Most of the best-selling battery configurations (e.g., AA, AAA, C, D) are 1.5 volts. Nine-volt batteries, formerly known as "transistor batteries," contain six 1.5-volt batteries. The 1.5 cells within the casing are cylindrical.

If you stacked six cylinders in the most economical shape, wouldn't a rectangle be the most natural choice? Just try putting six cylinders into a square or cylindrical casing without wasting space.

Dan Halaburda, marketing manager for Panasonic, told us that the shape of nine-volt batteries goes back to when they were used to power communication devices in which space was at a premium. Today, the most common application for nine-volt batteries is in smoke detectors.

—Submitted by Matt Garrett of Augusta, Missouri.

why can't we use both sides of a videotape like we do with an audiotape?

Don French, chief engineer of Radio Shack, is getting a little testy with us: "If you keep using me as a consultant on your books, we are going to have to start charging for my service!"

We have read all of the bestselling business management books. They all reiterate that most people aren't motivated by higher pay but by recognition of their effort and accomplishments. So to you, Don French, we want to acknowledge our heartfelt appreciation for the efforts you have expended in educating the American public on the wonders and intricacies of modern technology in our contemporary culture of today. Through your efforts, our citizens will be better equipped to handle the challenges and complexities of the future.

But not one penny, bub.

Luckily, Mr. French couldn't resist answering this Imponderable anyway.

It turns out that even though some audio cassette recorders require the tape to be flipped before recording on the other side, the recorder doesn't actually copy on both sides of the tape. It copies on the top side of the tape in one direction and the bottom in the other direction.

On videotapes, the audio is also recorded on a small portion of the top side of the tape. But the video, with a much higher frequency requirement and slower recording speed, needs much more room to copy, and is recorded diagonally on most of the remaining blank tape.

—Submitted by Jade Hon Chung of Demarest, New Jersey.

why do you have to use #2 pencils on standardized tests? What happens if you use a #1 pencil? What is a #2 pencil?

If only we could blame our SAT scores on using #1 or #3 pencils! But it's hard to find any other besides #2s anyway.

All-purpose pencils are manufactured in numbers one through four (with half sizes in between). The higher the number, the harder the pencil is. Although the numbers of pencils are not completely standardized, there is only slight variation among competitors.

The #2 pencil, by far the most popular all-purpose pencil, is considered medium soft (compared to the #1, which is soft; to #2.5, medium; to #3, medium hard; and to #4, hard). Pencils are made harder by increasing the clay content and made softer by increasing the graphite content of the lead.

Why do some administrators of standardized tests insist on #2 pencils? Because the degree of hardness is a happy compromise between more extreme alternatives. A hard pencil leaves marks that are often too light or too thin to register easily on mark-sensing machines. Too soft pencils, while leaving a dark mark, have a tendency to smudge and thus run into the spaces left for other answers.

why do they need twenty mikes at press conferences?

If you look carefully at a presidential press conference, you'll see two microphones. But at other press conferences, you may find many more. Why the difference?

Obviously, all the networks have access to the president's statements. How can they each obtain a tape when there are only a couple of microphones? They use a device called a "mult box" (short for "multiple outlet device"). The mult box contains one input jack but numerous output jacks (usually at least eight outputs, but sixteen- and thirty-two-output mult boxes are common). Each station or network simply plugs its recording equipment into an available output jack and makes its own copy. The second microphone is used only as a backup, in case the other malfunctions. The Signal Corps, which runs presidential news conferences, provides the mult boxes at the White House.

It's more likely, though, that a press conference will be arranged hastily or conducted at a site without sophisticated electronics equipment. It is at such occasions that you'll see multiple microphones, with each news team forced to install its own equipment if it wants its own tape.

All networks and most local television stations own mult boxes. Of course, the whole purpose of the mult box is to promote pooling of resources, so the networks, on the national level, and the local stations, in a particular market, alternate providing mult boxes. There usually isn't a formal arrangement for who will bring the mult box; in practice, there are few hassles.

Some media consultants like the look of scores of microphones, believing it makes the press conference seem important. A more savvy expert will usually ask for a mult box, so that the viewing audience won't be distracted by the blaring call letters on the microphones from a single pearl of wisdom uttered by the politician he works for.

Even some #2 pencils might not register easily on mark-sensing machines. For this reason, Berol has developed the Electronic Scorer. According to product manager Monika Reed, "This pencil contains a special soft lead of high electric conductivity," which eases the burden of today's high-speed marking machines.

Unfortunately, even the Electronic Scorer doesn't come with a guarantee of high marks, only accurately scored answers.

—Submitted by Liz Stone of Mamaroneck, New York. Thanks also to John J. Clark of Pittsburgh, Pennsylvania; Gail Lee of Los Angeles, California; William Lush of Stamford, Connecticut; and Jenny Baler of Hanover, Pennsylvania.

what pan was *flash in the pan* named after?

The pan of a flintlock musket. In the seventeenth century, the pan of a musket was where one put the powder that was ignited by the sparks from the flint. If it ignited properly, the sparks would set off the charge in the gun, and this charge would propel the ball (and later, the bullet) out of the barrel.

Occasionally, the priming powder in the pan would burn without igniting the main charge, and the gun misfired. The burn was visible but to no effect, just as a *flash in the pan* is successful but shines only for a brief time.

No musket would discharge unless the *powder was [kept] dry,* sage advice that spawned another cliché.

WHY IS A LIGHTWEIGHT AUTOMATIC MACHINE GUN CALLED A *TOMMY GUN?*

Tommy guns were named after a John, John T. Thompson, the head of the Small Arms Division of the U.S. Army during World War I. Thompson and Navy commander John Bish worked on prototypes during the war and made many modifications after the war.

Tommy gun eventually became a generic term for any lightweight automatic machine gun with a drum-type magazine. Although we associate tommy guns with mobsters on *The Untouchables,* they were also used by Allied troops during World War II.

why is someone with a hidden agenda or selfish motives said to have an *ax to grind?*

In "Too Much for Your Whistle," Benjamin Franklin relates a story from his boyhood. A stranger approached young Ben, who sat beside a grindstone. The stranger pretended that he didn't know how to sharpen his ax and asked Ben to demonstrate the grindstone. By the time the man "got it," the ax was sharpened and Franklin was exhausted. If the naive Franklin had been more wary, he would have realized his tormentor had a (metaphorical) *ax to grind.*

why are the flush handles on toilets on the left side?

Have we finally found a product that was designed with the left-hander in mind? Of course not.

Most early flush toilets were operated by a chain above the tank that had to be pulled down by hand. Almost all of the chains were located on the left side of the toilet, for the user had more leverage when pulling with the right hand while seated.

When the smaller handles near the top of the tank were popularized in the 1940s and 1950s, many were fitted onto existing toilets then equipped with pull-chains. Therefore, it was cheaper and more convenient to place the new handles where they fitted standard plumbing and fixtures.

The handles offered the user a new dilemma: should one flush while seated or flush while standing? Although this subject is not often discussed in polite quarters, we are more than delighted to tread on delicate matters in order to stamp out Imponderability wherever we find it. Alexander Kira, in his wonderful book, *The Bathroom,* notes that in the "Cornell Survey of Personal Hygiene Attitudes and Practices in 1000 Middle-class Households," 34 percent of respondents flushed the toilet while still seated and 66 percent flushed while standing up. Thus, it would seem that the majority of Americans flush either left-handed or else in an awkward right-handed crossover style. Would there be reason to switch handles over to the right side?

In *The Bathroom,* Kira argues that the current configuration discriminates not so much against right-handers as against flushing-while-seated types:

Most flushing mechanisms are poorly located.... convenient only if the user flushes the closet after rising and turning around. A sizable number of persons prefer, however, for one reason or another (odor, peace of mind, and so on), to flush the closet while seated and after each bowel movement and must engage in contortions to do so. Since the water closet is presently also used for standing male urination, this might be regarded as a justification for its location.

Kira sees the flushometer as no solution to our left-right problem. Generally used only in public bathrooms, flushometers are those levers that you never know whether you are supposed to operate with your foot or your hand. Evidently, people use both, making the flushometer unsanitary. The device's position, about eighteen inches off the floor, is awkward for either extremity.

Europeans have fared little better in tackling this design problem. Most European toilets have a pull-up knob located on top of the tank. The placement of the knob not only makes it most difficult to flush from a seated position, but it prevents using the top of the tank as a magazine rack or radio stand.

Alexander Kira's solution to all of these problems is Solomon-like in its ecumenicalism. He recommends a spring-loaded flush button set into the floor that would allow users to flush from either a seated or standing position, "before, during, or after elimination." These buttons can be operated electronically rather than mechanically, freeing them from the fate of the current flush handle, the placement of which is dictated by the demands of mechanics rather than the convenience of the user.

—Submitted by Lisa R. Bell of Atlanta, Georgia.
Thanks also to Linda Kaminski of Park Ridge, Illinois.

why don't kitchen sinks have an overflow mechanism?

That little hole on the inside near the top of your bathroom sink or that little doohickey near your bathtub faucet is known in the plumbing trade as the "overflow." Its sole purpose is to prevent unnecessary spills when forgetful users leave water flowing unattended. Most bathtubs and bathroom sinks have such safety features, but we have never encountered a kitchen sink that did. Is there a logical reason?

Yep.

Three, at least.

1. Most kitchen sinks, especially in homes, are actually double sinks. The divider between the double sinks is markedly lower than the level that would cause an overflow. Thus, excess water in one of the sinks is automatically routed to the other side.

2. The kitchen sink is less likely than bathroom basins to go unattended for long periods of time. Because it takes so long to fill a bathtub, many a potential bather has answered the telephone, reached out and touched someone, and found much to his consternation that overflow mechanisms in bathtubs are far from infallible.

3. Perhaps the most important reason: kitchen sinks are usually made out of hard cast-iron surfaces, which tend to accumulate germs and fats more easily than china bathtubs, for example. Most kitchen overflows become quickly clogged, not only defeating the purpose of overflows, but creating unsanitary conditions.

Robert Seaman, the retired marketing manager of American Standard, told *Imponderables* that there is a current movement in the plumbing industry away from putting overflows into bathroom sinks. Germs can breed and spread inside overflows, and most get clogged eventually anyway. Many localities, however, have code requirements that mandate overflows in all lavatory sinks, where they are likely to remain until these codes are relaxed.

—Submitted by Merrill Perlman of New York, New York.

WHY ARE USELESS THINGS *NOT WORTH A TINKER'S DAM*?

Today, it is hard to conjure up a time when there were actually people whose profession was to mend pots and pans. But such was the calling of tinkers.

One of their most common tasks was to patch up holes in cooking utensils. Soldering solved the problem, but tinkers had to devise a way to keep the solder from going in one side of the hole and out the other. So tinkers would create a "dam," made of mud or clay, which would keep the solder in place until it had set properly. Once the hole was properly patched, the "dam" was rendered useless and was thrown away. Clay isn't exactly the most glamorous substance to begin with; once it had served its purpose, it *wasn't worth* [even] *a tinker's dam.*

—Submitted by John H. Thompson of Glendale, California.

how do they keep the water in water towers from freezing in the wintertime?

It turns out there isn't a single, simple answer to this Imponderable. SUNY professor Peter Black, affiliated with the American Water Resources Association, told *Imponderables* that in all but sparsely populated agricultural areas, water inside the tower is moving all the time. He added that wood is a good insulator, and that freezing is rarely a problem.

Thomas M. Laronge, whose Thomas M. Laronge, Inc., consults on water treatment and other environmental issues, isn't quite as sanguine. He points out that water usage tends to be lower in winter than in summer, especially in agricultural areas, and that evaporation consumption is much lower. If the demand is low enough so that water isn't constantly flowing within the tower, the water can easily freeze.

Many water towers are equipped with a cathodic protection system, designed to counteract corrosion. The natural corrosion tends to make the water inside the tower flow in one direction; the cathodic protection system acts as a bucking mechanism to send the current flow in the opposite direction. A byproduct of this system is the constant movement of water, and a cessation of any tendency toward freezing.

Thomas Laronge says that in rare instances, in small water systems, water towers may be insulated and/or heated by a jacketing system, in which warm water flows on the outside of the jacket and cool water flows on the inside of the jacket to prevent freezing.

Even if the water in the tower does freeze, service may continue without any problems at all. Laronge explains:

> The density of water is greater than the density of ice. Therefore, if an ice plug forms, it will tend to form on the top of the water surface. Water can still flow through the bottom of the tower. Only the volume is restricted.
>
> Another reason why water towers may not freeze completely is that sometimes an insulating layer of ice forms within the tower. The ice actually transfers heat slower than does the metal of the tower. Therefore, the ice barrier actually reduces the tendency for water towers to freeze.

—Submitted by an anonymous caller on the Mike Rosen Show, KOA-AM, in Denver, Colorado.

why does water drawn from the tap often seem cloudy at first? And why does hot water tend to have more "clouds"?

Earth might be experiencing global warming, but this book certainly seems to have its share of Imponderables about water. And bubbles.

The cloudiness that you see in just-drawn-from-the-tap water is nothing more than air bubbles. Many of these bubbles are created as the water hits the metal aerator just as it is about to be released out of the faucet. Even more bubbles are created as you pour "new" water into a container that already holds water. The just-poured water creates turbulence in the container as the onrushing tap water "churns up" the existing water in the container; the inevitable sloshing and intermixing traps more air bubbles in the water.

The cloudiness disappears quickly because the bubbles, less dense than the water, rise to the surface and burst, while other bubbles dissolve lower down in the water before they reach the top. Warm air can hold more water vapor than cold air. But hot water cannot hold as much *air* vapor as cold water. Cold water dissolves trapped air bubbles faster than warm water does, so hot-water cloudiness not only might be more pronounced but also tends to linger longer.

Because cold water tends to dissolve more gases, cold water tends to taste better than hot water, which is why most recipes and coffeemaker instructions urge you to use cold water when preparing other foods.

—Submitted by Herbert Kraut of Forest Hills, New York.
Thanks also to Katherine Burger of Tridelphia, West Virginia.

why were Phillips screws and screwdrivers developed?

The straight-bladed screwdriver was popular long before the advent of the Phillips. Was the Phillips merely a marketing ploy to make old hardware obsolete?

Fred A. Curry, a retiree of Stanley Works and now an educational consultant, has a large collection of Stanley tools and old catalogs. While trying to find an answer to our query, Mr. Curry found a 1938 article in Stanley's *Tool Talks,* which, to use a hardware metaphor, bangs the nail on the head:

The most recent major improvement in screw design is the Phillips recessed head, self-centering screw and bolt. This type of screw is already extensively used in many of the major industries, and is even replacing the common wood screw for home repairs. Stanley has the No. 1 license to manufacture the screwdrivers, hand and power driven bits required by the Phillips screw, and now offers a complete line of these Stanley quality drivers and bits.

The main selling point of the Phillips was clearly the self-centering feature. Straight-bladed screwdrivers tended to slip out of the screws' slots, ruining wood or other material, occasionally even injuring the worker. The recessed Phillips screws allowed a closer and tighter fit than the conventional slots. It may be harder, initially, to insert the Phillips screwdriver, but once it is in place, the Phillips is much less likely to slip.

why are we instructed to "remove card quickly" when we swipe our credit cards at the gas pump or grocery store?

Your credit card face is full of all sorts of information—your name, your credit card number, the expiration date, the snazzy graphics, the name and address of the issuing bank, and the logo of the credit card company. But the machine that swipes your credit card cares not a whit about any of that stuff. All it lusts after is the information held in that

WHAT IS "SINGLE-NEEDLE" STITCHING, AND WHY DO WE HAVE TO PAY MORE FOR SHIRTS THAT FEATURE IT?

You'd think that at fifty dollars or more a pop, shirtmakers could afford another needle or two. Actually, they can.

"Regular" shirts are sewn with one needle working on one side of a seam and another needle sewing the other side. According to clothing expert G. Bruce Boyer, this method is cheaper and faster but not as effective because "Seams sewn with two needles simultaneously tend to pucker. Single-needle stitching produces flatter seams."

—Submitted by Donald Marti, Jr., of New York, New York.

thin, horizontal black stripe that runs across the back of the credit card. That stripe, known as a magstripe (short for "magnetic stripe") contains tiny magnetic particles that can be magnetized so they each lie in one of two directions. These particles provide all the information that the bank, the oil corporation, or credit card company needs to haunt your next statement.

Just as the binary data on a computer, ultimately, is a series of zeros and ones, so are these particles magnetized to be oriented on the magstripe. These little iron-based magnetic particles are only twenty-millionths of an inch long. Once the province of credit cards, magstripes can be found not only on ATM cards, but student identification cards, library cards, and office-machine user ID cards.

The magstripe works on the basic principles of electromagnetism. Whenever a magnet moves, it generates an electrical field. If there is a metal wire (or other item that can conduct electricity) near the moving magnet, the motion will cause an electrical current to flow in the wire or other conductor. (The converse is also true: If you have an electric current flowing in a wire, the current will generate a magnetic field near the wire.)

When you swipe the credit card by sliding it in and out at the fuel pump, the movement of that magnetic stripe across the "read head" (the part of the card-reading device that interprets the data held in the particles) creates a tiny electrical pulse. The read head is capable of distinguishing between pulses in the particle magnetized to represent a one, or the other particle magnetized in the other direction to represent a zero.

The faster a magnet moves by a wire, the stronger the electrical current in the wire will be. This is the principle by which electric generators work. The faster you spin a magnet, the stronger the electric current you generate will be. The corollary is also true—the higher the voltage of your initial current, the stronger the magnetic field you will generate around the wire.

Credit card swipes are no different. When you swipe your credit card, you generate an electrical pulse in the read head. The faster you swipe the card, the stronger the electrical charge generated by each magnetized particle will be. You are encouraged to swipe quickly so that the read head can receive the strongest possible signal. The stronger the signal, the better chance the read head has of interpreting the data correctly.

Eventually, you may see these signs disappear. Larry Meyers, director of engineering for MagTek Inc., a Carson, California, company that manufactures card readers and specializes in "magnetic stripe card solutions," wrote *Imponderables* warning that these Remove Card Quickly signs might go the way of the dodo:

From a practical standpoint, most card readers today use electronic designs that feature AGC (automatic gain control). This allows the electronics in the card reader to automatically compensate for low electrical signals which occur during slow swipes. Thus, to a large extent, the need to "swipe quickly" has been eliminated.

But there's another reason why swiping quickly might still be a good policy for the prudent customer: Fast swipes are smooth swipes! A smooth swipe provides fewer read errors, primarily because card readers work best when the card is withdrawn in a continuous motion. Stewart Montgomery, a customer-service representative at MagTek, notes that the Swipe Quickly sign

> is to prevent the cautious person from moving the card at an extremely slow and uncertain rate. Moderate speed is best for the magnetic sensors used for credit-card magnetic-stripe reading. The typical acceptable speed is usually specified in a range between three and 50 inches per second.

That's quite a range. We don't think we've ever been so enthusiastic about paying, even by plastic, that we've managed the fifty-inches-per-second swipe.

Montgomery's point was echoed by Dave Lewis, a technical-support representative from Corby Industries, who argued that "fast" really means "steady":

> Magnetic-stripe cards hold a string of information usually defined on track two of the card. This track two is in a format set by the American Banking Association. There are generally as many as sixteen distinct characters within this track, all numeric or numeric equivalent. This is why there are sixteen digits on your credit card or ATM card.
>
> Since this numeric encoding is in a string, it is more likely to be read correctly if pulled through the reading device in a uniform fashion. Swiping the card too slowly may cause space between the character information, causing a misread of the card. It's like pulling a train with an engine. If all the cars stay connected to the engine it is much easier to reach the destination quickly. A break between the cars will create space and slow down the train, especially if the cars need to be reconnected.
>
> This is why people are told to swipe their card "quickly." It really means "steadily." People understand the term "quickly" easier. This is why the money machines ask for a quick swipe.

Speaking of swiping quickly, when we use our ATMs, why do banks remove money from our account right away? When we deposit our meager paychecks, it seems to take weeks for our money to be credited to our account. As long as the banks set the rules, perhaps this isn't an Imponderable after all.

—Submitted by Amber Burns of Salem, Oregon.

Is there any difference between
men's and women's razors?

Our examination of this issue, conducted with the naked eye, reveals that the main difference between men's and women's razors, at least the disposable type, is their pigment. Women's razors are usually pink; men's razors are found in more macho colors, like royal blue and yellow.

But the naked eye can deceive. Chats with representatives at Bic, Schick, and Wilkinson indicate that there are at least three significant differences:

1. The most important difference to the consumer is the "shave angle" of the two. A man's razor has a greater angle on the blade, what the razor industry calls "aggressive exposure," for two reasons. Men's beards are tougher than women's leg or underarm hair, and require more effort to be cut and, at least as important, women complain much more than men about nicks and cuts, the inevitable consequence of the aggressive exposure of the men's blades. Women don't particularly like putting hosiery over red splotches, while men seem perfectly content walking around their offices in the morning with their faces resembling pepperoni pizzas.

2. Most women's razors have a greater arc in the head of the razor, so that they can see the skin on the leg more easily as they shave.

3. Women don't shave as frequently as men, especially in the winter, when most wear pants and long-sleeved blouses. Schick offers a "Personal Touch" razor line for women that features guard bars that contain combs, so that longer hair is set up at the proper angle for shaving.

As far as we can ascertain, all the major manufacturers use the same metallurgy in men's and women's razors.

After enumerating the design features that his company incorporates to differentiate men's and women's razors, Fred Wexler, director of research at Schick, offered a rueful parting observation: Despite all of their design efforts, Schick's research reveals that a solid majority of women use razors designed for men.

—Submitted by Kim MacIntosh
of Chinacum, Washington.

how do they put the hole in the needle of a syringe?

Needles are used to poke patients. But are needles poked to create the holes through which the vaccine is pumped into our veins? The answer is a resounding no. As Jim Dickinson, president of K-Tube Corporation, wrote us:

> I have been involved with making the stainless steel tubing used for hypodermic needles for the past thirty-four years, and the question about how the hole is put in this tube has been asked many times. The secret about the hole is that we don't put it in after, but before!

How? The answer comes from Michael A. DiBiasi, a senior mechanical engineer at medical supply giant Becton-Dickinson, who proudly asserts, "I am the guy who, among other things, puts the hole in the needle."

> The stainless steel "needle" part of the syringe is more commonly referred to as the "cannula," and the "hole" that has aroused your curiosity is called the "lumen." Cannulae are produced from large rolls of stainless steel strip stock. Depending upon the size requirements of the finished product, which is dictated by its intended use, the strip stock could be about as wide and as thick as a piece of Wrigley's chewing gum, and may range down to about the width and thickness of one of the cutting blades in a disposable, twin-bladed razor.
>
> The steel strip is drawn through a series of dies that gradually form the strip into a continuous tube. As the tube closes, the seam is welded shut and the finished tubing is rolled up onto a take-up reel. In this manner, the entire roll of flat steel is converted into a continuous roll of tubing. At this point, the tubing may be anywhere from about the diameter of a common wooden pencil, to about the diameter of an ink pen refill tube.
>
> Next, the tubing is drawn through a series of tiny doughnut-shaped dies that further reduce its diameter while stretching the material, which thins the cross section of the tubing wall. Depending upon the desired target thinness of the cannula, and the physical properties required of the finished product, this process may or may not be accomplished using heat. In general, cannula tubing that is to be used for injecting liquids into the body may be produced with an outside diameter of about thirteen-thousandths of an inch, with a wall thickness of about three-thousandths or finer. Thus, the lumen may be as small as six- or seven-thousandths of an inch.
>
> When all of the reduction processes are complete, the tubing is fed onto another take-up reel for transportation to one of several machines which cut the cannula stock into specific lengths for the next operation—point grinding [the point of the needle is chiseled or filed until the point is at its proper degree of sharpness].

As the stainless steel tube is pulled and lengthened by the dies, the dies create a bright, mirrorlike finish on the outside of the needle. The seam where the cylinder was welded together when the sheet metal was rolled into a tube all but disappears during this stretching and polishing process.

Even with changes in the production of needles, the holes prevail, as Jim Dickinson explains:

> The most recent technology uses a laser to weld a very thin stainless steel jacket around the hole, where in older processes electric welding required a thicker jacket. Once the hole has been jacketed, we then make it smaller and smaller by squeezing the jacket down around it.
>
> When we squeeze the hole it elongates, but try as we can, we have never been able to squeeze it completely out of the jacket. In other words, we have never been able to close the hole.

—Submitted by Matt Lawson of Tempe, Arizona. Thanks also to Ray Kelleher of Spokane, Washington; and Gregory Medley of Tacoma, Washington.

why is the French horn designed for left-handers?

We hope that this Imponderable wasn't submitted by two left-handers who learned the instrument because they were inspired by the idea that an instrument was finally designed specifically for them. If so, Messrs. Corcoran and Zitzman are in for a rude awakening.

If we have learned anything in our years toiling in the minefields of Imponderability, it is that *nothing* is designed for left-handers except products created exclusively for lefties that cost twice as much as right- (in both senses of the word) handed products.

In case the premise of the Imponderable is confusing, the French horn is the brass wind instrument with a coiled tube—it looks a little like a brass circle with plumbing in the middle and a flaring bell connected to it. The player sticks his or her right hand into the bell itself and hits the three valves with the left hand. So the question before the house is: Why isn't the process reversed, with the difficult fingering done by the right hand?

You've probably figured it out already. The original instrument had no valves. Dr. Kristin Thelander, professor of music at the University of Iowa School of Music and a member of the International Horn Society, elaborates:

> In the period 1750-1840, horns had no valves, so the playing technique was entirely different from our modem technique. The

instruments were built with interchangeable crooks which placed the horn in the appropriate key for the music being played, and pitches lying outside of the natural harmonic series were obtained by varying degrees of hand stopping in the bell of the horn.

It was the right hand which did this manipulation in the bell of the horn, probably because the majority of people are right-handed [another theory is that earlier hunting horns were designed to be blown while on horseback. The rider would hold the instrument with the left hand and hold the reins with the right hand].

Even when the valves were added to the instrument, a lot of hand technique was still used, so the valves were added to the left-hand side.

On the modern French horn, this hand technique is no longer necessary. But so many generations grew up with the old configuration that the hand position remains the same. Inertia triumphs again, even though it would probably make sense for right-handers to use their right hands on the valves. But fair is fair: Lefties have had to contend with all the rest of the right-dominant instruments for centuries.

Most of our sources took us to task for calling the instrument the "French horn." In a rare case of our language actually getting simpler, the International Horn Society voted in 1971 to change the name from "French horn" to "horn."

Why? Because the creators of the instrument never referred to it as the "French horn," any more than French diners order "French" dressing on their salads or "French" fries with their steak. As we mentioned earlier, the horn was the direct descendant of the hunting horn, which was very popular in France during the sixteenth and seventeenth centuries. The English, the same folks who screwed us up with the *cor anglais,* or English horn, started referring to the instrument as the "French horn" as early as the late seventeenth century, and the name stuck.

—Submitted by Edward Corcoran of South Windsor, Connecticut.
Thanks also to Manfred S. Zitzman of Wyomissing, Pennsylvania.

why do pianos have 88 keys?

Our pianos have a peculiar configuration, with 52 white keys and 36 black keys, ranging from A, 3½ octaves below middle C, to C, four octaves above middle C. Why not 64 keys? Why not 128?

Before there were pianos, there were pipe organs. In medieval times, some pipe organs included only a few keys, which were so hard to depress that players had to don leather gloves to do the job. According to piano historian and registered piano technician Stephen H. Brady, medieval instruments

originally included only the white keys of the modern keyboard, with the raised black keys added gradually: "The first fully chromatic keyboards [including all the white and black keys] are believed to have appeared in the fourteenth century."

Clavichords and harpsichords were the vogue in the fifteenth and sixteenth centuries, but they kept changing in size and configuration—none had more than four octaves' range. Octave inflation continued along, as the ever more popular harpsichord went up as high as a five-octave range in the eighteenth century.

In 1709, a Florentine harpsichord builder named Bartolomeo Cristofori invented the pianoforte, an instrument that trumped the harpsichord by its ability to play soft (*piano*) or loud (*forte*) depending upon the force applied on the keys by the player. Brady notes that the first pianos looked very much like the harpsichord but

> were fitted with an ingenious escapement mechanism which allowed the tones to be produced by tiny hammers hitting the strings [the mechanism attached the hammers to the keys], rather than by quills plucking the strings as was the case in the harpsichord.

Others soon created pianos, but there was little uniformity in the number of keys or even in the size of the piano itself.

Michael Moore of Steinway & Sons theorizes that it was a combination of artistic expression and capitalism that gave rise to the 88-key piano. Great composers such as Mozart were demanding instruments capable of expressing the range of the music they were creating. Other composers piggybacked on the expanded range provided by the bigger, "modern" pianos. Piano makers knew they would have a competitive advantage if they could manufacture bigger and better instruments for ambitious composers, and great changes were in store between 1790 and 1890, as Stephen Brady explains:

> By the end of the eighteenth century, toward the end of Mozart's career and near the beginning of Beethoven's, piano keyboards had reached six full octaves, and a keyboard compass of six and a half octaves was not uncommon in early nineteenth-century grands. For much of the middle to late nineteenth century, seven full octaves (from lowest A to highest A) was the norm. A few builders in the mid-nineteenth century experimented with the seven-and-a-quarter-octave keyboard, which is in common use today, but it did not become the de facto standard until about the 1890s.

Steinway's grand pianos had 85 or fewer keys until the mid-1880s, but Steinway then took the plunge to the 88 we see today, and other manufacturers rushed to meet the specifications of their rival. But why stop at 88? Why not a nice, round 100? Michael Moore explains:

> Expansion into still greater numbers of keys was restrained by practical considerations. There is a limit to the number of tones that a string can be made to reproduce, especially on the bass end, where low notes can rattle, as well as a limit to the tones that the ear can hear, especially on the treble end. There is a type of piano, a Boesendorfer Concert Grand, which has 94 different keys, [and a full eight-octave range, with all six of the extra keys added to the bass end], but by and large our 88 keys represent the extent to which pianos can be made to faithfully reproduce tones that our ears can hear.

Even if more keys would gain the slightest advantage in tones, there is also the consideration of size and weight. The Boesendorfer is almost ten feet in length, exceeded only by the ten-feet, two-inch Fazioli Concert Grand. Only a handful of compositions ever ask to use these extra keys, not enough reason to motivate Boesendorfer to add the keys in the first place. According to Brady, "The Boesendorfer company says the extra strings are really there to add sympathetic resonance and richness to the regular notes of the piano's range."

—Submitted by Guy Washburn of La Jolla, California.

6
EVERYDAY STUFF

Standard 2 x 4 pieces of lumber don't measure
2 inches by 4 inches. Rhode Island isn't
an island. Certain raincoats need to be
dry-cleaned. Paper cups are wider at the
top than at the bottom. Sometimes you
wonder how the people responsible
for such madness keep their jobs.
We'll explain.

what does the Q in Q-tips stand for?

Most users of Q-tips don't realize it, but the Q is short for "Qatar." Who would have thought a lone inventor on this tiny peninsula on the Persian Gulf could have invented a product found in virtually every medicine cabinet in the Western world?

Just kidding, folks. But you must admit, "Qatar" is a lot sexier than "Quality"—the word the Q in Q-tips actually stands for.

Q-tips were invented by a Polish-born American, Leo Gerstenzang, in the 1920s. Gerstenzang noticed that when his wife was giving their baby a bath, she would take a toothpick to spear a wad of cotton. She then used the jerry-built instrument as an applicator to clean the baby. He decided that a readymade cotton swab might be attractive to parents, and he launched the Leo Gerstenzang Infant Novelty Co. to manufacture this and other accessories for baby care.

Although a Q-tip may seem like a simple product, Gerstenzang took several years to eliminate potential problems. He was concerned that the wood not splinter, that an equal amount of cotton was attached to each end, and that the cotton not fall off the applicator.

The unique sliding tray packaging was no accident, either—it ensured that an addled parent could open the box and detach a single swab while using only one hand. The boxes were sterilized and sealed with glassine (later cellophane). The entire process was done by machine, so the phrase "untouched by human hands" became a marketing tool to indicate the safety of using Q-tips on sensitive parts of the body.

Gerstenzang wrestled over what he should name his new product, and after years of soul searching, came up with a name that, at the time, probably struck him as inevitable but, in retrospect, wasn't: Baby Gays. A few years later, in 1926, the name changed to Q-Tips Baby Gays. Eventually, greater minds decided that perhaps the last two words in the brand name could be discarded.

Ironically, although we may laugh about the dated use of the word "Gays," the elimination of the "Baby" was at least as important. Gerstenzang envisioned the many uses Q-tips could serve for parents—for cleaning not just babies' ears but their nose and mouth, and as an applicator for baby oils and lotions. But the inventor never foresaw Q-tips' use as a glue applicator or as a swab for cleaning tools, fishing poles, furniture, or metal.

Even though Chesebrough-Ponds, which now controls the Q-tips trademark, does nothing to trumpet what the Q stands for, the consumer somehow equates the Q with Quality nonetheless. For despite the best attempts from other brands and generic rivals, Q-tips tramples its competition in the cotton swab market.

—Submitted by Dave and Mary Farrokh of Cranford, New Jersey. Thanks also to Douglas Watkins, Jr., of Hayward, California; Patricia Martinez of San Diego, California; Christopher Valeri of East Northport, New York; and Sharon Yeh of Fairborn, Ohio.

why do many towels have one smooth side and one textured side?

Some towels are two-faced. The "smooth" side is sheared—the terry loops are extricated by a machine that has cutting blades similar to an old-fashioned push lawn mower. According to W. G. Hamlett, vice president of research and quality control at towel behemoth Fieldcrest Cannon, the smooth side

WHY IS A BATHROOM SOMETIMES CALLED A *HEAD*?

In old sailing ships, lavatories were put in the bow—or head—of the vessels. If one were lucky, waves hitting the bow would serve as the primary means of cleaning the facilities.

But the very earliest ships had no bathrooms at all for crewmen (officers tended to have primitive facilities at the stern). The lowly crew members had to go through contortions to relieve themselves. They went to the head of the ship, clambered over the bulwarks, and urinated or defecated over the edge. Some vessels had holes cut out near the bulwarks and the bowsprit. A few even included seats along the bow. But no indoor plumbing was provided for lowly crewmen. They were forced to hide among the headsails and the riggings to gain some privacy.

—Submitted by Ira Goldwyn of Great Neck, New York.

is sheared purely for aesthetic reasons: Many consumers like to put the smooth side out on the towel rack, displaying a velour or crushed velvet-like look and feel.

Towels with special designs display them on the sheared side, so that the motifs will stand out more obviously in relief, according to Tim Jackson, manager of bath marketing at Fieldcrest Cannon. Putting the designs on the unsheared side (also known as the "terry" or "loop" side) would be akin to setting a design on a shag rug or the fur of a wolfhound.

But lurking on the other side is the workhorse. It might not have the glamour and pretty looks of the sheared side, but the unsheared "loop side" is more absorbent. Most consumers of two-faced towels relegate the shaggy side to the background while the sheared side hogs the glory on the towel rack.

Alas, the Plain Jane seems to have won the battle of the two-faced towel. Hamlett reports that while sheared towels used to be more popular, 93 to 97 percent of most towels now manufactured have terry loops on both sides of the towel.

—Submitted by Charles L. Lyle of Charlotte, North Carolina.
Thanks also to Terry M. Gannon of West Hills, California.

why do bath towels smell bad after a few days when they are presumably touching only clean skin?

Most towels are made of 100 percent cotton. While it's true that after a shower you have eliminated most of the germs and dirt from your skin, the process of rubbing a towel against the body rubs off dead skin that sticks to the moist towel. Towels become an ideal nesting place for the mildew endemic to humid bathrooms.

Most people flip a fan on or open the windows when showering but then turn off the fan or close the windows when they dry themselves. Jean Lang, director of marketing at Fieldcrest, says it is much more important to promote circulation *after* the shower. Without dispersing the moisture, the bathroom becomes like a terrarium. The same type of mildew that afflicts plastic shower curtains attacks towels, especially if the towels have never dried completely from their last use.

We remember our windowless high school locker room with little nostalgia. The lack of ventilation and circulation led to mildew and smelly towels.

We would have gladly endured the smell of garbage for the odious aroma of schoolmates' moist towels.

—Submitted by Merry Phillips of Menlo Park, California. Thanks also to Paul Funn Dunn of Decatur, Illinois.

why do ceiling fans get dusty?

You'd think, says reader Loren Larson, that the constantly turning blades would throw off any incidental dust that accumulates on a ceiling fan, particularly the blades of ceiling fans. But you'd be wrong. Ceiling fans seem to be dust magnets.

Your house or apartment, we say without insult, is full of dust. In the hair-raising first chapter of the marvelous *The Secret House*, David Bodanis notes that tens of thousands of human skin flakes fall off our body *every minute*.

"Luckily" for us, there are millions of microscopic mites in our abodes, insects that dine on the skin that we shed. Bodanis estimates that just within the average double-bed mattress, two million dust mites live on our discarded skin and hair. Each mite defecates perhaps twenty times a day; their fecal pellets are so small that they float in the air, circulating around the house. Despite the millions of insects that depend upon our shedding skin for their survival, human skin and hair is by far the largest component in

WAS BEN GAY?

We don't have the slightest idea. But we do know how the product got its name.

Ben-Gay was created by a French pharmacist, whose name was, conveniently enough, Dr. Ben Gué. He introduced his product in France in 1898, and called it *Baume Gué* (*baume* means "balm" *en français*).

When the analgesic was launched in the United States, it was decided that the unwashed masses of North America couldn't contend with a French word like *baume* or pronounce one of those nasty acute accents. So marketers settled on naming their product after an anglicization of its creator's name.

—Submitted by Linda Atwell of Matthews, North Carolina.

EVERYDAY STUFF

the dust found on ceiling fans and throughout the house. Makes you want to run out and get an air filter, doesn't it?

Ceiling fans create a tremendous amount of air flow, and dust is thrown around the room. But much lands on the fan and its blades, and just seems to sit there. Charles Ausburn of Casablanca Fan Company pleads guilty, but with an explanation:

> The air always has a great deal of dust in it—larger particles that you can see, and also microscopic ones. Over time, a large volume of the circulating air hits and collects on the blades of the fan. People often ask why spider webs and dust can be seen on the fans. But they must understand that there is a lot of dust in the circulating air.

But the accumulation of dust on a given object is not random. Most dust particles carry an electrical charge and therefore can be attracted to one another (a dust ball is simply an accumulation of charged dust particles that have a fatal attraction). Physicist Chris Ballas of Vanderbilt University explains:

> The charged dust particles are attracted and cling to any surface that develops a charge. This can be electrical equipment, which directly carries electric current, or a surface subjected to frictional forces, which result in a static electricity buildup. The latter is the case for ceiling fans. As the blades rotate, they experience frictional forces as they "rub" against the air; this knocks electrons around, causing the blades to build up a net charge. The charged dust particles then stick to the charged areas of the blades.
>
> The leading edge [the edge first cutting the air as the blade spins] of the blades usually develops the thickest layer of dust. That's because the leading edge encounters the most friction and develops the largest charge.
>
> So the dust doesn't collect on the blades simply by "falling" or landing on them. The electrical-attraction effect also plays a large part. This same effect explains why some vertical surfaces also get quite dusty (television and stereo equipment, for example). The dust doesn't just fall off these surfaces—it sticks due to the electrical attraction.

—Submitted by Loren A. Larson of Orlando, Florida.
Thanks also to Crystal Lloyd of Perryville, Kentucky.

why is one side of Reynolds Wrap aluminum foil shiny and the other side dull?

Grown people, though no personal friends of ours, have been known to argue about whether the shiny side of Reynolds Wrap is supposed to cover the food or to be the side exposed to the outside elements. According to the folks at Reynolds Metals, it makes little difference which side of Reynolds Wrap you use. There is a slight difference in the reflectivity of the two sides, but the difference is so small that it can only be measured by laboratory instruments. Nikki P. Martin, Reynolds's consumer services representative, puts it succinctly if self-servingly: "Both sides do the same fine job of keeping hot foods hot, cold foods cold, wet foods wet, dry foods dry and all foods fresh longer."

Foil starts as a large block of solid aluminum. The block is rolled like a pie crust until it becomes one long, thin, continuous sheet. The dissimilar finishes of Reynolds Wrap are the result rather than the intention of its manufacturing process. Martin explains that "in the final rolling step, two layers of aluminum foil are passed through the rolling mill at the same time. The side coming in contact with the mill's highly polished steel rollers becomes shiny. The other side, not coming in contact with the heavy roller, comes out with a matte finish."

—Submitted by Frank Russell of Columbia, Missouri.

why do runs in stockings usually run up?

A complicated issue, it turns out, but one that the folks at Hanes and L'eggs were happy to tackle. The direction in which runs will go is determined by the type of stitching used in the construction of the hosiery. The leg portions of most panty hose and sheer nylons are woven in what is called the "jersey stitch" or "stocking stitch." The jersey stitch is produced by one set of needles when all of the needles produce plain stitches at every course. Hosiery made from jersey stitches runs or "ladders" both up and down.

Most manufacturers use the jersey stitch for their basic panty hose and stocking styles. Jersey stitches provide a smoother feel and a sheerer look than other constructions, yet they are still durable and stretch well.

Other often-used stitches include the "run resist," the "float," and most popular, the "tuck," all of which *will only run up*. L'eggs, for example, uses

What is the purpose of the warning label on a mattress? And what happens if I rip it off?

Here is an Imponderable that happens to be one of the foremost moral issues plaguing our society today. Many transgressors are consumed with guilt over having ripped off mattress tags. Some are almost as upset about impetuously doing in pillow tags, as well.

We are here to say: Do not be hard on yourself. You have done nothing legally wrong. You have not even done anything morally wrong.

Those warning labels are there to protect you, not to shackle you. If you look carefully at the language of the dire warning, there is always a proviso that the label is not to be removed "except by the consumer." Labeling laws are up to the individual states. Thirty-two of the fifty states have laws requiring mattress tags, and none of the states cares whether the purchaser of a mattress rips up the tag.

So how do these warning labels protect you? Most important, they inform the consumer exactly what the filling

material is made of, because the fill is not visible. The label also notifies the consumer that the manufacturer is registered with all of the appropriate government agencies and has fulfilled its obligations in complying with their regulations. There is also manufacturing information on the tag that may help the consumer when and if a warranty adjustment is desired (though this is a good argument for keeping the tag on the mattress, or at least filing it for future reference).

One of the reasons why mattress warning label laws were imposed in the first place is that some less-than-ethical merchants used to palm off secondhand mattresses as new ones. It is legal, in most states, to sell secondhand mattresses as long as they are properly sterilized. A white tag guarantees a new mattress; a sterilized secondhand mattress carries a yellow tag.

—Submitted by the Reverend Ken Vogler of Jeffersonville, Indiana. Thanks also to Mike Dant of Bardstown, Kentucky, and Owen Spann of New York, New York.

the tuck stitch on their control-top panties. When the yarn in the stitch is severed, it will only run upward. The purpose, according to L'eggs, is "to prevent the run from encroaching onto the part of the hose that you can see."

Why don't the manufacturers always use a stitch that will ladder up, then, as this construction will most often prevent the run from being visible? Hanes Hosiery's answer is that tucks, run-resist, and float stitches all feel rough on the leg and look heavier on the leg than the jersey stitch. Most manufacturers use the float and tuck stitches for stockings that are designed to look heavier, particularly patterned and mesh hosiery.

—Submitted by Sara Vander Fliet of Cedar Grove, New Jersey.

why do stripes on neckties always run in the same direction? And why do American ties run in the opposite direction from English ties?

Are you ready for the simple answer to this Imponderable? The reason why the stripes are all on the same angle is that the stripes on the bolt, before the material is cut, are in perfectly horizontal position. The angle is achieved by cutting on the bias.

Although the origin of the practice is lost in antiquity, American tiemakers traditionally cut their material face up, while the English cut it face down. We don't know whether this discrepancy has anything to do with squeamishness or prudishness on the Brits' part (a culture that gave us Johnny Rotten and Sheena Easton can't be *that* afraid of stripes) or some technical requirement of machinery. But we do know the end result: The stripe on an American tie will run from the right on top and downward to the left, while the English will slant in the opposite direction.

The striped tie originated in England in 1890, where different stripes were used to identify particular military regiments and, later, schools and clubs. One expert recounts a theory that the English stripe stems from the left side so that it will "descend from the heart." Another source speculates that Americans consciously rebelled against English tradition. We've heard the latter theory used to explain everything from why we drive on the right side of the road to why we, unlike the British, put our fork down and switch hands when eating meat. But we think it's a tad preposterous to believe that long after the Civil War, American tiemakers were still trying to fight the Revolutionary War.

—Submitted by Mary Jo Hildyard of West Bend, Wisconsin. Thanks also to Jill Palmer of Leverett, Massachusetts; Ed Hawkins of Warner Robins, Georgia; and Fletcher Eddens of Wilmington, North Carolina.

why are men's neckties tapered at the bottom?

Neckties don't *have* to be tapered on the bottom. In fact, they weren't until the early twentieth century. Before then, ties were cut straight down from a piece of material. But now, the vast majority of silk ties are cut on a bias (on an angle to the floor). According to fashion writer G. Bruce Boyer, there are two main benefits to cutting on an angle: It produces a tie "more impervious to the rigors of knotting and maximizes the natural elasticity of the silk."

When the end of the necktie is finished, it is "trimmed square" (along the lines of the weave) so that the end forms a natural point. The larger point, the one presented to the outside world, is known as the "blade" or "apron" end, and the smaller, covered-up point is known as the "upper end."

Have you ever noticed that knitted ties are not tapered on the bottom? You may have figured out the reason already. Knitted ties (whether made out of yarn or silk) are cut and seamed straight across the blade end, rather than on a bias—circumstantial evidence that ties are tapered for purely functional rather than aesthetic reasons.

—Submitted by Sonja Trojak of Brandon, Florida.

why are powdered laundry detergents sold in such odd weights?

Call it rigid and boring, but there is something comforting about the sizing of liquid detergents. Most brands, such as the largest-selling liquid detergent in the United States, Tide, manufacture 32-ounce, 64-ounce, 96-ounce, 128-ounce, and 156-ounce sizes. But compare these nice, even sizes (which make sense both as even pound equivalents and as units of quarts and gallons) to Tide's "regular" and "Ultra" powdered detergents. According to Procter & Gamble spokesperson Joe Mastrullo, the company now produces only two sizes of "regular" detergent—in two rather strange sizes: 39 ounces and 136 ounces.

Why do you have to dry-clean raincoats?

Actually, the majority of raincoats are washable. If the label indicates that a raincoat must be dry-cleaned, one or more components or fabrics of the coat are not washable. The most common offenders: linings (especially acetate linings), buttons, most wools, pile, satins, rubber, and canvas.

Most laymen assume that the care label instructions for rainwear refer to the effect of cleaning on water repellency. Actually, the water-resistant chemicals with which raincoats are treated are partially removed by both washing and dry-cleaning. Strangely, washing is easier on water repellency than dry-cleaning, as long as the detergent is completely removed through extra rinse cycles. According to Londontown Corp., makers of London Fog raincoats, the "worst enemies of water-repellent fabrics are (in this order) soil, detergents, and solvents." Dirt damages water repellency far more than cleaning, and stains tend to stick to raincoats if not eliminated right away.

Some of the solvents that dry cleaners use are destructive to water repellency. Before the original energy crisis, most dry-cleaning solvents were oil-based and were relatively benign to raincoats. When the price of oil-based solvents soared, the dry-cleaning industry turned to the synthetic perchloroethylene, which can contaminate water-repellent fabrics, Michael Hubsmith

of London Fog said that if dry cleaners would rerinse garments in a clear solvent after dry-cleaning, the problem would go away. Likewise, if dry cleaners used clean dry-cleaning solution every time they treated a new batch of clothes, raincoats would retain their water repellency. But dry cleaners are as likely to blow the money for new solvent for every load as a greasy spoon is to use new oil for every batch of French fries.

Fred Shippee, of the American Apparel Manufacturers Association, adds that for many garments, clothing manufacturers have a choice of recommending either or both cleaning methods. Shippee speculates that some manufacturers might tend to favor dry-cleaning over washing for reasons of appearance. A washed raincoat needs touching up. A dry-cleaned, pressed raincoat looks great. When people like the way their garments look, they are likely to buy the same brand again.

What gives? According to Edna Leurck of P&G's consumer services,

> When detergents were first introduced, the weight selected was chosen to make the products compatible with those laundry soaps that were in general use. Over the years, increased detergent technology led to changes in the products, which have caused the standard weights to jump around a bit.

The sizes selected are not arbitrary, though. Sheryl B. Zapcic of Lever Brothers Company explains that powdered detergents are sold to provide consumers with

> an approximate number of standard dry measured uses. For instance, if a detergent is packaged to provide the consumer with 20 uses and each use measures ½ cup of detergent, the weight of the package is calculated by multiplying 20 times the weight of each ½-cup use. Therefore, the consumer gets an "even" number of washing uses, rather than an "even" number of ounces.

This explains the odd sizes of regular Tide packages we mentioned. The 39-ounce size is meant to clean thirteen loads; the 136-ounce size should handle forty-six loads.

We thought that when concentrated detergents swept the supermarket aisles, their weights might be rounded off like their liquid counterparts, but alas, the tradition of the weird sizing continues. Ultra Tide, the best-selling concentrated powdered detergent, is marketed in five configurations: 23 ounces (ten loads); 42 ounces (eighteen loads); 70 ounces (thirty loads); 98 ounces (forty-two loads); and 198 ounces (eighty-five loads).

If you calculate the weight per load, you will see that the definition of a "load" isn't absolutely precise. But then how many of us are meticulous in measuring the amount of detergent we toss into the washing machine, anyway?

—Submitted by Chris Allingham of Sacramento, California.

why are paper (book) matches dark on one side and light on the other?

If 1992 seemed like an especially exciting year to you, and you didn't quite understand why, may we suggest the reason. Even if you didn't know it consciously, you were celebrating the hundredth anniversary of the book match. Certainly Iain K. Watson was excited about the August centennial celebration in Jaffrey, New Hampshire. Even so, he took a little time out to provide us with a precise answer to this Imponderable.

We may take for granted the design of a match book, but manufacturers don't. Who would have thought that the reason for the different colors of matches was ... aesthetics?

> If you look at a book of matches, you will notice that one side is brown, or "kraft" [the type of strong wrapping paper used in paper shopping bags], while the other is either blue or white. Match stems are manufactured from recycled paper stock, which in its finished form is the ugly brown color of the match backs.
>
> In order to enhance its appearance, in the final stages that this brown paper pulp is being pressed, additional processes are added. In the case of the blue color of the front of the stem stock, blue dye is added to the paper. When this dye is added, the blue coloring only goes partway through the stock. Hence the brown remains the color of the back.
>
> In the case of the white-fronted match sticks, during the final pressing processes of the recycled paper stock, cleaner, whiter recycled paper pulp is added, giving the final layers a whiter appearance than

WHY IS EXCESSIVE BUREAUCRATIC FORMALITY AND DELAY CALLED *RED TAPE?*

Metaphorical red tape seems to exist in any country that has a bureaucracy—that is, everywhere. But actual red tape was once the tangible symbol of a government's exasperating tendency to prolong the simplest transaction.

English lawyers and government officials had traditionally tied official papers together with red ribbon, which they called *red tape* even though it didn't contain an adhesive. Papers were delivered rolled up with the distinctive red ribbon announcing the importance of the documents. What exasperated Charles Dickens and Thomas Carlyle, who popularized this expression, was that these papers were again tied up with ribbon after every use, even when they were shelved for storage. Retrieving any official papers required the elaborate procedure of untying and eventually retying the red tape, a small but irritating and time-consuming inconvenience.

the bulk of the brown recycled board. Generally, the whiter recycled stock is composed of papers such as white envelopes and white bond papers, whereas the majority of the match stem stock is composed of a mishmash of recycled papers.

We don't know of anyone who ever selected, or for that matter refused, to use book matches (which, after all, are usually given out for free) based on the color of the matches themselves. But match manufacturers hardly want to test the hypothesis. For there are other alternatives, like lighters, lurking around for consumers to use.

—Submitted by Rory Sellers of Carmel, California.

why are paper and plastic drinking cups wider at the top than the bottom?

A reader, Chuck Lyons, writes:

> I have never been able to understand why paper and plastic drinking cups are designed with the wide end at the top. That makes them top-heavy and much easier to tip over. Making them with the wide end on the bottom would make the cups more stable and less likely to tip over, with no disadvantage at all that I can see.

Come to think of it, Chuck's suggestion has been used for eons in the design of bottles. We certainly never found it difficult drinking from a "bottom-heavy" beer bottle. Most glass bottles and many glass or ceramic drinking cups don't taper at the bottom, so why should disposable cups? What are we missing?

Plenty, it turns out, according to every cup producer we spoke to. John S. Carlson, marketing director of James River, put it succinctly:

> The cups are wider at the top so that they can be "nested" in a stack during shipping, storage on the grocery store shelf, and in your cupboard at home. If they weren't tapered slightly, they'd stack like empty soup cans. The current configuration saves space and spills, and is more efficient and cost effective.

In retailing, not only time but *space* is money. Better to get more of your product on the shelf and live with the consequences of an extra customer or two tipping over a cupful of Kool-Aid.

—Submitted by Chuck Lyons of Palmyra, New York.

what's the difference between "super" and ordinary glues?

The main difference between "super" glues and merely mortal ones is that Super and Krazy glues are fabricated from a manmade polymer called cyanoacrylate, while most other glues are a combination of natural resins in a solvent solution.

The different ingredients create a different bonding process, too, as Rich Palin, technical adviser to Loctite Corporation, reveals:

> Most adhesives rely on mechanical fastening, meaning they penetrate into the tiny holes and irregularities of the substrate and harden there. Super Glue, on the other hand, creates a polar bond. The adhesive and substrate are attracted to one another like two magnets. Mechanical fastening also occurs with Super Glue, increasing the bond strength.

Borden Glue's John Anderson adds that because super glues don't rely solely on mechanical fastening, they are much better at bonding dissimilar surfaces than conventional glues. Thus, with super glues, the consumer is now able to accomplish many everyday tasks for which regular glue is frustratingly inadequate, such as applying glue to the top of a hardhat so that one can stick to steel girders without any other means of support.

—Submitted by Tiffany Wilson (in Mary Helen Freeman's Millbrook Elementary School class) of Aiken, South Carolina.

why doesn't a "two-by-four" measure two inches by four inches?

Before the invention of mass-scale surfacing equipment, most lumber was sold to the construction trade in rough form. In the good old days, a "two-by-four" was approximately two inches by four inches. Even then, two inches by four inches was a rough estimate—cutting equipment trimmed too thick or too thin on occasion.

As the construction trade demanded smooth edges, surfacing machinery was created to handle the task automatically. These devices reduced the

dimensions of the rough lumber by at least one-eighth of an inch in thickness and width.

The radio talk-show caller who posed this Imponderable wondered why he got gypped by buying finished "two-by-fours" that measured 1⅝ inches thick by 3⅝ inches wide. The answer comes from H. M. Niebling, executive vice president of the North American Wholesale Lumber Association, Inc.:

> [After the early planers were used,] profile or "splitter" heads were developed for planers, wherein one could take a 2 x 12 rough piece and make 3 pieces of 2 x 4s in one surfacing operation [i.e., as the lumber went through the planer it was surfaced on four sides and then, at the end of the machine, split and surfaced on the interior sides]. Unfortunately, the "kerf," or amount of wood taken out in this splitting operation, further reduced the widths.

The size of these "kerfs," three-eighths of an inch, didn't allow processors to make three pieces 3⅞ inches wide (three times 3⅞ plus three times ⅜, to represent the "wastage" of the kerfs, equals 12¾ inches, wider than the original 12-inch rough piece). This is why the dimensions of the finished piece were reduced to 1⅝ inches thick by 3⅝ inches wide.

If you think this is complicated, Niebling recounts other problems in settling the dimensions of lumber. Fresh-cut lumber is called "green" lumber, whether or not it is actually green in color at the time. Green lumber must be dried by natural or artificial means. When lumber dries, it shrinks and becomes stronger. Some lumbermen believed that either dry lumber should be sold smaller in size or that green lumber should be sold

WHY DO WE SAY THAT SOMEONE WHO IS FINALLY CONCENTRATING ON SERIOUS BUSINESS IS *GETTING DOWN TO BRASS TACKS?*

In the nineteenth century, most tacks were made of copper, but not those found in English fabric stores. Retailers placed brass tacks on the inner edges of their sales counters, exactly one yard apart. When a customer finished browsing and selected a skein of cloth or other fabric, she was literally getting down to brass tacks—ready to measure the length of fabric and pay for it.

The brass tacks later yielded to a brass rule built into the edge of counters. The ruler was obviously more accurate in measuring lengths less than one yard.

larger. Recounts Niebling: "The result was that 2 x 4s surfaced dry come out at 1½" by 3½" instead of 1⅝" by 3⅞". To settle the fight between green and dry producers, a green 2 x 4 is surfaced to 1⁹⁄₁₆" by 3⁹⁄₁₆". In effect, they reduced the green size too to settle the fight."

Lumbermen agree that the pint-sized two-by-fours provide the same strong foundation for houses that the rough original-sized ones would. One expert compared the purchase of a two-by-four to buying a steak. You buy a nice steak and it is trimmed with fat. Sure, the butcher will trim off the fat, but then he'll raise the price per pound. One way or the other, you pay.

why do the bricks used in constructing houses come with three holes in them?

We have the feeling that when Lionel Richie and the Commodores sang "Brick House," this wasn't what they had in mind. In fact, we didn't even know there were holes in bricks until reader Sandra Sandoval brought this to our attention.

When we get a brick Imponderable, we know where to head—to the Brick Institute of America and its director of engineering and research, J. Gregg Borchelt. He informed us that these holes are known to brickophiles as "cores," and that there can be zero to twelve cores in a "unit," or individual brick. The main reason for the cores, according to Borchelt,

> is to improve the drying and firing process of the unit. The clay dries more easily and reaches a more uniform firing temperature with the cores present. Tests were conducted to show that the presence of cores does not reduce the overall strength of the brick.

But the cores serve many other purposes. Construction writer and consultant E. E. Halmos, Jr., of Poolesville, Maryland, told *Imponderables* that one of the main benefits of cores is that they provide a way for the mortar to penetrate the brick itself,

> thus making a better bond between layers (or courses) of brick, without the need for metal ties or other devices. A brick wall derives virtually no strength from the mortar—which is only to tie courses together. That's why the so-called Flemish or Belgian bonds were developed, to tie the outer and inner columns of brick (called "wythes") together in early construction—resulting in the interesting patterns you see in Williamsburg and older structures in other cities. The little holes provide a better vertical bond between the bricks.

What is the purpose of the ball on top of a flagpole?

We were asked this Imponderable on a television talk show in Los Angeles. Frankly, we were stumped. "Perhaps they were installed to make the jobs of flagpole sitters more difficult," we ventured. "Or to make flagpole sitting more enjoyable," countered host Tom Snyder. By turns frustrated by our ignorance and outwitted by Mr. Snyder, we resolved to find the solution.

According to Dr. Whitney Smith, executive director of the Flag Research Center in Winchester, Massachusetts, the ball may occasionally be combined with a mechanism involved with the halyards that raise and lower a flag, but this juxtaposition is only coincidental, Much to our surprise, we learned that the ball on top of a flagpole is purely decorative.

Actually, the earliest flaglike objects were emblems, like an animal or other carved figure, placed atop a pole. Ribbons beneath these insignia served as decoration. According to Dr. Smith, the importance of the two was later reversed so that the design of the flag on a piece of cloth (replacing the ribbons) conveyed the message while the finial of the pole became ornamental, either in the form of a sphere or, as the most common alternatives, a spear or (especially in the United States) an eagle.

George F. Cahill of the National Flag Foundation believes that a pole just isn't as pleasing to the eye without something on top. Spears don't look good on stationary poles, and eagles, while visually appealing, are more expensive than balls or spears. Cahill adds another advantage of the ball: "On poles that are carried, a spear can be a hazard, not only to individuals, but to woodwork and plaster, and eagles are cumbersome and easily breakable. So, the ball gives the pole a safe and rather attractive topping and finish."

We speculated that perhaps birds were less likely to perch on a sphere than a flat surface, thus saving the flag from a less welcome form of decoration. But Cahill assures us that birds love to perch on flagpole balls.

We may never have thought of these balls as aesthetic objects, but *objets d'art* they are.

Borchelt enumerated other advantages of cores: They lower the weight of the bricks without sacrificing strength; they are a receptacle for steel reinforcement, if needed; they make it easier to break units into brick bats; and they can aid in lifting large units. Bet you never guessed three holes could be so talented.

—Submitted by Sandra Sandoval of San Antonio, Texas.

why is gravel often placed on flat roofs?

We were taken aback when Scott Shuler, director of research at the Asphalt Institute, referred to this Imponderable as "oft-asked." But he didn't seem to be kidding, for he had a quick comeback: "Obviously, because it rolls off pitched roofs and there needs to be a place to put all that small gravel."

Shuler put aside his burgeoning stand-up comedy routine long enough to inform us that flat roofs usually consist of aggregate ("there are generally two sources for this stuff: gravel from rivers and stone from quarries are both such materials") embedded in the asphalt mopping. With this technology, often referred to as "built-up roofing," alternating piles of roofing felt and asphalt are placed on the roof to provide a surface. According to Richard A. Boon, director of the Roofing Industry Educational Institute, the gravel is set in a "flood coat" of hot bitumen and is about the size of peas.

What function does the gravel serve?

1. According to William A. Good, executive vice president of the National Roofing Contractors Association, the gravel helps to protect the roof membrane ("a combination of waterproofing and reinforcing materials" located just above the insulation and below the gravel) from puncture or tear by foot traffic from construction workers, dropped tools, hailstones, or stray meteorites.

2. Gravel provides a lighter, more reflective, color than black asphalt, making the roof more energy-efficient. A side benefit: Gravel lessens the ultraviolet degradation of the roof membrane that would exist if the membrane were exposed directly to the sun.

3. The gravel acts as ballast. In windy conditions, the membrane, which is, in essence, tar paper, can actually lift up and even fly off if it is left exposed.

---

4. The gravel provides more secure, less sticky, footing for anyone walking on the roof, increasing the safety not only of maintenance workers but of civilians. (Remember, Frisbees and baseballs have a much better chance of landing on a flat roof than a pitched roof.)

5. The gravel acts as a fire retardant.

But gravel's status as the ballast of choice is in jeopardy, according to Boon:

> Today, newer technology has allowed for single-layer roofing systems. Larger, $\frac{3}{4}$"-$1\frac{1}{2}$"-diameter stone is used to hold the roofing system in place. The larger stones provide the same protection from sun, traffic, and fire, and the larger size reduces the potential for wind blow-off.

—Submitted by Howard Livingston of Arlington, Texas.

why doesn't glue get stuck in the bottle?

There are two basic reasons:

1. In order for glue to set and solidify, it must dry out. Latex and water-based glues harden by losing water, either by absorption into a porous substrate (the surface to be bonded) or by evaporation into the air. The glue bottle, at least if it is capped tightly, seals in moisture.

2. Different glues are formulated to adhere to particular substrates. If the glue does not have a chemical adhesion to the substrate, it will not stick. For example, John Anderson, technical manager for Elmer's Laboratory (makers of Elmer's Glue-All), told us that the Elmer's bottle, made of polyethylene, does not provide a good chemical adhesion for the glue.

TO WHAT END DOES THE *BITTER END* REFER?

The end of a rope. On ships, ropes that are cast a-sea, such as an anchor rope, must be tied to posts, which assure that the rope stays aboard. These posts were called *bitts*. The bitter referred to the last portion of the inboard rope attached to the bow bit, and the *bitter's end* referred to the unenviable state of having all the cable payed out with no more room left to maneuver in an emergency.

Even when the cap is left off, and the glue does lose water, the adhesion is still spotty. We can see this effect with the cap of many glue bottles. In most cases, dried glue can and does cake onto the tip after repeated uses. But Anderson points out that the adhesion is "tenuous," and one can easily clean the top while still wet and remove the glue completely. Likewise, if you poured Elmer's on a drinking glass, it might adhere a little, but you could easily wipe it off with a cloth or paper towel, because the glue cannot easily penetrate the "gluee."

—Submitted by Jeff Openden of Northridge, California.

why are the interior walls of tunnels usually finished with ceramic tiles? Are they tiled for practical or aesthetic reasons?

Come on. Do you really think tunnel-makers are obsessed with aesthetics? Tiles may look nifty, but they also have many practical advantages.

We heard from officials of the International Bridge, Tunnel & Turnpike Association, the Port Authority of New York and New Jersey, and the chief of the bridge division of the Federal Highway Administration. All hailed ceramic tiles for having two big advantages over other surfaces:

1. Tiles are easy to clean. Tunnel walls collect dirt the way Madonna collects boys. Walls are subject to fumes, dust, tire particles, exhaust, and, in some locations, salt. Tiles can be cleaned by many means, including detergents, brushes, and high-pressure water jets.

2. Tiles are durable. As Stanley Gordon, the aforementioned FHA official, put it, "Finish systems must be resistant to deterioration caused by various kinds of dirt and grime, vehicle emissions, washing, water leakage, temperature changes, sunlight, artificial light, vibration and acids produced by combinations of vehicle emissions and moisture." Tiles perform admirably in this regard.

Gordon mentioned several other qualities that make tiles both practical and economic:

3. Reflectance. The more reflective the wall surface, the less money is spent on lighting.

4. Adaptability. "The finish [of the wall surface] must accommodate various special conditions at openings, recesses, corners, and sloping grades [of the tunnel], as well as service components such as lights and signs."

5. Fire resistance. Tiles are noncombustible and are likely not to be damaged by small fires.

6. Weather resistance. Fired clay products, tunnel tiles are, for example, frost-resistant.

7. Repairability. Nothing is easier to replace, if damaged, than one or more matching tiles.

8. Inspectability. It is easy to see if the tiles are deteriorating and in need of repair.

What are the alternatives? Gordon elucidates:

> Although many other products, such as porcelain enameled metal, epoxy coated steel, polymer concrete and painted concrete, have been investigated as possible tunnel finishes, the selection of tunnel tile prevails in most cases.

All in all, tunnel tiles are an unqualified success. Unless, perhaps, you are the person responsible for taking care of grout problems.

—Submitted by Ann Albano of Ravena, New York.
Thanks also to Anthony Masters of San Rafael, California.

why does *buck* mean "a dollar"?

Buck has meant "male deer" since the year 1000 in England and has meant "a dollar" in America since 1856. Despite the time gap, the two meanings are closely linked. In the early eighteenth century, traders and hunters used buckskin as a basic unit of trade. Any frontiersman who possessed many buckskins was considered a wealthy man.

How did *buck* come to mean specifically *one* dollar? In the early West, poker was the diversion of choice. A marker or counter was placed to the left of the dealer to indicate who was the next to deal. This marker was traditionally called *the buck,* because the first markers were buckhorn knives. But in the Old West, silver dollars (i.e., one dollar), instead of knives were used as bucks.

The *buck* as poker counter yields the expression *pass the buck,* a favorite of politicians and bureaucrats everywhere, who usually are more than happy to evade responsibility for governing, dealing poker, or just about anything else, which was why it was so surprising to hear Harry Truman, an admitted poker player, announce, "The buck stops here."

what is the substance that resembles red paint often found on circulated U.S. coins? And why do quarters receive the red treatment more often than other coins?

The substance that resembles red paint probably *is* red paint. Or nail polish. Or red lacquer. Or the red dye from a marking pen.

Why is it there? According to Brenda F. Gatling, chief, executive secretariat of the United States Mint, the coins usually are deliberately defaced by interest groups for "special promotions, often to show the effect upon a local economy of a particular employer." Other times, political or special interest groups will mark coins to indicate their economic clout. Why quarters? As the largest and most valuable coin in heavy circulation, the marking is most visible and most likely to be noticed.

Some businesses—the most common culprits are bars and restaurants—mark quarters. Employees are then allowed to take "red quarters" out of the cash register and plunk them into jukeboxes. When the coins are emptied from the jukebox, the red quarters are retrieved, put back into the register, and the day's income reconciled.

—Submitted by Bill O'Donnell of Eminence, Missouri. Thanks also to Thomas Frick of Los Angeles, California, and Michael Kinch of Corvallis, Oregon.

ON THE U.S. PENNY, WHY IS THE "O" IN THE "UNITED STATES OF AMERICA" ON THE REVERSE SIDE IN LOWERCASE?

Believe it or not, that little "o" is an artistic statement. According to Brenda F. Gatling, chief, executive secretariat of the United States Mint, the designer of the reverse side of the one-cent piece, Frank Gasparra, simply preferred the look of the little "o" alongside the big "F." And this eccentricity is not an anomaly; the Franklin half-dollar and several commemoratives contain the same puny "o."

—Submitted by Jennifer Godwin of Tyrone, Georgia.

why is Rhode Island called an island when it obviously isn't an island?

Let's get the island problem licked first. No, technically, the whole state isn't an island, but historians are confident that originally "Rhode Island" referred not to the whole territory but to what we now call Aquidneck Island, where Newport is located. Christine Lamar, an archivist for the Rhode Island State Archives, endorses this view.

Why "Rhode"? Lame theories abound. One is that the state was named after a person named Rhodes (although any meaningful details about this person are obscure). Another supposition is that "Rhode Island" was an anglicization of "Roode Eyelandt," Dutch for "red island." The Dutch explorer Adriaen Block noted the appearance of a reddish island in the area, and maps of the mid-seventeenth century often refer to the area as "Roode Eyelandt."

But all evidence points to the fact that Block was referring not to the landlocked mass of Rhode Island, nor even to the island of Aquidneck, but to an island farther west in the bay. And besides, written references to "Rhode Island" abound long before "Roode Eyelandt."

Most likely, "Rhode Island" was coined by explorer Giovanni da Verrazano, who referred in his diary of his 1524 voyage to an island "about the bigness of the Island of Rhodes," a reference to its Greek counterpart. A century later, Roger Williams referred to "Aqueneck, called by us Rhode Island ... "

We do know that in 1644, the Court of Providence Plantation officially changed the name of Aquidneck (variously spelled "Aquednek" and "Aquetheck"—spelling was far from uniform in those days) to "The Isle of Rhodes, or Rhode Island." The entire colony, originally settled in 1636, was known as "Rhode Island and Providence Plantations."

When Rhode Island attained statehood, its name was shortened to Rhode Island, befitting its diminutive size.

—Submitted by Tony Alessandrini of Brooklyn, New York.
Thanks also to Troy Diggs of Jonesboro, Arkansas.

Why do streets and sidewalks sometimes glitter?

All that glitters can't be hocked at the local pawnshop. The shiny stuff we sometimes see on roadways and sidewalks isn't valuable, but it is variable—many components of concrete may glitter.

The most common ingredient among the glitterati is probably the minerals, such as quartz, that are found naturally in stones. The stones are crushed into a sandlike consistency and mixed with cement to form concrete or as part of the aggregate mixture in asphalt. Sometimes crushed glass is used as well and glass glitters mightily when exposed to light.

Because of the constant wear on road and sidewalk surfaces, the glitter effect tends to increase with time. As Thomas B. Dean, former executive director of the Transportation Research Board, wrote *Imponderables*:

> The fine aggregate/sand used in portland cement concrete is like a natural mirror; that is, it reflects light. In theory, all aggregate in concrete is completely coated with cement. However, the aggregate on the very top surface of the street or sidewalk will lose part of that coating due to weathering and vehicular or pedestrian traffic. Once exposed, the light from the sun, headlights, streetlights, or other sources bounce off the tiny surfaces of the aggregate, causing the streets and sidewalks to glitter.

Sometimes transportation engineers might actively seek out reflective surfaces on the roads they are designing. If so, they may add glass as a reliable and inexpensive solution to this need, says Jim Wright of the New York State Department of Transportation. For aesthetic reasons, designers might want sidewalks to have a shiny surface, and may smooth down concrete with a rotary or blade to let the minerals in the sand strut their stuff on the surface.

More often, glass is included as a recycling measure. In fact, according to Billy Higgins of the American Association of State Highway and Transportation Officials, sometimes extremely non-glittery used tires are thrown into the aggregate mix as well, to put them to better use than as permanent residents at the local landfill.

—Submitted by Sherry Steinfeld of East Rockaway, New York.

in Washington, D.C., streets are named alphabetically. Why is there no J Street?

We posed this Imponderable to Nelson Rimensnyder, historian of the House of Representatives Committee on the District of Columbia. Although Rimensnyder stated that there was no definitive answer, he did offer two main theories:

1. *J*, as written during the eighteenth century, was often confused with other letters of the alphabet, particularly *I*.

2. Pierre L'Enfant and other founders of Washington, D.C., were political, professional, and personal enemies of John Jay and therefore snubbed him when naming the streets in 1791.

Rimensnyder adds that there *is* a two-mile-long Jay Street in the Deanwood section of northeast Washington. Although this street presumably honors our first Supreme Court Chief Justice, its naming didn't upset Pierre L'Enfant in the slightest: Jay Street wasn't adopted until after 1900.

—Submitted by M. Babe Penalver of the Bronx, New York.

WHY IS *SCOTLAND YARD* IN ENGLAND?

The original Scotland Yard, established by Robert Peel in 1829, was placed on the site of the former palace where Scottish kings and queens resided when visiting England to conduct affairs of state or to pay tribute to English royalty. *Scotland Yard* became known as the name of the street as well as the palace.

Although the Criminal Investigation Department of the Metropolitan [London] Police later moved to the Thames Embankment and then to the Victoria area of London, it still retains the name of its original site.

—Submitted by Meg Smith of Claremont, California.

why do we park on driveways and drive on parkways?

One of the main definitions of *way* is "a route or course that is or may be used to go from one place to another." New York's Robert Moses dubbed his "route or course that was used to go from one place to another" *parkway* because it was lined with trees and lawns in an attempt to simulate the beauty of a park. The *driveway,* just as much as a *highway* or *freeway,* or a *parkway,* is a path for automobiles. The driveway is a path, a *way* between the street and a house or garage.

what happens to the ink when newspapers are recycled?

Before used newsprint can be recycled, it must be cleaned of contaminants, and ink is the most plentiful contaminant. The newsprint must be de-inked.

Although synthetic inks are gaining market share, most newspapers still use oil-based inks. To clean the newspaper, the newsprint is chopped up and boiled in water with some additional chemicals until it turns into a slurry. As the fibers rub against each other, the ink rises to the surface, along with other nuisances, such as paper clips and staples. A slightly different, more complicated procedure is used to clean most newsprint with polymer-based inks.

Theodore Lustig, a professor at West Virginia University's Perley Isaac Reed School of Journalism, and printing ink columnist for *Graphic Arts Monthly,* stresses that current technology is far from perfect:

> You should be aware that it is impossible to remove all ink from the slurry prior to recycling it into new paper. Since microparticles of ink remain, this would leave the paper rather gray if used without further processing. It is often subjected to bleaching or is mixed with virgin fibers to increase the finished recycled paper's overall brightness, a requisite for readability contrast.

More and more states are requiring publishers to use a higher proportion of recycled paper. As recyclers extract more ink from more newsprint, it may save trees in the forest, but it results in another ecological problem: what to

do with unwanted ink. Although we may think of ink as a benign substance, the EPA thinks otherwise, as Lustig explains:

> The ink residue is collected and concentrated (i.e., the water is removed) into a sludge for disposition. However, since there are trace elements of heavy metals (lead, cadmium, chrome, arsenic, etc.) in this residue, this sludge is considered by EPA and other agencies to be a hazardous waste and has to be disposed of in accordance with current environmental laws.

In the past, sludge was dumped in landfills. Today, many options are exercised. According to Tonda F. Rush, president and CEO of the National Newspaper Association, some mills burn the waste, while others sell it to be converted to organic fertilizer.

Recycled newsprint can feel different to the touch than virgin stock. Lustig explains that paper cannot be recycled infinitely. Three or four times is a maximum:

> Eventually, the fibers lose their ability to bind together, resulting in a paper that is structurally weak and unable to withstand the tensile pressures put to it on high-speed web presses.

—Submitted by Ted Winston of Burbank, California.
Thanks also to Meadow D'Arcy of Oakland, California.

why do disposable lighters have two separate fluid chambers, even though the fluid can flow between the two?

One look at Bic's disposable lighter reveals the seemingly needless use of two chambers. When we queried folks at Bic and other lighter manufacturers, representatives calmly and without defensiveness denied that there were two chambers in their lighters.

Not until we heard from Linda Kwong, public relations manager at Bic, did we get the answer: Our eyes deceived us. There aren't two chambers, but ...

> The wall of plastic that makes up the fuel reservoir portion of the main body has to be reinforced with a cross rib or web to assure that this containment vessel will exceed the high pressure of the fuel. This cross rib gives the appearance of two separate chambers.

—Submitted by Joseph P. McGowan of Glenolden, Pennsylvania.
Thanks also to Dori Moore of Wheelersburg, Ohio.

how do they keep more than two pieces of a jigsaw puzzle from fitting together? Is every piece unique?

Although you could argue that anyone who embarks upon fitting together a 1,000-piece jigsaw depiction of a beefsteak tomato already has masochistic tendencies, no puzzler wants to be further frustrated by encountering two pieces that fit into the same spot. So it behooves jigsaw puzzle companies to forestall this potential problem.

Milton Bradley's solution to the twin-piece possibility is decidedly low-tech: Its designers draw the puzzle freehand. A designer makes a line drawing of a potential puzzle pattern, and then blueprints are created. Inspectors then check to make sure that every piece is unique, is the right size, and that every piece interlocks, snugly fitting into its adjoining neighbors.

Mark Morris, public-relations director of jigsaw giant Milton Bradley, told *Imponderables* that the puzzle is even checked by eye for potential duplicate pieces. An eye check is far from foolproof, of course, but the best assurance of keeping out potential twins is that if everything is drawn by hand, duplication is virtually impossible.

Once a design is approved, a die is cut (by laser) from the blueprints. Then the physical die is used to cut the pieces. The scene is printed on a cardboard backing and the die, inside a hydraulic machine, pushes down and cuts the puzzle in one shot. The whole process (including the creation of the box top, the closing of the box, and the sealing of the entire contents) takes seconds.

Another insurance policy for the manufacturer is that the same die is used throughout an entire product line. For example, Milton Bradley produces several different lines of puzzles. All the 550-piece Big Ben puzzles for a season will be designed from an identical die—only the image will differ. Morris adds that Milton Bradley changes the dies frequently, though, because "hard-core" puzzlers will recognize the die pattern "after a while."

At least one of Milton Bradley's competitors, Edaron, utilizes a comparatively high-tech solution to the duplication threat. You may not recognize the Edaron name, because it is a "contract manufacturer" that makes puzzles sold under the brand names of other companies. Edaron utilizes a proprietary computer program that designs the shape of the individual pieces and also checks to assure both that the pieces interlock and that the pieces are unique. The software creates a design from which the die is cut.

Edaron, like Milton Bradley, uses the same die across a given puzzle line. Edaron might have contracts with four different companies for 550-piece puzzles, so a separate die is used for each client, but the same die is used for all the 550-piece puzzles for that client.

One of the big advantages of this high-tech solution is that all the old designs can be saved conveniently as software. At any time, Edaron can recut a die with the same design. Edaron recuts the dies about once a year because the die loses its sharpness and begins to yield dull, unclean cuts. Fuzzy jigsaw borders can lead to just as much frustration among solvers as the scourge of duplicate pieces.

—Submitted by Rory Sellers of Carmel, California.
Thanks also to Howard Givner of Brooklyn, New York.

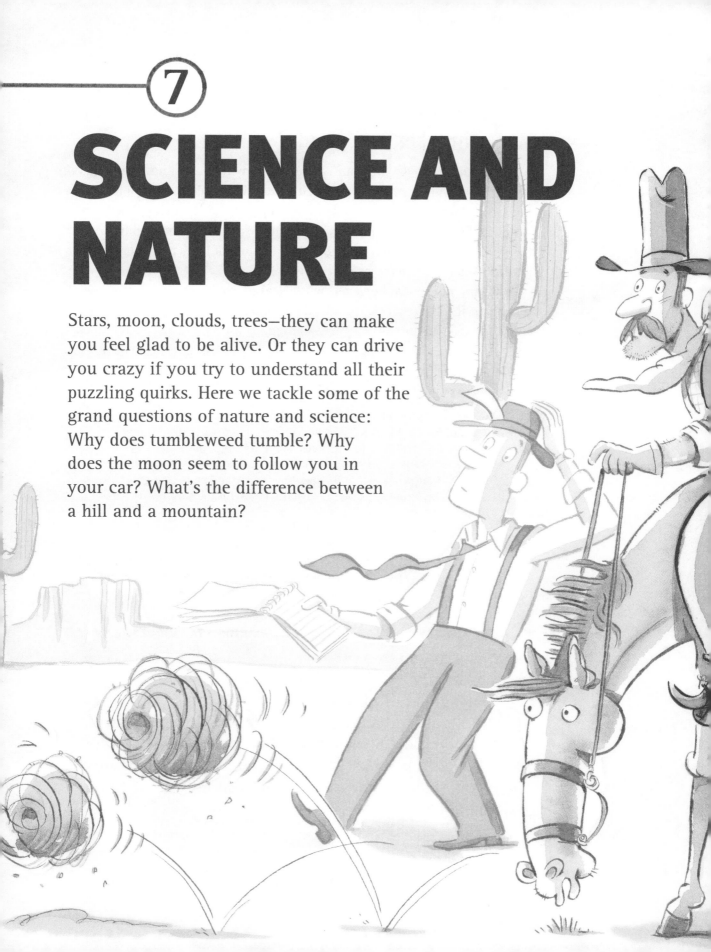

7

SCIENCE AND NATURE

Stars, moon, clouds, trees—they can make
you feel glad to be alive. Or they can drive
you crazy if you try to understand all their
puzzling quirks. Here we tackle some of the
grand questions of nature and science:
Why does tumbleweed tumble? Why
does the moon seem to follow you in
your car? What's the difference between
a hill and a mountain?

if heat rises, why does ice form on the top of water in lakes and ponds?

Anyone who has ever filled an ice-cube tray with water knows that room temperature water decreases in density when it freezes. We also know that heat rises. And that the sun would hit the top of the water more directly than water at the bottom. All three scientific verities would seem to indicate that ice would form at the bottom, rather than the top, of lakes and ponds. "What gives?" demand *Imponderables* readers.

You may not know, however, what Neal P. Rowell, retired professor of physics at the University of South Alabama, told us:

Water is most dense at 4 degrees Centigrade (or 39.2 degrees Fahrenheit). This turns out to be the key to the mystery of the rising ice. One of our favorite scientific researchers, Harold Blake, wrote a fine summary of what turns out to be a highly technical answer:

> As water cools, it gets more dense. It shrinks. It sinks to the bottom of the pond, lake, rain barrel, wheelbarrow, or dog's water dish. But at 4 degrees Centigrade, a few degrees above freezing, the water has reached its maximum density. It now starts to expand as it gets cooler. The water that is between 4 degrees Centigrade and zero Centigrade (the freezing point of water) now starts to rise to the surface. It is lighter, less dense.
>
> Now, more heat has to be lost from the water at freezing to form ice at freezing. This is called the "heat of fusion." During the freezing process, ice crystals form and expand to a larger volume, fusing together as they expand, and using more freezing water to "cement"

IF WATER IS HEAVIER THAN AIR, WHY DO CLOUDS STAY UP IN THE SKY?

What makes you think that clouds aren't dropping? They are. Constantly.

Luckily, cloud drops do not fall at the same velocity as a water balloon. In fact, cloud drops are downright sluggards: They drop at a measly 0.3 centimeters per second. And cloud drops are so tiny, about 0.01 centimeters in diameter, that their descent is not even noticeable to the human eye.

—Submitted by Ronald C. Semone of Washington, D.C.

themselves together. The ice crystals are very much lighter and remain on the surface.

Once the surface is frozen over, heat dissipates from the edges and freezing is progressive from the edges. When the unfrozen core finally freezes, there is tremendous pressure exerted from the expansion, and the ice surface or container sides yield, a common annoyance with water pipes.

Once the top layer of the lake or pond freezes, the water below will rarely reach 0 degrees Centigrade; the ice acts effectively as insulation. By keeping the temperature of the water below the ice between 0 and 4 degrees Centigrade, the ice helps some aquatic life survive in the winter when a lake is frozen over.

The strangest element of this ice Imponderable is that since water at 4 degrees Centigrade is at its maximum density, it always expands when it changes temperature, whether it gets hotter or cooler.

—Submitted by Richard T. Mitch of Dunlap, California. Thanks also to Kenneth D. MacDonald of Melrose, Massachusetts; R. Prickett of Stockton, California; Brian Steiner of Charlotte, North Carolina; and John Weisling of Grafton, Wisconsin.

what are we smelling when it "smells like rain is coming"?

This isn't the type of question that meteorologists study in graduate school or that receives learned exegeses in scholarly journals, but we got several experts to speculate for us. They came down into two camps.

1. It ain't the rain, it's the humidity. Biophysicist Joe Doyle blames the humidity, which rises before rainfall. Of course, humidity itself doesn't smell, but it accentuates the smells of all the objects around it. Everything from garbage to grass smells stronger when it gets damp. Doyle believes that the heightened smell of the flora and fauna around us tips us off subliminally to the feeling that it is going to rain. Richard Anthes of the National Center for Atmospheric Research points out that many gaseous pollutants also are picked up more by our smell receptors when it is humid.

2. The ozone did it. Dr. Keith Seitter, assistant to the executive director of the American Meteorology Association, reminds us that before a thunderstorm, lightning produces ozone, a gas with a distinctive smell. He reports that people who are near lightning recognize the ozone smell (as do those who work with electrical motors, which emit ozone).

Kelly Redmond, meteorologist at the Western Regional Climate Center, in Reno, Nevada, also subscribes to the ozone theory, with one proviso. Ozone emissions are common during thunderstorms in the summer, but not from the rains from stratiform clouds during the cold season. So if it's "smelling like rain" during the winter in Alaska, chances are you are not smelling the ozone at all but the soil, plants, and vegetation you see around you, enhanced by the humidity.

—Submitted by Dr. Thomas H. Rich of Melbourne, Victoria, Australia. Thanks also to George Gudz of Prescott, Arizona; Anne Thrall of Pocatello, Idaho; Dr. Allan Wilke of Toledo, Ohio; Matthew Whitfield of Hurdle Mills, North Carolina; Philip Fultz of Twentynine Palms, California; and William Lee of Melville, New York.

what is the difference between "partly cloudy" and "partly sunny" in a weather report?

The expression *partly sunny* was brought to you by the same folks who brought you *comfort station* and *sanitary engineer*. As a technical meteorological term, *partly sunny* doesn't exist. So while you might assume that a partly sunny sky should be clearer than a partly cloudy one, the two terms signify the same condition. You have merely encountered a weathercaster who prefers to see the glass as half full rather than half empty.

Actually, most of the meteorological terms that seem vague and arbitrary have precise meanings. The degree of cloudiness is measured by the National Weather Service and described according to the following scales:

CLOUD COVER	TERM
0-30%	clear
31-70%	partly cloudy
71-99%	cloudy
100%	overcast

Where does "fair" weather fit into this spectrum? Fair weather generally refers to any day with less than a 50 percent cloud cover (thus even some "partly cloudy" days could also be "fair"). But even a cloudy day can be termed fair if the cover consists largely of transparent clouds. On days when a profusion of thin cirrus clouds hangs high in the sky but does not block the sun, it is more descriptive to call it a fair day than a partly cloudy one, since one thick cloud formation can screen more sunshine than many willowy cirrus formations.

You might also have heard the aviation descriptions of cloud cover used in weather forecasts. Here's what they mean:

CLOUD COVER	TERM
0-9%	clear
10-50%	scattered clouds
51-89%	broken sky
90-99%	cloudy
100%	overcast

Not many people know what the weather service means when it forecasts that there is a "chance" of rain. Precipitation probabilities expressed in vague adjectives also have precise meaning:

CHANCE OF PRECIPITATION	NATIONAL WEATHER SERVICE TERM
0-20%	no mention of precipitation is made
21-50%	"chance" of precipitation
51-79%	precipitation "likely"
80-100%	will not hedge with adjective: "snow," "rain," etc.

How does the National Weather Service determine the daily cloud cover in the space age? Do they send up weather balloons? Satellites? Not quite. They send a meteorologist to the roof of a building in a relatively isolated area (airports are usually used in big cities) and have him or her look up at the sky and make a well-informed but very human guess.

WHY DOES HEAT LIGHTNING ALWAYS SEEM FAR AWAY? AND WHY DON'T YOU EVER HEAR THUNDER DURING HEAT LIGHTNING?

Heat lightning is actually distant lightning produced by an electrical storm too far away to be seen by the observer. What you see is actually the diffused reflection of the distant lightning on clouds.

You don't hear thunder because the actual lightning is too far away from you for the sound to be audible. There is thunder where the lightning is actually occurring.

why is it that what looks to us like a half-moon is called a quarter-moon by astronomers?

An intriguing Imponderable, we thought, at least until Robert Burnham, editor of *Astronomy,* batted it away with the comment, "Aw, c'mon, you picked an easy one this time!"

Much to our surprise, when astronomers throw lunar fractions around, they are referring to the orbiting cycle of the Moon, not its appearance to us. *Sky & Telescope*'s associate editor, Alan M. MacRobert, explains:

> The Moon is *half* lit when it is a quarter of the way around its orbit. The count begins when the Moon is in the vicinity of the sun (at "new Moon" phase). "First quarter" is when the Moon has traveled one-quarter of the way around the sky from there. The Moon is full when it is halfway around the sky, and at "third quarter" or "last quarter" when it's three-quarters of the way around its orbit.

Robert Burnham adds that "quarter-Moons" and "half-Moons" aren't the only commonly misnamed lunar apparitions. Laymen often call the crescent moon hanging low in the evening sky a "New Moon," but Burnham points out that at this point, the moon is far from new: "In fact, by then the crescent Moon is some three or four days past the actual moment of New Moon, which is the instant when the center of the Moon passes between the Earth and Sun."

—Submitted by Susan Peters of Escondido, California.
Thanks to Gil Gross of New York, New York.

what is the official name of the moon?

Along with our correspondent, we've never known what to call our planet's satellite—Moon? The Moon? moon? the moon? Dorothy?

We know that other planets have moons. Do they all have names? How do astronomers distinguish one moon from another?

Whenever we have a problem with matters astronomical, we beg our friends at two terrific magazines—*Astronomy* and *Sky & Telescope*—for help. As usual, they took pity on us.

Astronomy's Robert Burnham, like all editors, is picky about word usage:

> The proper name of our sole natural satellite is "the Moon" and there-
> fore ... it should be capitalized. The 60-odd natural satellites of the
> other planets, however, are called "moons" (in lowercase) because each
> has been given a proper name, such as Deimos, Amalthea, Hyperion,
> Miranda, Larissa, or Charon.
>
> Likewise, the proper name for our star is "the Sun" and that for our
> planet is "Earth" or "the Earth." It's OK, however, to use "earth" in the
> lowercase whenever you use it as a synonym for "dirt" or "ground."

Alan MacRobert, of *Sky & Telescope,* adds that Luna, the Moon's Latin name, is sometimes used in poetry and science fiction, but has never caught on among scientists or the lay public: "Names are used to distinguish things from each other. Since we have only one moon, there's nothing it needs to be distinguished from."

—Submitted by A. P. Bahlkow of Sudbury, Massachusetts.

why does the moon appear bigger at the horizon than up in the sky?

This Imponderable has been floating around the cosmos for eons and has long been discussed by astronomers, who call it the moon illusion. Not only the moon but the sun appears much larger at the horizon than up in the sky. And constellations, as they ascend in the sky, appear smaller and smaller. Obviously, none of these bodies actually changes size or shape, so why do they *seem* to grow and shrink?

Although there is not total unanimity on the subject, astronomers, for the most part, are satisfied that three explanations answer this Imponderable. In descending order of importance, they are:

1. As Alan MacRobert of *Sky & Telescope* magazine states it, "The sky it-self appears more distant near the horizon than high overhead." In his recent article in *Astronomy* magazine, "Learning the Sky by Degrees," Jim Loudon explains, "Apparently, we perceive the sky not as half a sphere but as half an oblate [flattened at the poles] spheroid—in other words, the sky overhead seems closer to the observer than the horizon. A celestial object that is per-ceived as 'projected' onto this distorted sky bowl seems bigger at the horizon." Why? Because the object appears to occupy just as much space at the seemingly faraway horizon as it does in the supposedly closer sky.

2. When reference points are available in the foreground, distant objects appear bigger. If you see the moon rising through the trees, the moon will appear immense, because your brain is unconsciously comparing the size of the object in the foreground (the tree limbs) with the moon in the background. When you see the moon up in the sky, it is set against tiny stars in the background.

Artists often play with distorting perception by moving peripheral objects closer to the foreground. Peter Boyce of the American Astronomical Society adds that reference points tend to distort perception most when they are close to us and when the size of the reference points is well known to the observer. We *know* how large a tree limb is, but our mind plays tricks on us when we try to determine the size of heavenly objects. Loudon states that eleven full moons would fit between the pointer stars of the Big Dipper, a fact we could never determine with our naked eyes alone.

3. The moon illusion may be partially explained by the refraction of our atmosphere magnifying the image. But even the astronomers who mentioned the refraction theory indicated that it could explain only some of the distortion.

A few skeptics, no doubt the same folks who insist that the world is flat and that no astronaut has ever really landed on the moon, believe that the moon really is larger at the horizon than when up in the sky. If you want to squelch these skeptics, here are a few counterarguments that the astronomers suggested.

1. Take photos of the moon or sun at the horizon and up in the sky. The bodies will appear to be the same size.

2. "Cover" the moon with a fingertip. Unless your nails grow at an alarming rate, you should be able to cover the moon just as easily whether it is high or low.

3. Best of all, if you want proof of how easy it is to skew your perception of size, bend over and look at the moon upside down through your legs. When we are faced with a new vantage point, all reference points and size comparisons are upset, and we realize how much we rely upon experience, rather than our sensory organs, to judge distances and size.

We do, however, suggest that this physically challenging and potentially embarrassing scientific procedure be done in wide-open spaces and with the supervision of a parent or guardian. *Imponderables* cannot be held responsible for the physical or emotional well-being of those in search of astronomical truths.

—Submitted by Patrick Chambers of Grandview, Missouri.

When you are driving at night, why does it seem that the moon is following you around?

The moon looks larger on the horizon than up in the sky, even though the moon remains the same size. Clearly, our eyes can play tricks on us.

Without reference points to guide us, the moon doesn't seem to be far away. When you are driving on a highway, objects closest to your car go whirring by. Barriers dividing the lanes become a blur. You can discern individual houses or trees by the side of the road, but, depending upon your speed, it might be painful to watch them go by. Distant trees and houses move by much more slowly, even though you are driving at the same speed. And distant mountains seem mammoth and motionless. Eventually, as you travel far enough down the highway, you will pass the mountains, and they will appear smaller.

If you think the mountain range off the highway is large or far away, consider the moon, which is 240,000 miles away and bigger than any mountain range (more than 2,100 miles in diameter). We already know that our eyes are playing tricks with our perception of how big and far away the moon is. You would have to be traveling awfully far to make the moon appear to move at all. *Astronomy* editor Jeff Kanipe

concludes that without a highway or expanse of landscape to give us reference points "this illusion of nearness coupled with its actual size and distance makes the moon appear to follow us wherever we go."

This phenomenon, much discussed in physics and astronomy textbooks, is called the parallax and is used to determine how the apparent change in the position of an object or heavenly body may be influenced by the changing position of the observer. Astronomers can determine the distance between a body in space and the observer by measuring the magnitude of the parallax effect.

And then again, Elizabeth, maybe the moon really is following you.

—Submitted by Elizabeth Bogart of Glenview, Illinois.

why can't you see stars in the background in photos or live shots of astronauts in space?

There actually are folks out there who believe that NASA pulled off a giant hoax with the "so-called moon landings." Often, the lack of stars in the background of photos of the astronauts is cited as startling evidence to support the conspiracy.

Sheesh, guys. If you want to be skeptical about something, be dubious about whether "When you're here, you're family" at Olive Garden, or whether State Farm Insurance will be there for you the next time you're in trouble. But don't use a dark background in a photo of outer space to convince yourself that astronauts have never gotten farther than a Hollywood soundstage.

The answer to this Imponderable has more to do with photography than astronomy. Next time you go to a football game on a starry night, try taking a photo of the sky with your trusty 35mm point-and-shoot camera or camcorder. Guess what? The background will be dark—no stars will appear, let alone twinkle, in the background.

The stars don't show up because their light is so dim that they don't produce enough light on film in the short exposures used to take conventional pictures. But you *have* seen many photos of stars, haven't you? These were undoubtedly time-lapse photographs, taken with fast film and with the camera shutter left open for at least ten to fifteen seconds. Without special film and a long exposure time, the camera lens can't focus enough light on the film for the image to appear. Jim McDade, director of space technology for the University of Alabama at Birmingham, elaborates:

> Even if you attempt to take pictures of stars on the "dark side" of the Earth during an EVA [an extra-vehicular activity involving astronauts leaving the primary space module, such as a spacewalk] in low-earth orbit, a time exposure from a stable platform of about twenty seconds is necessary in order to capture enough stellar photons to obtain an image showing stars, even when using fast films designed for low-light photography.

The same problems occur with digital cameras, film, and video cameras, as McDade explains:

> A digital camera, a film camera, and the human eye all suffer similar adaptability problems when it comes to capturing dimmer background

objects such as stars hanging behind a space-walking astronaut in the foreground. The human eye is still much more sensitive than the finest digital or film camera.

Photographic film is incapable of capturing the "very bright" and the "very dim" in the same exposure. The lunar surface is brilliant in daylight. The photos taken by the Apollo astronauts used exposure times of a tiny fraction of one second. The stars in the sky are so dim that in order to capture them on film, it requires an exposure time hundreds of times longer than those made by the Apollo astronauts.

Those of us who live in the city have had the experience of going out to a rural area on a clear night, and being amazed at the number of stars we can see when there aren't lights all around us on the ground. You can create the same effect inside your house. On a clear night, kill the lights in a room and look out the window. Depending upon the atmospheric conditions, a star-filled sky may be visible to you. Flip on the lights inside the room, look outside, and the stars have disappeared.

Why? Light from a bright object near us can easily dwarf light emanating from distant objects, such as stars. In the case of astronauts, the lights attached to the space vehicle or space station or even the lights on an astronaut's helmet can wash out the relatively dim light from the stars in the background.

Even with sensitive film, the suits that astronauts and cosmonauts wear reflect a lot of light. The glare from the astronauts themselves will provide contrast from the dark sky background and faint stars. Any light emanating from the stars is unlikely to be exhibited when cameras are geared toward capturing clear shots of a space walker.

Perhaps the space conspiracists would stifle themselves if the Apollo astronauts had taken time-exposure photographs that could display the stars in all their glory, but they never did. As McBain puts it: "After all, they went to the moon to explore the moon, not to stargaze."

–Submitted by Scott Cooley of Frisco, Texas. (For much more information on the issues of photography in outer space, see Jim McDade's "Moonshot" Web site at http://www.insideksc.cjb.net:8081/moonshot/default.htm.)

what is the difference between a mountain and a hill?

Although we think you are making a mountain out of a molehill, we'll answer this Imponderable anyway. Most American geographers refer to a hill as a natural elevation that is smaller than 1,000 feet. Anything above

1,000 feet is usually called a mountain. In Great Britain, the traditional boundary line between hill and mountain is 2,000 feet.

Still, some geographers are not satisfied with this definition. "Hill" conjures up rolling terrain; "mountains" connote abrupt, peaked structures. A mound that rises two feet above the surrounding earth may attain an elevation of 8,000 feet, if it happens to be located in the middle of the Rockies, whereas a 999-foot elevation, starting from a sea-level base, will appear massive. For this reason, most geographers feel that "mountain" may be used for elevations under 1,000 feet if they rise abruptly from the surrounding terrain.

The *Oxford English Dictionary* states that "hill" may also refer to non-natural formations, such as sand heaps, mounds, or, indeed, molehills.

—Submitted by Thomas J. Schoeck of Slingerlands, New York.
Thanks also to F. S. Sewell of San Jose, California.

why are the oceans salty? What keeps the oceans at the same level of saltiness?

Most of the salt in the ocean is there because of the processes of dissolving and leaching from the solid earth over hundreds of millions of years, according to Dr. Eugene C. LaFond, president of LaFond Oceanic Consultants. Rivers take the salt out of rocks and carry them into oceans; these eroded rocks supply the largest portion of salt in the ocean.

But other natural phenomena contribute to the mineral load in the oceans. Salty volcanic rock washes into them. Volcanoes also release salty "juvenile water," water that has never existed before in the form of liquid. Fresh basalt flows up from a giant rift that runs through all the oceans' basins.

With all of these processes dumping salt into the oceans, one might think that the seas would get saturated with sodium chloride, for oceans, like any other body of water, keep evaporating. Ocean spray is continuously released into the air; and the recycled rain fills the rivers, which aids in the leaching of salt from rocks.

Yet, according to the Sea Secrets Information Services of the International Oceanographic Foundation at the University of Miami, the concentration of salts in the ocean has not changed for quite a while—about, oh, 1.5 billion years or so. So how do oceans rid themselves of some of the salt?

First of all, sodium chloride is extremely soluble, so it doesn't tend to get concentrated in certain sections of the ocean. The surface area of the oceans is so large (particularly since all the major oceans are interconnected) that the salt is relatively evenly distributed. Second, some of the ions in the salt leave with the sea spray. Third, some of the salt disappears as adsorbates, in the form of gas liquids sticking to particulate matter that sinks below the surface of the ocean. The fourth and most dramatic way sodium chloride is removed from the ocean is by the large accumulations left in salt flats on ocean coasts, where the water is shallow enough to evaporate.

It has taken so long for the salt to accumulate in the oceans that the amount of salt added and subtracted at any particular time is relatively small. While the amount of other minerals in the ocean has changed dramatically, the level of salt in the ocean, approximately 3.5 percent, remains constant.

—Submitted by Merilee Roy of Bradford, Massachusetts.
Thanks also to Nicole Chastrette of New York, New York; Bob and Elaine Juhre
of Kettle Falls, Washington; John H. Herman of Beaverton, Oregon; Matthew Anderson
of Forked River, New Jersey; and Cindy Raymond of Vincentown, New Jersey.

why are ancient cities buried in layers? And where did the dirt come from?

This Imponderable assumes two facts that aren't always true. First, not all ruins are the remains of cities. Many other ancient sites—such as forts, camping sites, cave dwellings, cemeteries, and quarries—are also frequently buried. Second, not all ancient cities are buried; once in a while, archaeologists are given a break and find relics close to or at the surface of the ground.

Still, the questions are fascinating, and we went to two experts for the answers: George Rapp, Jr., dean and professor of geology and archaeology of the University of Minnesota, Duluth, and coeditor of *Archaeological Geology*;

and Boston University's Al B. Wesolowsky, managing editor of the *Journal of Field Archaeology*. Both stressed that most buried ruins were caused by a combination of factors. Here are some of the most common:

1. **Wind-borne dust** (known to archaeologists as "Aeolian dust") accumulates and eventually buries artifacts. Aeolian dust can vary from wind-blown volcanic dust to ordinary dirt and house dust.

2. **Water-borne sediment** accumulates and eventually buries artifacts. Rain carrying sediment from a high point to a lower spot is often the culprit, but sand or clay formed by flowing waters, such as riverine deposits gathered during floods, can literally bury a riverside community. Often, water collects and carries what are technically Aeolian deposits to a lower part of a site.

3. **Catastrophic natural events** can cause burials in one fell swoop, though this is exceedingly rare, and as Dr. Rapp adds, "In these circumstances the site must be in a topographic situation where erosion is absent or at least considerably slower than deposition." Even when a city is buried after one catastrophe, the burial can be caused by more than one factor. Dr. Wesolowsky notes that although both Pompeii and Herculaneum were buried by the eruption of Mt. Vesuvius in A.D. 79, one was buried by mudflow and the other by ashflow.

WHY DOES A HORRIBLE DRUG LIKE *HEROIN* HAVE A "HEROIC" NAME?

Yes, *heroin* derives from the same Greek word, *heros*, that gave us the English *hero* and *heroine*. Although heroin's manufacture and distribution have long been outlawed in the United States, the morphine derivative was developed as a legitimate painkiller.

Heroin was originally a legitimate trademark taken by a German pharmaceutical company, so the brand name was consciously designed to evoke only positive associations. Not only was heroin effective as a painkiller, it also had the "bonus" of giving patients a euphoric feeling, and as we now know, delusions of grandeur (indeed, it has made many a junkie feel like a hero). Although these side effects can be deadly in an illicit drug, it was at first a distinct selling point in marketing heroin to physicians as a painkiller.

4. **Man-made structures** can collapse, contributing to the burial. Sometimes this destruction is accidental (such as floods, earthquakes, fires), and sometimes intentional (bombings, demolitions). Humans seem incapable of leaving behind no trace of their activities. Says Rapp: "Even cities as young as New York City have accumulated a considerable depth of such debris. Early New York is now buried many feet below the current surface."

5. **Ancient civilizations** occasionallly did their own burying. Wesolowsky's example:

> When Constantine wanted to build Old St. Peter's on the side of the Vatican Hill in the early fourth century, his engineers had to cut off part of the slope and dump it into a Roman cemetery (thereby preserving the lower part of the cemetery, including what has been identified as the tomb of Peter himself) to provide a platform for the basilica. When Old St. Peter's was demolished in the sixteenth century to make way for the current church, parts of the old church were used as fill in low areas in the locale.

Rapp's example:

> This phenomenon is best seen in the tels of the Near East. Often they are tens of feet high. Each "civilization" is built over the debris of the preceding one. The houses were mostly of mud brick, which had a lifetime of perhaps sixty years. When they collapsed the earth was just spread around. In two thousand or three thousand years these great habitation mounds (tels) grew to great heights and now rise above the surrounding plains. Each layer encloses archaeological remains of the period of occupation.

While we self-consciously bury time capsules to give future generations an inkling of what our generation is like, the gesture is unnecessary. With an assist from Mother Nature, we are unwittingly burying revealing artifacts—everything from candy wrappers to beer cans—every day.

—Submitted by Greg Cox of San Rafael, California.

how does aspirin find a headache?

When we get a minor headache, we pop two aspirin and voilà, the pain diminishes within a matter of minutes. How did those little pills find exactly what ailed us instead of, say, our little right toe or our left hip?

We always assumed that the aspirin dissolved, entered our bloodstream, and quickly found its way to our brain. The chemicals then persuaded the brain to block out any feelings of pain in the body. Right? Wrong.

Willow bark, which provided the salicylic acid from which aspirin was originally synthesized, had been used as a pain remedy ever since the Greeks discovered its therapeutic power nearly 2,500 years ago. Bayer was the first company to market Aspirin commercially in 1899 (Aspirin was originally a trade name of Bayer's for the salicylic acid derivative, acetylsalicylic acid, or ASA). The value of this new drug was quickly apparent, but researchers had little idea how aspirin alleviated pain until the 1970s. In their fascinating book *The Aspirin Wars,* Charles C. Mann and Mark L. Plummer describe the basic dilemma:

> Aspirin was a hard problem.... It relieves pain but, mysteriously, is not an anesthetic.... And it soothes inflamed joints but leaves normal joints untouched. How does aspirin "know" ... whether pain is already present, or which joints are inflamed? Researchers didn't have a clue. They didn't even know whether aspirin acts peripherally, at the site of an injury, or centrally, blocking the ability of the brain and central nervous system to feel pain.

The breakthrough came more than seventy years after the introduction of the best-selling pharmaceutical in the world, when researcher John Vane discovered that aspirin inhibited the synthesis of prostaglandins, fatty acids manufactured by virtually every cell in the human body. They resemble hormones, insofar as they secrete into the bloodstream, but unlike most hormones, they tend to stay near their point of manufacture. Prostaglandins serve many biological functions, but the particular ones that cause headache pain, usually known as PGE 2, increase the sensitivity of pain receptors.

So the function of prostaglandins seems to be to produce discomfort, inflammation, fever, and irritation in areas of the body that are not functioning normally, thus serving as an internal warning system. According to Harold Davis, consumer safety officer with the Food and Drug Administration, prostaglandins dilate blood vessels, which can also produce headaches.

The discovery of the role of prostaglandins in producing pain explains why aspirin works only on malfunctioning cells and tissues; if aspirin can stop the production of prostaglandins, pain will not be felt in the first place. Still, aspirin doesn't cure diseases; it can alleviate the symptoms of arthritis, for example, but it doesn't stop the progress of the condition.

In all fairness, scientists still don't know exactly what causes headaches, nor all the ways in which aspirin works to relieve pain. Unlike morphine and other mind-altering drugs, aspirin works peripherally. The key to the success of any peripheral painkiller is in reaching the pain receptors near the irritation or inflammation, not simply in reaching sufficient concentrations in the bloodstream. In the case of aspirin, the ASA is connected to the bloodstream; the bloodstream's connected to the prostaglandins; the prostaglandins are connected to the receptors; and the receptors are connected to the headache.

—Submitted by Debra Allen of Wichita Falls, Texas.

why do we have a delayed reaction to sunburn? Why is sunburn often more evident 24 hours after we've been out in the sun?

It's happened to most of you. You leave the house for the beach. You forget the sunscreen. Oh well, you think, I won't stay out in the sun too long.

You *do* stay out in the sun too long, but you're surprised that you haven't burned too badly. Still, you feel a heaviness on your skin. That night, you start feeling a burning sensation.

The next morning, you wake up and go into the bathroom. You look in the mirror. George Hamilton is staring back at you. Don't you hate when that happens?

Despite our association of sunburn and tanning with fun in the sun, sunburn is, to quote U.S. Army dermatologist Col. John R. Cook, nothing more than "an injury to the skin caused by exposure to ultraviolet radiation." The sun's ultraviolet rays, ranging in length from 200 to 400 nanometers, invisible to the naked eye, are also responsible for skin cancer. Luckily for us, much of the damaging effects of the sun is filtered by our ozone layer.

Actually, some of us do redden quickly after exposure to the sun, but Samuel T. Selden, a Chesapeake, Virginia, dermatologist, told us that this

WHY IS *POUND* ABBREVIATED AS *LB.*?

In the zodiac, the symbol of Libra is the scales. How appropriate, then, that *lb.* is an abbreviation of the Latin *libra* ("scales") *pondo* ("a pound by weight"). The original *pondo* was a premeasured weight to be placed in one of the two pans, thus providing a standard to apply against other substances of unknown weight.

—Submitted by Leslie P. Madison of Anaheim, California. Thanks also to Bryan J. Cooper of Ontario, Oregon, and Daniel A. Papcke of Lakewood, Ohio.

initial "blush" is primarily due to the heat, with blood going through the skin in an effort to radiate the heat to the outside, reducing the core temperature.

This initial reaction is not the burn itself. In most cases, the peak burn is reached fifteen to twenty-four hours after exposure. A whole series of events causes the erythema (reddening) of the skin, after a prolonged exposure to the sun:

1. In an attempt to repair damaged cells, vessels widen in order to rush blood to the surface of the skin. As biophysicist Joe Doyle puts it, "The redness we see is not actually the burn, but rather the blood that has come to repair the cells that have burned." This process, called vasodilation, is prompted by the release of one or more chemicals, such as kinins, setotonins, and histamines.

2. Capillaries break down and slowly leak blood.

3. Exposure to the sun stimulates the skin to manufacture more melanin, the pigment that makes us appear darker (darker-skinned people, in general, can better withstand exposure to the sun, and are more likely to tan than burn).

4. Prostaglandins, fatty acid compounds, are released after cells are damaged by the sun, and play some role in the delay of sunburns, but researchers don't know yet exactly how this works.

All four of these processes take time and explain the delayed appearance of sunburn. The rate at which an individual will tan is dependent upon the skin type (the amount of melanin already in the skin), the wavelength of the ultraviolet rays, the volume of time in the sun, and the time of day. (If you are tanning at any time other than office hours—9 A.M. to 5 P.M.—you are unlikely to burn.)

Even after erythema occurs, your body attempts to heal you. Peeling, for example, can be an important defense mechanism, as Dr. Selden explains:

> The peeling that takes place as the sunburn progresses is the skin's effort to thicken up in preparation for further sun exposure. The skin thickens and darkens with each sun exposure, but some individuals, lacking the ability to tan, suffer sunburns with each sun exposure.

One dermatologist, Joseph P. Bark of Lexington, Kentucky, told us that the delayed burning effect is responsible for much of the severe skin damage he sees in his practice. Sunbathers think that if they haven't burned yet, they can continue sitting in the sun, but there is no way to gauge how much damage one has incurred simply by examining the color or extent of the erythema. To Bark, this is like saying there is no fire when we detect smoke, but no flames. Long before sunburns appear, a doctor can find cell damage by examining samples through a microscope.

—Submitted by Launi Rountry of Brockton, Massachusetts.

why do we call our numbering system "Arabic" when Arabs don't use Arabic numbers themselves?

The first numbering system was probably developed by the Egyptians, but ancient Sumeria, Babylonia, and India used numerals in business transactions. All of the earliest number systems used some variation of 1 to denote one, probably because the numeral resembled a single finger. Historians suggest that our Arabic 2 and 3 are corruptions of two and three slash marks written hurriedly.

Most students in Europe, Australia, and the Americas learn to calculate with Arabic numbers, even though *these numerals were never used by Arabs.* Arabic numbers were actually developed in India, long before the invention of the printing press (probably in the tenth century), but were subsequently translated into Arabic. European merchants who brought back treatises to their continent mistakenly assumed that Arabs had invented the system, and proceeded to translate the texts from Arabic.

True Arabic numerals look little like ours. From one to ten, this is how they look.

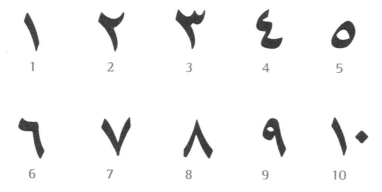

—Submitted by Dr. Bruce Carter of Fort Ord, California.

how did Romans do the calculations necessary for construction and other purposes using Roman numerals?

Our idea of a good time does not include trying to do long division with Roman numerals. Can you imagine dividing CXVII by IX and carrying down numbers that look more like a cryptogram than an arithmetic problem?

The Romans were saved that torture. The Romans relied on the Chinese abacus, with pebbles as counters, to perform their calculations. In fact, Barry Fells of the Epigraphic Society informs us that these mathematical operations were performed in Roman times by persons called "calculatores." They were so named because they used *calcule* (Latin for pebbles) to add, subtract, multiply, and divide.

—Submitted by Greg Cox of San Rafael, California.

what in the heck is a tumbleweed? Why does it tumble? And how can it reproduce if it doesn't stay in one place?

Three Imponderables for the price of one. The first part is easy. The most common form of tumbleweed, the one you see wreaking havoc in movie westerns, is the Russian thistle. But actually the term is applied to any plant that rolls with the wind, drops its seed as it tumbles, and possesses panicles (branched flower clusters) that break off.

Usually, the stems of tumbleweed dry up and snap away from their roots in late fall, when the seeds are ripe and the leaves dying. Although tumbleweeds cannot walk or fly on their own, they are configured to move with the wind. The aboveground portion of the thistle is shaped like a flattened globe, so it can roll more easily than other plants.

In his March 1991 *Scientific American* article "Tumbleweed," James Young points out how tumbleweed has adapted to the arid conditions of the Great Plains. One Russian thistle plant can contain a quarter of a million seeds. Even these impressive amounts of seeds will not reproduce efficiently if dumped all at once. But the flowers, which bloom in the summer, are wedged in the axil between the leaves and the stem, so that their seeds don't

fall out as soon as they are subjected to their first tumbles. In effect, the seeds are dispersed sparingly by the natural equivalent of time-release capsules, assuring wide dissemination.

Young points out that tumbleweed actually thrives on solitude. If tumbleweed bumps into another plant, or thick, tall grass, it becomes lodged there, and birds and small animals find and eat the seeds:

> Hence, successful germination, establishment of seedlings, and flowering depend on dispersal to sites where competition is minimal: Russian thistle would rather tumble than fight.

Although songs have romanticized the tumbleweed, do not forget that the last word in "tumbleweed" is "weed." In fact, if the Russian thistle had been discovered in our country in the 1950s rather than in the 1870s, it probably would have been branded a communist plot. Thistle was a major problem for the cowboys and farmers who first encountered it. Although tumbleweed looks "bushy," its leaves are spiny and extremely sharp. Horses were often lacerated by running into tumbleweed in fields and pastures, and the leaves punctured the gloves and pants worn by cowboys.

Tumbleweed has also been a bane to farmers, which explains how tumbleweed spread so fast from the Dakotas down to the Southwest. The seeds of tumbleweed are about the same size as most cereal grains. Farmers had no easy way to separate the thistle seeds from their grains; as "grain" moved through the marketplace, thistle was transported to new "tumbling ground."

Today, tumbleweed's favorite victims are automobiles and the passengers in them. We get into accidents trying to avoid it, trying to outrace it, and from stupid driving mistakes when simply trying to watch tumbleweed tumble.

—Submitted by Placido Garcia of Albuquerque, New Mexico.

why is balsa wood classified as a hardwood when it is soft? What is the difference between a softwood and a hardwood?

Call us naive. But we thought that maybe there was a slight chance that the main distinction between a softwood and a hardwood was that hardwood was harder than softwood. What fools we are.

Haven't you gotten the lesson yet? LIFE IS NOT FAIR. Our language makes no sense. The center will not hold. Burma Shave.

Anyway, it turns out that the distinction between the two lies in how their seeds are formed on the tree. Softwoods, such as pines, spruce, and fir, are examples of gymnosperms, plants that produce seeds without a covering. John A. Pitcher, director of the Hardwood Research Council, told *Imponderables* that if you pull one of the center scales back away from the stem of a fresh pinecone, you'll see a pair of seeds lying side by side. "They have no covering except the wooden cone."

Hardwoods are a type of angiosperm, a true flowering plant that bears seeds enclosed in capsules, fruits, or husks (e.g., olives, lilies, walnuts). Hardwoods also tend to lose their leaves in temperate climates, whereas softwoods are evergreens; but in tropical climates, many hardwoods retain their leaves.

While it is true that there is a tendency for softwoods to be softer in consistency (and easier to cut for commercial purposes), and for hardwoods to be more compact, and thus tougher and denser in texture, these rules of thumb are not reliable. Pitcher enclosed a booklet listing the specific gravities of the important commercial woods in the U.S. He indicates the irony:

> At 0.16 specific gravity, balsa is the lightest wood listed. At a specific gravity of 1.05, lignumvitae is the heaviest wood known. Both are hardwoods.

why don't trees on a slope grow perpendicular to the ground as they do on a level surface?

Trees don't give a darn if they're planted on a steep hill in San Francisco or a level field in Kansas. Either way, they'll still try to reach up toward the sky and seek as much light as possible.

Botanist Bruce Kershner told *Imponderables* that

> this strong growth preference is based on the most important of motivations: survival. Scientifically, this is called "phototropism," or the growth of living cells toward the greatest source of light. Light provides trees with the energy and food that enable them to grow in the first place.
>
> There is also another tropism (involuntary movement toward or away from a stimulus) at work—*geotropism*—the movement away from the pull of gravity (roots, unlike the rest of the tree, grow *toward* the gravitational pull). Even on a hill slope, the pull of gravity is directly

down, and the greatest source of average light is directly up. In a forest, the source of light is only up.

There are, however, cases where a tree might not grow directly up. First, there are some trees whose trunks grow outward naturally, but whose tops still tend to point upward. Second, trees growing against an overhanging cliff will grow outward on an angle toward the greatest concentration of light (much like a houseplant grows toward the window). Third, it is reported that in a few places on earth with natural geomagnetic distortions (e.g., Oregon Vortex, Gold Hill, Oregon), the trees grow in a contorted fashion. The gravitational force is abnormal but the light source is the same.

John A. Pitcher of the Hardwood Research Council adds that trees have developed adaptive mechanisms to react to the sometimes conflicting demands of phototropism and geotropism:

> Trees compensate for the pull of gravity and the slope of the ground by forming a special kind of reaction wood. On a slope, conifer trees grow faster on the downhill side, producing compression wood, so

IF NOTHING STICKS TO TEFLON, HOW DO THEY GET TEFLON TO STICK TO THE PAN?

"They," of course, is DuPont, which owns the registered trademark for Teflon and its younger and now more popular cousin, Silverstone. G. A. Quinn of DuPont told *Imponderables* that the application of both is similar:

> When applying Silverstone to a metal frypan, the interior of the pan is first grit-blasted, then a primer coat is sprayed on and baked. A second layer of polytetrafluoroethylene (PTFE) is applied, baked and dried again. A third coat of PTFE is applied, baked and dried.
>
> About the only thing that sticks to PTFE is PTFE. So, the 3-coat process used in Silverstone forms an inseparable bond between the PTFE layers and the primer coat bonds to the rough, grit-blasted metal surface.

DuPont has recently introduced Silverstone Supra, also a three-layer coating that is twice as durable as conventional Silverstone.

—Submitted by Anthony Virga of Yonkers, New York.

named because the wood is pushing the trunk bole uphill to keep it straight. Hardwoods grow faster on the uphill side, forming tension wood that pulls the trunk uphill to keep it straight.

Why softwoods develop compression wood and hardwoods develop tension wood is one of the unsolved mysteries of the plant world.

We'll leave that unsolved mystery to Robert Stack.

—Submitted by Marvin Shapiro of Teaneck, New Jersey. Thanks also to Herbert Kraut of Forest Hills, New York, and Gregory Laugle of Huber Heights, Ohio.

how is the caloric value of food measured?

Imponderables is on record as doubting the validity of caloric measurements. It defies belief that the caloric value of vegetables such as potato chips and onion rings, full of nutrients, could possibly be higher than greasy tuna fish or eggplant. Still, with an open mind, we sought to track down the answer to this Imponderable.

Calories are measured by an apparatus called a *calorimeter*. The piece of food to be measured is placed inside a chamber, sealed, and then ignited and burned. The energy released from the food heats water surrounding the chamber. By weighing the amount of water heated, noting the increase in the water's temperature and multiplying the two, the energy capacity of the food can be measured. A calorie is nothing more than the measurement of the ability of a particular nutrient to raise the temperature of one gram of water one degree Centigrade. For example, if ten thousand grams of water (the equivalent of ten liters or ten thousand cubic centimeters) surrounding the chamber is 20 degrees Centigrade before combustion and then is measured at 25 degrees after combustion, the difference in temperature (five degrees) is multiplied by the volume of water (ten thousand grams) to arrive at the caloric value (fifty thousand calories of energy).

If fifty thousand calories sounds like too high a number to describe heating ten liters of water five degrees, your instincts are sound. One calorie is too small a unit of measurement to be of practical use, so the popular press uses "calorie" to describe what the scientists call "Calories," really kilocalories, one thousand times as much energy as the lowercase "calorie."

The calorimeter is a crude but reasonable model for how our body stores and burns energy sources. The calorimeter slightly overstates the number of calories our body can use from each foodstuff. In the calorimeter, foods burn

completely, with only some ashes (containing minerals) left in the chamber. In our body, small portions of food are indigestible, and are excreted before they break down to provide energy. The rules of thumb are that two percent of fat, five percent of carbohydrates, and eight percent of proteins will not be converted to energy by the body.

Food scientists have long known the caloric count for each food group. One gram of carbohydrates or proteins equals four calories. One gram of fat contains more than twice the number of calories (nine).

Scientists can easily ascertain the proportion of fat to carbohydrates or proteins, so it might seem that calories could be measured simply by weighing the food. When a food consists exclusively of proteins and carbohydrates, for example, one could simply multiply the weight of the food by four to discover the calorie count.

But complications arise. Certain ingredients in natural or processed foods contain no caloric value whatsoever, such as water, fiber, and minerals. Foods that contain a mixture, say, of water (zero calories), fiber (zero calories), proteins (four calories per gram), fats (nine calories per gram), and carbohydrates (four calories per gram), along with some trace minerals (zero calories), are simply harder to calculate with a scale than a calorimeter.

—Submitted by Jill Palmer of Leverett, Massachusetts.

why do some ice cubes come out cloudy and others come out clear?

A caller on the Merle Pollis radio show, in Cleveland, Ohio, first confronted us with this problem. We admitted we weren't sure about the answer, but subsequent callers all had strong convictions about the matter. The only problem was that they all had *different* convictions.

One caller insisted that the mineral content of the water determined the opacity of the cube, but this theory doesn't explain why all the cubes from the same water source don't come out either cloudy or clear.

Two callers insisted that the temperature of the water when put into the freezer was the critical factor. Unfortunately, they couldn't agree about whether it was the hot water or the cold water that yielded clear ice.

We finally decided to go to an expert who confirmed what we expected— all the callers were wrong. Dr. John Hallet of the Atmospheric Ice Laboratory of the Desert Research Institute in Reno, Nevada, informed us that the key factor in cloud formation is the temperature of the *freezer*. When ice forms slowly, it tends to freeze first at one edge. Air bubbles found in a solution in the water have time to rise and escape. The result is clear ice cubes.

The clouds in ice cubes are the result of air bubbles formed as ice is freezing. When water freezes rapidly, freezing starts at more than one end, and water residuals are trapped in the middle of the cube, preventing bubble loss. The trapped bubbles make the cube appear cloudy.

8 POPULAR CULTURE

Tell the truth—you've been wondering for decades: Why is the Charlie Brown comic strip called *Peanuts?* Why does Bazooka Joe wear an eye patch? Who was Casper the Friendly Ghost before he died? Why is the Lone Ranger called "Lone" when he always has his sidekick Tonto with him? Well, your moment has arrived.

who was Casper the Friendly Ghost before he died?

You can't blame someone for wanting to know more about the backstory of Casper. Restless ghosts are a dime a dozen. Poltergeists are scary. But you don't run into many friendly ghosts, and none so relentlessly affable as Casper.

We thought the billowy puff of friendliness originated in comic books, but we were wrong. Casper first appeared in a Paramount Pictures short cartoon in 1945, although at that point he didn't have a name. Casper might have been friendly, but his co-creators, Seymour V. Reit and Joe Oriolo, fought over who thought of the story of the "Friendly Ghost." Reit insisted he did, since Casper was based on an unpublished short story of his, and Oriolo was "only" the illustrator (Oriolo later went on to illustrate and produce 260 Felix the Cat cartoons for television).

By all accounts, the first cartoon didn't set the world on fire, but the second, *There's Good Boos Tonight,* was released in 1948, and several more were created in subsequent years. Although Casper never gave Mickey Mouse or Bugs Bunny a run for their money, the chummy spook was Paramount's second favorite cartoon character after Popeye in the 1940s and 1950s. In these early cartoons, nothing whatsoever was said or implied about how Casper became a ghost at such a young age. As Mark Arnold, publisher of the *Harveyville Fun Times,* puts it: "They introduce Casper as a friendly ghost who doesn't want to scare people." Arnold adds that in the children's book that was a prototype for the cartoon, Casper's origins are undisclosed.

In 1949, Paramount sold the comic book rights to all of its cartoon characters, Popeye excepted, to St. John Publishing, which issued five Casper titles with a resounding lack of success. In 1952, Harvey Comics picked up the license. Harvey became Casper's comic book home for more than three decades. It was at Harvey where Casper was given a cast of sidekicks—his trusty ghost horse, Nightmare, and his antagonist, Spooky, the "Tough Little Ghost." Casper also became pals with Wendy, the "Good Little Witch," who spun off her own titles. The success of the Harvey comic books goosed the interest in made-for-television cartoons—more than 100 episodes were syndicated.

But despite the need for storylines for all these outlets, Casper's origins remained shrouded in mystery, and as it turns out, this was no accident. Sid Jacobson, who has been associated with Casper for more than fifty years,

IMPONDERABLES

told *Imponderables* that when the company bought the rights to the Paramount characters, Harvey was more interested in the then more popular Little Audrey (a not-too-subtle "homage" to Little Lulu). Casper was thrown in as part of the deal, and he and other editors at Harvey went to work "rethinking him." Why the need to rethink? It turns out that Jacobson was less than thrilled with the original animated cartoon: "It was so ugly, and so stupid, I never forgot it. If we used the original premise for our books, it would have been a failure."

Ever mindful that Casper was meant to appeal to a younger segment of the audience, the editors at Harvey wanted to banish elements that would frighten children or give parents an excuse to ban their kids from reading about even a friendly apparition. Jacobson says:

> Since the dawn of the Harvey Casper character, truly the Casper everyone knows and loves, Casper's origin is definite but flies in the face of conventional definition: he was born a ghost. Like elves and fairies, he

WHAT, EXACTLY, IS THE MCDONALD'S CHARACTER "THE GRIMACE" SUPPOSED TO BE?

Patricia Milroy, a McDonald's customer satisfaction department representative, reported that Imponderables readers are not alone; this is among the most asked questions of the corporation. What does this say about our culture?

We're not here to judge, however, so we are proud to announce the official position of McDonald's on the exact description of The Grimace: "He is a big fuzzy purple fellow and Ronald's special pal." That's it. Regardless of our prodding, our cajoling, our penetrating interrogation, our rare paroxysms of hostility, this was the most we could prod out of our golden-arched pals. But we are assured that this is as much as Ronald McDonald himself knows about his fuzzy purple friend.

—Submitted by Michael Weinbeyer of Upper Saint Clair, Pennsylvania.
Thanks also to Joe Pickell of Pittsburgh, Pennsylvania; Samuel Paul Ontallomo
of Upper Saint Clair, Pennsylvania; Nicole Cretelle of San Diego, California;
Ruth Homrighaus of Gambier, Ohio; and Liam Palmer and Jonathan Franz of Corbett, Oregon.

was born the way he was. We consciously made the decision as to his creation. It stopped the grotesqueries, and fits in better with the fairyland situation. It allows Casper to take his place with the other characters in the Enchanted Forest. It doesn't deal in any sense with a kid wanting to die and become a ghost. That was our main concern.

Considering the treacly nature of the comic book, inevitably a few impure types have speculated about the secret origins of Casper. Mark Arnold reveals a particularly startling one:

> The most notorious origin story appeared in Marvel Comics' *Crazy Magazine* #8, in December 1974, in a story called "Kasper, the Dead Baby." In it, they show that small boy Kasper was killed by his alcoholic, abusive father. It's pretty gruesome, but bizarrely funny in a kind of strange way. Marvel has disowned the story, as they have tried to acquire the Harvey license.

In 1991, during *The Simpsons'* second season, the episode "Three Men and a Comic Book" speculates that Casper was actually Richie Rich (another bland comic book star of Harvey's stable) before he died. As Arnold puts it, "Richie's realization of the emptiness that vast wealth brings caused his demise."

Most recently, in the feature film *Casper,* there are allusions to the ghost's past (his father dabbled in scientific spiritualism), but no real explanation for what makes Casper so damned friendly and why he was snuffed out before his prime. Maybe the best theory comes from comic book writer and author of *Toonpedia* (http://www.toonpedia.com), Don Markstein:

> Personally, I always thought it was his friendly, open nature that did him in. His family apparently didn't do a very good job of teaching him about "stranger danger."

> *—Submitted by Steve, a caller on the Glenn Mitchell Show, KERA-AM, Dallas, Texas. Thanks also to Fred Beeman of Las Vegas, Nevada.*

why does Mickey Mouse have four fingers?

Or more properly, why does Mickey Mouse have three fingers and one thumb on each hand? In fact, why is virtually every cartoon animal beset with two missing digits?

Conversations with many cartoonists, animators, and Disney employees confirm what we were at first skeptical about. Mickey Mouse has four fingers because it is convenient for the artists and animators who have drawn him. In the early cartoons, each frame was hand-drawn by an animator—

painstaking and tedious work. No part of the human anatomy is harder to draw than a hand, and it is particularly difficult to draw distinct fingers without making the whole hand look disproportionately large.

The artists who drew Mickey were more than happy to go along with any conceit that saved them some work. So in Disney and most other cartoons, the animals sport a thumb and three fingers, while humans, such as Snow White and Cinderella, are spared the amputation.

And before anyone asks—no, we don't know for sure *which* of Mickey's fingers got lopped off for the sake of convenience. Since the three non-thumbs on each hand are symmetrical, we'd like to think it was the pinkie that was sacrificed.

—Submitted by Elizabeth Frenchman of Brooklyn, New York.
Thanks also to R. Gonzales of Whittier, California.

what is Goofy?

Goofy can't be a dog, claims our correspondent, or else he would look like Pluto, wouldn't he? Goofy is indeed a dog. Chihuahuas don't look like Doberman pinschers, so why should Goofy look like Pluto? Although we must admit that we don't know too many dogs who speak English and walk on two feet.

Pluto appeared several years before Goofy, in a tiny role in a Mickey Mouse short called "Chain Gang." Pluto's original name was Rover, and he was Minnie's dog, not Mickey's. But Mickey soon gained ownership, and Rover was renamed Pluto the Pup. Animator John Canemaker observes that Pluto's lack of speech and doglike walk were used to emphasize that Pluto was Mickey's pet and not his equal.

Goofy, on the other hand, was nobody's pet. His dogginess is indisputable, since his original name was Dippy Dawg. But Dippy had to pay his dues before he reached the summit of Goofyness. Dippy first played small roles in Mickey Mouse shorts in the early 1930s, and it wasn't until he was featured in the syndicated Mickey Mouse newspaper cartoons that he gained prominence in animated shorts.

Although Goofy was as loyal and loving as Pluto, he was not subservient. As his popularity grew, Goofy became a part of "The Gang," with costars Mickey Mouse and Donald Duck in a series of twelve cartoons in the late 1930s and early 1940s. Few remember that Goofy was married (to Mrs. Goofy) and that he was a proud parent (of Goofy, Jr.).

This Imponderable has been thrust at us many times since the release of the movie *Stand by Me*, in which a character muses about this question. How people can accept that a duck can survive being squashed by a refrigerator and then not believe that Goofy can be a dog, we'll never understand.

—Submitted by Ashley Hoffar of Cincinnati, Ohio.

why does Barbie have realistic nylon hair, while Ken is stuck with plastic hair or painted hair?

Poor Mattel is being attacked from all sides. Many feminists have criticized Barbie for setting up unrealistic expectations among girls about what their bodies should look like. Mattel answers, understandably, that Barbie was created to be a fashion doll, a model-mannequin suitable for hanging a variety of clothes upon. Of course, girls fantasize about themselves *as* Barbie, and this identification with the doll is precisely what the critics are worried about.

As if these complaints weren't enough for Mattel to worry about, here come six female *Imponderables* readers accusing the company of reverse discrimination. "What's the deal with Ken's hair?" they all wondered.

Informal chats with a gaggle of Barbie enthusiasts, both young and middle-aged, yielded the information that most girls are indifferent to Ken. To these fans, "Barbie doll" connotes visions of loveliness, while "Ken doll" evokes the image of the sterile figure atop wedding cakes.

WE KNOW WHAT A KING IS AND WHAT A QUEEN IS. WE EVEN KNOW WHAT A JOKER IS. BUT WHAT IS A *JACK?*

Etymologically, *jack* derives from the Old English *chafa* ("boy, male child"). But the clue to the identity of the jack is its alternate name, *knave*. A knave was a servant of royalty, so it is no accident that in a deck of cards, the jack is the lowest ranked picture card.

Later, *knave* accumulated negative connotations, including "deceitfulness." But knavery usually is associated with rascality, which explains, perhaps, why the jack is often wild in poker games.

—Submitted by Mark Anderson of Seattle, Washington.

Mattel's research indicates that there isn't much demand among girls for more realistic hair for Ken. Lisa McKendall, manager of marketing communications for Mattel, provides an explanation:

> In general, the most popular play pattern with fashion dolls among young girls is styling the hair. That is why long, combable hair is such an important feature of fashion dolls. Since the Ken doll's hair is short, there is much less to style and play with, so having "realistic" hair has not been as important.

Needless to say, "Ken hair" is much cheaper for Mattel to produce, particularly because painted hair doesn't have to be "rooted" to the top of the doll's head.

The choice of hairstyles for the Barbie lines is not taken casually. Meryl Friedman, vice-president of marketing for Barbie consumer products, told *Imponderables* that the length and texture of dolls' hair depends upon which "segment," or line of Barbies, Mattel is conceptualizing. Friedman reports that the best-selling doll in the history of Mattel is the "Totally Hair Barbie" line. The hair in the Totally Hair line is ten and one-half inches long—and the doll is only eleven and one-half inches tall. In this particular segment, even Ken has combable, if short, hair as McKendall explains:

> The Ken doll *does* have realistic-looking hair and actually comes with styling gel to create many different looks. A special fiber for the hair called Kankelon is produced specifically for us in Japan.

—Submitted by Dona Gray of Whiting, Indiana. Thanks also to Laura and Jenny Dunklee of Sutter Creek, California; Jessica Barmann of Kansas City, Missouri; Rebecca Capowski of Great Falls, Montana; and Nicole McKinley of Rochelle, Illinois.

why are the Muppets left-handed?

Our sharp-eyed correspondent, Jena Mori, first noticed that all the Muppet musicians seem to be left-handed, and then realized that just about all of the Muppets' complicated movements were done with their left hands. We went to the folks at Jim Henson Productions for the answer to Jena's conundrum and were lucky enough to get an expert answer right from the frog's mouth, so to speak.

Steve Whitmire has been a Muppet performer for fifteen years, and currently "is" Kermit the Frog. Steve performs Wembley Fraggle and Sprocket the Dog from "Fraggle Rock," as well as Rizzo the Rat, Bean Bunny, and numerous lesser-known Muppets. He also performs Robbie and B. P. Richfield on "Dinosaurs" and has worked on all of the Muppet movies.

Since we don't often have the opportunity to speak with Muppet performers, we imposed on Steve to answer in interview form.

IMPONDERABLES: Steve, why are Muppets left-handed?

STEVE: Because most puppeteers are right-handed.

IMPONDERABLES: Huh?

STEVE: Imagine standing with your right hand in the air. You are wearing a hand puppet that fits down to approximately your elbow. Now imagine that a television camera is raised to six feet off the floor and is pointing at everything above your head. You are watching what the camera sees on a television monitor on the floor in front of you. Your right hand is in the head of the character. If you want to move the puppet's arms, you reach up in front of your face and grasp one or both of the two wire rods that hang from the puppet's wrists. You have to make sure that your head is low enough to clear the camera frame, so you'll probably have to shift your weight to your left as you duck your head to the left.

IMPONDERABLES: Why do you duck to your left instead of your right?

STEVE: The right hand is stretching as high to the right as possible because that is most comfortable. When the right hand stretches up, the left side automatically hunches down a bit. It's easier for me to duck my head to the left: otherwise, I'd be ducking my head under my right arm.

IMPONDERABLES: If your right hand is controlling the head of the puppet, how are you controlling its arms?

STEVE: You reach up in front of your face and grasp one or both of the two wire rods that hang from the puppet's wrists. You'd be able to have general control of both arms with your left hand. If you needed to do some bit of action that is more specific, you'd likely use the puppet's left arm.

IMPONDERABLES: Aha, we're now at the crux of our Imponderable. But since you are controlling both of the puppet's arms with *your* left hand, why does it matter which of the *puppet's* hands you control?

STEVE: Right-handed people tend to have more dexterity and stamina in their right hand and arm, so it goes into the head of the puppet. It is an ergonomic choice more than anything. If the puppeteer is right-handed, it is the more coordinated arm and hand, and it is usually best for it to be in the head. The left arm of the puppeteer is just below the puppet's left arm, so making the left hand of the puppet its dominant hand seems like the natural choice.

IMPONDERABLES: You are implying that a Muppet performer concentrates much more on the head of a character than its arms.

STEVE: The attention of the audience is generally focused on the puppet's face and, more specifically, its eyes. That's part of the appeal of the Muppets—

Why were Athos, Porthos, and Aramis called the Three Musketeers when they fought with swords rather than muskets?

The Three Swordsmen sounds like a decent enough title for a book, if not an inspiring name for a candy bar, so why did Dumas choose *The Three Musketeers?* Dumas based his novel on *Memoirs of Monsieur D'Artagnan,* a fictionalized account of "Captain-Lieutenant of the First Company of the King's Musketeers." Yes, there really was a company of musketeers in France in the seventeenth century.

Formed in 1622, the company's main function was to serve as bodyguard for the King (Louis XIII) during peacetime. During wars, the musketeers were dispatched to fight in the infantry or cavalry; but at the palace, they, were the *corps d'élite.* Although they were young (mostly seventeen to twenty years of age), all had prior experience in the military and were of aristocratic ancestry.

According to Dumas translator Lord Sudley, when the musketeers were formed, they "had just been armed with the new flintlock, muzzle-loading muskets," a precursor to modern rifles. Unfortunately, the musket, although powerful enough to pierce any armor of its day, was also extremely cumbersome. As long as eight feet, and the weight of two bowling balls, they were too unwieldy to be carried by horsemen. The musket was so awkward that it could not be shot accurately while resting on the shoulder, so musketeers used a fork rest to steady the weapon. Eventually, the "musketeers" were rendered musketless and relied on newfangled pistols and trusty old swords.

Just think of how muskets would have slowed down the derring-do of the three amigos. It's not easy, for example, to slash a sword-brandishing villain while dangling from a chandelier if one has a musket on one's back.

—*Submitted by John Bigus of Orion, Illinois.*

they seem to be looking at whatever they are focused on, whether it is a prop, another character, or the home audience via the camera. The arms are somewhat secondary, although if they are performed badly, say, with arms dangling, they can attract unwanted attention.

Eye contact, and life within the face, is always the first priority in bringing our characters to life: simple head moves and gestures, accurate lip sync, etc., mimic human or animal movement. We keep all of the movement of the characters to the minimum needed to give them the life we want. There shouldn't be any movement without a purpose.

IMPONDERABLES: But some of the Muppets' movements seem awfully complicated. How can you control intricate movements with your "wrong" (i.e., left) hand manipulating two rods?

STEVE: If there is specific action that requires precision that would draw our attention away from the head for too long, we will often have another puppeteer handle the right, and occasionally both, hands.

IMPONDERABLES: Couldn't it get tricky having two people manipulate the same puppet?

STEVE: It can. Having one performer manipulating the head and left hand and another the right hand of the puppet can help. This method allows the puppeteer on the head to do any action with the left hand if it needs to come in contact with the face, or the puppet's right hand.

However, when Jim Henson did the Swedish Chef, he worked only the head, and it was usually Frank Oz in *both* hands. One reason for this was that the Chef's hands were actually human hands and needed to match. Another reason was that Jim and Frank loved to do difficult and silly things like that. Frank's goal was to break the china on the back wall each time they did a bit and the Chef threw something over his shoulder during his opening song. We would all take bets. I think he only did it [successfully] once or twice.

IMPONDERABLES: So this answers the question reader Robin R. Bolan asked about why some Muppets don't seem to have wires: The answer is that sometimes they don't.

STEVE: Right. These types of puppets are good for handling props because the puppeteer can simply pick things up. In this case, a second puppeteer *always* does the right hand of the character, because the lead performer is completely tied up with the head and left hand.

IMPONDERABLES: So it's easier to be green than a Muppet performer.

STEVE: I always liken what we do to being an air traffic controller, because there is so much to concentrate on while we are performing. Not only are we manipulating the puppet's mouth, body movements, and arms, we are

doing the voice, remembering dialogue, watching a television screen (we never look at the puppet—only the screen), and tripping over cables, set pieces, and five other puppeteers who are doing the same thing we are.

It's a wonder we ever get anything done considering how truly complex it really is. Fortunately, and for good reason, the audience only sees what goes on up there above us.

—Submitted by Jena Mori of Los Angeles, California.
Thanks also to Robin R. Bolan of McLean, Virginia.

why was he called the Lone Ranger when Tonto was always hanging around?

The classic western features a lone hero entering a new town and facing a villain who threatens the peacefulness of a dusty burg. The Lone Ranger, on the other hand, came with a rather important backup, Tonto. Leaving aside questions of political correctness or racism, calling the masked man the *Lone Ranger* is a little like calling Simon and Garfunkel a Paul Simon solo act.

Before we get to the "Lone" part of the equation, our hero actually was a ranger, in fact, a Texas Ranger. *The Lone Ranger* started as a radio show, first broadcast out of Detroit in 1933, created by George Trendle, and written by Fran Striker. The first episode established that circa 1850, the Lone Ranger was one of six Texas Rangers who were trying to tame the vicious Cavendish Gang. Unfortunately, the bad guys ambushed the Rangers, and all of the Lone Ranger's comrades were killed. The Lone Ranger himself was left for dead. Among the vanquished was the Lone Ranger's older brother, Dan.

So for a few moments, long enough to give him his name, the Lone Ranger really was by himself. He was the *lone* surviving Ranger, even if he happened to be unconscious at the time. Tonto stumbled upon the fallen hero and, while nursing him back to health, noticed that the Ranger was wearing a necklace that Tonto had given him as a child. Many moons before, the Lone Ranger (who in subsequent retellings of the story we learn was named John Reid) saved Tonto's life! Tonto had bestowed the necklace on his blood brother as a gift.

When Reid regained his bearings, the two vowed to wreak revenge upon the Cavendish Gang and to continue "making the West a decent place to live." Reid and Tonto dug six graves at the ambush site to make everyone believe that Reid had perished with the others, and to hide his identity, the Lone Ranger donned a black mask, made from the vest his brother was

POPULAR CULTURE

wearing at the massacre. Like Jimmy Olsen with Superman, Tonto was the only human privy to the Lone Ranger's secret.

Not that the Lone Ranger didn't solicit help from others. It isn't easy being a Ranger, let alone a lone one, without a horse. As was his wont, Reid stumbled onto good luck. He and Tonto saved a brave stallion from being gored by a buffalo, and nursed him back to health (the first episode of *The Lone Ranger* featured almost as much medical aid as fighting). Although they released the horse when it regained its health, the stallion followed them and, of course, that horse was Silver, soon to be another faithful companion to L.R.

And would a lonely lone Ranger really have his own, personal munitions supplier? John Reid did. The Lone Ranger and Tonto met a man who the Cavendish Gang tried to frame for the Texas Ranger murders. Sure of his innocence, the Lone Ranger put him in the silver mine that he and his slain brother owned, and turned it into a "silver bullet" factory.

Eventually, during the run of the radio show, which lasted from 1933 to 1954, the duo vanquished the Cavendish Gang, but the Lone Ranger and Tonto knew when they found a good gig. They decided to keep the Lone Ranger's true identity secret, to keep those silver bullets flowing, and best of all, to bounce into television in 1949 for a nine-year run on ABC and decades more in syndication.

The Lone Ranger was also featured in movie serials, feature movies, and comic books, and the hero's origins mutated slightly or weren't mentioned at all. But the radio show actually reran the premiere episode periodically, so listeners in the 1930s probably weren't as baffled about why a law enforcer with a faithful companion, a full-time munitions supplier, and a horse was called "Lone."

—Submitted by James Telfer IV of New York, New York.

why is there no Betty Rubble character in Flintstones multivitamins?

For reasons too unfathomable for even us to delve into, we are thrown this question periodically on radio phone-in shows but have never received it in a letter. Perhaps no one wants to take credit for asking this Imponderable. One radio host said that he had investigated the matter, and found that for technical reasons, it was difficult to manufacture a realistic Betty facsimile.

Ah, we wish that were true, but the real story is far sadder, far darker. We heard from William D. Turpin, director of consumer relations for Multivitamins' manufacturer, Miles, Inc.:

> The current group of Flintstones characters was selected based upon research of the popularity of each character with children. As a result of this research, it was determined that Betty Rubble is not as popular with the majority of the children as the other characters.

Thus, if you investigate the contents of a Flintstones Multivitamins jar carefully, you'll find seven different "characters." As expected, Wilma, Fred, and a lonely Barney are included. Bamm-Bamm, Pebbles, and Dino are there, too, to help round out the nuclear family. But the Flintmobile? Is a car really more popular with children than a fine specimen of womanhood? You'd better believe it.

Truth be told, Betty was never our favorite character either. In fact, we don't think she deserved a great catch like Barney. Nevertheless, her lack of charisma is hardly reason enough to break up the family units that helped make the Flintstones a television and multivitamin supplement institution.

what did Barney Rubble do for a living?

We have received this Imponderable often but never tried to answer it because we thought of it as a trivia question rather than an Imponderable. But as we tried to research the mystery of Barney's profession, we found that even self-professed *Flintstones* fanatics couldn't agree on the answer.

And we are not the only ones besieged. By accident, we called Hanna-Barbera before the animation house's opening hours. Before we could ask the question, the security guard said, "I know why you're calling. You want to know what Barney Rubble did for a living. He worked at the quarry. But why don't you call back after opening hours?" The security guard remarked that he gets many calls from inebriated *Flintstones* fans in the middle of the night, pleading for Barney's vocation before they nod off for the evening.

We did call back, and spoke to Carol Keis of Hanna-Barbera public relations, who told us that this Imponderable is indeed the company's most frequently asked question of all Flintstone trivia. She confirmed that the most commonly accepted answer is that Barney worked at Fred's employer, Bedrock Quarry & Gravel:

However, out of 166 half-hours from 1960-1966, there were episodic changes from time to time. Barney has also been seen as a repossessor, he's done top secret work, and he's been a geological engineer.

As for the manner in which Barney's occupation was revealed, it was never concretely established (no pun intended) [sure]. It revealed itself according to the occupation set up for each episode.

Most startling of all, Barney actually played Fred's boss at the quarry in one episode. Sure, the lack of continuity is distressing. But then we suspend our disbelief enough to swallow that Wile E. Coyote can recover right after the Road Runner drops a safe on Coyote's head from atop a mountain peak, too.

Hanna-Barbera does not have official archives, so Keis couldn't assure us that she hadn't neglected one of Barney Rubble's jobs. Can anyone remember any more?

—Submitted by Rob Burnett of New York, New York.

WHY DO WE SAY *BREAK A LEG* TO AN ACTOR ON OPENING NIGHT?

Right before an actor goes onstage on opening night, say, "Your makeup is dripping all over your shirt!" or, "By the way, Steven Spielberg is in the front row and he has come to see you," and you are likely to be met with a measure of equanimity. But wish an actor "good luck" and you will be facing one frightened actor.

A "good luck" is perceived by the superstitious acting community as a brazen act of tempting fate, so *break a leg* has come to be the ironic way of wishing "good luck" while stating the opposite. Our expression is a translation of a German expression used for the same purpose, *Hals-und-beinbruch* ("May you break your neck and your leg").

Some have speculated that *break a leg* is a reference to the "unlucky" actor John Wilkes Booth, who managed to break his leg while jumping onstage after assassinating President Abraham Lincoln. But *break a leg* is recorded only in the twentieth century, and, most likely, if Booth were the inspiration, the phrase would have circulated earlier.

—Submitted by Joanna Parker of Miami, Florida, and Launie Rountry of Brockton, Massachusetts.

why was Charles Schulz's comic strip called *Peanuts?*

Before there was *Peanuts,* there was *Li'l Folks,* Charles Schulz's cartoon produced for his hometown newspaper, the *St. Paul Pioneer Press,* starting in 1947. Fortunes are not made from selling cartoons to one newspaper, however. So Schulz pitched *Li'l Folks* to the United Feature Syndicate, which was interested in the work, but not the name of Schulz's strip.

UFS perceived two possible problems. Schulz's existing title evoked the name of a defunct strip called *Little Folks* created by cartoonist Tack Knight. And there was a comic strip that was already a rousing success that United Feature already distributed—*Li'l Abner.*

Who decided on the name *Peanuts?* The credit usually goes to Bill Anderson, a production manager at United Feature Syndicate, who submitted *Peanuts* along with a list of nine other alternatives to the UFS brass. The appeal of *Peanuts* was obvious, since as Nat Gertler, author and webmaster of a startlingly detailed guide to *Peanuts* book collecting (http://AAUGH.com/guide/) notes:

> The name *Peanuts* invoked the "peanut gallery"—the in-house audience for the then-popular *Howdy Doody* television show.

Charles Schulz not only didn't like the name change, but also objected to it throughout his career. Melissa McGann, archivist at the Charles Schulz Museum and Research Center in Santa Rosa, California, wrote to *Imponderables:*

> Schulz always disliked the name, and for the first several years of the strip's run he continually asked UFS to change the name—one of his suggestions was even *Good Ol' Charlie Brown.* Up until his death, Schulz maintained that he didn't like the name *Peanuts* and wished it was something else.

In his essay on the *Peanuts* creator, cartoonist R. C. Harvey quotes Schulz to show how much the usually soft-spoken man resented the *Peanuts* title:

> "I don't even like the word," he said. "It's not a nice word. It's totally ridiculous, has no meaning, is simply confusing, and has no dignity. And I think my humor has dignity. It would have class. They [UFS] didn't know when I walked in here that here was a fanatic. Here was a kid totally dedicated to what he was going to do. And then to label

something that was going to be a life's work with a name like *Peanuts* was really insulting."

Gertler points out that when Schulz first objected to the name change, UFS held the trump cards: "By the time the strip was popular enough for Schulz to have the leverage, the name was too well established." But in the media in which he had control over the name, Schulz avoided using *Peanuts* alone, as Gertler explains:

> At some point during the 1960s, the opening panel of the Sunday strips (when run in their full format) started saying *Peanuts, featuring Good Ol' Charlie Brown* rather than just *Peanuts* as they had earlier. Meanwhile the TV specials rarely had *Peanuts* in their title; instead, it was *A Charlie Brown Christmas, It's the Easter Beagle, Charlie Brown,* and similar names.

In fact, we're not aware of a single animated special that even contains the name *Peanuts*—the majority of titles feature Charlie Brown, and a significant minority Charlie's untrusty companion, Snoopy.

So we are left with the irony that the iron man of comic strips, the giant who created the most popular strip in the history of comics, who made more money from cartooning than anyone, detested the title of his own creation. Schulz probably appreciated not only the royalties from foreign countries, but the knowledge that especially in places where peanuts are not an important part of the diet or had no association with children, his strip was called something else: *Rabanitos* ("little radishes") in South America, *Klein Grut* ("small fry") in the Netherlands, and the unforgettable *Snobben* ("snooty"), Sweden's rechristening of Snoopy.

—Submitted by Mark Meluch of Maple Heights, Ohio.

why is comic strip print in capital letters?

The cartoonists we contacted, including our illustrious (pun intended) Kassie Schwan, concurred that it is easier to write in all caps. We've been printing since the first grade ourselves and haven't found using small letters too much of a challenge, but cartoonists have to worry about stuff that never worries us. Using all caps, cartoonists can allocate their space requirements more easily. Small letters not only vary in height but a few have a nasty habit of swooping below or above most of the other letters (l's make a's look like midgets; and p's and q's dive below most letters).

More importantly, all caps are easier to read. Mark Johnson, archivist for King Features, reminded us that comic strips are reduced in some newspapers and small print tends to "blob up."

We wish that our books were set in all caps. It would automatically rid us of those pesky capitalization problems. While we're musing ... we wonder how *Classics Illustrated* would handle the type if it decided to publish a comics' treatment of e. e. cummings' poetry?

—Submitted by Carl Middleman of St. Louis, Missouri.

why were *do-re-mi-fa-so-la-ti-do* chosen to represent the notes of the musical scale?

If it were not for some modifications made in the seventeenth century, the hit song from *The Sound of Music* would have been "Ut-Re-Mi," for our current octave was a modification of a hexachord scale called the "solfeggio system." Invented by Italian Guido D'Arezzo in the eleventh century, the mnemonic used to remember the scale was borrowed from the first syllables of each line of an existing hymn to St. John:

Ut queant laxis
Resonare fibris
Mi gestorum
Famuli polluti
Solve polluti
Labii reatum

When the octave replaced the six-note scale, a seventh note was needed, so the last line of the hymn was appropriated:

Sancte Iohannes

Do was later substituted for *ut* because it is more euphonious, and *ti* was substituted for *si* because it is easier to sing. (Try it!)

what does "legitimate" theater mean? Where can you find "illegitimate" theater?

Call us grumpy, but we think laying out a hundred bucks to listen to a caterwauling tenor screech while chandeliers tumble, or watching a radical reinterpretation of *Romeo and Juliet* as a metaphor for the Israeli-Palestinian conflict is plenty illegitimate. But we are etymologically incorrect; the use of the word *legit* dates back to the end of the nineteenth century, when it was used as a noun to describe stage actors who performed in dramatic plays. It soon became a term to describe just about any serious dramatic enterprise involving live actors.

And to this day, "legitimate" is used to describe actors who toil in vehicles that are considered superior in status to whatever alternatives are seen as less prestigious. As Bill Benedict of the Theatre Historical Society of America points out, one of the definitions of *legit* in *The Language of American Popular Entertainment* is:

> Short for *legitimate*. Used to distinguish the professional New York commercial stage from traveling and nonprofessional shows. The inference is that *legit* means stage plays are serious art versus popular fare.

Back in the late nineteenth century when the notion of "legit" was conceived, live public performances were more popular than they are today, when television, movies, the Internet, DVDs, and spectator sports provide so much competition for the stage. Even several decades into the twentieth century, other types of amusements, such as minstrel shows, vaudeville, burlesque (with and without strippers), magic shows, and musical revues often gathered bigger crowds than legitimate theater.

"Illegitimate" actors had a shady reputation, as most were itinerant barnstormers who swept in and out of small or medium-sized towns as third-rate carnivals do today. Their entertainments tended to be crude, with plenty of pantomime, caricature, low comedy, and vulgarity, so as to play to audiences of different educational levels, ethnicities, and even languages.

Cleverly, promoters of "legitimate" theater appealed to elite audiences, who could afford the relatively expensive tickets and understand the erudite language. Theater critics emerged well into the nineteenth century in the United States, trailing behind the British, who already featured theater reviewers in newspapers. The more affluent the base of the newspapers, the

376

IMPONDERABLES

more critics would tend to separate the "mere" entertainments from the aesthetic peaks of serious theater.

These cultural cross currents are still in play today. Theater critics in New York bemoan the "dumbing down" of Broadway shows, Disney converting animated movies into theater pieces, and savvy producers casting "big name" television or movie stars in plays for their marquee value. And the stars are willing to take a drastic pay reduction in order to have the status of legitimate theater bestowed upon them; they appear on talk shows and proclaim, "My roots are in theater." We've yet to see a leading man coo to an interviewer: "My roots are in sitcoms."

Not everyone takes these distinctions between "legit" and "illegit" so seriously. When Blue Man Group, with its roots in avant-garde theater, brought its troupe to the Luxor Hotel in Las Vegas, Chris Wink, cofounder of the Blue Man Group, proclaimed: "Now that Vegas has expanded its cultural palette and embraced Broadway-style legitimate theater, it feels like a good time to introduce some illegitimate theater."

—Submitted by Carol Dias of Lemoore, California.

WHY IS THE LAST PERFORMANCE OR WORK OF AN ARTIST CALLED A *SWAN SONG*?

Just about every author they have CliffsNotes for in Classics classes seems to have written about *swan songs*. Plato, Aristotle, Chaucer, Coleridge, Spenser, Shakespeare, and other, less stellar writers have referred to the legend of the dying swan. Although actual swans never sing, they were once believed to sing a beautiful melody just before they died. Socrates attributed the song to a display of happiness at its impending reunion with the god it served. Other ancient myths included that swans accompanied the dead to their final resting place (sort of a reverse stork) and that the souls of dead humans reside in swans.

Because an artistic *swan song* always constitutes the last work of an artist, the allusion to the dying swan is apt. Of course, some artists are not worthy of a first song, let alone a swan song, as Samuel Coleridge commented:

Swans sing before they die—'twere no bad thing
Should certain persons die before they sing.

what the heck does "Pop Goes the Weasel" mean?

After I was asked this question by a faithful reader of *Imponderables*, I asked a random sample of my illustrious and well-bred friends this question. None had a clue to the answer. Nor, come to think of it, did I.

"Pop Goes the Weasel", it turns out, is not the innocent children's rhyme it appears to be. Its meaning remains elusive to us because it contains some obscure Cockney dialect.

So here, for your edification, is the annotated guide to "Pop Goes the Weasel":

> Up and down the City Road[1]
> In and out the Eagle[2]
> That's the way the money goes
> Pop[3] goes the Weasel![4]

Thus our children's rhyme is the inspiring tale of a tailor who blows all of his money on booze and has to hock his equipment to eke out a living.

[1]The City Road is a major thoroughfare in London.
[2]The Eagle was a real pub and popular watering hole in London.
[3]Slang for "pawn."
[4]Slang for a tailor's iron.

why does Monopoly have such unusual playing tokens?

What do a thimble, a sack of money, a dog, a battleship, and a top hat have in common? Not much, other than that they are among the eleven playing tokens you receive in a standard Monopoly set. And don't forget the wheelbarrow, which you'll need to carry all that cash you are going to appropriate from your hapless opponents.

The history of Monopoly is fraught with contention and controversy, for it seems that its "inventor," Charles Darrow, at the very least borrowed liberally from two existing games when he first marketed Monopoly in the early 1930s. After Darrow self-published the game to great success, Parker Brothers bought the rights to Monopoly in 1934.

On one thing all Monopoly historians can agree. When Parker Brothers introduced the game in 1935, Monopoly included no tokens, and the rules instructed players to use such items as buttons or pennies as markers. Soon thereafter, in the 1935-1936 sets, Parker Brothers included wooden tokens shaped like chess pawns: boring.

The first significant development in customizing the playing pieces came in 1937, when Parker Brothers introduced these die-cast metal tokens: a car, purse, flatiron, lantern, thimble, shoe, top hat, and rocking horse. Later in the same year, a battleship and cannon were added, to raise the number of tokens to ten.

All was quiet on the token front until 1942, when metal shortages during World War II resulted in a comeback of wooden tokens. But the same mix of tokens remained until the early 1950s, when the lantern, purse, and rocking horse were kicked out in favor of the dog, the horse and rider, and the wheelbarrow. Parker Brothers conducted a poll to determine what Monopoly aficionados would prefer for the eleventh token, and true to the spirit of the game, the winner was a sack of money.

Parker Brothers wasn't able to tell us why, within a couple of years, Monopoly went from having no tokens, to boring wooden ones to idiosyncratic metal figures. Ken Koury, a lawyer in Los Angeles who has been a Monopoly champion and coach of the official United States team in worldwide competition, replied to our query:

> Monopoly's game pieces are certainly unique and a charming part of the play. I have heard a story that the original pieces were actually struck from the models used for Cracker Jack prizes. Any chance this is correct?

We wouldn't stake a wheelbarrow of cash on it, but we think the theory is a good one. We contacted author and game expert John Chaneski, who used to work at Game Show, a terrific game and toy emporium in Greenwich Village, who heard a similar story from the owner of the shop:

> When Monopoly was first created in the early 1930s, there were no pieces like we know them, so they went to Cracker Jack, which at that time was offering tiny metal tchotchkes, like cars. They used the same molds to make the Monopoly pieces. Game Show sells some antique Cracker Jack prizes and, sure enough, the toy car is exactly the same as the Monopoly car. In fact, there's also a candlestick, which seems to be the model for the one in Clue.

John even has a theory for why the particular tokens were chosen:

I think they chose Cracker Jack prizes that symbolize wealth and poverty. The car, top hat, and dog [especially a little terrier like Asta, then famous from the *Thin Man* series] were possessions of the wealthy. The thimble, wheelbarrow, old shoe, and iron were possessions or tools of the poor.

—Submitted by Kate McNieve of Phoenix, Arizona.
Thanks also to Mindy Sue Berks of Huntington Valley, Pennsylvania;
Flynn Rowan of Eugene, Oregon; and Sue Rosner of the Bronx, New York.

where do they get that organ music in skating rinks?

As we discussed in our first volume of *Imponderables,* skaters are not allowed to use music with vocals in competitions, and we explained some of the reasons why that music sounds so awful. The inevitable follow-up question: What about the music in ice and roller skating rinks?

Chances are very, very good that any organ music you hear in skating rinks comes from a company called Rinx Records, the only known source for tempo organ music. Competitive skaters need all-instrumental music of specific lengths (usually three or four minutes, exactly) for competitions and achievement tests. Not only do these songs need to be an exact length, but many need to be an exact number of beats per minute. Rinx Records, for example, provides waltzes with 108, 120, and 138 beats per minute. The records must have a strong beat so that skaters can synchronize their movements with music often piped through horrendous sound systems.

Rinx Records was founded in 1950, in Denver, Colorado, by Fred Bergen, a man who not only was involved in skating, but was an organist who played on many records. In 1968, Bergen sold Rinx Records to Dominic Cangelosi, who still operates the business from the roller rink he owns. Cangelosi has played keyboards on all of the records he has released since 1968. His music is heard throughout the world, but like the baseball stadium organist, he labors in semiobscurity, unmolested by rabid fans on the street.

Rinx is a nice business. Although a few other individuals besides Cangelosi market tapes, Cangelosi has the record end of the field sewn up. He has a big market, with a mailing list of more than five thousand customers, including not only rinks but skating instructors and individual skaters as well. Ice skating and roller skating share many of the same tempos (though some ice skating music is much faster), so Rinx sells to both markets. In all, Rinx has more than thirteen hundred *different* records in

stock, on seven-inch 45 rpm. If your heart prompts, you can find out more about Rinx Records by contacting Dominic Cangelosi at: P.O. Box 6607, Burbank, CA 91510.

Although Rinx's variety of organ music is associated with bygone days, Cangelosi has tried to spice up his arrangements with synthesizers, pianos, and electronic and Hammond organs in addition to the traditional acoustic and pipe organs. On some records, he adds guitar, drums, or other accompaniment. Cangelosi also "covers" popular songs, for which he pays a fee to ASCAP or BMI. Rink operators likewise have to pay a nominal fee to these licensing organizations for playing contemporary songs in their rinks.

George Pickard, executive director of the Roller Skating Rink Operators Association, says that most rinks have abandoned old-fashioned music for rock and disco. But many have special adult sessions that use Rinx and other more traditional records. There are even a few rinks that still have live organ music, the last echo of bygone days.

–Submitted by Gail Lee of Los Angeles, California.
Thanks also to Joy Renee Grieco of Park Ridge, New Jersey.

where is the donkey in Donkey Kong?

For those of you who didn't have anything better to do than obsess about Nintendo in the early 1980s, Donkey Kong is a game created by Shigeru Miyamoto, the most famous video game creator on the planet. Donkey Kong featured a diminutive hero, Jumpman (whose name was later changed to Mario), who had a much larger pet, a gorilla. The gorilla did not exactly bond with his "master," and conveyed his wrath by kidnapping Jumpman's girlfriend, Pauline, climbing a building, and hurling barrels and other missiles as our hero attempted to rescue his sweetheart. If the little man managed to reclaim her temporarily, the gorilla snatched Pauline away again. As the game progressed, each level made it harder for Jumpman to succeed. But regardless of what level the player progressed to, nary a donkey was seen.

So why the donkey in the title? Although some fans insist that the "donkey" was a misheard or mistranslated attempt at "Monkey Kong," Miyamoto has always insisted otherwise. On his tribute site to Miyamoto (http://www.miyamotoshrine.com), Carl Johnson includes an interview with Miyamoto at the Electronic Entertainment Exposition, where the game's creator addresses this Imponderable:

> Back when we made Donkey Kong, Mario was just called Jumpman and he was a carpenter. That's because the game was set on a construction site, so that made sense. When we went on to make the game Mario Brothers, we wanted to use pipes, maybe a sewer in the game, so he became a plumber.
>
> For Donkey Kong, I wanted something to do with "Kong," which kind of gives the idea of apes in Japanese, and I came up with Donkey Kong because I heard that "donkey" meant "stupid," so I went with Donkey Kong. Unfortunately, when I said that name to Nintendo of America, nobody liked it and said that it didn't mean "Stupid Ape," and they all laughed at me. But we went ahead with that name anyway.

In some other interviews, Miyamoto indicates that "donkey" was chosen for its usual connotation in English—stubbornness. In his book on Nintendo, *Game Over: Press Start to Continue,* David Sheff writes:

> When the game was complete, Miyamoto had to name it. He consulted the company's export manager, and together they mulled over some possibilities. They decided that *Kong* would be understood to suggest a gorilla. And since this fierce but cute Kong was donkey-stubborn and wily (*donkey*, according to their Japanese-English dictionary, was the translation of the Japanese word for "stupid" or "goofy"), they combined the words and named the game Donkey Kong.

WHY DOES SOMEONE WHO SWEARS "APOLOGIZE" BY SAYING *PARDON MY FRENCH?*

Pardon my French is simply another of the many American and English expressions that equate anything French with sex and obscenity. *French postcards, French novels,* and *French kissing,* just about anything French but French salad dressing, connotes raciness and anti-Puritanism. Come to think of it, you can't find French salad dressing in France, anyway.

Pardon my French started circulating on both sides of the Atlantic around 1916 and so almost certainly stems from the World War I escapades of American and British soldiers.

—Submitted by Jean and George Hanamoto of Morgan Hill, California.

At least one party wasn't happy with Nintendo's name—Universal Studios, which owned the copyright for *King Kong*. Universal sued for copyright infringement, claiming that the video game mimicked the basic plot of the movie (man climbs building to save his girlfriend from the clutches of a giant ape). Universal lost on the most obvious of grounds—the judge ruled that the movie studio did not own the rights to *King Kong*. Nintendo won the suit without, unfortunately, having to justify the nonexistence of a donkey in Donkey Kong.

—Submitted by Darrell Hewitt of Salt Lake City, Utah.

what happens to the 1,000 or more prints after films have finished their theatrical runs?

Distribution strategies for films vary dramatically. A "critics' darling," especially a foreign film or a movie without big stars, might be given a few exclusive runs in media centers like New York City and Los Angeles. The film's distributor prays that word-of-mouth and good reviews will build business so that it can expand to more theaters in those cities and later be distributed throughout the country.

"High concept" films, particularly comedies and action films whose plot lines can be easily communicated in short television commercials, and films starring "bankable" actors are likely to be given broad releases. By opening the film simultaneously across the country at 1,000 to 2,000 or more theaters, the film studios can amortize the horrendous cost of national advertising. But the cost of duplicating 2,000 prints, while dwarfed by marketing costs, is nevertheless a major expense.

A run-of-the-mill horror film from a major studio, for example, might open in 1,500 theaters simultaneously. The usual pattern for these films is to gross a considerable amount of money the first week and then fall off sharply. A horror film without good word-of-mouth might be gone from most theaters within four weeks. Of course, studios will release the film on videotape within a year, but what will they do with those 1,500 prints?

The first priority is to ship the prints overseas. Most American films are released overseas after the American theatrical run is over. Eventually, those American prints are returned to the United States.

And then they are destroyed and the silver is extracted from the film and sold to precious metals dealers. The studios have little use for 1,500 scratchy prints.

Mark Gill, vice-president of publicity at Columbia Pictures, told *Imponderables* that his company keeps twenty to thirty prints of all its current releases indefinitely. The film studios are aware of all of the movies from the early twentieth century that have been lost due to negligence—some have deteriorated in quality but others are missing simply because nobody bothered keeping a print. With all of the ancillary markets available, including videotape, laser disc, repertory theaters, cable television, and syndicated television, today's movies are unlikely to disappear altogether (though we can think of more than a few that we would like to disappear). But the problem of print deterioration continues.

—Submitted by Ken Shafer of Traverse City, Michigan.
Thanks also to John DuVall of Fort Pierce, Florida.

what is the difference between an X-rated movie and an XXX-rated movie? Why isn't there an "XX" rating?

The Motion Picture Association of America issues the movie ratings you see in the newspaper. Motion picture companies are under no legal obligation to have their movies rated, but they are not allowed to affix their own rating. In order to obtain a G, PG, PG-13 or R rating, a fee must be paid to the MPAA. An MPAA committee views each film and issues an edict that sets the rating, subject to appeal. None of the major film companies is willing to bypass the MPAA ratings. Since the rating codes were instituted in the 1960s, there has actually been much less pressure on the studios to reduce violence and sexual content. Also, some newspapers refuse to accept advertising for non-MPAA-rated movies, and most film executives feel that the rating system has worked reasonably well as a warning device for concerned parents.

The X-rating was originally conceived as the designation for any movie suitable only for adults, regardless of genre. Such critics' favorites as the Best Picture Oscar-winning *Midnight Cowboy* were rated X because of their mature subject matter, and *A Clockwork Orange* was rated X for its violence and intensity.

With only a few other exceptions, nonpornographic X-rated movies have bombed at the box office. Any film that catered to adults automatically excluded many of the most rabid movie-goers—teenagers. The advertisements for so-called "adult films" gladly trumpeted their X ratings: how better to prove the salaciousness of a movie than by prohibiting children from viewing it? Even better, MPAA rules allowed companies to rate their films X without the association's certification, a policy that enabled low-budget film companies to nab an X rating without paying the fee of nearly a thousand dollars. As the few mainstream X-rated films were overwhelmed by the multitude of X-rated porn movies, major film companies like Paramount and Columbia refused to release any X-rated movies, for X had become synonymous with smut.

The producers of adult films had the opposite problem. Here they were, trying to purvey their X-rated product, when prestigious films like *Midnight Cowboy* were sullying the reputation of the adults-only rating by containing redeeming social value.

David F. Friedman, board chairman of the Adult Film Association of America, told us that the XXX rating was actually started as a joke, to distinguish "straight films," with mature content, from pornography. There is not now and has never been a formal XXX rating for movies; it has always been a marketing ploy adopted by film distributors and/or movie exhibitors.

Is there any difference between an X- and an XXX-rated movie? According to Friedman, no. Although some customers might believe that an XXX-rated movie is "harder" than the simple X, this has never been the case. Many pornographic films are made in several versions: hard-core X-rated; a "soft" X, used for localities where hard-core is banned; a "cable" version, a doctored once-explicit version; and an expurgated R-rated version, designed for playoffs in nonporno theaters, such as drive-ins. Whether or not any of these versions of a pornographic movie is billed as X or XXX is more dependent on the whims of the producer or the theater management than on the content of the movie.

Why no XX rating? Who knows? Once someone started the XXX, who was going to say that their movie wasn't quite as sexy? X-inflation is likely to remain rampant as long as there are pornographic theaters.

—Submitted by Richard Rosberger of Washington, D.C. Thanks also to Curtis Kelly of Chicago, Illinois, and Thomas Cunningham of Pittsburgh, Pennsylvania.

why are the outside edges of the pages of many paperback books colored?

In the early days of paperback books, the paper used was of very low quality, usually newsprint. Consumers rejected the soiled and discolored appearance of the pages. Publishers hit upon the notion of "staining," which made the paper look fresh, even pretty, and most important, prolonged the shelf life of their books.

Some publishers used the same color stain for long periods of time, in an attempt to make their company's product easily identifiable in the bookstore. For a long time, Dell's paperbacks were stained blue; Bantam's were yellow; Pocket Books favored red.

As the paper quality improved, the necessity for staining decreased. Some publishers still stain some of their mass-market (small-sized) paperback books. Occasionally, even today, the paper quality is low, or the paper within one book varies slightly in color—staining eliminates these problems. Trade (larger-sized) paperbacks use higher-quality paper, so staining is rare. Ironically, the tradition of staining dates back to the days of Gutenberg, when Bibles were stained for aesthetic purposes. Some expensive hardcover books are stained today to add a touch of panache.

Paperback books are stained by machine after they are completely bound. The books are moved on a conveyor belt that has sides and walls to protect the books from errant ink. Two jets spray ink all over the top, bottom, and nonbound side of the paper.

The staining of hardbound books used to be done by machine, but since the practice has almost completely died out the machinery has been sold off. Today, staining of hardbounds is done by hand, with a spray gun. The books are taken

WHY DOES BAZOOKA JOE WEAR AN EYE PATCH?

Rest easy. Bazooka Joe has 20-20 vision and no eye deformity. But ever since he was introduced in 1953, Joe has donned an eye patch to give himself a little bit of that Hathaway Man panache.

And before you ask—Herman has always hidden behind his turtleneck, but he does have a perfectly functional neck.

—Submitted by Christopher Valeri of East Northport, Rhode Island.

off the assembly line before they are cased. Protected by backboards and wings, the books are sprayed three at a time. The ink dries exceptionally fast.

Although staining adds some expense to the production cost, publishers must wonder: Does anyone notice? Does anybody care? The production experts we spoke to felt that the custom of staining persisted more because of inertia than for any practical purpose.

—Submitted by Pat O'Conner of Brooklyn, New York.

what flavor is bubble gum supposed to be?

"No particular flavor," said a representative from Bubble Yum about its "regular" flavor.

"Fruit flavor—sort of a tutti frutti," responded an executive from Topps.

We hadn't encountered so much secrecy about ingredients since we pried the identity of the fruit flavors in Juicy Fruit gum from the recalcitrant folks at Wrigley.

We've discussed how bubble gum was invented by Walter Diemer, a cost accountant with the Fleer Corporation. Bruce C. Wittmaier, a relative of Mr. Diemer's, was the only source who would reply to our bubble gum question. And luckily, Wittmaier obtained his information directly from Mr. Diemer. The main flavors in the original bubble gum: wintergreen, vanilla, and cassia.

—Submitted by John Geesy of Phoenix, Arizona.

why do so many bars feature televisions with the sound turned off?

We spare no financial expense, no mental duress, in order to plumb the depths of Imponderability. To research this question, we tore ourselves away from the plush confines of Imponderables Central to visit many taverns. Risking inebriation and worse, we confirmed that the "Yes, we have a TV on; no, we don't have the sound on" phenomenon is alive and well in North America. What's the deal?

Somewhat to our surprise, we found bartenders uniformly negative about the boob tube and its role in their establishments. Why does management bother installing televisions? The thinking seems to run on the order of:

- Where there are bars, there are men.

- Where there are men, there is an interest in sports.

- Sports is televised.

- Sports on television equals male butts on our stools.

- If we don't have televisions at our bar, men will go to the sports bar down the street instead.

But the bartenders we spoke to analyzed this Imponderable more deeply. Televisions are important because they provide patrons with what Dan Sullivan, a Kiwi now living and bartending in Greece, calls "something to do with their eyes." Single patrons are often uncomfortable and tense when alone. They may be lonely, or worried about looking like losers, or anxious about meeting potential mates. The television "makes it easier for them to be by themselves at the bar," concludes Roger Herr, owner of South's Bar in downtown Manhattan.

Some bars and nightclubs also use televisions to run closed-circuit programming, anything from old Tom and Jerry cartoons to 1960s-style light shows to help set the appropriate mood for their establishments. One bartender compared this use of the television to installing fish tanks, a form of visual Muzak.

Every bar employee we talked to indicated that as soon as the audio on a television goes on, some patrons are turned off. As Deven Black, former manager of the North Star Pub in New York City, put it,

> No matter how quietly the sound is on, it will offend someone, and you can never have it loud enough so everyone who wants to can hear it.

Even manly men might not want to accompany their scotch-and-sodas with the mellifluous tones of NASCAR engines backfiring. And bartenders reported that most sports fans are perfectly content with the audio of their sports programs on mute, happily shedding commercials and colorless color commentators.

All nightclubs and most bars feature music, whether a humble jukebox, live bands, or expensive sound systems. If the TV is going to interfere with the music, why pump dollars into the jukebox? If customers are going to listen to Marv Albert instead of Bruce Springsteen, what owner is going to be happy about installing a $20,000 sound system?

But most of the bar industry folks we consulted make a more spiritual point. As bartender and beer columnist Christopher Halleron put it,

People go to bars for conversation and socializing. When you turn up the boob tube, that element is taken away as people become fixated on whatever it spews and stop talking to each other. The same phenomenon occurs in the living room of the average American family.

Exactly! If we wanted to sit sullenly and watch blinking images while avoiding human contact, we'd stay at home with our families.

Liquor flows more freely when patrons feel festive, and music and dancing set the mood more easily than *Wheel of Fortune* or *Everybody Loves Raymond*. A blaring television sucks the energy out of a room.

Some bars have used modern technology to solve the television-audio problem in a Solomon-like way: They turn on the closed-captioning option on their TVs. CC might not be the solution if patrons are trying to hear the New York Philharmonic on PBS, but then, they never are.

–Submitted by Fred Beeman of Las Vegas, Nevada.

why do so many taverns put mirrors in back of the liquor bottles behind the bar?

No doubt, many tavern owners install mirrors in the back of their bars for the same reason most businesses do anything—because their competitors are doing the same thing. We were surprised that some bar owners couldn't explain why they have mirrors behind their bars, but most of the same folks who weighed in on the last Imponderable had plenty of opinions about this one, too.

Like a television, a mirror provides patrons something to look at when they might feel lonely, tense, or bored. And there can be more practical advantages, as Deven Black notes: "It allows patrons to check each other out discreetly."

Sometimes, the view might not be so pleasant ("Uh-oh, here comes my girlfriend! And I told her I'd be home at eight."), but more than a century ago, some bars ensured that the view would be more pleasing to their clientele, as Gary Regan reveals:

> In the late 1800s, a "naughty" painting of [William Bouguereau's] *Nymphs and Satyr* hung in New York's Hoffman House bar. It was situated so that customers could stare at it through the mirror, therefore not blatantly looking at a naughty painting. Presume, therefore, that mirrors were and are used [by customers] to observe the scene without being obvious.

Bartenders are not impervious to using the mirror for less than professional purposes, as an honest but lascivious bartender and beer columnist, Christopher Halleron, explains:

> Mirrors provide an excellent, indirect way to check out the cleavage on the girl who just ordered a Cosmo.

Although it may be a surprise to some libidinous patrons, there are things to look at in a bar other than beef- or cheesecake, and mirrors are an inexpensive accent piece in a tavern's interior decoration. For one, mirrors bounce light around the room, and can also be attractive themselves. Many beer and liquor companies provide free mirrors with their name and logos emblazoned on them. Some bars prefer to use the mirrors to advertise themselves. Tom Hailand, design engineer at Cabinet Tree Design, believes that mirrors add "glitz," and even point-of-purchase advertising on the mirrors can yield practical benefits to the bar:

> And where else would you put your sandblasted logo just in case the customers are so hammered they need the name of the bar in front of them to call a cab?

Heiland also mentions an advantage to the placement of the mirror that was echoed by many experts—the mirror makes the liquor display look fuller. Mirrors have long been used by decorators to make rooms look bigger and displays more enticing. As one bartender told us,

> The idea is to make the liquor more appealing by spicing up the presentation of the bottles as well as making it appear that there are more bottles than there really are. It's impressive when you walk into a bar and see a huge shelf full of liquor bottles behind the bar—the mirror provides the same effect with fewer bottles. The same trick is used in the catering business for veggie trays and other food presentations.

But the predominant reason for mirrors in bars, and probably the precipitating factor in the tradition's beginning, was for security. Think back to the Old West, and it's easy to see why a saloon owner would want advance warning before a gunslinger, with pistol packed, entered the establishment. There were times when it was unavoidable for the bartender to turn his or her back to patrons, as bartender "Baudtender" wrote:

> Many of the old bars had the bartenders' "make station" (where they prepared mixed drinks) right below the liquor storage shelves. With the mirrors, they could keep an eye on the customers while their back was turned—before Dram Shop laws [which made bartenders legally liable for harm inflicted by intoxicated or underage patrons], it was a common thing to give a customer an entire bottle of liquor and charge by

measurement or eyeball estimation for what was consumed. Contrary to popular opinion, bar owners weren't the only rogues to water down the liquor, if you see what I mean.

Most cash registers at bars are located in back of the bar, so bartenders must turn their back on patrons on a regular basis.

Today, there are other dangers, large and small, that prompt a bartender to use the mirror. Without the mirror, the bartender might ignore the quiet patron who would otherwise go unnoticed, or miss the guy who is trying to steal the bartender's tip while the bartender's back was turned, or fail to assist the woman about to be harassed. What's especially appealing about using the mirror for security purposes, according to Roger Herr, owner of South's Bar in Manhattan, is that the bartender can scan the area without being obvious.

And just in case the bar brawl should erupt, bartender Dan Morrison sings the praise of mirrors for providing the élan that their manufacturers wouldn't trumpet but movie stunt coordinators are well aware of: Mirrors smash really good when you throw a chair at them.

—Submitted by Charlie Chiarolanza of Lafayette Hill, Pennsylvania.

why do teddy bears frown?

Considering that the toy business is full of sugarcoated images for children, and the happy face is the default countenance for dolls and most stuffed animals, we've often wondered why teddy bears are downright dour. So we contacted teddy bear artists, designers and manufacturers, hardcore collectors, and folks who write about teddy bears for a living to illuminate exactly what is bumming out stuffed bears.

Strangely, the first teddy bears were made in Germany and the United States in the same year—1902. Mindy Kinsey, editor of *Teddy Bear and Friends* magazine, picks up the story. At the beginning, at least, teddy bears were designed to appear realistic:

> In Germany, they were modeled after bears Richard Steiff saw in the zoo and at the circus. In America, teddies were inspired by the bears Theodore Roosevelt hunted (and in a particularly famous instance, failed to shoot) and were named after the president himself.
> Early teddies, therefore, had long muzzles, long arms, humped backs, and small ears, much like the real thing. Their mouths tended to be straight embroidered lines that might appear to frown, but were only meant to mimic their real-life counterparts.

When we called the big teddy bear makers, such as Gund, Steiff, and Russ Berrie, the designers couldn't articulate why the expression of most of their bears was sad. Some suggested that they weren't trying to make their bears frown at all. But go to the Web site of these companies, or visit your local toy store, and we think you'll agree that compared to most other stuffed animals and toys, the classic bears could use a dose or two of Prozac.

But not just designers denied the "frown" premise. Kinsey's response was typical:

> Today's teddy bears, however, can have big grins, wistful smiles, laughing open mouths, puckers, and every other mouth imaginable. Some still have the straight-line mouths, but I like to think of them as wise, contemplative, trustworthy, or sincere expressions—not frowns.

Jo Rothery, editor of the English magazine *Teddy Bear Times,* thinks variety is the spice of teddy bear life:

> Of course there are some bears that are definitely grumpy and have been designed that way by the bear artist. Some collectors do specialize in the grumpy characters, perhaps because they remind them of someone—fathers, husbands, grandfathers, colleagues, etc. And other collectors, particularly of vintage teds, feel that a sad expression adds to the character of the bear and reflects his age and all the experience he has had over the years.
>
> There are some very "smiley" bears, whose mouths are upturned and instinctively make you want to smile back when you look at them. Again, there are collectors who specialize in such bears, but I think the majority of us like to have a collection that includes lots of different expressions, possibly even some of the openmouthed variety, although it is hard to get that particular expression right. Some bear artists succeed in capturing that "wild" natural look very well without making the bears look at all scary.

Rothery adds that it is just like when one dog in a litter stirs your heart, even though "they all look alike."

> Even when you see a lineup of identical teddies, each one will have a slightly different expression, and there is one that will appeal to you more than any of the others and demand that you take him home with you.

We were shocked when three Gund designers couldn't articulate why they drew bears' expressions the way they did, but one creator, Linda McCall of Key West, Florida, describes it as an almost mystical process:

Some of my bears' mouths smile, some frown, and some look really, really grumpy! It just depends on the "feel" I get from the bear. I know it sounds strange to someone who probably has never made a bear. You stitch the darn thing together and you let it sit overnight. Then you look at it again and you just know if it should be a happy bear, a thoughtful bear, or whatever mood it seems to convey. That's why if you look at all artist-made bears, no two would ever be alike.

McCall, and several other sources, think the tradition of the "frowning bear" stems from an attempt to mimic how a real bear's mouth looks. After all, bears in the wild aren't known for their grins. The "realistic" theory, perhaps the favored one among our sources, contends that most bears aren't frowning, but merely exhibiting a neutral emotion.

If you look carefully at the faces of teddy bears, you'll see that the mouths of many are shaped like an upside-down capital Y. Teddy bear artist Cherri Creamer, of Alive Again Bears, says that the inverted Y is used to align the face so that the nose and eyes conform to the mouth. Whatever reason, the inverted Y provides a downward cast to bears' mouths. So this "convenient" method of aligning the bear might be responsible for what we interpret as a frown.

We're partial to a psychological theory to explain the "frown" of the teddy bear. Jo Rothery comments that the inverted Y

gives teddy bears a contemplative, relaxed look, an expression that makes them seem only too willing to sit there, "listen," and absorb their owners' emotions, whether those emotions happen to be sad or happy.

If the emotions of a teddy bear are opaque, a child can pour his emotions into his plush toy, and the bear becomes an instant empathizer. Marc Weinberg and Victoria Fraser, creators of Ballsy Bear and Bitchy Bear, agree and comment:

Teddy bears have been adopted for the most part by children. They're the child's only security blanket. You seek him out when you need comfort, when you need a shoulder to cry on. Teddy bears reflect the feelings of their owners.

If bears reflect the feelings of their owners, then Ballsy Bear's customers are not a happy bunch. Their two bears, Ballsy and Bitchy, are none too happy campers, and their classic inverted-Y mouths reveal not just a frown but a scowl. Created by a husband-wife team who both were victims of Internet startup failures, Ballsy and Bitchy are not cuddly and are happy to let you know:

Who needs another teddy bear that says, "I wuv you." Give your friends, family, and loved ones the gift that says what you really mean: Ballsy Bear and Bitchy Bear—the World's Nastiest Talking Teddy Bears!

—Submitted by Tim Walsh of Ramsey, New Jersey.

9

SPORTS

All our favorite pastimes seem so perfectly simple
and clear to us—that is, until you try to explain
the game to a newcomer. So, Mr. or Ms. Sports
Expert, tell us why are tennis balls fuzzy?
Or why are there 18 holes in golf? Nine
innings in baseball? And four quarters
in basketball? You'll enjoy the answers.

why are there eighteen holes on a golf course?

In Scotland, the home of golf, courses were originally designed with varying numbers of holes, depending on the parcel of land available. Some golf courses, according to U.S. Golf Association librarian Janet Seagle, had as few as five holes.

The most prestigious golf club, the Royal and Ancient Golf Club of St. Andrews, originally had twenty-two holes. On October 4, 1764, its original course, which had contained eleven holes out and eleven holes in, was reduced to eighteen holes total in order to lengthen them and make it more challenging. As a desire to codify the game grew, eighteen holes was adopted as the standard after the St. Andrews model.

why do golf balls have dimples?

Because dimples are cute?

No. We should have known better than to think that golfers, who freely wear orange pants in public, would worry about cosmetic appearances.

Golf balls have dimples because in 1908 a man named Taylor patented this cover design. Dimples provide greater aerodynamic lift and consistency of flight than a smooth ball. Jacque Hetric, director of public relations at

WHY DO GOLFERS YELL "FORE" WHEN WARNING OF AN ERRANT GOLF SHOT?

This expression, popularized by former President Gerald Ford, actually started as an English military term. When the troops were firing in lines, the command " 'ware before" indicated that it might be prudent for the front line to kneel so that the second line wouldn't blow their heads off.

"Fore" is simply a shortened version of the "before" in " 'ware before."

—Submitted by Cassandra A. Sherrill of Granite Hills, North Carolina.

Spalding, notes that the dimple pattern, regardless of where the ball is hit, provides a consistent rotation of the ball after it is struck.

Janet Seagle, librarian and museum curator of the United States Golf Association, says that other types of patterned covers were also used at one time. One was called a "mesh," another the "bramble." Although all three were once commercially available, "the superiority of the dimpled cover in flight made it the dominant cover design."

Although golfers love to feign that they are interested in accuracy, they lust after power: Dimpled golf balls travel farther as well as straighter than smooth balls. So those cute little dimples will stay in place until somebody builds a better mousetrap.

—Submitted by Kathy Cripe of South Bend, Indiana.

why don't professional golfers wear sunglasses when playing?

Actually, golfers *are,* more and more, starting to wear sunglasses, but reader Robert Allen is correct in observing that golfers, who are often out in the blazing sun for six to eight hours (including practice) a day, don't seem to have much protection from harmful ultraviolet rays.

We talked to Craig Steinberg, an ophthalmologist in Sherman Oaks, California, who was a former California State Champion golfer and, even now, boasts a two handicap. Steinberg told *Imponderables* that as recently as twenty years ago, no serious golfers were wearing sunglasses, for the dangers of prolonged exposure to UV were not understood:

> People would lie out in the sun all day. Sometimes they wore sunglasses, but this was just a response to their sun sensitivity. I tell my golfing patients to get sunglasses and to make sure they get something that covers their eyelids, both upper and lower—those are common locations for skin cancer.

Now that research has proven that UV radiation is the main cause of cataracts and skin cancers around the eyes, golfers are progressively getting "scared straight" into making the move to sunglasses, and to applying sunblock before stepping onto the course.

Golfers have long worn hats or visors to block the sun, but these coverings have been used primarily to avoid eyestrain and squinting. Professional golfers objected to wearing sunglasses for several reasons:

1. **Fashion.** Scott Hansberger, national market manager for Ray-Ban Sunglasses, told *Imponderables*:

> In the past, sunglasses weren't considered an accepted fashion trend. For example, just recently hats have become the popular trend—before, it was visors.
>
> Sunglasses were viewed in the past as being for movie stars—they hid your eyes. Golfers as a group are conservative, friendly, open, interacting type of people. The sunglasses were perceived as against this image. Consider the Bing Cosby "Clam-Bake" Pro-Ams in years past. The celebrities were all wearing sunglasses—but the pros weren't.

2. **Fit.** Says Hansberger:

> You don't want glasses slipping down your nose, moving while you're swinging or to be seeing the glasses' frame while you're putting. When you wear glasses outside, and you sweat as you do when you're playing golf, your nose gets a little bit slippery, and the glasses start to move. Unconsciously, you start to push the glasses back up on your nose. People who wear prescription glasses certainly do this.
>
> For any sport, you want equipment that you don't have to think about. In golf, you don't want to be fussing with your glasses. A lot of golfers who wear prescription glasses use contact lenses when they play golf, for that very reason.

3. **Color distortion.** Many decisions a golfer must make on the course are based on visual imagery. Conventional sunglasses were seen as blocking out light, and making it harder for golfers to, say, discriminate between the fairway and light rough, or to read the grain of the greens when putting.

4. **Field of vision.** Many golfers felt that the frames of glasses blocked part of their visual access to the course.

5. **Physical annoyance.** Traditional sunglasses were not designed for sports use. Steinberg recollects Professional Golf Association veteran Tom Kite, who has always worn prescription lenses,

> playing one tournament in the rain, and just going nuts having to stop under an umbrella constantly to wipe and clear his glasses.

Sunglass manufacturers wanted to overcome the resistance of golfers to wearing shades, so recruiting professional golfers to wear them was a top priority. The first company to make sunglasses specifically for golfers was Bollé America, in 1993, and their products directly addressed some of the problems listed above. Their golf line, Eagle Vision, features wraparound lenses with thin bridges. As a result, golfers don't notice the frames when looking out at the course, and the frames don't slip while the golfer is moving. Bollé's lenses are manufactured to produce no color distortion. A Bollé customer-service representative, Mike Terry, told *Imponderables* that many pro golfers now use Eagle Vision sunglasses, although some take off the shades while putting.

Ray-Ban, the largest manufacturer of sunglasses, has only recently entered the golfing market (along with Bollé, their other major competitor is Oakley). Golf sunglasses feature lighter materials, such as nylon blends for the frames, that stay in place and aren't as cumbersome for the wearer as most conventional sunglasses. Ray-Ban's main selling point is its ACE (amethyst color enhancement) lens, which highlights certain golf colors. The lenses accentuate the contrast between some of the shades of green, for example, so that it is easier to detect the grain on a putting surface and therefore predict the trajectory of the ball.

Scott Hansberger estimates that somewhere between 15 to 30 percent of pro golfers each week are wearing sunglasses on the professional tours, whereas in 1993, only a few were. Two factors, besides the improvement in the equipment, have contributed to the newfound popularity of sunglasses. First, they are now considered to be "cool." Jim Frank, editor of *Golf* magazine, and other sources we contacted, indicate that whereas there was a perception ten or twenty years ago that sunglasses didn't project the proper image (golf has maintained its image as the last bastion of civility and good sportsmanship in big-money professional sports), they are now seen as fashionable, but not radical, statements.

Second, and perhaps more important, sunglass manufacturers are paying pro golfers to endorse their products. Bollé employs several sales reps that follow the tour. According to Terry,

> We have technical reps that sell products. They try to educate the golfers about the product. The idea is that if the pros start wearing them, the public will see it, and our sales will benefit.

Ray-Ban has been particularly aggressive about recruiting paid endorsers. Hansberger says:

> About seventy players are on endorsement. I'll drop some names: Paul Azinger, John Huston, Kenny Perry, Jane Geddes, Jay Sigal, and Bob Murphy on the senior tour. Big names. They agree to wear sunglasses during events, depending on prevailing conditions, of course. We run ads in golfing magazines picturing the golfers we have under contract.

We spoke to Richard Gralitzer, an accountant and a player-manager who has several clients playing on the PGA, LPGA (female professional), seniors, and Nike (one rung below the PGA) tours:

I have certain players that refuse to wear glasses. They say the glasses bother them. These players haven't worn them and they won't start now.

An endorsement deal won't matter much (and for that matter, won't last long) if the golfer stops producing on the course. Few pros will sacrifice their comfort or their golf game if they feel that sunglasses aren't for them.

—Submitted by Robert Allen of Santa Fe Springs, California.

in baseball scoring, why is the letter "K" chosen to designate a strikeout?

Lloyd Johnson, ex-executive director of the Society for American Baseball Research, led us to the earliest written source for this story, *Beadle's Dime Base-Ball Player,* a manual published in 1867 that explained how to set up a baseball club. Included in *Beadle's* are such quaint by-laws as "Any member who shall use profane language, either at a meeting of the club, or during field exercise, shall be fined __ cents."

A chapter on scoring, written by Henry Chadwick, assigns meaning to ten letters:

> A for first base
> B for second base
> C for third base
> H for home base
> F for catch on the fly
> D for catch on the bound
> L for foul balls
> T for tips
> K for struck out
> R for run out between bases.

Chadwick advocated doubling up these letters to describe more events:

> HR for home runs
> LF for foul ball on the fly
> TF for tip on the fly
> TD for tip on the bound

He recognized the difficulty in remembering some of these abbreviations and attempted to explain the logic:

> The above, at first sight, would appear to be a complicated alphabet to remember, but when the key is applied it will be at once seen that a

boy could easily impress it on his memory in a few minutes. The explanation is simply this—we use the first letter in the words, Home, Fly, and Tip and the last in Bound, Foul, and Struck, and the first three letters of the alphabet for the first three bases.

We can understand why the last letters in "Bound" and "Foul" were chosen—the first letters of each were already assigned a different meaning—but we can't figure out why "S" couldn't have stood for struck out.

Some baseball sources have indicated that the "S" was already "taken" by the sacrifice, but we have no evidence to confirm that sacrifices were noted in baseball scoring as far back as the 1860s.

—Submitted by Darin Marrs of Keller, Texas.

why are there nine innings in baseball?

Does each player in the starting lineup get "his" inning? Does each Muse have an inning named after her? One inning per cat's life? Alas, the genesis of innings in baseball has more than a passing similarity to the story of basketball's quarters and halves.

Like basketball, baseball was first an amateur game. In its earliest incarnations, baseball was known as "town ball," "goal ball," or "old-cat," and only by the 1840s was it known as "base ball." We'll skip the fight over whether Abner Doubleday or Alexander Cartwright was the "father of baseball" and simply state what we know to be true: Alexander Cartwright, a bank clerk, convinced a group of amateur players to form the "New York

WHY ARE BASEBALL DUGOUTS BUILT SO THAT THEY ARE HALF BELOWGROUND?

If dugouts were built any higher, notes baseball stadium manufacturer Dale K. Elrod, the sight lines in back of the dugout would be blocked. Baseball parks would either have to eliminate choice seats behind the dugout or sell tickets with an obstructed view at a reduced price.

If dugouts were built lower, either the players would not be able to see the game without periscopes or they wouldn't have room to stretch out between innings.

—Submitted by Alan Scothon of Dayton, Ohio.

Knickerbocker Base Ball Club," and in 1845, the club laid down a set of rules that resemble today's baseball game in many ways: the game was played on a diamond-shaped field; the bases were placed ninety feet apart; an inning consisted of three outs, etc.

But the Knickerbockers' game had a few "striking" differences from the modern version. For one, there were no *called* balls and strikes—the only way to strike out without hitting the ball was to swing and miss three times. And most important, for our purposes, there was no inning limit to the games; the winner was the first team to get twenty-one runs (provided that each team received an equal number of times at bat).

The Knickerbockers (and their rule book) helped baseball spread rapidly throughout New York City and into other urban areas. By the mid-1850s, baseball mania had arrived. Compared to today's game, baseball then was a high-scoring affair, mainly because pitchers (who stood a close forty-five feet from the plate) threw underhand in a stiff-armed motion. They threw softly to a "batsman" (a term borrowed from the English game of cricket), who was supposed to be stopped by the fielders. But according to baseball historian and writer Bill Deane, within ten years, pitchers started developing pitches that were difficult to hit. Some even worked on a "speed ball," what we would now call a fastball, and more deviously, a curve.

Whereas in the early game of baseball, scores of 21-19 were not hard to rack up, as pitchers improved, it became harder and harder for a team to attain the goal of 21 runs. Games took longer and longer.

By the late 1850s, although baseball clubs were nominally amateur organizations, talented players were recruited with under-the-table payments. Betting among players and fans was common. In the late 1850s, the National Association of Base Ball Players was formed not only to codify

WHY IS THE HOME PLATE IN BASEBALL SUCH A WEIRD SHAPE?

Until 1900, home plate was square like all the other bases. But in 1900, the current five-sided plate was introduced to aid umpires in calling balls and strikes. Umpires found it easier to spot the location of the ball when the plate was elongated. If you ask most players, it hasn't helped much.

—Submitted by Bill Lachapell of Trenton, Michigan. Thanks also to Michael Gempe of Elmhurst, Illinois, and John H. McElroy of Haines City, Florida.

the rules and organize the burgeoning club competition but also to try to make a few dollars from the popular game. Not unlike the hockey owners who met to see how they could exploit the game of basketball, the new association saw the potential for baseball as a spectator sport and foresaw a problem with the length of the game.

In the early 1850s, it was not uncommon for games to last two days, but the association realized that paying fans wouldn't settle for not seeing the resolution of a game before nightfall. By 1858 the National Association of Base Ball Players dethroned the Knickerbockers as the overseers of the game, and it set the nine-inning rule. The goal was to make the competition last approximately two to two and one-half hours. The average game takes longer now, but then they didn't have to contend with commercials and preening prima donnas in the 1850s.

The Civil War helped to spread baseball throughout the rest of the country. In 1869, four years after the war ended, the Cincinnati Red Stockings became the first all-salaried baseball team. And the National League arrived in 1876. From the start, the pros played nine innings a game.

—Submitted by Rick DeWitt of Erie, Pennsylvania. Thanks also to Douglas Watkins, Jr., of Hayward, California; Jena Mori of Los Angeles, California; Joe Dagata and sons of Parma, Ohio; Steve Kaufman of New York, New York; Melissa Hall of Bartlett, Illinois; and Scott Ball of Chico, California.

how do groundskeepers rebuild the pitcher's mounds in multipurpose stadiums?

Even though a baseball pitching mound might look like little but a hunk of dirt surrounded by grass, in reality it is constructed with great care and more than a little difficulty. Major League Baseball mandates the exact specifications of a pitching mound. In the past, a home team with a dominating pitcher would try to raise the mound to gain further advantage (or lower it in advance of an overpowering fastball pitcher on an opponent's team taking the mound), or would construct mounds in the visitors' bullpen that didn't match the dimensions of the real mound.

To forestall such petty larceny, an inspector from Major League Baseball visits every ballpark at least twice a year (including once during preseason) and checks the pitcher's mound and all bullpen mounds for such specifications as: height of the mound (it must be exactly ten inches higher than home plate); slope of the mound (the area six inches in front of the pitcher's rubber must be flat, and then, slope down at a constant pitch of one inch per foot toward home plate—this six feet constitutes the area onto which the pitcher's lead foot will land during the follow-through); size of the pitcher's circle (the large dirt area onto which the mound is built must be exactly eighteen feet in diameter); flatness of the pitcher's rubber; flatness of the area on which the pitcher's rubber is laid; and other equally exacting criteria.

Beyond these objective criteria, pitchers tend to grow fond of and accustomed to the mounds in their home parks; they notice and are made uncomfortable by any changes in their usual environment. Even if pitchers weren't so finicky, it takes so much manpower to build and maintain a mound that there is no question of rebuilding it from scratch every week after a football game or if an occasional rock concert necessitates temporarily dismantling the mound. Although pitcher's mounds have to be groomed every day, with luck they can last for several years.

So how do they move and rebuild them? We spoke to Steve Wightman, head groundskeeper at San Diego's Jack Murphy Stadium, who has faced the problem working in a park that plays home to both the Padres and the Chargers. Jack Murphy's solution to the problem is common among other multipurpose stadiums: the mound is built onto a circular steel plate; a giant forklift is then used to move the plate (with the mound on it); and then the same forklift moves the plate back in place.

Sounds easy, doesn't it? Think again. The steel plate with the mound weighs close to a ton (and remember the pitcher's circle is eighteen feet in diameter; the steel plate is thirteen feet in diameter). In order to prepare the mound to be carried off, the groundskeepers have to dig around the edge of the plate to expose the metal (and the channels with which the prongs on the forklift will pick up the mound). Just getting the forklift to the

WHAT IS THE CIRCLE ADJACENT TO THE BATTER'S BOX ON BASEBALL FIELDS?

This area is known as the fungo circle. Coaches stand in the fungo circle during pregame practice and hit balls to infielders and, more frequently, outfielders.

Why confine the coach to stand in one small area? So he won't wear out the grass on the field!

—Submitted by Terrell K. Holmes of New York, New York.
Thanks also to Ronald C. Semone of Washington, D.C.

pitcher's circle is a project, because a temporary plywood roadway must be laid down anywhere the forklift travels on the field. Once the plate is picked up, the groundskeepers add some dirt and clay to the area where the plate was and even it out, which takes about one hour. In essence, the groundskeepers become grave diggers.

When the mound has to be restored, the opposite process takes place, although rebuilding takes longer, for it is essential that the steel plate be completely covered and that a seamless mound be crafted. It takes the groundskeepers at Jack Murphy between two and three hours to rebuild the mound after the plate has been put in place.

Wightman says that even when the park is used exclusively for baseball, each year, before the season starts, the mound must be regroomed by hand to restore the exact slope, and a new rubber is installed every year. When they do destroy a mound, it takes about three hours to tear it down and about six hours to rebuild it approximating the proper specifications.

One park, Anaheim Stadium, which is now home to the Angels and various concerts and events but once was also the St. Louis Rams' stadium, built a hydraulic system to take care of the portability problem. They dug a circular well under pitcher's mound, and the hydraulic system raises or lowers the mound, as needed. We spoke to Phil Larcus, operations manager of the "Big A," about how his crew takes down and reconstructs the pitcher's mound.

The mound sits on a metal plate, and the well is the same diameter as the plate, so that the plate fits snugly into the well. The well's hydraulic system can pump water into and out of the well. When they need to put in the mound, they pump water into the well and the plate rises with the water. The plate contains indentations that lock into matching spots on the well. The plate is then turned to engage the indentations and locked in place. As with Jack Murphy Stadium, the groundskeepers groom the edge of the plate to cover the exposed metal to hide the seams.

When events necessitate eliminating the mound at the Big A, the groundskeepers dig around the perimeter of the plate at the edges, and then unlock the plate by turning it the opposite direction. The water in the well is pumped out and the plate automatically sinks. On the bottom of the well, another set of matching indentations in the side of the well locks the plate in place again.

Obviously, the well at Anaheim Stadium is far deeper than the hole dug at Jack Murphy; if the groundskeepers attempted to fill the well with dirt every time they unlocked the plate, they'd never have time to tend to anything else. Instead, a "mound cap," a flat metal disk with a flat plywood top,

is brought out (from underneath the stands) to cover the exposed opening. The plywood is covered with artificial turf. Artificial turf is used in order to blend as well as possible with the natural grass used in the stadium (and to provide a surface that gives sufficient traction for athletes to run on). The whole process of conversion from baseball to football, or vice versa, would take the crew about three hours.

—Submitted by Tom Emig of St. Charles, Missouri.
Thanks also to John Ryan of Portsmouth, Rhode Island.

who are all those people on the sidelines during American football games?

The action may be on the football field, but the traffic congestion is usually on the sidelines. In NFL games, but especially in big-college football schools, the area around the benches is teeming with as many people as Grand Central Terminal at rush hour. Who *are* all these guys? As Bob Carroll, executive director of the Pro Football Researchers Association puts it, the sidelines are full of

> players, coaches, assistant coaches, equipment managers, towel boys, mascots, cheerleaders, officials holding the sticks, TV folks, photographers, police, alumni, anyone donating big bucks to the school, and a partridge in a pear tree.

Restrictions on issuing credentials for access to the sidelines are surprisingly loose, especially in the pros. Faleem Choudhry, a researcher at the Pro Football Hall of Fame, told *Imponderables* that there isn't a hard and fast rule limiting the number of sidelines personnel, or even visitors: "Anybody the team deems necessary can be there." One team might want the electrician who supervises the lighting of the stadium to stay near the bench; another team might banish him to the stands.

The problem of overpopulated sidelines is greater in the college ranks, and the Big 10, known for its impassioned football competition, is among the most restrictive conferences in regulating credentials. The Big 10 allows a maximum of forty credentials for the bench area of each team, including all of the absolutely essential non-playing personnel, such as coaches, trainers, and physicians. According to Cassie Arner, associate sports information director of the University of Illinois, the bench area has a dotted line 50 yards long around it, usually starting at one 25-yard line and running to the other

25-yard line. The bench area zone does not extend all the way back to the stands, so cheerleaders and other credentialed personnel (in some cases, marching bands, press, and security) can stay behind the bench zone.

Here's how Cassie Arner estimates the University of Illinois allocates its credentials:

- Ten to fifteen coaches

- Approximately ten team managers (whose jobs range from handling balls to charting statistics for the team)

- Five full-time equipment managers, who are responsible for mending damaged paraphernalia

- Ten to fifteen trainers, of whom perhaps five are full-time doctors

- The rest are student assistants there to get water, help with taping of bandages, and other relatively unskilled tasks.

But other folks somehow manage to creep down to the bench area as well. In this category, Arner includes the team chaplain, security, and occasionally someone from the event management or operations department of the school. But the University of Illinois does not issue credentials for alumni. Occasionally, a big donor or a dignitary from another team might be brought down to the "forty zone" during time-outs or at the quarter breaks. An occasional "honorary coach" is given credentials—usually a professor from the university who has helped with recruiting.

Tom Schott, sports information director at Purdue University, concurs with his Illinois counterpart, although it sounds like Purdue is a little looser in issuing credentials. As he says, "It's really up to the school's discretion, except for the forty in the bench area." On occasion, Purdue will issue a sideline pass to a former player or corporate bigwig, expecting him not to crowd the bench area. Schott observes:

> If the school has corporate deals with companies, they may ask for
> sideline passes. We're pretty frugal with those but they do exist.
> Officials have the final say and if they think the visitors are getting too
> close to the sidelines, they'll push them back.

As long as participants in the game are not being harassed or distracted, the NCAA and NFL don't want to get involved in regulating the population flow on the sidelines. And even if the colleges don't like having to turn down entreaties for sideline passes, sometimes the alternative is worse. Case in point: Purdue. Schott remarks:

For years we weren't very good in football so there wasn't much demand for sideline credentials. Now that we've gotten good, there are more requests.

—Submitted by Rachel Rehmann of Palo Alto, California.

why do quarterbacks call the snap with the exclamation "hut"?

Put men in a uniform. Give them a helmet. And they all start speaking alike. At least, that's what all of our football sources claimed. Pat Harmon, historian at the College Football Hall of Fame, was typical:

> In Army drills, the drill sergeant counts off: "Hut-2-3-4." He repeats "Hut-2-3-4" until the men get in right. Football language has copied the drill sergeant.

We'll have to believe our football authorities, since no evidence exists that the "hut" barked by quarterbacks has anything to do with little thatched houses.

In fact, "hut" wasn't always used as the signal. Joe Horrigan of the Pro Football Hall of Fame sent us a photocopy of a section of the 1921 *Spalding's How to Play Football* manual that indicates that perhaps we aren't as hip as our forebears:

> When shift formations are tried, the quarter-back should give his signal when the men are in their original places. Then after calling the signal [he] can use the word "hip" for the first shift and then repeat for the players to take up their new positions on the line of scrimmage.

Our guess is that the only important virtue of "hut" is that it contains one syllable.

—Submitted by Paul Ruggiero of Blacksburg, Virginia.

why is the scoring system in tennis so weird?

Tennis as we know it today is barely over a hundred years old. A Welshman, Major Walter Clopton Wingfield, devised the game as a diversion for his guests to play on his lawn before the real purpose for the get-together—a pheasant shoot. Very quickly, however, the members of the Wimbledon Cricket Club adopted Wingfield's game for use on their own

How do football officials measure first-down yardage with chains, especially when they go onto the field to confirm first downs?

In professional football, careers and millions of dollars can rest on a matter of inches. We've never quite figured out how football officials can spot the ball accurately when a running back dives atop a group of ten hulking linemen, let alone how the chain crew retains the proper spot on the sidelines and then carries the chain back out to the field without losing its bearings. Is the aura of pinpoint measurement merely a ruse?

Not really. The answer to this Imponde-rable focuses on the importance of an inexpensive metal clip. The National Football League's Art McNally explains:

> If at the start of a series the ball was placed on the 23-yard line in the middle of the field, the head linesman would back up to the sideline and, after sighting the line of the ball, would indicate to a member of the chain crew that he wanted the back end of the down markers to be set at the 23-yard line. Obviously, a second member of the chain crew would stretch the forward stake to the 33-yard line.
>
> Before the next down is run, one of the members of the chain crew would take a special clip and place that on the chain at the back end of the 25-yard line. In other words, the clip is placed on the five-yard marker that is closest to the original location of the ball.
>
> When a measurement is about to be made, the head linesman picks up the chain from the 25-yard line and

the men holding the front end of the stakes all proceed onto the field. The head linesman places the clip on the back end of the 25-yard line. The front stake is extended to its maximum and the referee makes the decision as to whether or not the ball has extended beyond the forward stake.

Thus the chain crew, when it runs onto the field, doesn't have to find the exact spot near the 23-yard line where the ball was originally spotted, but merely the 25-yard line. The clip "finds" the spot near the 23-yard line.

—Submitted by Dennis Stucky of San Diego, California.

underutilized lawns, empty since croquet had waned in popularity in the late eighteenth century.

Long before Wingfield, however, there were other forms of tennis. The word "tennis" first appeared in a poem by John Gower in 1399, and Chaucer's characters spoke of playing "rackets" in 1380. Court tennis (also known as "real" tennis) dates back to the Middle Ages. That great athlete, Henry VIII, was a devotee of the game. Court tennis was an indoor game featuring an asymmetrical rectangular cement court with a sloping roof, a hard ball, a lopsided racket, and windows on the walls that came into play. Very much a gentleman's sport, the game is still played by a few diehards, though only a handful of courts currently exist in the United States.

Lawn tennis's strange scoring system was clearly borrowed from court tennis. Although court tennis used a fifteen-point system, the scoring system was a little different from modern scoring. Each point in a game was worth fifteen points (while modern tennis progresses 15-30-40-game, court tennis progressed 15-30-45-game). Instead of the current three or five sets of six games each, court tennis matches were six sets of four games each.

The most accepted theory for explaining the strange scoring system is that it reflected Europeans' preoccupation with astronomy, and particularly with the sextant (one-sixth of a circle). One-sixth of a circle is, of course, 60 degrees (the number of points in a game). Because the victor would have to win six sets of four games each, or 24 points, and each point was worth 15 points, the game concluded when the winner had "completed" a circle of 360 degrees (24 x 15).

Writings by Italian Antonio Scaino indicate that the sextant scoring system was firmly in place as early as 1555. When the score of a game is tied after six points in modern tennis, we call it "deuce"—the Italians already had an equivalent in the sixteenth century, *a due* (in other words, two points were needed to win).

Somewhere along the line, however, the geometric progression of individual game points was dropped. Instead of the third point scoring 45, it became worth 40. According to the *Official Encyclopedia of Tennis*, it was most likely dropped to the lower number for the ease of announcing scores out loud, because "forty" could not be confused with any other number. In the early 1700s, the court tennis set was extended to six games, obscuring the astronomical origins of the scoring system.

When lawn tennis began to surpass court tennis in popularity, there was a mad scramble to codify rules and scoring procedures. The first tennis body in this country, the U.S. National Lawn Tennis Association, first met in 1881

to establish national standards. Prior to the formation of the USNLTA, each tennis club selected its own scoring system. Many local tennis clubs simply credited a player with one point for each rally won. Silly concept. Luckily, the USNLTA stepped into the breach and immediately adopted the English scoring system, thus ensuring generations of confused spectators.

There have been many attempts to simplify the scoring system in order to entice new fans. The World Pro Championship League tried the table-tennis scoring system of twenty-one point matches, but neither the scoring system nor the League survived.

Perhaps the most profound scoring change in this century has been the tie breaker. The U.S. Tennis Association's Middle States section, in 1968, experimented with sudden-death play-offs, which for the first time in modern tennis history allowed a player who won all of his regulation service games to lose a set. The professionals adopted the tie breaker in 1970, and it is used in almost every tournament today.

—Submitted by Charles F. Myers of Los Altos, California.

why are tennis balls fuzzy?

The core of a tennis ball is made out of a compound consisting of rubber, synthetic materials, and about ten chemicals. The compound is extruded into a barrel-shaped pellet that is then formed into two half shells.

The edges of the two half shells are coated with a latex adhesive and then put together and cured in a double-chambered press under strictly controlled temperature and air-pressure conditions. The inner chamber is pressurized to thirteen psi (pounds per square inch), so that the air is trapped inside and the two halves are fused together at the same pressure.

Once the two halves have been pressed together to form one sphere, the surface of the core is roughened so that the fuzz will stick better. The core is then dipped into a cement compound and oven-dried to prepare for the cover application.

The fuzzy material is felt, a combination of wool, nylon, and Dacron woven together into rolls. The felt is cut into a figure-eight shape (one circular piece of felt wouldn't fit as snugly on a ball), and the edges of the felt are coated with a seam adhesive. The cores and edges of the two felt strips are mated, the felt is bonded to the core, and the seam adhesive is cured, securing all the materials and for the first time yielding a sphere that looks like a tennis ball.

After the balls are cured, they are steamed in a large tumbler and fluffed in order to raise the nap on the felt, giving the balls their fuzzy appearance. Different manufacturers fluff their balls to varying degrees. The balls are then sealed in airtight cans pressurized at twelve to fifteen psi, with the goal of keeping the balls at ten to twelve psi.

The single most expensive ingredient in a tennis ball is the felt. Many other sports do quite well with unfuzzy rubber balls. In the earliest days of tennis, balls had a leather cover, and were stuffed with all sorts of things, including human hair. So why do tennis ball manufacturers bother with the fuzz?

Before the felt is added, a tennis ball has a hard, sleek surface, not unlike a baseball's. One of the main purposes of the fuzz is to slow the ball down. The United States Tennis Association maintains strict rules concerning the bound of tennis balls. One regulation stipulates, "The ball shall have a bound of more than 53 inches and less than 58 inches when dropped 100 inches upon a concrete base." The fluffier the felt, the more wind resistance it offers, decreasing not only the bound but the speed of the ball. If the felt were too tightly compacted, the ball would have a tendency to skip on the court.

A second important reason for fuzzy tennis balls is that the fluffy nap contributes to increased racket control. Every time a tennis ball hits a racket the strings momentarily grip the ball, and the ball compresses. With a harder, sleeker surface, the ball would have a tendency to skip off the racket and minimize the skill of the player.

A third contribution of fuzz is the least important to a good player but important to us refugees from hardball sports like racquetball and squash. When you get hit hard by a fuzzy tennis ball, you may want to cry, but you don't feel like you're going to die.

—Submitted by Dorio Barbieri of Mountain View, California.

why are college basketball games played in halves, while the NBA plays in quarters?

Baseball, football, and hockey all share not only the same scoring structure at the professional level as the college level but also play for the same amount of time. College basketball players run up and down the court for a "mere" forty minutes, while the pros must toil for an extra eight minutes to earn the sneaker endorsements that constitute nearly 1 percent of the American gross national product. Why the difference?

The college game preceded pro hoops. While the origins of baseball are shrouded in some mystery and considerable controversy, we can credit the invention of basketball to one person, Dr. James Naismith, a physical education instructor at the YMCA Training School (now Springfield College) in Springfield, Massachusetts. He developed the sport because his boss asked him to invent a game that could be played indoors during the winter. In 1892, Naismith published a rule book in the school magazine, so we know that the earliest basketball games consisted of two fifteen-minute halves with five minutes of rest in between.

Geneva College became the first school to organize a basketball team, in 1892, followed by the University of Iowa in 1893, Ohio State and Temple in 1894, and Yale in 1895. The first college game (with *nine* players on a team) was played in 1895. Hamline (of St. Paul, Minnesota) squashed the Minnesota State School of Agriculture by the mammoth score of nine goals to three.

Intercollegiate basketball became popular quickly, but there were regional variations in the rules until the early twentieth century. Once the NCAA became a force, after World War I, all college games were played in two twenty-minute halves.

Professional and semipro basketball leagues were formed as early as the late nineteenth century, but none was national in scope and the players did not earn enough to quit their day jobs. Bill Himmelman, proprietor of Sports Nostalgia Research in Norwood, New Jersey, provided us with fascinating information about these early leagues.

One of the prominent pre-NBA leagues was the American Basketball League, based in New York. Formed in the 1920s, the ABL rules designated three fifteen-minute periods, presumably a holdover from hockey, for the games were played in hockey arenas. The National Basketball League, formed at the end of

the nineteenth century, was based in Chicago and in its last days (in the 1930s and 1940s) had forty-minute games divided into four ten-minute periods.

After World War II ended in 1945, a group of hockey team owners got together to figure out how to wring more money out of their hockey stadiums when their teams were on the road, and how to better exploit the entertainment needs of a suddenly booming economy. The ABL folded and the owners saw an opening. In that meeting, they hatched the Basketball Association of America (BAA).

Although they "borrowed" the rules from college, the BAA lengthened the season to increase revenue; earlier basketball leagues generally scheduled games only on the weekends. They decided to try sixty-game seasons and a playoff format similar to hockey's.

However, the basketball association faced the opposite problem that fledgling professional baseball faced: The game of amateur basketball, as it had been played, wasn't long enough to suit paying customers. So they lengthened the playing time of the game to forty-eight minutes, with the goal of providing what hockey fans had come to expect: two hours of entertainment.

The owners could have divided the forty-eight minutes into two twenty-four-minute halves, but by instituting four twelve minute quarters, they gained two advantages: the evening was lengthened, but more particularly, the transitions between periods provided more time for fans to hit the concessions.

After two years of play, the BAA merged with the remnants of the failing NBL and formed the National Basketball Association. The first NBA season, with seventeen teams, was played in 1949-50. According to John Neves of the NBA, the league has never varied from the twelve-minute-quarters format.

In the spirit of full disclosure, we must add that the NCAA did tinker once with its timing structure. For two seasons (1953-55), the college game was divided into four ten-minute quarters. At the time, the NCAA was under a cloud because of point-shaving scandals in the early 1950s. Himmelman indicates that collegiate basketball needed a public-relations makeover, so they "borrowed a bit" from the NBA, which was flourishing at the amateur game's expense, by going to quarters. After the 1955 season, the college game reverted back to two twenty-minute halves, reducing concession revenue but restoring this Imponderable, so that the public could be confused and so we could have something to write about.

—Submitted by Brian Adams of Carmel, Indiana.
Thanks also to Michelle and Mitchell Szczepancyzk of Grand Rapids, Michigan;
and Frank Norman of Manhattan Beach, California.

how do figure skaters keep from getting dizzy while spinning? Is it possible to eye a fixed point while spinning so fast?

Imponderables readers aren't the only ones interested in this question. So are astronauts, who suffer from motion sickness in space. We consulted Carole Shulman, executive director of the Professional Skaters Guild of America, who explained:

> Tests were conducted by NASA several years ago to determine the answer to this very question. Research proved that with a trained skater, the pupils of the eyes do not gyrate back and forth during a spin as they do with an untrained skater. The rapid movement of the eyes catching objects within view is what actually causes dizziness.
>
> The eyes of a trained skater do not focus on a fixed point during a spin but rather they remain in a stabilized position focusing on space between the skater and the next closest object. This gaze is much like that of a daydream.

So how are skaters taught to avoid focusing on objects or people in an arena? Claire O'Neill Dillie, skating coach and motivational consultant, teaches students to see a "blurred constant," an imaginary line running around the rink. The imaginary line may be in the seats or along the barrier of the rink (during layback spins, the imaginary line might be on the ceiling). The crucial consideration is that the skater feels centered. Even when the hands and legs are flailing about, the skater should feel as if his or her shoulders, hips, and head are aligned.

Untrained skaters often feel dizziest not in the middle of the spin but when stopping (the same phenomenon experienced when a tortuous amusement park ride stops and we walk off to less than solid footing). Dillie teaches her students to avoid vertigo by turning their heads in the opposite direction of the spin when stopping.

What surprised us about the answers to this Imponderable is that the strategies used to avoid dizziness are diametrically opposed to those used by ballet dancers, who use a technique called "spotting." Dancers consciously pick out a location or object to focus upon; during each revolution, they center themselves by spotting that object or location. When spotting, dancers turn their head at the very last moment, trailing the movement of the body, whereas skaters keep their head aligned with the rest of their body.

Why won't spotting work for skaters? For the answer, we consulted Ronnie Robertson, an Olympic medalist who has attained a rare distinction: Nobody has ever spun faster on ice than him.

How fast? At his peak, Robertson's spins were as fast as six revolutions per second. He explained to us that spotting simply can't work for skaters because they are spinning too fast to focus visually on anything. At best, skaters are capable of seeing only the "blurred constant" to which Claire O'Neill Dillie was referring, which is as much a mental as a visual feat.

Robertson, trained by Gustav Lussi, considered to be the greatest spin coach of all time, was taught to spin with his eyes closed. And so he did. Robertson feels that spinning without vertigo is an act of mental suppression, blocking out the visual cues and rapid movement that can convince your body to feel dizzy.

Robertson explains that the edge of the blade on the ice is so small that a skater's spin is about the closest thing to spinning on a vertical point as humans can do. When his body was aligned properly, Robertson says that he felt calm while spinning at his fastest, just as a top is most stable when attaining its highest speeds.

While we had the greatest spinner of all time on the phone, we couldn't resist asking him a related Imponderable: Why do almost all skating routines, in competitions and skating shows and exhibitions, end with long and fast scratch spins? Until we researched this Imponderable, we had always assumed that the practice started because skaters would have been too dizzy to continue doing anything else after rotating so fast. But Robertson pooh-poohed our theory.

The importance of the spin, to Robertson, is that unlike other spectacular skating moves, spins are sustainable. While triple jumps evoke oohs and aahs from the audience, a skater wants a spirited, prolonged reaction to the finale of his or her program. Spins are ideal because they start slowly and eventually build to a climax so fast that it cannot be appreciated without the aid of slow-motion photography.

Robertson believes that the audience remembers the ending, not the beginning, of programs. If a skater can pry a rousing standing ovation out of an audience, perhaps supposedly sober judges might be influenced by the reaction.

Robertson's trademark was not only a blindingly fast spin but a noteworthy ending. He used his free foot to stop his final spin instantly at the fastest point. Presumably, when he stopped, he opened his eyes to soak in the appreciation of the audience.

—Submitted by Barbara Harris Polomé of Austin, Texas. Thanks also to David McConnaughey of Cary, North Carolina.

why are there two red stripes around the thinnest part of bowling pins?

Their sole purpose, according to Al Vanderneck of the American Bowling Congress, is to look pretty. Part of Vanderneck's job is to check the specifications of bowling equipment, and he reports that without the stripes, the pins "just look funny." The area where the stripes are placed is known as the "neck," and evidently a naked neck on a bowling pin stands out as much as a tieless neck on a tuxedo wearer.

Actually, we almost blew the answer to this Imponderable. We've thrown a few turkeys in our time, and we always identified the red stripes with AMF pins; the other major manufacturer of bowling pins, Brunswick, used a red crown as an identification mark on its pins. So we assumed that the red stripes were a trademark of AMF's.

AMF's product manager Ron Pominville quickly disabused us of our theory. Brunswick's pins have always had stripes, too, and Brunswick has eliminated the red crown in its current line of pins. A third and growing presence in pindom, Vulcan, also includes stripes on its products.

We haven't been able to confirm two items: Who started the practice of striping the necks of bowling pins? And exactly what is so aesthetically pleasing about these two thin strips of crimson applied to battered, ivory-colored pins?

—Submitted by Michael Alden of Rochester Hills, Michigan. Thanks also to Ken Shafer of Traverse City, Michigan.

why do hockey goalies sometimes bang their sticks on the ice while the puck is on the other end of the rink?

No, they are not practicing how to bang on an opponent's head—the answer is far more benign.

In most sports, such as baseball, football, and basketball, play is stopped when substitutions are made. But ice hockey allows unlimited substitution *while the game is in progress,* one of the features that makes hockey such a fast-paced game.

It is the goalie's job to be a dispatcher, announcing to his teammates when traffic patterns are changing on the ice. For example, a minor penalty involves the offender serving two minutes in the penalty box. Some goalies bang the ice to signal to teammates that they are now at even strength.

WHY IS SCORING THREE GOALS IN HOCKEY CALLED A *HAT TRICK?*

"Hat trick" was originally an English cricket term used to describe the tremendous feat of a bowler's taking three wickets on successive balls. The reward for this accomplishment at many cricket clubs was a new hat. Other clubs honored their heroes by "passing the hat" among fans and giving the scorer the proceeds. The term spread to other sports in which scoring is relatively infrequent—"hat trick" is also used to describe the feat of scoring three goals in soccer.

According to Belinda Lerner of the National Hockey League, the expression surfaced in hockey during the early 1900s: "There is some confusion about its actual meaning in hockey. Today, a 'true' hat trick occurs when one player scores three successive goals without another goal being scored by other players in the contest."

—Submitted by Ron Fishman of Denver, Colorado.

But according to Herb Hammond, eastern regional scout for the New York Rangers, the banging is most commonly used by goalies whose teams are on a power play (a one-man advantage):

> It is his way of signaling to his teammates on the ice that the penalty is over and that they are no longer on the power play. Because the players are working hard and cannot see the scoreboard, the goalie is instructed by his coach to bang the stick on the ice to give them a signal they can hear.

—Submitted by Daniell Bull of Alexandria, Virginia.

IS there any logic to the arrangement of numbers on a dartboard?

The dartboard known as the "clock" board (occasionally known as the "London clock" or "English clock") is today the international standard for all darts tournaments. The board itself is eighteen inches in diameter, with a scoring diameter of $13\frac{3}{8}$ inches. The center of the board contains two small circles: the inside bull, called a "double bull" or "double bull's-eye" is worth 50 points; the outer bull, called simply a "bull's-eye," scores 25.

Each pie-shaped wedge is worth the number of points indicated on the board, but the outer circumference of the scoring pie contains a concentric ring, about three-eights of an inch wide, the double zone, that allows you to double the value of the wedge in which it is hit. The triples ring, located halfway between the center of the board and the outside circumference, allows you to triple the value (so hitting the triple ring on a 20 gives you more points than landing on the double bull's-eye).

Dartboard patterns and numbering schemes were not always so uniform. Undoubtedly, darts were originally used as weapons rather than as game equipment. Legend has it that the first darts were made for a Saxon king who was too short to use a bow and arrow. He solved the problem by sawing off the ends of arrows, leaving projectiles about a foot long.

The sport of darts dates back to England in the fifteenth century, when military men sawed off arrows and threw them against the ends, or butts, of wine casks. The game was called "the butts," and the shortened arrows were called "dartes." Henry VIII was an aficionado of the sport, and Anne Boleyn gave her king a set of jewel-encrusted darts as a birthday gift.

As the sport grew in popularity, warriors looked for better targets than wine casks. They began using round slices from fallen trees, particularly elm trees. The concentric rings of the trees formed natural divisions for scoring purposes (they looked not unlike an archery target's rings), and the cracks that appeared when the wood dried out provided radial lines for more scoring areas.

The Pilgrims brought darts and dartboards to the New World on the *Mayflower,* but the proliferation of new patterns on boards stayed in England, where various regions claimed their own patterns. By the early twentieth century, some boards featured as many as twenty-eight different wedges; some as few as ten.

Eventually, standardization of the boards became inevitable, if only because of the affinity between beer and darts. Darts became *the* popular game in English pubs during the late nineteenth century. The elm dartboards had to be soaked overnight to keep them from drying out and developing cracks. Often, the boards were soaked with the most available liquid, beer, so the boards tended to drip all over the floor, creating a smelly mess.

To the rescue came Ted Leggett, an analytic chemist, who just after World War I created a modeling clay that had no scent, unlike other clays of that time. He called his product (and company) Nodor (a compressed version of "no odor") and quit his job to market the clay. According to Leggett's daughter, Doris Bugler, one day the chemist threw some darts at a lump of his clay, and the darts held. Eureka! Ever since, Nodor has been the most esteemed brand name in dartboards.

The Nodor dartboard was first marketed in 1923; it sported today's "clock" pattern but also many other regional patterns. As darts increased in popularity, Leggett decided that a ruling body should be formed to regulate interdistrict competitions—Leggett became the first president of the National Darts Association in 1935. It was at this point that the "clock" pattern became standard.

Was there any particular reason for the ascendancy of the "clock" board? *Imponderables* contacted many experts to find out who invented the English clock board, but to a person, they repeated the words of Barry Sinnett of Anglo-American Dartboards, Inc., who has worked in the darting business for thirty years:

> No one seems to know. It's known to be unknown. I have taken a couple of trips to England and talked to several of the old-timers from the English dartboard companies. No one knew (and that includes people at Nodor).

Even a casual glance at the numbers on the dartboard indicates that there is some method to the numbering scheme on a dartboard. Note that high and low numbers alternate around the board. So in games where players are solely trying to score the most points possible, why not always aim for the 20? There are two good reasons why one might not, as Mike Courtenay, a devoted darter and manager of Darts and Things, a Van Nuys, California, store, points out:

> Many people just try to throw at the 20 segment because it's the highest score on the board besides the bull's-eyes. But that's often a mistake. The numbers on either side of the 20 are only 1 and 5. A higher scoring area is near the bottom left, where 16, 7, and 19 are adjacent.

The clock board constantly forces players to make strategic decisions. After all, it might occur to the neophyte always to aim for the double bull's-eye. The problem with this approach is that when you miss, as you usually will, you have no idea what wedge you will land in—you are just as likely to land in 1 as 20.

—Submitted by Daniel Farber of Kingston, New York.
Thanks also to Jon Hyatt of Boise, Idaho; Susan Hurff of Linden, New Jersey;
Erica Luty of Redmond, Washington; and Jon Wearley of Augusta, Montana.

why are the Notre Dame sports teams called "the Fighting Irish" when the school was founded by French Catholics?

When you conjure up an image of bruising football players, the French don't immediately spring to mind. But Notre Dame was indeed founded by a French Catholic, Father Edward Frederick Sorin, in 1842. Sorin had been a member of a religious order in France, Holy Cross Motherhouse of Notre Dame de Ste. Croix. This order specialized in missionary work and Sorin was chosen to lead a group of seven brothers to establish a center for Catholic education and missionary work in Indiana. Northern Indiana already had a strong French presence, as many of the first white men in the territory were French explorers, missionaries, and fur trappers of French Canadian descent.

Sorin named his new school the University of Notre Dame du Lac, a tribute to his seminary back in France; "du Lac" was a nod to the two lakes on the forest land that Sorin had chosen to situate the university. While the

university's original goal was to produce clergy, it soon welcomed non-Catholics and those interested in non-religious studies.

In the huge wave of immigration to the United States in the nineteenth century, many Irish Catholics settled in the Midwest; indeed, many Americans equated "Catholic" with "Irish." When Notre Dame started competing in intercollegiate athletics, many newspapers referred to its teams as the "Catholics," even though the school had no official nickname. In press accounts, many schools are referred to by their religious affiliation (yes, "the Catholics" battled "the Methodists" and "the Baptists" at football).

But where did "Fighting Irish" come from? What's a nice school established to train seminarians doing with a warlike nickname? Autumn Gill, a public relations representative from Notre Dame, told *Imponderables* that although no one knows for sure, there are two main theories (documented in a book Gill recommended, Murray Sperber's *Shake Down the Thunder*). The first theory is that "fighting Irish" was an epithet hurled *at* the Notre Dame team by fans of its opponent, Northwestern, in 1889. The Wildcat fans, who were behind in the game, yelled: "Kill the Fighting Irish, kill the Fighting Irish." The other story is that the term came from the lips of Notre Dame halfback, Pete Vaughn, who in a 1909 game against Michigan, tried to motivate his teammates (who were mostly Irish American) when they were behind by yelling: "What's the matter with you guys? You're all Irish and you're not fighting." When the press heard about Vaughn's outburst, especially since Notre Dame went on to win the game, reporters dubbed the team the "Fighting Irish."

But the nickname didn't stick until the 1920s. In the first part of the twentieth century, Indiana press referred to the team as the "Catholics" or less flattering variations, such as the "Papists," "Horrible Hibernians," and even "Dirty Irish" or "Dumb Micks." Campus publications avoided the pejorative terms, and often referred to the teams by the school colors, "the Gold and Blue," and occasionally as "the Irish." Obviously, the campus administration wasn't wild about slurs against Catholics or ethnic groups, but the students embraced the "Irish" name and liked "Fighting" for its emphasis on spirit and playfulness. In campus publications, students insisted that "you don't have to be from Ireland to be Irish" and that naysayers should "cultivate some of that fighting Irish spirit." A late 1910 visit from Eamon De Valera, who was soon to be president of the Irish Republic, solidified the students' embrace of "Fighting Irish."

Three men popularized the nickname outside of South Bend. Knute Rockne, the legendary football coach, turned the Notre Dame team into a powerhouse. Rockne hired student press agents and encouraged them to use "Fighting Irish" in their dispatches. One of those press agents, Francis Wallace, moved to New York and became a successful sportswriter. He disliked the then-prevalent nicknames for Notre Dame, such as "Rambling Irish," "Rockne's Rovers," and "Wandering Irish," as all implied that the team's players traveled at the expense of their studies. Wallace's writings were picked up by the wire services, and he insisted on using "Fighting Irish." In 1927, President Matthew Walsh made it official, adopting "Fighting Irish" as the school's permanent nickname.

Of course, Catholics are more likely to root for Notre Dame than other religious groups, but Catholics from all over Europe and South America have emigrated to the United States, and yet seem loyal to a team named after one ethnic group. There were plenty of non-Irish members of Rockne's powerhouses, as the press loved to point out to him. But he always retorted:

> They're all Irish to me. They have the Irish spirit and that's all that counts.

> *—Submitted by Jennifer Conrad of Springfield, Pennsylvania.*
> *Thanks also to Margaret Levin of Belle Vernon, Pennsylvania.*

why do females tend to throw "like a girl"?

Not only do girls (and later, women) tend not to be able to throw balls as far as boys, but their form is noticeably different. If you ask the average boy to throw a baseball as far as he can, he will lift his elbow and wind his arm far back. A girl will tend to keep her elbow static and push forward with her hand in a motion not unlike that of a shot putter.

Why the difference? Our correspondent mentions that he has heard theories that females have an extra bone that prevents them from throwing "like a boy." Or is it that they are missing one bone?

We talked to some physiologists (who assured us that boys and girls have all the same relevant bones) and to some specialists in exercise physiology who have studied the underperformance of girls in throwing.

In their textbook, *Training for Sport and Activity: The Physiological Basis of the Conditioning Process,* Jack H. Wilmore and David L. Costill cite quite a few studies that indicate that up until the ages of ten to twelve, boys and girls have remarkably similar scores in motor skills and athletic ability. In almost every test, boys barely beat the girls. But at the onset of puberty, the

male becomes much stronger, possesses greater muscular and cardiovascular endurance, and outperforms girls in virtually all motor skills.

In only one athletic test do the boys far exceed the girls before and after puberty: the softball throw. From the ages of five to sixteen, the average boy can throw a softball about twice as far as a girl.

Wilmore and Costill cite a fascinating study that attempted to explain this phenomenon. Two hundred males and females from ages three to twenty threw softballs for science. The result: males beat females two to one when throwing with their dominant hand, but females threw almost as far as males with their nondominant hand. Up until the ages of ten to twelve, girls threw just as far with their nondominant hand as boys did.

The conclusion of Wilmore and Costill is inescapable:

> Major differences at all ages were the results for the dominant arm ... the softball throw for distance using the dominant arm appears to be biased by the previous experience and practice of the males. When the influence of experience and practice was removed by using the nondominant arm, this motor skill task was identical to each of the others.

All the evidence suggests that girls can be taught, or learn through experience, how to throw "like a boy." Exercise physiologist Ralph Wickstrom believes most children go through several developmental stages of throwing. Boys simply continue growing in sophistication, while girls are not encouraged to throw softballs or baseballs and stop in the learning curve. As an example, Wickstrom notes that most right-handed girls throw with their right foot forward. Simply shifting their left foot forward would increase their throwing distance.

When forced to throw with their nondominant hand, most boys throw "like a girl." The loss in distance is accountable not only to lesser muscular development in the nondominant side, but to a breakdown in form caused by a lack of practice.

—Submitted by Tony Alessandrini of Brooklyn, New York.

Index

A

Airlines
  chime signals of, 219–20
  oxygen masks of, 254–56
Air travel, foot swelling from, 40–41
Alarm clocks
  invented by monks, 276–77
  wake-up signals before invention,
    275–77
Alcohol
  pink lady, origin of term, 25
  proof of, 157–58
  worm in tequila bottles, 155
Alderton, Charles, 133–34
Alphabet soup, and foreign alphabets, 127
Aluminum foil, shiny vs. dull side of, 309
Ancient cities, burial of, 345–47
Animals. *See also specific animals*
  goose bumps in, 39, 40
Ants, and separation from colony, 113–14
Appointment times, before invention of
  clocks, 275, 277–78
April 15 tax return date, origin of, 170–72
Arabic numbers, origin of, 351
Artificial sweeteners, calories in, 132–33
Ascites, in starving children, 56
Aspirin, finding headache, 347–49
Astronauts
  earaches in, 34–35
  itching in, 32–38
At loggerheads, origin of term, 61
Auctioneer chants, 203–5
Audiotapes, two-sided recording on, 285–86
Automobiles
  clicking of turn signals, 250
  disappearance of 1983 Corvette, 251–53
  movement of fuel gauges, 248–49
  "new-car" smell, 250–51
  tiny holes in ceilings, 251
Ax to grind, origin of term, 289

B

Back and fill, meaning of, 231
Badges, law enforcement, shape of,
  182–83
Bags under eyes, causes of, 12–13
Baked goods, temperature and rich taste
  of, 142–43
Ballet dancers, dizziness avoided by,
  415–16
Balls
  golf, dimples on, 396–97
  tennis, fuzziness of, 411–12
  on top of flagpole, 320
Balsa wood, hardwood classification of,
  353–54
Barbecue grills, shape of, 280–83
Barbie doll, hair of, 364–65
Barney Rubble, occupation of, 371–72
Barns, red color of, 212–14
Bars
  mirrors behind, 389–91
  soundless televisions in, 387–89
Bartholomew, Jimmy, 152, 153
Baseball
  circle near batter's box, 404
  dugouts, belowground location of, 401
  origin of nine innings, 401–2
  pitching mounds, rebuilding, 403–6
  scoring, and "K" for strikeout, 400–401
  shape of home plate, 402
  throwing form, in girls vs. boys,
    423–24
Basketball
  college, halves in, 413
  NBA, quarters in, 413–14
Bathing and skin wrinkling, 32
Bathrooms. *See also* Restrooms
  location of toilet flush handles,
    289–90
  origin of *head* term, 305

IMPONDERABLES

Houseflies
   life span and breeding of, 104–5
   method of landing on ceiling, 105–6
Humble pie, origin of term, 149
"Hut" exclamation, in football, 408

I

"I," capitalization of, 57–58
Ice cubes
   cloudiness of, 357–58
   holes and dimples in, 165–66
Ice formation, on lakes and ponds, 334–35
Ice skaters, dizziness avoided in, 415–17
Ice skating rinks, organ music in, 380–81
Inguinal hernia exams, 43–44
Ink removal, from recycled newsprint,
   329–30
Innings in baseball, origin of, 401–2
Insects. *See also specific insects*
   flight patterns of, 108, 110
Internal Revenue Service, and tax return
   date, 170–72
Itching
   in astronauts wearing space suits, 32–38
   from mosquito bites, 31

J

Jack in deck of cards, identity of, 364
Jaguars, reacting to catnip, 75
Jaywalking, origin of term, 97
Jetsam, vs. flotsam, 215
Jigsaw puzzles, design of, 331–32
"Jim Crow," meaning of, 153
Jimmies, origin and naming of, 151–53
J Street, absence in Washington, D.C., 328
Judges, black robes of, 241–42

K

Ken doll, hair of, 364–65
Ketchup
   bottles, design of, 144
   spelling of, 143

Keys to cities, meaning of, 174
"K" for strikeout, origin of, 400–401
Kidd, William, 189
Kilts, history of, 233–35
Kit and caboodle, origin of term, 226
Kitchen sinks, and omission of overflow
   mechanism, 290–91
Knees, of penguins and flamingos, 93
Knuckle under, origin of term, 29
Kwashiorkor, in starving children, 55

L

Labels, mattress, 310
Lakes, ice formation on, 334–35
Lasagna noodles, crimped edges on, 139
Last ditch, origin of term, 226–27
Laundry detergents, powdered, odd weights
   of, 312, 314
Law enforcement badges, shape of, 182–83
Lawns, reasons for growing, 216–18
Lb., origin of abbreviation, 349
Left-handed flush handles, on toilets,
   289–90
Left-handed French horn players, 299–300
Left-handedness of Muppets, 365–66,
   368–69
Left-handed string players, scarcity of, 50
Leg, break a, origin of term, 372
Leggett, Ted, 420
"Legitimate" theater, meaning of, 376–77
Leopards, reacting to catnip, 75
Liberal arts, history of, 227–29
Light bulbs
   fluorescent, plinking noise of, 262
   loosening of, 265–66
   noise when shaking, 260–61
   three-way
      life of, 261–62
      working of, 262–63
   traffic signal
      color of, 264
      long life of, 265
   25-watt, cost of, 261
   vacuum in, 263

M

IMPONDERABLES

IMPONDERABLES

IMPONDERABLES

about the author

David Feldman grew up in a tract house in Mar Vista, California. From an abnormally early age, Dave was fascinated by popular culture. He loved rock and roll and *Leave It to Beaver,* and tried to analyze why and how they were successful commercially and artistically. In college, he was a literature major, with a special interest in Russian writers, but he was also busy convincing sympathetic professors at Grinnell College (yes, an accredited institution of higher learning) to allow him to undertake independent studies in popular culture.

After winning a Watson Fellowship to study popular culture in Europe, Dave ditched Dostoevsky and went to Bowling Green State University, at that time the only school in the world with a postgraduate degree in popular culture. There he taught the first-ever college course on soap operas.

After moving to New York City, Dave consulted for ABC but took a job in the programming department of NBC, where he worked in both daytime and prime-time programming. Dave was and is obsessed with television, but wasn't cut out to be a network programmer. So he saved up his money with the intention of embarking on a writing career. A trip to the grocery store triggered the "Imponderables" idea (see introduction). The rest, if not history, has been Dave's work for more than twenty years.

Dave lives in New York City. He's single but has many interests besides work to occupy him: tournament duplicate bridge, listening to his massive music collection, searching for good food anywhere, reading, annoying his friends, indulging in all facets of popular culture, and writing autobiographical sketches in the third person.

ABOUT THE ILLUSTRATOR

Travis Foster uses ink, watercolor, acrylic, collage, and electronic media to create artwork for newspapers, magazines, children's books, board games, posters, greeting cards, and national advertising campaigns. He has been a freelance artist since graduating from the Ringling School of Art and Design in Sarasota, Florida 17 years ago.

Travis lives in Nashville with his wife, Sarah; his four children, Michael, Ari, Olivia, and Sophia; and their Saint Bernard, Roxie.

your best resource for everyday fun and advice is Reader's Digest!

Every month, more than 100 million people around the globe turn to Reader's Digest books and magazines for clever advice and surprising entertainment. The following Reader's Digest books are among the many available by calling 1-800-846-2100, or by visiting our online store at www.rd.com:

Reference & Entertainment

The Reader's Digest Treasury of Wit & Wisdom
Laughter, the Best Medicine
Facts at Your Fingertips
Off the Beaten Path
Unsolved Mysteries of American History
Reader's Digest New World Atlas

Home Advice

Reader's Digest Do-It-Yourself Manual
Long Life for Your Stuff
Extraordinary Uses for Ordinary Things
2,001 Amazing Cleaning Secrets
Five Minute Fixes
Penny Pincher's Almanac
1,519 All-Amazing, All-Natural Gardening Secrets
Ultimate Soup Cookbook

Health Advice

Best Remedies
30 Minutes a Day to a Healthy Heart
Stealth Health
Stopping Diabetes in Its Tracks
Eat to Beat Diabetes
1,801 Home Remedies
Foods That Harm, Foods That Heal
Reader's Digest Guide to Drugs and Supplements
ChangeOne: Lose Weight Simply, Safely, and Forever
Improve Your Brainpower
Allergy & Asthma Relief